Gentlemen, players and politicians

Dalton Camp

Gentlemen, players and politicians

Dalton Camp

McClelland and Stewart Limited Toronto/Montreal

0-7710-1865-7

The Canadian Publishers
McClelland and Stewart Limited
25 Hollinger Road, Toronto 374

Printed and bound in Canada by
The Hunter Rose Company

For my wife who endured all this, including the retelling.

Foreword

I wanted to write a book free of myth, make-believe, mystery, and moonshine, which would be about Canadian politics and Canadian politicians, which would be neither cynical, smart-alec, dishonest, nor self-serving–to write what I saw and heard for myself, not what I wished, suspected, or gathered from gossip, and to write without hindsight, if I could, and with as much charity, compassion, and candour as an affectionate admirer of our political system could muster. No one else is responsible other than myself for such failure of intentions as readers may detect on reading this book.

Even so, I have been mightily helped: by Queen's University, which bestowed the honour of a Skelton Clark Fellowship which allowed the essential time to begin this first of a two volume work; by Professors John Meisel and Hugh Thorburn of the Department of Political Studies, who gave essential encouragement and criticism; by Flora MacDonald, whose memory of political events is, so far as I know, incomparable; and, no means least, by Bonnie Langley, who provided invaluable assistance in preparing, editing, and proof-reading the manuscript.

In a highly original sense, to experience the politics of Canada is not only to discover one's country, but equally to discover one's self. It has occurred to me that little of signal importance in the global scheme of things has ever been at issue, much less determined, as a result of the Canadian political process. So that what is recorded for our posterity is not the chronicle of awesome events, but the memory of how individuals responded to personal crisis, challenge, and opportunity, how power affected them, how low they would stoop, or how tall they would stand, in order to conquer.

Finally, I hope it will be obvious the sense of kinship, if not comradeship, which the author feels for most of those who trouble themselves with politics and public service, only a few of whom are encountered in this volume, but who are found among the vanquished as well as victors, and among foes as well as friends.

Dalton Camp

Robertson's Point, N.B.
August 31, 1970.

1

WAS IT 1947? I'M NOT SURE:

The National Liberal Federation is assembled in the Chateau Laurier; it is nearing the luncheon hour when the tall rear doors are drawn apart. Starting from the back and moving to the front, like a wave racing to the shore, the audience rises, and with it the sound of mounting applause.

A pale, colourless, little man, clad in the aura of indestructibility, moves slowly down the centre aisle, his inscrutable, featureless face as familiar as a worn five-cent piece, like an animated icon whose eyes emit refracted glints of secret pleasures, cynicism, and wisdom.

William Lyon Mackenzie King, Prime Minister, for twenty-one years a leader without peer, speaks to his followers in the compressed, slight voice, the oddly forgettable voice with its spare, pedestrian prose, and although one does not recall afterwards what he has said, all are drenched in the awe of the occasion. Soon we have heard enough, and the light is too strong to endure.

Then he has gone, retired to the vaulted, hidden labyrinth of power, the big room seems emptier and darker, as though he had come and taken away the essence of the day.

We Liberals spoke of Mackenzie King with a mixture of wonder and uneasiness, but sparingly. He was less a person, more a presence. To the Liberal Party he had become a familiar mystery–like Communion wine–to be seen, partaken of, believed in, never fully understood; King conjured visions of mystical powers, eternal triumph, and an omnipotence beyond the ken of ordinary men.

Those around him, his ministers and principal supporters, had more identifiable and endearing qualities, and their mannerisms and foibles were subjects for lively discussion. But as for King, one could end a conversation by beginning to talk about him. No one knew quite what to say.

Now, in the summer of 1948, Mackenzie King had summoned his party to choose his successor. It took getting used to, the thought of replacing King. He had been there for so long, the processes by which he would be succeeded had been almost forgotten. The New Brunswick delegation, travelling to Ottawa by sleeper and chair car, amused themselves over cards or stared at the countryside, shimmering in the white sunlight. Few of us had ever been to a national leadership convention; the last one had been in August, 1919. Leadership conventions were for Tories.

1

The prospect of going to the Ottawa convention was appealing, especially after the one-sided victory of John B. McNair's Liberal Party in the June general election. With the fresh prestige of a recent and complete triumph, there were rumbles about renewing in Ottawa a half-forgotten cry–Maritime rights.

New Brunswick Liberals had political muscle. Of the fifty-two seats in the provincial legislature, McNair's party held forty-seven of them; of the ten seats in the federal parliament, seven were Liberal. This, despite southern New Brunswick's acknowledged Tory inclinations, gave lustre to the reputation of the delegation from New Brunswick. Or so we thought.

Such things as electoral victories seemed to matter in Ottawa, where everyone was patronized by someone and was patronizing to someone else in turn. Ontario's delegates were the most patronized of all; they were out of power provincially and, in the federal context, their province provided the opposition with most of its seats. Ontario delegates were leaderless, poor-mouthing, and gauche. (It seemed appropriate then, just as Mackenzie King was bidding his party a last farewell and the hall was hushed in respectful silence, that the rear doors should suddenly burst open and a rabble of Ontario supporters plunge into the back of the hall, shouting slogans about drafting Paul Martin. Only Ontario Liberals could be so crudely inept, so preposterously vulgar.)

There was the usual jocular rivalry among the provincial delegations, the same restless silence when French was spoken, the same tributes to parochialism, and the usual drunken conviviality – the pawing, back-slapping, handshaking, and fond embracing which characterize political meetings in Ottawa or anywhere else.

Politics is much too serious a business to be taken seriously by too many people. Party democracy is essentially ritual, and here, as Mackenzie King stepped down, the partisans dutifully acted out their parts. Everyone – or almost everyone – knew his place and kept it.

The old patronized the young, which is their habit, and when a feeble protest was made by some of the Young Liberals, I was abruptly called out of the Resolutions Committee to the platform, one of three Young Liberals chosen by persons unknown to address the convention. We were asked–Vernon Singer, Roland Le Francois, and I–to present "the Young Liberal point of view" to a hall of chattering, distracted delegates. Although I arrived on the platform last, I was the first called upon to speak by the chairman, who signalled our presence with words I found embarrassingly gratuitous, and almost completely false:

I do not know what they wish to talk about, but when there are three or four men who say they have something important to say to a Convention of this kind we should hear them. They have asked for only three minutes apiece. If they stick to three minutes they must be very good. We have accepted their request to speak to you for three minutes . . . .

I had the feeling of being on the end of a string looped around someone's fingers, helplessly manipulated, obliged to respond without thought or calculation to the urgencies of unknown or unseen forces. What, I asked myself, looking out over the crowd, did they want from me? Where was the revolt our presence was calculated to quell? Why was I being tokenized?

While thinking, I began talking, saying the first and most natural thing to come to mind, which proved to be an elaborate tribute to the Liberalism of John B. McNair, whose side I had just left and for whose personal circumstances I felt an overwhelming, undifferential sympathy. Such sentiments evoked applause, which sounded like the rustling of wind through treetops, but whatever I said came from a distracted mind, annoyed by the patronizing introduction, puzzled by my selection, and ignorant of any purpose.

Somehow, and God only knows how, I had the notion that power was compassionate and sympathetic. Where the idea came from I cannot say, perhaps from the fact that men who possessed it seemed, as individuals, to be gentle in nature and recognizably human. It was not until now in this dark, noisy, confused hall, and in the corridors and stuffy little rooms where groups of men gathered, that I sensed that power is a blind and omnipresent force, that it is indiscriminate and amoral, and that men who wield it are also prisoners of it. The young cannot have power, for if they possessed it, they would only despise it.

In the press the next day I read a headline saying, "Recognize Us, Or Another Party Will" and in the story below Dalton Camp was quoted as saying, "If you will not listen to the younger members of this party, then they will leave and join another party."*

But at least some listened on that day. And when I sat down and Vern Singer followed me to the podium, they were still listening, because they booed something he said, which I did not hear for I had suddenly realized that Mackenzie King was sitting on the platform too, and I had said nothing in my remarks to acknowledge his presence or to pay tribute to him on this occasion of his retiring from office.

Then someone came over and tugged my sleeve and said the Prime Minister wished to speak to me. I got up and walked over to Mr. King. He shook my hand warmly and said I had made a fine speech.

Immediately I apologized for my oversight, saying that I had not seen him when I had come to the platform from outside the hall. He dismissed this, and repeated that he appreciated my speech "very much indeed."

*Montreal *Star,* Aug. 7, 1948.

I never saw him again. Two years later, I watched his coffin, borne on a gun carriage, pass from the Parliament Buildings, down the gentle slope of the Hill and out through the gates for the last time.

I returned to the Resolutions Committee, taking my place beside McNair, who, along with the rest of the New Brunswick members of the committee,* was waiting for some pertinence to come to the proceedings. Ontario Liberals quarrelled with one another and with Quebec and western delegates. Within the Quebec group, a visible struggle was underway between Jean Lesage and Hugues Lapointe for the leadership of that delegation. Each vied with the other for prominence, position, and the floor.

McNair bore all this with inexhaustible patience. Some of us knew of his wife's illness. So there was both languor and tension among the New Brunswick delegates, but we were all good listeners.

There was a protracted discussion on the question of a Canadian flag. The Liberal Party was not without its quota of traditionalists and colonialists with strong views as to whether a new flag should have the Union Jack on it, or the Fleur de Lis, or the Coat of Arms, or something else, or nothing.

On the edge of exasperation, McNair turned to C. T. Richard, a North Shore M.P. and an Acadian: "Clovis, did you ever hear so much nonsense?"

With a huge shrug, Clovis threw up his hands. "What's wrong with the flag we got?"

Doug Anglin, an Ontario Rhodes Scholar-elect, and I were delegated to draft a resolution on the flag, which we did; the committee, its interest waning, passed it without protest. The resolution stood as Liberal policy on that matter, unchanged and unresolved, until 1964.

There were heated discussions on taxation and federal surpluses. A number of the committee thought taxes were too high, and resistance to the view seemed minimal, although Senator Cairine Wilson protested, "The trouble with so many of our people, especially the younger ones, is that they believe what they read in the Tory press. The *Globe and Mail,* for example." (There has since come to be an identical view on this in the Tory Party.)

Finally, the Finance Minister appeared before us, sitting with legs crossed at the knee, an arm casually draped over the back of his chair, relaxed and smiling, a boardroom portrait of bland and effortless efficiency.

"Well, Mr. Chairman," Doug Abbott said, his light voice buoyant with confidence and genial candour, "let me just say this to you. It doesn't matter what resolutions you pass here. Pass any resolutions

*Saint John *Telegraph-Journal;* August 4, 1948. "Premier McNair, Hon. Milton Gregg, Senator Copp, G. T. Mitton, Hon. J. G. Boucher, Dalton Camp, Hon. J. J. Hayes Doone, Hon. A. C. Taylor, Hon. Dr. F. A. McGrand and C. T. Richard, M.P."

you like. But I am the Minister of Finance and so long as I am, I will do what I think is right."

Saying that, he smiled–a handsome, radiant, ear-to-ear smile.*

People liked Abbott, admired his poise and insouciance, especially in Parliament. He had always seemed different from the others–an ambition so well contained as to be undetected, a directness of manner that forbade misunderstandings, and yet, even so, the suggestion that he could not somehow take himself too seriously. But now he was making a serious point in a cheerful, almost exuberant way, and he was telling them all – the critics, the worriers, the *Globe and Mail* readers – to go to hell. He was one of the few, the very few, who could do it, and no one could have done it more nicely.

But most of us, sitting around McNair, took little note of it; there was a barely audible exhalation of breath after Abbott's brief remarks, like wind spilling from sails, and when I looked up again, he was gone. As Maritimers, we had other strategies in mind and these did not, or so we thought, involve Mr. Abbott.

McNair was writing a speech that would place in nomination for the leadership of the Liberal Party the name of Angus L. Macdonald, Premier of Nova Scotia, former wartime Minister for the Navy, and the most prestigious and powerful of the three Maritime premiers. It was, to us, an appealing strategy. McNair was to nominate Macdonald, Senator Wishart Robertson of Nova Scotia was to be the seconder, and Macdonald's task would be to articulate the policy recommendations being advanced at the convention by the Maritime delegates. Having done this, which we were certain would seize the attention of the convention, the press, and the unseen radio audience, Macdonald would withdraw as a candidate.

It seemed an entirely plausible, effective, and even dramatic way to make our views known and to demonstrate the unity and strength in which they were held. We could then return home in good conscience, convinced we had achieved something of substance for those we claimed to represent.

New Brunswick and Prince Edward Island had caucused together, and agreed with the purpose and the plan. We assumed that since Angus L. had agreed to be nominated the matter was settled. When the Resolutions Committee adjourned its activity, the drafting of McNair's nominating speech was nearly completed, and a spirit of rising anticipation spread throughout the New Brunswick delegation.

In the corridors, I met one of the Nova Scotia provincial organizers, and we paused to exchange mutual congratulations on our combined strategy. As we were speaking, Robert Winters, then a Member of Parliament for Lunenburg-Queens, N.S., joined us.

*Later, to a citizens' group protesting a 25 per cent rent increase: "I hope you don't think that mass demonstrations go in Canada."

"Isn't it great?" I said to him. "McNair is nominating Angus L. and we're going to put our Maritime resolutions on the floor."

Winters' handsome face conveyed only his displeasure. Whether he was surprised or not, I could not tell. But he turned away from us, saying as he moved off, "In a pig's ass."

The Nova Scotia organizer quickly disappeared, propelled by sudden awareness of fresh and unforeseen circumstances. Left alone in a fluctuating stage of shock and alarm, I hastened to find McNair.

It soon enough became clear that the unity of the Maritime delegation had come apart. McNair had laboured in vain over his speech. There was a mood of gloom and despair, with sympathy for McNair, and resentment for Winters.

As for Macdonald, dissuaded by a determined Winters and by others, including Henry Hicks, he declined his part in the strategy, and, without him and his delegation, there was nothing. Winters was soon to enter the reconstructed cabinet, and Macdonald's disruption of the installation proceedings of Louis St. Laurent would be an unwelcome embarrassment, to say the least. As for Hicks, he opposed Macdonald's standing in nomination because he suspected that Macdonald's motive was not so much for the cause of Maritime unity as to enjoy one last occasion to harass Mackenzie King.

It was more serious than that; had Macdonald gone through the first ballot, as some suspected he might, he would only have needed the votes of loyal Maritimers to threaten St. Laurent's first-ballot victory. It was enough to close a number of hands on a lot of wrists; no one wanted a second ballot.

Few of us knew of these intricacies which so quickly surrounded what had seemed to us a rather uncomplicated undertaking. Few of us knew that Macdonald had not forgiven King for his treatment of Ralston (and himself), and few of us thought Winters would see in our idealistic and innocent strategy a direct challenge to his own authority and prestige in Nova Scotia.

It was astonishing how quickly and totally the plan was abandoned. Ruefully, wordlessly, McNair stuffed his longhand speech notes in the inner pocket of his suitcoat. The fragile wall of resolve many of us had so laboriously improvised was easily breached by a numberless horde whose interests and ambitions lay with the new order. The deeper realities of politics left us exposed, armed with only good intentions, while men who, hours earlier, had lent their applause and endorsement to the effort were now rationalizing their change of mind. In the ellipses of their speech one glimpsed a more profound self-interest.

New Brunswick caucused once again before the leadership balloting. McNair, weary and distant, left his delegates without instruction or direction, and they scattered themselves throughout the convention.

6

Later, McNair addressed the convention, as did Macdonald.* The Maritime resolutions were tidily appended to the policy statement, accepted with perfunctory dispatch by the party, and as quickly forgotten. It had been made clear that nothing was to be allowed to stand in the way of the business-like efficiency of the convention. The surrogates from the principalities had been treated with a dispassionate, if cordial, firmness.

The Liberal Party was now a corporate dynasty, and its board of directors was not lacking in zeal for good shareholder relations. No delegate felt himself pushed or driven, but gently directed by some benevolent guidance system, deflected in the mists of his confusion from the possibility of harmful collision with more powerful purpose and authority.

What one had come to marvel at most in Canadian Liberalism was its efficiency, its splendid imperturbability, the infallibility of both its fortune and its genius. The convention had been summoned to decide everything–to ratify the decision of the directors as to its management for the next decade–and to decide nothing (or as little as possible) and to demonstrate that there are ways to maintain fealty other than through commitment to a cause. It was a new politics of pragmatism made more compelling for its graceful power.

Discipline, ritualism, tokenism, the intelligent, flexible application of a suggested promise to a suspected interest, and a deft, skilful manipulation–man-management–these made Liberalism function. At the centre, men of unique experience could calculate with exquisite precision the tolerances and stresses of the adjuvant relationships they were obliged to supervise.

The chief purpose of the convention, St. Laurent's first-ballot election, was merely a fitting ceremony to close the proceedings. Earlier, Mr. King had bid his farewell, and each delegate was given a recording of his valedictory. Now, Mr. St. Laurent appeared to respond to his nomination: distinguished, white-haired, finely tailored, impeccably precise in gesture and expression, shifting fluidly from one language to the other. Standing above the crowd on the raised platform, he seemed impervious and invulnerable. To the quiet, graceful reassurance which his assumption of power provided, the delegates paid homage, certain they would not see him again so close at hand, a mere few feet above them. The Dauphin was now become King.

I voted for Charles G. "Chubby" Power, a vote not against St. Laurent, I told myself, but against the establishment. (I marvel that I made such a distinction.) Power's nomination speech had impressed me. As I came increasingly to sense the authoritarian bent of the

*And Angus L. had his say: "Let us not think the Liberal Party has a divine right to govern Canada, that it can remain in power indefinitely no matter what it may do."

Liberal Party, at least I understood Power, if no one else.

He had been viciously maligned. Political parties seethe with underground gossip, and that gossip which is most persistent often has, as its genesis, responsible, credible sources. Thus, over tall glasses of your preference, in the Chateau suites where the party elite were gathered and discreetly canvassed, it was remarked that Power was a drunkard, that he had been indiscreet and had bibulously leaked cabinet secrets during the war.

Power had come to the convention to challenge the establishment and to appeal to Liberals. His appeal for me was a mixture of sympathy, respect, and communality of attitude. In his nomination speech, he said:

I am wondering, however, if a whitewash of the past and a blank cheque for the future will give any reassurance to Liberalism throughout the country that the trend of the Party has in any way changed its orientation.

To those among us who feel that in the field of political reform Liberalism can rest upon its laurels, that we have reached the last word in responsible government, and that we can now safely turn our energies towards fiscal reform, or social security, I should like to say here that, however much we may favour these two fundamentals, almost nothing can be accomplished unless we proceed vigorously along the lines of reforming, first, our electoral system; secondly, our parliamentary system; and, thirdly, our administrative ministerial system; to make these more readily responsive to the will of the people. I mean from bottom to top, from voter to Prime Minister. Our parliamentary system of democracy threatens to run down and collapse. It must be reformed.

I begin with electoral reform.

There must be a complete and final disappearance from our electoral manners, customs and morals of wasteful, unnecessary and often scandalously corrupt political expenditure.

With that, at least one delegate from New Brunswick heartily concurred.

On the eve of the balloting, I had visited the "hospitality suite" of the third candidate, the Hon. James Gardiner, King's Minister of Agriculture, who was known to have Saskatchewan as his fief. When I arrived in the room no one was there but his son, Wilf, whom I knew among the Young Liberals, and when I left, some twenty minutes later, I left him alone again.

I concluded that Gardiner was a stalking horse–or a Judas goat –for the establishment. His function was to draw potential support

8

away from Power; coming from Western Canada and representing the rural interests, Gardiner was attractive to those delegates for whom St. Laurent had little appeal, either because of his being French Canadian, or a Roman Catholic, or corporation lawyer, or simply because he was a stranger to them.

Although St. Laurent's election was a certainty, to make the triumph absolute, and sweeter, it was important that King's principal detractor and the Liberal Party's principal, if not its only, critic, Chubby Power, should enjoy as few votes as possible. Gardiner's candidacy ideally served such purposes; he was neither so serious a candidate as to challenge the predetermined result of the convention, nor so unlikely a one as to be incredible to those who might resist St. Laurent.

In the balloting, St. Laurent had 848 votes and Gardiner 323; Power had fifty-six votes, one of them mine.

Six years later, I met Power for the first time in the dining room of the Chateau Laurier where, sooner or later, everyone in Canadian politics meets. He had by then entered the Senate and I had entered the Conservative Party—different purgatories for similar heresies. When I told him I had voted for him at the 1948 convention, he expressed his belated appreciation and said he was coming to the conclusion that he should have asked for a recount. Many more delegates to the convention, he said wryly, had claimed they voted for him than the number of ballots attributed to him had indicated.

Near the end of his life, Power occupied the Skelton-Clark Chair in Political Science at Queen's while he wrote his autobiography. Later when I, too, became a Skelton-Clark Fellow, someone showed me a copy of an article I had written in 1947 for the Liberal Review, the party publication of the New Brunswick Liberals, which he had found among Power's papers. My article contained some criticisms of Liberalism of the day, and those paragraphs had been marked in Power's hand.

Smiler McFadgen was not a bad man by any measure. He did for the political chiefs what they did not want to do themselves—the numberless, small, but cumulatively vital tasks of dispensing what is collected, for appropriate purposes and maximum effect, among the party's forces and elsewhere. For while the victories belong to the politicians those with their names on the ballots—the totals are compiled and the majorities fashioned at the polls under the shrewd and watchful management of men like McFadgen, who adopt whatever means seem most likely to achieve the best results.

Occasionally, Smiler would walk along the main street of Fredericton dispensing two-dollar bills among his constituents, men who clustered on the corners, in their frayed Mackinaw or denim jackets, wool shirts open at the throat, the bottoms of their trousers tucked loosely into tops of pink-soled, gum-rubber boots. Smiler not only knew most of them by name, he knew where they lived, where they had worked, and how many votes were in the family.

He knew the taxi-drivers, the winos, and those who drifted in and out of the city from the countryside, and he had an honest, direct relationship with them all that was neither cunning nor cynical but, in a Calvinistic way, compassionate. He was the unofficial almsman of the Liberal Party.

For the balance of the summer of 1948, after the convention, I wrestled with a growing uneasiness about politics and with the New Brunswick Liberal organization. A half-dozen Young Liberals had been recruited by Donald Cochrane, who was a local member in the provincial house, vice-chairman of the Power Commission, and McNair's political organizer.

We were employed ostensibly to organize the party's youth which, in a summer immediately following a provincial election, seemed next to impossible. Some of us made occasional and brief excursions into the field, but for most of the time we sat about in the party's second-floor offices, awaiting instructions, inspiration, or leadership. None was forthcoming. We played cards.

We all knew where we were headed, which was back to college, or law or medical school. I had been selected as a Beaverbrook Overseas Scholar and would be going to the London School of Economics. Between games of cutthroat forty-fives, I read the old *Synoptic Reports* I found in the office.

I marvelled at the elaborate, mysterious irrelevance of the New Brunswick legislature, the interminable hours of meaningless debate, and the dramatic, highly stylized interventions of McNair. He only spoke on occasions of special significance–the budget, the Throne Speech, the estimates for his department, and yet the yellowing pages of the *Reports* seemed to crackle with his caustic wit and bitter irony, all directed at make-believe adversaries in a world of illusion.

It was not for me, I concluded. It was much too dark and mysterious a business to fathom. Something about being a part of it deprived you of your balance, like damage to the inner ear, so that you walked in anxious fear of falling and developed a hesitancy in speech, as though frankness would have your tongue. Politicians, I decided, were afflicted by some rare, obscure passion which they could neither understand nor consummate, and they were doomed to lonely lives devoted to failing in the effort.

I finally went to see McNair and, facing him across his desk, looking over his shoulder at the thick cover of maple leaves shading the open windows behind him, I told him I had come to dislike politics. I could not catalogue my reasons, but I had come even to dislike his party, since much of my experience in it had been, to my dismay, distasteful.

It was probably a puzzling and unconvincing confession, and something McNair was unlikely to have heard before. He seemed lost for words. Finally, after the long silence, during which we could hear the leaves chafing one another in the breeze outside, he advised me, in his dour, absent, bemused way, to enjoy the balance of the New Brunswick summer, profit from my year overseas and, when I returned, perhaps I would feel differently about it.

The impression I took with me, leaving his office, was that he had other things on his mind. Tweedie and I parted cheerfully; I suspect he was glad to see his most difficult protégé on his way to a year's absence from his purview.

Drifting idly along the main street, I reflected on this abrupt change in my circumstances. Passing Smiler McFadgen's friends standing on the corners, I considered the deliberateness of this summary act and the vagueness of its motivation. We all seek to idealize our motives: but what if the act is clear but the motives are non-existent? I felt I had made a major decision, as though I had responded to some warning signal whose source was unknown but whose strength and persistence had been profound.

I went back to the party office to say goodbye to my colleagues. When I entered the room, Don Cochrane was there, distributing the weekly pay cheques for services rendered, or otherwise. He produced envelopes for everyone but me.

When his pale blue eyes met mine, he said, "You've already had yours."

I never knew what Donald Cochrane meant. Perhaps he had heard of my conversation with McNair, and this was a means of showing his displeasure. In any event, it meant that I had been summarily and retroactively removed from the payroll of the Liberal Party. How could one put a value on a week's card-playing?

Or perhaps Donald Cochrane wished to bring me to my senses— a sharp reminder that those smiling teeth of the political boss could also bite. But how strange it seemed, and strangest of all the sudden, desperate, irrational feeling of being trapped, imprisoned in that close, dust-coated office with its creaking floors, battered furniture, and peeling walls, caught up in the desperate pride and wants and avarice of others. And in being trapped, knowing that the feeling was not pain but humiliation, as though you were called to be a silent spectator at your own degradation.

How quickly one's thoughts were juxtaposed, from the ritualistic pageantry of the Ottawa convention to this crude and basic confrontation in the committee rooms: Louis St. Laurent, standing above the crowd, praising famous men and glorious deeds of Liberalism; Smiler

McFadgen cruising the streets of Fredericton, shaking hands with dollar bills in his palm; Donald Cochrane, in wrinkled brown gabardine, his eyes the colour of new blueberries, orderly rows of false teeth flashing a compulsive smile, paying off his collection of card-playing collegians. Except me.

I hitch-hiked back to the family cottage at Robertson's Point and quickly dived into the water. The placid, mirrored surface of the lake reflected the slanting rays of a late August sun. The summer was ending, and with it, I thought, a brief career in politics. I had quit the Liberal Party.

2

During the violent interregnum of the war, New Brunswick had given generously of her sons. Or New Brunswick's sons had given generously of themselves. Once again, despite the coarse and brutish suffering of their fathers, the sons had rushed to take up arms, although some said the first to go were largely derelicts of the depression.

One early autumn day in 1945, I stood on the station platform in Fredericton, awaiting a passenger on an arriving train. There were others around me, on similar missions, including a wife and family beside me, prepared to greet a husband and father home from overseas.

He came off the day coach first, pausing on the top step, crisp and fresh in a new uniform, the bright red patch of the First Division on his sleeve, his face cruelly smashed in the war, the lower jaw all but gone, one cheek sunken beneath the eye.

A stranger quickly turned away; the soldier's children did the same, crying out in terrible anguish.

"Oh my God," one of them said. "Look at him. Oh God."

POLITICS SO EASILY CREATES A SENSE OF COMPLACENCE AMONG ITS practitioners. Deceptively, insidiously, the more successful the politician, the more settled and satisfying the world seems. A party securely in power carries with it a musk of well-being and reeks with the essence of its affluence and comfort. Men quickly learn to shift their gaze from that which they do not want to see, or to view with indifference things to which they have become strangely accustomed.

Among New Brunswick's God-fearing, uncomplaining, law-abiding people, men in power can soon persuade themselves that all is well, even while things are perhaps only better, in a statistically quantitative way if at all.

There was, certainly, after the long years of depression and war, more of everything in New Brunswick. More hard-surfaced, dust-free roads, more welfare, more classrooms and teachers, more homes and farms serviced by electricity, more pensions and allowances for more people. But, of course, there was also more for the quick and the sleek, for the cozened, comfortable few who served politics and who were served, in turn, by politics. Indeed, a hell of a lot more.

As a result, many came to be, and remained, Liberal, not because of any private convictions, but because their ordinary lives depended upon it. Nor were these only the select in the higher organizational echelons, nor merely the contractors and entrepreneurs. They included

13

the numberless people who subscribed to the Liberal Party in recognition of whatever they got from it.

They included the aged, assured their pensions would be guaranteed; businessmen, who enjoyed the efficient means by which political matters were handled; sundry agents and suppliers, whose partisanship had become fatefully married to their profits; and the men Smiler McFadgen met on the main street, to whom politics was a mystery except for the dim awareness that somehow some got pensions, others got jobs, and still others, on a lucky day, found money on the street.

The innocent are not corrupt, nor are they corruptible. The society of New Brunswick remained an egalitarian one; the only aristocracy was power. What had ennobled Liberalism was its charity and compassion; what now corrupted it was its expedience and the haunted insecurity that led it to accompany humanitarianism with the menace of fear. This became the gist of Liberalism—everyone was better off being Liberal, everyone would be worse off being anything else. The philosophy was not so simply pejorative as that; it had been refined and tailored for countless applications, wherever uncertainty could be seeded, whenever there was fear to be fostered. Liberalism had become not a faith but a command.

It seemed that it had to be; no party on earth could treat so many claimants. For despite the steady, unending out-migration of each generation, off to Montreal, Toronto, and "the Boston States," there were still too many at home – too many old, too many ignorant, too many poor, too many bruised and damaged by the great convulsions of society, depressions and wars – and for all of them there was too little opportunity.

In 1946 a stranger came to the door of my converted barracks apartment, designated by the University of New Brunswick as a married student veterans' quarters, and introduced himself as Robert Tweedie, private secretary to the Premier of New Brunswick. Politics was a foreign country to me, and politicians were distant, alien figures one saw in the simplistic, one-dimensional black and white of newspaper half-tones. The atmosphere seemed rare, and besides, one politician seemed very like another, a suspicion strengthened by the evidence that while the governments changed, nothing else did. It would have been embarrassing to both of us had he asked me if I had an interest in politics.

Instead, he asked me if I would like to go to Ottawa on the invitation of Premier McNair and the Hon. Frank Bridges, federal Minister of Fisheries. They had been impressed, I was told, by some of my editorials in the college weekly, and Mr. Bridges and some of his colleagues would like to meet me.

So I went, travelling in unaccustomed style, in a sumptuous bedroom and chair car, to be met at the station by the first in an endless line of

14

ubiquitous men described as executive assistants to the ministers, and to be shown my room in the Chateau Laurier, with two beds, and big overstuffed chairs and a gleaming white tiled bathroom. On the dresser was a bottle of Scotch, for which I had not the nerve to confess I had not yet acquired a taste. It was clear that I had arrived, both in Ottawa and somewhere–on some upper rung–of the Liberal ladder.

Frank Bridges proved to be an uncut gem of a man–huge, homely, gregarious, robustly entertaining. I lunched with him in the parliamentary restaurant and dined in the Chateau Grill. I sat in his hotel room while white-jacketed waiters hustled in and out bearing pails of ice and pots of coffee and trays of food, meeting people with names that echoed somewhere in the mind, people who seemed to be enjoying their lives, which consisted of politics and the company of men like Frank Bridges. In the hotel, in the offices on Parliament Hill, wherever they gathered, the carpets were wall-to-wall, the smiles ear-to-ear, the talk man-to-man.

And before leaving, I had sat in the gallery and looked down on the gently lit, softly coloured chamber below. At its burnished desks and seats sat identical men, in charcoal greys and blacks and navy blues, drumming on their desks in unison, laughter rising in throats like a chorus. Their responses were orchestrated by a single member standing by his desk, swaying slightly, his thin, reed-like voice intoning on the condition of his constituents in some distant place known only to him. Finally, the House fell silent around him, in a frozen tableau broken only by the pages, flitting like starlings about the Speaker's Chair and along the front row desks, and by the distant, liturgical sound of the lonely voice.

Then the leisurely journey homeward; solicitous farewells behind me, memories of making a little speech at a private luncheon off the parliamentary dining room, in the company of men like Percy Burchill and Neil MacLean, who were senators and looked it, and members of Parliament, like Wesley Stewart of Charlotte, while the Minister of Fisheries beamed approvingly and someone said, "Hear, hear."

"Well," I asked Tweedie when I got home, "what am I supposed to do now?"

"Don't worry about that, my friend," he said. "Something will occur to you."

Something did. I began to write a column for the *Liberal Review*: "A Young Liberal Looks at Politics," it was called.

Politics is the study of irony.

Before going to Ottawa, I had gone to see Milton Gregg, the president of the university, to ask his advice and approval. "Don't get too involved," he warned. "Politics can be a terrible waste of time."

Within six months, Frank Bridges was dead at forty-five, the promising career abruptly ended in mid-course. I mourned him as a likable stranger. Now, York-Sunbury was without a member and the province was without representation in the cabinet.

There is an apocryphal version of how Milton Gregg came to be chosen as Bridges' successor: King telephoned McNair to discuss possible successors. "How about Greg?" he asked.

McNair welcomed the suggestion and immediately approached the president of the university. Only later, when it was too late, did he learn that King had meant Greg Bridges, the brother of Frank.

The choice was McNair's anyway; King could appoint his man, but only McNair could elect him. It was the reality of New Brunswick politics that the sole political organization was McNair's.

The University of New Brunswick was, like all of Canada's universities, overrun by the returning war veterans. Despite the inevitable confusion and overcrowding, and the threat to standards, the university survived and flourished. Milton Gregg was a principal reason. While there were occasional unkind references, from the expected sources, to the president's lack of academic qualifications, Gregg was universally admired and respected by the students.

He was not an academic, nor even a conspicuous success as an administrator, but neither was he a martinet, which one might have thought his army career would have made of him. Slight of build, hesitant in speech, instantly disarming, he was simply one of nature's gentlemen.

Without regard to Gregg's earlier warning, my own involvement in politics had both deepened and broadened, so that when my wife and I went for tea at his flat on the campus, while he was struggling with McNair's invitation to enter politics, he greeted me by saying, ruefully, "Camp, you're the fellow responsible for getting me into all this."

He had, he said, spent a night "back on the mountain" wrestling with his decision. I was all for it, although I felt I knew more about Milton Gregg than I knew about politics. We would both soon be learning more about politics.

King called the by-election for October 25, 1947. In August, as was the custom of the Prime Minister, he had already sworn Gregg into his cabinet as Minister of Fisheries.

I was to enroll in Columbia University before polling day, but the organization invited me to participate in the campaign while I could. I was eager to do so. There was the sensible supposition that the Tories would charge that Gregg had selfishly abandoned the veterans of the university in the interest of high political office. I was to offer rebuttal to that view.

As expected, the opposition was General Ernest W. Sansom– "Fightin' Ernie"–a decent, honourable man but an ineffective campaigner, backed by an even more ineffective organization. Although it caused neither comment nor interest at the time, Richard A. Bell, the

Tory National Director, appeared in Fredericton to direct Sansom's campaign.

In early September, the Liberals held their first public meeting, in a country hall at Burtts Corner, York County, about ten miles from the city. The site was deliberately chosen, for it was here that McNair had begun his many victorious campaigns. Such winning customs are impossible to break; Milton Gregg and I made our maiden political speeches together at Burtts Corner.

As we drove out in his dusty, rattling car, Gregg expressed his uncertainty as to what he should say. I was equally unsure, and both of us were plainly nervous, a novel circumstance for Gregg, who held the Victoria Cross and Military Cross and Bar, and was surely one of the bravest of men. But politics makes the strongest pale, at least until they come to know it.

Mackenzie King's Minister of Fisheries was attired in baggy grey flannels and a well-worn, brown tweed jacket with leather padding at the elbows. Even I, in my only shiny suit, felt no disadvantage. We drove the last few miles of our journey in silence, arriving to find both sides of the road and the field adjoining the hall lined with cars. It was an ominous sight, but no more so than had there been none.

We were late, the hall was filled, and Cochrane was first on his feet. I followed, looking down at the leathered, summer-browned faces, a thousand upraised eyes, feeling the heavy, breathless silence of curiosity and anticipation. I praised Gregg, as a man, damned the Tories as a party, and said that the people of York-Sunbury ought to have Milton Gregg in Ottawa to work with our Premier, John McNair. I added that the young people, like myself, were all for both of them.

I had not been slow to learn the litany.

Gregg spoke as I did, without notes and without much idea of what he wanted to say. The principal reason for his accepting this new charge, he said, was "to do something for the old sweats," the veterans of two wars. It sounded as though he meant it. But to the more familiar political patois of New Brunswick politics, he had nothing to contribute. His audience seemed puzzled by this man whose reputation as war hero, university president, and now federal cabinet minister seemed unconfirmed by his modest demeanour, simple speech, and undistinguished appearance.

We drove back through the warm summer night to party headquarters, a dim-lit room over Staples Drug Store on York Street. There a reception committee awaited the candidate.

One was Smiler McFadgen. Gregg had returned from Burtts Corner with the notion that he had done rather well, as had I. McFadgen had another opinion. "For Jesus' sake, Milton," he said, as soon as we entered the door, "haven't you got a decent suit of clothes? You can't go around the country looking like a tramp. You're a cabinet minister and people expect you to look like one. If you don't own a decent suit, we'll buy one for you."

Gregg, I thought, took this outburst remarkably well. With thumb and forefinger he thoughtfully stroked his nose, and then quietly promised to improve his sartorial presentation.

McNair, leaving nothing to chance, entered the campaign and his organization began its exhaustive canvass. By the end of September, the only signs of opposition were the defiant posters of "Fightin' Ernie" Sansom, nailed high on the hydro poles along the river road. Otherwise, it was quiet, and growing quieter as the days passed.

Gregg won by 4,118 votes; only twice before had anyone carried the seat by a greater margin and that had been R. B. Hanson himself. In New York, I received Gregg's cordial telegram announcing the result of his substantial victory. He had been well and truly launched on the bottomless, trackless seas of politics.

Despite Gregg's by-election success, and my first direct involvement in federal politics, the New Brunswick provincial scene seemed more interesting and vital. The difference was probably McNair, seen through my eyes and those of Bob Tweedie.

The New Brunswick legislature was a dark, musty, cavernous chamber, smelling of Dustbane and varnish and damp, in which the proceedings seemed less a series of debates than a program of recitations. Members did not speak from notes, but read directly from prepared texts, many of them ground out in Tweedie's office. Afterwards, the *Synoptic Report* published the texts verbatim, as did the *Daily Gleaner*. Parliamentary democracy was carefully planned and managed. Little was left to chance.

The Tory opposition, under Hugh Mackay, did not appear to me to represent an organized party so much as members of a break-away congregation, some obscure sect of dissidents, who were plainly baffled by McNair, perhaps intimidated as well. They seemed a strange lot (indeed a good deal more so than I knew at the time).

McNair treated them very much as though they were not there, save only on occasions when he would wind up a debate, cowing them into silence with the precision of his debating skill and the cutting edge of his wit. Today, it would be considered overkill.

Politics had become stylized to the point of ritual. The great depression, "Tory hard times," the balm of Liberal welfare, the politics of paving, the cultivated suspicions of "Tory Toronto" and "Bay Street" had all become basic parts of the ceremonial incantation. In this idiom, McNair was a master. The word "Tory" was an epithet which he used to prompt amusement or fear, or as a call to arms. He never tired of quoting from Hugh Mackay's maiden and disastrous speech in the legislature as Conservative leader, nor did he weary of cataloguing the

18

numerous directorships Mackay held which linked him to the sinister
financial citadels of Montreal and Toronto:

Why, Sir, it was those reactionary forces which, according to his own
statements in this House in 1941, already quoted, induced my
honourable friend, the Leader of the Opposition, in 1939, to come
back to New Brunswick and enter the political field. Had his party
won the general election of that year he would have been Premier
in my place.

In the opinion of the financial magnates of this country our Province
was then bankrupt. They had been crying it around every club and
meeting place in St. James and Bay Streets. We had built too many
roads and bridges, constructed too many hydro extensions, paid too
many old age pension cheques, were paying too much to our blind,
were doing too much for the people of New Brunswick.

... It was in those days that my honourable friend, the Leader of the
Opposition, made his famous offer of cooperation. He volunteered
to go with me to the citadels of high finance and straighten matters
out. Mr. Speaker, it was not cooperation he was offering; it was
terms of unconditional surrender.

In spite of all the prophecies of those days the affairs of this Province
have prospered at the hands of the Liberal Party. The lot of our people
was never better; the credit of New Brunswick never stood higher.
Our critics from outside have had the grace to acknowledge those
things. We are grateful to them. I have yet to hear, however,
one word of general commendation from any gentleman opposite.

But, Sir, in their present extremities I can forgive them much. They
know not whither they are going, nor when. With a captain whom
they do not trust–

Mr. McInerney: Oh no.

Hon. Mr. McNair:—and running without lights, on a journey which
is leading nowhere, their plight calls for our commiseration.

Mr. Perry: Don't you think we'll land over there?

Hon. Mr. McNair: Not in this world.

... For my part, I believe that New Brunswick is on the eve of a
fresh era of expansion, in which she will march shoulder to shoulder

with the rest of Canada in building up on this continent a still greater and mightier nation. It should be our common purpose in the days that lie ahead to unite with our fellow countrymen, from sea to sea, without distinction of class, race or creed, to make of our country a land where justice will reign and the social and economic lot of every man will be the concern of all.*

With relish, McNair improvised countless versions of this theme, his supporters hearing each of them with appropriate manifestations of enthusiasm, the more so for their familiarity.

Tweedie would argue the necessity of this ritual, but he was the first to warn me of the danger of excessive partisanship. His policy was not political warfare, but disarmament. Courtesy, consideration, and civility were, in Tweedie's view, the only essential weapons of government. It suited his nature and he practised what he preached; he considered the bloody-minded partisans and the narrow-minded Grits, as "damned fools" and sought always to temper excesses in either reaction, strategy, or speech.

Barring some apocalyptic event, he believed governments need never be defeated, even though they might live constantly on the brink of defeat–usually nearer than they knew. What defeated governments, in his opinion, were the "damn fools" whose stupidity and cupidity violated reason and common sense, inviting the hostility of decent people.

In New Brunswick, in the summer of 1948, Liberalism could do no wrong and Conservatism could do no right. The Liberals were un-challenged on the French-speaking North Shore; McNair ruled York and Sunbury Counties by personal fiat: in Charlotte County, Liberal supremacy was forged in the powerful combination of McNair's politi-cal shrewdness and the feudal entrenchment of the Connors Brothers fisheries along the Fundy shores. This left Carleton, Saint John City and County, and Kings to the Tories. For McNair, a prudent democrat, that was fair enough.

Politics in New Brunswick comes cruelly close to the bone. Life for most of its people is a hard struggle. The provincial government was, still is, the largest employer. Patronage, a matter of political favour and partisan right, is often a matter of survival as well. Work on the roads, jobs as foremen, road supervisors, distillers' representatives, government suppliers, or appointments to boards and commissions, even to the Senate and courts–the allotment of all these jobs is a vital concern, and can produce private disappointment, resentment, and public suspicion.

McNair's Liberal Party "looked after its own." It had become an inexorably thorough, all-conquering political machine. And it began

*Hon. J. B. McNair, *Synoptic Report,* 1946. Pgs. 307-8.

20

to acquire a life and style of its own, apart from party policy or purpose. The profound urge to sustain itself, nourish its power, feed its own desires came to dominate McNair's organization until, in fact, it became a kind of court, dispensing favour, rough justice, and even grace. I came to fear the machine and to burden Tweedie with my concern.

It made no difference to argue that the Tories, in power, would have been the same—or perhaps worse—for in politics, at least, it is the act of corruption that matters, not the contemplation of it. As for McNair, a careful, diligent, and frugal man, there were other pre-occupations—increasing demands upon his energies, already overtaxed, rising from the conspicuous lack of talent in his caucus and cabinet, the growing realization that the province was nearing a financial crisis, and the looming personal tragedy of his wife's illness.

I did not know many of McNair's cabinet members. My impression of them was close to the received opinion; few had the capacity to make a significant contribution, either to the government or to the politics of New Brunswick. McNair had no obvious successor, but, as with all personal dynasties, there was the underlying assumption that he had a number of good years left in him yet, and the matter of who would replace him was never discussed.

The ginger man of McNair's organization and the New Brunswick Liberal Party was one of the four York County members, Donald Cochrane, a former employee of the Marysville cotton mill, a short, thick-set, blue-eyed, pallid-complexioned man in his thirties, with a smooth bald head, a constant smile, and a gift for political oratory. He was McNair's chief political organizer and, as Vice-Chairman of the New Brunswick Hydro Commission, he was strategically placed for such responsibilities.

Cochrane knew what made the wheels turn and he did not like those that squeaked. I met him often, coming in and out of the Premier's office, at political gatherings, and in the legislature. (Tweedie thought him a powerful speaker and would give me advance notice when Cochrane was to perform.) Our relationship was an uneasy one. I was apprehensive about him, and I had no doubt the feeling was reciprocal.

After a year in New York at Columbia University, I returned to Fredericton, one degree better educated, with a Beaverbrook Overseas Scholarship in hand and a provincial general election in progress. On McNair's invitation and Tweedie's urging, I plunged into the campaign with enthusiasm.

Tweedie pretended to be concerned about the outcome, even though the Conservatives, led again by Hugh Mackay, began the election by conceding the five seats in Gloucester County, a French-speaking Liberal bastion. I became, once more, the voice of "youth," speaking at a rally in the old IOOF Hall in Fredericton, with McNair and Gregg,

21

and at "public meetings" in places like Marysville and Napadogan, where the proceedings were, by tradition, interminable. The meagre audiences, gathered in the dark, cheerless community halls, sat on hard benches to listen intently, if with restraint, to candidates and itinerant orators like myself, who recited the Liberal liturgy out of the campaign handbook. (I was struck by the fact that almost everyone made better –and briefer–speeches than did the candidates.) I also spoke on radio, and the favourable reaction led me to question the wisdom of ever speaking again in places like Napadogan.

McNair directed the campaign from the Premier's office in Fredericton, assisted by a tireless Tweedie and two men representing Walsh Advertising Ltd., Toronto. Scott Faggans, a creative, tough-minded art director, and Larry Jones, an experienced copywriter and public relations consultant, occupied a suite of rooms in the Lord Beaverbrook Hotel. After first meeting them in the Premier's office, I spent a good deal of time in their improvised offices watching Faggans labour over the drawing board and Jones batter out copy on his typewriter. I listened, fascinated, to their telephone conversations with their Toronto office, conducted in the unintelligible idiom of their trade. They were as sanguine about the outcome of the campaign as I, although considerably busier. What was more difficult to estimate was the effect of all their labours on the election.

The participation of the professional advertising agency in election campaigns was new to politics; indeed, due to Tweedie's initiative, New Brunswick's Liberal Party had been the innovator of the practice in the 1944 general election.

Whatever material Jones and Faggans prepared was always subjected to the cautious scrutiny of McNair and Tweedie. Occasionally they invited my opinion, which I gave reservedly, awed by the confident efficiency and expertise of the Liberal Party's advertising counsel. I had less hesitation in other matters. I went home to Carleton County one weekend, and in that Tory redoubt formed the opinion that we could win one of the three seats. Jock Fraser, the most promising of the Liberal candidates, was popular, presentable–and new to politics.

I had visited Liberal headquarters in Woodstock and come away dismayed by the unfamiliar lethargy of the organization. During my ten-minute visit, no one came into the office and the telephone remained ominously silent. The campaign manager relaxed behind his desk, peeling paint from the arms of his chair with dirty fingernails as he reminisced on past political wars.

All this is less disturbing and more familiar now, as are the symptoms of nascent political upsets. The local Tories were quarrelling among themselves. They had no confidence in their overall election prospects in the province and little more in their leader, Hugh Mackay. While certain that Hugh John Flemming would lead the poll in Carleton, they were less sure of the election of Gladstone Perry, and not at all certain of the third member on the ticket, Fred Squires.

In the verisimilitude of small town politics, personalities mattered, as did personal attitudes toward the candidates. Everyone liked Jock Fraser–at least, few could be found who disliked him. The same could not be said for Squires, who had enjoyed the longest experience and, with it, a growing residue of unpopularity.

I reported to Tweedie, knowing his native interest in the politics of Carleton County. He sent me immediately into McNair's office. I gave the Premier a true report on the condition of his organization in Carleton and the opinion that while Flemming could not be defeated, Fraser could be elected.

McNair promptly picked up his telephone and asked for Ed Mair, a prominent Woodstock merchant. When he reached him, he asked an innocent, general question as to the state of the campaign. Then he said, "Young Dalton Camp tells me we can elect Fraser if you people make the effort. We've done a lot for you people up there and now I want you to get off your rear ends and do something for us."

After that, McNair listened with brief impatience before saying, "All right, get moving." And he hung up.

I was impressed. No one knows what action followed McNair's call, but Flemming and Gladstone Perry were re-elected, while Squires lost to Jock Fraser, in an unprecedented rash of cross-balloting among the voters of Carleton County.

Everywhere the election was a disaster for the Tories. Of the fifty-two legislative seats they won only five – three in Kings County, including Mackay's, and just two in Carleton. The rest of their candidates were engulfed in the Liberal tide.

After the returns were in, I visited McNair's home to congratulate him. I found him in his shirtsleeves, strangely unelated, even somewhat rueful. The Liberals had won all four seats in Saint John City, a prize, he said, he could have done without. During the years of his premiership, he had slowly dismantled the provincial government facilities which had previously been in Saint John, moving them to Fredericton, to the delight of his own constituents, and in the sensible interest of improved administration. But he preferred to have the opposition party in Saint John. Now they were no longer there. He did not bother to conceal his disappointment.

On that warm June evening, as Frederictonians drew their blinds against the darkness and privately celebrated McNair's victory, no one could have reckoned the election result four years in the future, the McNair government hurled from office, McNair personally defeated, and Hugh John Flemming the new Premier-elect of New Brunswick. Myself, least of all.

3

One Monday in May, 1949, an impersonal female voice telephoned from the Daily Express. Lord Beaverbrook, I was informed, wished to see me at Cherkley on Sunday next. I would take the 10:30 train from Paddington, arrive at Leatherhead at 11:05, and be met by Lord Beaverbrook's chauffeur.

The female voice called on Wednesday: had I got the times right? Ten-thirty at Paddington. Eleven-five at Leatherhead? Right.

She called again on Friday. Lord Beaverbrook was expecting me at Cherkley on Sunday. Was I going? Just checking.

The train ride seemed brief; the journey in the back seat of the silent black Rolls was nearly endless. Moving up the long driveway leading to the house, under an archway of old trees, I had conflicting feelings of anticipation and apprehension.

Beaverbrook had just come back from France, where he had been photographed, along with Churchill, playing in the surf. He looked rested and tanned, and his welcome was cordial.

I had found him seated in the middle of a row of chairs on the porch, looking over the Surrey hills, and he was not alone. Three chairs away from him sat another man, in a white sleeveless shirt which revealed long, thin forearms the colour of milk. The man had a face of utter mystery, and a black patch over one eye. He was reading the Sunday papers and we were not introduced. Occasionally, while we talked, Beaverbrook would address him, calling him "Captain."

"What is the name of that fellow in Naval Research, Captain, the one who . . . ."

"How the hell would I know," retorted the Captain, not looking up from his paper.

"Captain, where is Mountbatten now?"

"How the hell would I know, Max," replied the Captain, turning a page of his newspaper.

Meanwhile, Beaverbrook cross-examined me. "I hear you are staying in England and going into politics."

No, I was going home after the summer.

"What do you think of Harold Laski?"

One of the greatest teachers I had ever known.

"Anti-Christ!" Beaverbrook said. "How do you like my new shoes?"

In Canada, we call them sneakers.

"Come for a walk while I try them out."

"What's new?" he asked a young man who presented himself out of nowhere. The young man told him about Berlin.

24

"There will be war in Germany within a year," Beaverbrook said aloud, but to himself. The young man vanished.

"Camp, do you want to have lunch in the sun or in the shade?"

Whichever you like, sir.

"Captain? Will you sit in the sun or the shade?"

"I don't give a damn where I sit, Max."

"Nurse? Where would you like to sit?"

"Don't worry about me," she said. "I'll sit anywhere."

"I don't know why none of you can make up your minds where you want to sit," Beaverbrook complained.

While I thought out answers to possible questions, Beaverbrook was on the telephone.

To the Daily Express: "I want more editorials on agriculture. Who's there?"

To the Research Department: "I want you to tell me who thought up the scheme for Habakkuk. I think it was Haldane."

"What? Habakkuk – h-a-b-a-k-k-u-k – it's a book in the Bible. But you wouldn't know that. If you can't find out in ten minutes, don't bother calling back."

To a telephone operator, hidden elsewhere: "I want Lord Baldwin of Bewdley."

To Lord Baldwin: "I want to know if you've done with my bull. . . . I said, has my bull finished servicing your cows? I want him back."

"Captain, wasn't Haldane mixed up with that Habakkuk scheme?"

"I told you Max, I don't know."

After lunch, the limousine took me back to the station and the train back to Paddington. When I got home, my wife asked me about my visit to Cherkley.

"I met the most amazing man," I told her. "I think he must be Beaverbrook's masseur. His name is Wardell, and the Beaver calls him 'Captain.' "

What I did not know, of course, was that this "most amazing man" was to become the owner and publisher of the Fredericton Gleaner and would be on his way to New Brunswick no later than I would be, that we would struggle to achieve a common political result, but that we would also disagree with each other.

IN THE DYING WEEKS OF 1949, LOOKING DOWN FROM A HOTEL WINDOW upon the snow-banked streets of Fredericton and the Saint John River locked in ice, I struggled to formulate reasons to substantiate a reckless impulse. Before me was a telegram from the president of the New Brunswick Progressive Conservative Party, a proposal both alluring and forbidding, like a sudden invitation to climb Mount Everest:

PLEASE ADVISE DATE YOU CAN ACCEPT POSITION EXECUTIVE SECRETARY
PROGRESSIVE CONSERVATIVE PARTY STOP APPOINTMENT APPROVED
AT SALARY STATED STOP IN REPLY CONFIRM OUR UNDERSTANDING

25

AND ADVISE IF YOU WISH ME SECURE ACCOMMODATION AND YOUR
REQUIREMENTS REGARDS–E C ATKINSON PRESIDENT

In the top left corner of the telegram was a sticker: "Sender is awaiting a speedy ANSWER."

Atkinson's wire had found me in Upper Montclair, New Jersey, where I had been examining the prospects of living in the United States. I had returned to New Brunswick, slowly, by train. I was met at Fredericton Junction by Aulder Gerow, the Young Progressive Conservative president, and secreted in the Lord Beaverbrook Hotel. I had yet to meet Atkinson, our first contact having been a telephone conversation. On arrival, I was informed he had suddenly been taken ill and was in the hospital recovering from the first of a series of heart attacks this indefatigable man was to survive, until the final one nineteen years later.

In the gathering darkness of that late afternoon, I tried to imagine the life one would have as a member of a despised, irrelevant minority – a Tory in New Brunswick! Tweedie, a director of the hotel, and thus closely informed as to its visitors, had telephoned me. In our brief, strained conversation he had left only a cordial warning, "Don't do anything foolish, my boy." Otherwise, silence, save only occasional calls from Gerow, testing my mood and inclination.

I had sought other advice, and it was negative. I had visited a trusted friend and a fellow cottager at Robertson's Point, K. L. Golding. A shrewd, kindly man with a spectator's interest in politics, Golding could only warn me of the dismal circumstances of the Conservative Party. (He was himself what was called "a McNair Tory," a professed Conservative who voted for McNair.) He stressed the dangers of association with Atkinson, a rather unpredictable and volatile politician. My wife and her family were gravely concerned; not that they disapproved of my departing the Liberal Party, but of my returning, as a result, to New Brunswick to serve in the Tory Party.

I was once told of a system allegedly employed by the Chinese in reaching difficult decisions; the method consisted of drawing a line down a sheet of paper and writing advantages and disadvantages on opposite sides of the line. When the exercise had been completed, the lengthier column would indicate the proper decision.

I set to work with painful deliberation. One side of the paper was filled with reasons for declining Atkinson's offer. Opposite were only three reasons for accepting it, and they were all I could think of:

1. Return to Canada
2. Live in New Brunswick
3. Teach Tories how to fight Grits.

There was, as well, an inarticulate idealism about politics, absorbed from Laski at the London School of Economics and the British experience, and a sense of outrage which the cold, pervasive New Brunswick winter rekindled, much of it directed at the Liberal Party. I had walked the streets of Woodstock and Fredericton, seeing once more the wasted men, the withering years upon them, bundled against the cold, resolutely cheerful as ever, asking nothing more from life than another day of it. Men consumed by idleness, their women worn by harsh routine, bearing the pallor of self-neglect, the children with bad teeth, the early beginning of a life cycle of decay; store windows displaying the hideous litter of cheap merchandise, malevolently designed for lives of quiet despair, for an existence amid an abandoned culture, in a ghetto of memory. And the city, its ordered rows of houses now banked and shuttered for the winter, the smoke rising silent and straight from the chimneys – all unchanged and unchanging, clinging to survival's shelf, the occupants seemingly content within.

Charity and compassion, cynicism and greed lived side by side. If there were other places that were much better, well, there were still other places that were much worse. The merchant class took few risks but prospered, and among the risks it did not take was an involvement in politics. Community responsibility was more safely expressed through the multitudinous activities of churches, charities, and service organizations whose good works proliferated among countless citizens' committees.

Government and commerce remained at peace, exchanging tributes with graceful facility and tacit understanding. Each agreed to avoid colliding in the other's jurisdiction, an undertaking that had historic sanction in New Brunswick. Politics was left to the lawyers, business to the merchants. New wealth came to those who glided in between, advertising a common usefulness. It was a classic kind of liberalism, satisfying and rewarding to the principals, stultifying to the people, suffocating to the province.

Yet something else. To the political process – the ways of democracy, if you like – had come the consequences of a long-darkening attrition. McNair was among those who had dimly seen in the British North America Act the unreality of its allocation of powers. There was a growing gap between provincial resources and provincial responsibilities; while New Brunswick held title to sovereign responsibilities under the constitution, providence had not provided for the means to discharge them. New Brunswick was becoming, for all purposes save only in the empty language of the constitution, a ward of the federal state.

The erosion was gradual enough, accompanied by indifference and the distraction of a routine rhetoric. Nevertheless, these were crucial years for New Brunswick: the painful discovery of a constitutional incapacity and the bankruptcy of a political system. If politics and the parliamentary system are a meaningless ritual, merely a crude public deception, then argument could be made that the condition of New

27

Brunswick, in 1949, was its natural state. The party system had collapsed, the public become fatalistically passive, while the capacity for protest, the vigour of dissent, and the claims of the aggrieved had all been abandoned, indeed, had devolved upon less than a half-dozen men, no more, each of whom, for one reason or another, lacked the strength, skill, or competence to discharge so large a responsibility. In New Brunswick, the party system was dead.

Fresh from Britain and the London School of Economics, steeped in the values of political partisanship, inspired by Laski as to the value of individual dissent, I looked upon the politics of New Brunswick as a personal challenge and a private duty.

What I knew of the Conservative Party, which was little enough, provided only one morsel of tenuous optimism – its lot could scarcely become worse. In the crushing defeat a year ago, it had received only twenty-six per cent of the vote.* I scarcely knew any of its five legislative members (other than by their modest reputations), had never met its leader, and only now was I to meet its provincial president.

To Ewart Atkinson, in his hospital bed, the future was bright indeed. McNair, he told me, was soon to go to the Bench. A gigantic scandal was about to break over the head of the government. A serious revolt was fomenting within the Liberal caucus. I was impressed not so much by his information as by the restless energy of this unusual man who, though ailing and requiring rest, was still keen for combat and full of encouraging rumour.

He was the first professional, vintage Tory I had ever met and the experience was nearly overwhelming. As I came to know him, I found he was all that Ken Golding had said of him. And more. Short, stocky, entirely bald, Atkinson was celebrated as an able courtroom lawyer, a shrewd businessman, and an unforgettable character. He could not bear silence, especially his own. Words tumbled from him in a breathless torrent, the sentences preceded by a declaratory, "Now lookit here," and finished by a conclusive, "you see!"

When he stood, he assumed the half-crouch of a boxer in the ring, the neck withdrawn into rounded shoulders, feet apart, restless eyes darting from face to face, fixing with a sudden fierce intensity on the object of his argument. He must have terrified juries into acquittals for his clients.

In the life of Ewart Atkinson, politics was his Klondike. A one-time winner, a perennial loser, he pursued the next election, always confident of victory, never conceding defeat. Optimism was his creed and he preached it with fervour. Later on, Atkinson was to apologize to his friend, John Diefenbaker, for recruiting me to Toryism, but for

*Popular vote: Liberals 332,321; Conservatives 145,028; CCF 35,514;
Independent 25,500; S.C. 3,134; Total 540,497.

28

this moment, on our first meeting, I was to him the herald of certain victory for the New Brunswick Conservative Party.

Already he had made arrangements for my office, conveniently adjacent to his own. But to begin this new career of awesome responsibility, he had booked fifteen minutes of radio time on the following evening. All I had to do was fill it.

I left him, along with Gerow, eager to escape the intensity of his enthusiasm, anxious only to ponder the dimensions of my decision. And glad that Atkinson had more days in hospital for recuperation. We both would need it.

On station CFNB, Monday, December 5, 1949, I said:

The business of politics is looked upon by many of us in this province as a practice somewhat unhealthy and sinister. That this is so is in itself mute indictment of the present party in power. It should be of little comfort to us that a national Canadian magazine* recently listed elections in New Brunswick as among the most corrupt in Canada.

Let me make it clear that the professional Liberal, in power today, is opposed to the Collectivist State. He is also self-dedicated to freedom. But the professional Liberal will sell any principle, as he has done throughout history and looks like doing today–if the selling will yield him increased power. If professional Liberalism means anything today, it means an ability to hold power, by the subtle exploitation of fear and suspicion.

I hope we do not have a sales tax in New Brunswick. We cannot afford it. We do not want it. But a sales tax is the logical result of the government's postwar fiscal policy.

Unemployment is growing in the province. Let no one say that this is welcomed by any party. But all parties will welcome government action to remedy it. We have all been told that Liberalism means full employment and continuous prosperity. But today, the Liberal Utopia trembles.

The attitude of the present provincial government towards labour is totally unreal. In fact, this government is anti-labour. Its declaration of the minimum wage for labourers in the woods this winter is shocking. Since most of these men work ten hours a day in the woods, their wage is lower than the minimum wage of 45 cents an hour.

The growth of free trade unions in this province–and the Tory Party supports this growth–has been frustrated and denied by the do-nothing policy of the Provincial Minister of Labour.

Let us look briefly at our Legislature. The Liberal Party has 46

*Maclean's.

sitting members. I am not doubting the motives nor the sincerity of these members. But when we set aside the leader of the Liberal Party and look at the crowded benches behind him, we see a startling array of nonentities–collected together for the purpose of governing a modern state.

My friends, you may disagree with me as to whether a Liberal Government or a Tory one might best meet the needs of our province. But surely we have not endorsed one-man government, nor a one-party state. A political machine has been put together in our province, highly skilled in the subtle art of patronage. A wealthy machine; a smooth machine. The masters of this machine do not sit in the Legislature; we do not elect them. They do not seek office, but the spoils of office.

The greatest task at hand is to crush this machine.

After the broadcast, Atkinson telephoned his enthusiastic congratulations. The Liberal Party reacted in customary fashion; by the following day the party line had it that I left the Liberals because McNair had refused to appoint me as director of the New Brunswick Travel Bureau, or had failed to support my alleged ambition to become editor of the *Daily Gleaner*. Erstwhile Liberal friends crossed the street or ducked into the nearest store to avoid meeting me. It had earlier been suspected I had gone off to Britain and returned a socialist, or worse. Now it seemed confirmed; it was worse.

4

THE WEEKS AND MONTHS TO COME WERE FILLED WITH PAINFUL PERsonal discovery. My ignorance of the condition of New Brunswick's Conservative Party was soon enough replaced by an accelerated education–like learning about gravity by falling over a cliff.

The Tory Party was racked by dissension, soured by intrigue, demoralized, spiritless, and fragmented. It needed not so much an organizer as an embalmer. It was a loose alliance of local power blocs in various provincial enclaves.

To my amazement, Atkinson had not informed Hugh Mackay, the party leader, of his plans for me. Thus, the flurry of publicity about the appointment came as a surprise to Mackay and alarmed his personal assistant, Ken Carson, the single, all-purpose servant of the organization.

There were three competing principalities in the provincial party: foremost, of course, Mackay in Saint John, with his dedicated and competent assistant, Carson, and two Kings County legislative colleagues, John Woods and Doctor Kennedy. These three elected members comprised a majority of the five-man caucus, and since Mackay was a wealthy man and financed the party personally, somewhat in the tradition of R. B. Bennett, his authority was more than titular.

The second was Carleton where Hugh John Flemming maintained correct and cordial relations with his leader. As the undeclared but obvious successor to Mackay, Flemming's general attitude was cautious and noncommital, and while he was accessible for consultation, he remained reluctant to give opinion.

The third group was centred in Fredericton and York County, and reached into neighbouring Queens and Sunbury Counties. Because the government was a constant presence in the city, Fredericton Tories seemed better informed, livelier and more relevant. The Fredericton faction had little confidence in Mackay and much of its energy was consumed in competing against the influence of the Saint John faction.

In Moncton, the way station to the North Shore, there was a number of disparate personalities, quarrelling among themselves, though united in a common dislike of Mackay and sharing a mutual hostility towards Atkinson and "the Fredericton clique."

All together, this general mood of intransigence and recalcitrance expressed an inevitable political law–the dimmer a party's prospects, the more numerous are its factions. In New Brunswick, it was not a defeated army, but a ragged assortment of guerilla bands, as I discovered when I assumed my uncertain duties in Fredericton.

Yet, there were, as testimony to the durability of the Conservative ethos, some 65,000 citizens who had, only recently, voted for the party, despite its condition and its prospects. The great majority of these lived along the Saint John River, from the border of Madawaska and Victoria Counties to the river's mouth at Saint John. Descendants of Loyalists and the English yeomanry, they lived on the more prosperous and productive land, proudly self-sufficient, historically suspicious of their Irish and Acadian compatriots, holding profound, deeply rooted allegiance to the Crown and the Old Country.

Their lands, their church, and their station in life came to them by inheritance, as did their Conservatism. If they sometimes were brought to question its spokesmen, they never doubted its traditional virtues. Urbanization and the resultant deterioration of the rural society were still a decade from their beginnings. The sons took their politics from their fathers, the wives from their husbands, and all took them seriously.

There were demographic distinctions in the Conservative community: few were Roman Catholics, fewer still were French-speaking. Youth were scarce, the aged more prevalent. But as important, it seemed to me, were offsetting graces—strong loyalties, a sturdy self-reliance and, common to all minorities, a tribal sense of kinship and hospitality. With their hardy conviction of political rectitude went an uncomplaining and dutiful compliance with a life of persistent disappointment marked by fifteen years in New Brunswick of enervating defeats, of sharing an inner sense of having been outwitted, outmanoeuvred, and deprived by history, as though democracy allotted to the Conservative only the functional privilege of serving in opposition. It was a life of responsibility without authority and service without reward.

Shortly after I had settled into the office of the Fredericton wing of the Tory Party, McNair called a by-election in Charlotte, setting the date for January 9. Hon. J. J. Hayes Doone had gone to the Senate, leaving a legislative seat vacant in the four-member constituency of Charlotte County. McNair was under no obligation to fill the seat, and with his unprecedented majority it seemed only remarkable that he would trouble to do so. To complicate the desperate condition of the opposition party, it was now confronted with a contest in strongly held government territory, in the heart of winter, and the prospect of campaigning during Christmas and New Year holidays. McNair was not one to be magnanimous.

While Atkinson lusted for the fray, my own appraisal provided the disturbing intelligence that only he and I were of like mind. Mackay was against contesting the seat, and the caucus supported his view. The party executive, with the notable exception of Atkinson, was indifferent, while the organization in Charlotte County seemed willing to concede. If I had once imagined that my chief contribution to this strange, disordered political instrument would be to sharpen its sword and improve its tactics–in view of its record and reputation not nearly so grandiose an ambition as it might appear–it seemed now that the basic problem was in motivating it to draw its sword at all.

Atkinson could be belligerently persuasive. He insisted, summoning his vociferous energies from his hospital bed, that the Charlotte County executive meet, that I consult its members and urge them to contest the by-election. The executive was willing, at least, to consider the matter, and we arranged a meeting in the town of St. Stephen, the county seat of Charlotte.

"Lookit here," Atkinson said to me, "you tell those bastards we're going to fight this by-election if I have to run myself. I could win that seat, make no mistake about it. We're going to fight it and we're going to win it, you see?"

In the general election, little more than a year previous, all four Liberals had been easily elected, the fourth-place Liberal receiving 6,391 votes while the leading candidate on the Tory ticket received 4,793 votes. In the face of Mackay's obvious reluctance, local apathy, the lack of issues, and the inconveniences of a winter campaign, only Atkinson could find grounds for optimism.

Sensing Atkinson's defiant mood, Mackay himself came to St. Stephen for the meeting, accompanied by Carson, Hugh John Flemming, and Flemming's Carleton colleague, the venerable Gladstone Perry. Twenty or so local Tories were assembled in a dingy room of undetermined utility, on the second storey of a crumbling wood-frame building on the main street of St. Stephen. The old building leaned precariously to the river, its oiled board floors creaking underfoot, December's winds infiltrating the sills of the soot-stained windows. A bare, dim bulb, strung from the ceiling, illuminated the stoic faces of the assembled Charlotte County Tory executive.

The chairman brought the meeting to order, welcomed each of us by name, and called upon Mackay to speak. Hearing him for the first time outside the House, I felt a rush of genuine sympathy. Ruddy-faced, grey-haired, dressed in a crisply tailored light-grey suit, white shirt, and blue polka dot bow tie, gold-rimmed spectacles slipping down the bridge of his nose, Mackay plainly showed the burden of his office; the ordinary exertions extracted by the movements of his soft, overly fleshed body echoed in his strained, harsh voice. It was easily possible to visualize Hugh Mackay in the Seigniory Club, or among his peers on St. James Street, buying and selling, focusing his shrewdness and experience on the simple possibilities for increment. But it was difficult to see him here, in St. Stephen, without feeling compassion for his ordeal.

He was a blunt, plain-speaking man. "If you want to contest this by-election, go ahead," Mackay was saying without rancour or emotion,

33

"but you won't get a goddamned cent from me. I'm still paying for the last election."

No one could doubt the truth of this assertion, nor argue the logic of the leader's position. In the consideration before them, Mackay told his followers, they must keep in mind the fact that the party could not even afford to advance the election deposit of the candidate. "It's as simple as that."

The chairman knew of my dissenting opinion and asked me to express it. I advanced the possibility, unproven by any personal experience, that an election could be fought without money, purely with volunteers, but with the knowledge that we would force a contest upon the Grits and in so doing would also force upon them their usual, substantial expense. I favoured fighting them at every turn, a war of attrition. I was careful not to provoke Mackay by being too aggressive, even more careful not to hint at any possibility of winning. Indeed, as the argument wore on, an important question seemed to be whether the party could afford the $100 deposit, the common assumption being that it would, in all likelihood, be lost.

Hugh John Flemming was invited to speak to the question. He provided a masterful demonstration of his highly developed capacity for seeming to deliver an opinion without appearing to disagree with either side. A youthful, handsome man, he sat cross-legged and relaxed, leaning back in his chair, holding all eyes, speaking in a quiet, thoughtful tone. His words were accompanied by a slight smile, as he marshalled arguments for both sides, agreeing with each, discounting neither, meanwhile absently cleaning the fingernails on one hand with the other.

He had made clear his sympathy and support for Mackay, and his respect for those whose combative instinct might be to fight the seat. His personal opinion—"just my opinion, mind you"—was that the seat could not be won, although he cited precedents for electoral miracles. He alluded to the difficulties of winter campaigning and of being without funds for poll workers or cars on election day, but at the same time he was quick to admit more money was always spent on elections than necessary, and he regretted the party workers' habit of expecting remuneration.

When he had finished this careful and exhaustive analysis, silence flooded the room, the executive shifting uneasily in their chairs, a negative consensus groping toward the edge of resolution. Finally, the chairman invited a show of hands on whether Charlotte County Tories should field a candidate. The majority of hands were raised against it and the business seemed to be done.

"Mr. Chairman!"

Consensus is like a fog, susceptible to the gusts of dissenting spirits. In countless meetings of this kind, decisions made suddenly become

34

decisions challenged. It is one of the rude habits of democracy. Invariably, the challenge will come from heretofore silent members in the back of the hall. And so it did now. We all turned to see a taciturn man named Stewart, from Deer Island, and another named Everett, from St. Andrews, who had exchanged brief, hoarse whispers before Everett rose to speak, unfolding himself languidly from his chair.

"Mr. Chairman," he said again, in a voice of such surprising resonance one wondered how it could have been silent for so long. "I just want to say something on behalf of myself and Mr. Stewart. I want to say first how much I respect Mr. Mackay and appreciate all he has done to hold this party together. But the time has come when we Conservatives in Charlotte County have got to fight our own battles.

"I thought you'd like to know, Mr. Chairman, that between Mr. Stewart and myself, one of us is going to be a candidate in this election. And between us we're going to put up the deposit. And if the party here don't support us that's fine, and if they do that's even better. But we're going to flip a coin and the winner—or the loser—is going to take on the Grits right here in this election, Mr. Chairman."

When the applause had subsided, Stewart followed Everett to confirm their joint enterprise. More applause.

"I think it's goddamn foolishness," rumbled Mackay, "but if that's what you want it's all right with me."

Hugh John Flemming smiled approvingly.

And Doug Everett became the Progressive Conservative candidate for the January 9 by-election. Mackay was disappointed. Atkinson would be elated, and very likely McNair would be astounded. But the Tory Party had decided to fight.

The Charlotte County by-election, seemingly a hopeless cause, offered some appealing compensations. There was the opportunity, inherent in defeat, of investing in future victory. In the search for campaign issues, both for present purposes and future advantages, at least two presented themselves—the possibility of a provincial sales tax, probably to be introduced in the spring session; and the obvious need for election reforms, in which Charlotte County could be expected to provide singular example for illustration.

We had little time and smaller resources. Mackay, true to his word, could provide no support, and I detected in Carson a disconcerting feeling of resentment and rivalry. There would be neither aid nor encouragement from Saint John. Atkinson reached into his own pocket to produce the total budget for the campaign—$75. It did not take long deciding how it should be spent.

I prepared my first political advertisement, the only one of the campaign, a wordy challenge to the Liberal candidate to declare himself for or against the "inevitable sales tax." Oddly enough, he obliged by responding to this modest provocation with a publicized statement declaring that he knew nothing about the possibility of a sales tax. Between the lines one gleaned ample confirmation of what was to come, but none of us, beleaguered, impoverished, and struggling to survive, knew how near our campaign rhetoric was to future reality.

Politics demands a harsh apprenticeship, at least in the Conservative Party. Docility conditioned by repeated defeat, the brooding presence of an unexpressed frustration which permeates all discussion and infects every activity, and the feeling of the oppressive strength of a government seasoned by power and accustomed to victory–these were, for me, both unfamiliar and hard to bear. For a Tory novitiate in my first encounter against the Liberal Party, these were by far the hardest weeks of my political life.

My assessment of Everett was coloured by a warm appreciation of him for his stubborn resolve to run. But he was a unique character and an entirely original candidate. He was personally popular in his home town of St. Andrews (a fact confirmed in the results–he carried the poll), but I had no success in drawing him out into the county to campaign.

I was determined that our candidate would not lose his deposit, and with that minimal objective in mind I made a nuisance of myself prodding the organization on in St. Stephen, where the Tory vote was traditionally heavy, and imploring Everett to show himself elsewhere than in St. Andrews. After spending Christmas in New Jersey with my wife and child, I spent the balance of the campaign in St. Stephen, each day of it an unrelieved experience of frustration and despair.

All that sustained me was a fierce cloak of defiance–and unintentional encouragement from my old friend, Senator J. J. Hayes Doone, whom I had known in my Liberal days.

I stayed at a gloomy, mouldering hotel on the main street of St. Stephen, near to the party's headquarters, occupying a small, tattered room; it was more than half filled by a huge, tarnished brass bed equipped with a mattress, stuffed, I suspected, with straw. Here I slept, fitfully, and took my meals. One morning, while I was reading the *Telegraph-Journal,* searching in vain for news of the campaign, the waitress put a bowl of cornflakes before me. I looked down to see a long, sturdy cockroach emerge from under the flakes, march across the table, and proceed up the wall.

In politics, more than in normal life, men can see themselves in the centre of things. The ego searches for satisfaction, achievement, consolation; the self demands expression and finds it in the party circle.

Politics is the only human activity in which there is significance simply in assertion. If you are a party member and you say, despite incontrovertible evidence to the contrary, that the world is flat, you become a force to be reckoned with nonetheless, and the party organism will respond and react in countless ways, in elaborate complexity, taking notice of a disturbing presence. As will opposing parties, should they sense a danger.

So it was in St. Stephen when, driven from the stultifying closeness of my hotel room, I walked through the lobby in pursuit of fresh night air. I encountered a body of twenty or more men emerging from the hotel dining room, adjusting their clothes, lighting cigarettes, belching, yawning, scratching, mellow in good fellowship, exuding confidence in their prowess and glowing with satisfaction in their cause. These were the Charlotte County Grits, assembled for communion on the eve of battle.

In their midst stood Senator J. J. Hayes Doone, having pronounced the benediction, the first man to be struggling into his coat and taking his leave. For some at his side, it was one of the more important functions of their lives: to be in the local chieftain's presence, commanded into service, to be praised and valued, given the recognition and authority that comes rarely to men whose lives are centred in inescapable routine, on the land, behind the counter, or in the mill. The Senator, glowing with goodwill, puffing slightly from his familial exertions, but with the peripheral vision of the veteran politician, saw me pass.

"By heavens," he shouted, "Dalton Camp!"

We clasped hands and he introduced me around.

"Gentlemen," he said, smiling, "let me give you a warning. If you make any mistakes in this campaign—any mistakes—this fellow Camp will make you regret it!"

There was laughter, the moment enriched by this unexpected partisan confrontation. I could only thank my old friend for his flattery and depart. Outside, walking on the deserted, darkened street, I imagined myself as the principal adversary of the New Brunswick Liberal Party. Perhaps I was. Anyway, Doone had been an unexpected tonic to my morale.

In Charlotte County, the first citizen was the sardine. Along the shore were the fishing villages—Letang, Lepreau, Letete—and Blacks Harbour, where the fish plant of Connors Bros. Ltd. processed and tinned the community catch.

During the war, the Department of National Defence had built both an army and an air force base in the county, two nearly adjacent installations, separated by the thin spine of Pennfield Ridge. The air force base, for Commonwealth Air Training, was said to be inoperative half the time because of persistent coastal fogs. The army base, ironically called Camp Utopia, was set down in the midst of an enormous blueberry bog. (Part I Orders were issued annually forbidding soldiers to eat of the forbidden fruit, but as they tramped and crawled over them in season, they ate them anyway.) The army was Canadian, the air force largely British, and they mixed seldom, other than in

37

occasional street brawls in the neighbouring town of St. George.

As a result of a prolonged stay at Camp Utopia, I knew the geography of Charlotte County, having patrolled its coastline in all weather, at all hours, guarding against spies who might be dispatched ashore from enemy submarines. (One had, it was told, landed at nearby New River Beach early in the war.) And, on training exercises, the troops dined on army K-rations, the most edible part of which were sardines from Connors Bros. Ltd., Blacks Harbour.

Connors Bros. Ltd. was owned and operated by "the MacLeans," who owned Blacks Harbour, controlled fish prices, and held the individual fishermen, and the community, in their thrall. The MacLeans owned the Blacks Harbour weekly newspaper, and a radio station in Saint John which carried the strongest signal to Charlotte County. Members of the firm were strategically placed; Neil MacLean was a senator in Ottawa, J. J. Hayes Doone had been provincial secretary-treasurer in the McNair administration in Fredericton, before he also became a senator. His successor for the vacated seat in Charlotte was W. N. Campbell, a management official for Connors Bros. from the town of St. George.*

The grip of Connors Bros. Ltd., as applied by the MacLeans on the Liberal Party of Charlotte County, was firm and unshakable. In the company town of Blacks Harbour, Tory organizers could not find workers. Indeed, the polls went unmanned by local Conservatives on election day, and representatives had to be dispatched from St. Stephen to represent the party. They brought back tales of incredible practices, including that of voters casting their ballots, in full view of the deputy returning officers, without entering the booths. In the by-election, the Liberal vote was 725 and the Tory eighty in Blacks Harbour.

St. Stephen held a stubborn core of Tory voters, most of them so silent as to be anonymous. The town was helped by an income from tourism (it was the major border crossing point between the Maritimes and New England), a struggling cotton mill, and, as the home of Ganong's Chocolates, whose management was believed to be Conservative, a faith which served to bolster Tory morale but also never seemed to be tested for its validity.

In January, 1950, stubborn weeds had long since pushed through the tarmac on the abandoned airbase; bitter winds swept around the empty barracks at Utopia; the countryside lay quiet in the grasp of winter and of Connors Bros. Ltd., and Liberalism was like a spell cast upon the land.

St. Andrews was some exception; in winter, the formidable anachronism of the elegant Canadian Pacific Hotel loomed silently over

---

*Still another MacLean was to represent Charlotte in the federal Parliament, from 1962 to 1968, and another became president of the New Brunswick Liberal Association.

the pleasant town, having seen its better days as a fashionable watering place for prospering Montrealers, but still looking forward to another opening season when the Americans would come. The conventioneers, along with a few of the old families, would return to their perennial summer homes, and such as Sir James Dunn, Rt. Hon. C. D. Howe, and Lt. Gov. Larry McLaren would be seen on the streets of the town, or at the St. Andrews Men's Club, at the dockside.

It was the logical place for the Tory candidate to come from. Doug Everett, in his white Stetson and driving a war-surplus jeep, campaigned in leisurely style among the townsfolk, comfortable in their familiar company. When I advised him of the fifteen minutes of broadcast time offered free by the Fredericton station, he quickly accepted, and I accompanied him on the sixty-mile drive to the provincial capital.

We sped over back country roads in his jeep, making a narrow corridor of light through the forbidding darkness and the piercing cold. As he drove, Everett sang aloud, mostly cowboy ballads, and occasionally we discussed what he might say in his radio address. I suggested he renew the sales tax issue, and outlined for him the sort of argument he might make, pledging himself to represent all those who would be opposed to such a tax, whatever their politics.

"Well," Everett said, between snatches of song, his voice rising over the high-pitched whine of the jeep's engine, "I think I should talk about the United Nations."

Which he did.

On the eve of the by-election, a winter storm moved up the Atlantic seaboard and swept over Charlotte County, depositing a fresh cover of snow. On election day, the streets of the town and the country roads were heavy and slow underwheel, and temperatures stayed around the freezing mark. We sat in the overheated offices of our temporary headquarters and watched "Liberal cars" churning to and fro on their busy rounds. We had few cars to dispatch and few calls for them. It is a long day when you are awaiting defeat.

Before noon, we had reports that some of the polls established by the returning officers were missing—two, to be exact. One of our stout-hearted supporters, an elderly lady, who had struggled to her place of voting only to find it abandoned, went off to search for its location, stumbling through drifts and battling the cold. Exhausted, she finally gave up and went home, and telephoned us to protest.

When the polls closed, the election result was soon clear.

| Campbell (Liberal) | 5,547 |
| Everett (P.C.) | 3,156 |

It was a light vote, but in view of all circumstances a tribute to the hardy spirit of the people of Charlotte—and to the Liberal organization which, I had no doubt, hauled many of our voters to the polls. And despite the sour predictions of some of our Tory friends, Everett did not lose his deposit. For Ewart Atkinson's investment of $75, it was neither a bad showing nor such a bad campaign, all things considered.

I sent a telegram to McNair:

The Government has dismally mismanaged the administration of this Charlotte County by-election. The proclamation of notice of grant of a poll was not posted nor issued in accordance with the instructions under Section 48 of the act respecting elections to the Legislative Assembly.

Polling stations have been moved as late as polling day without due and proper notice being given to the voters. One polling station was moved on polling day to a house situated within the boundaries of another polling division, contrary to Section 49 (1).

By its lack of responsibility the government has impinged upon the rights and privileges of the voters of Charlotte County. We protest the complete inadequacy of government preparations for the election as defined in the provincial Elections Act. We demand full investigation of the gross abuses and violations of the provincial Elections Act.*

The Premier, content with the result, seemed only puzzled by this unexpected sign of defiance. He told the press, "Mr. Camp's telegram suggested lack of understanding on his part of the electoral laws of New Brunswick . . . the electoral laws of the province do not permit the conduct or direction of an election by the government of the day."**

In reply to that, "Mr. Camp said the Premier was assuming the Progressive Conservative Party was protesting the election under the Controverted Elections Act. Mr. Camp said the party did not protest the election result, but would persist in its demand for a full inquiry into the manner in which the election was conducted. . . . If the rights of the voters were violated, directly or indirectly, by design or accident, the government had the right and duty to make an inquiry."

Well, cut your losses. To the Tory Party, the Charlotte County by-election was simply another defeat in a numbing rain of blows. The business about election irregularities seemed esoteric; everyone assumed elections were corrupt, and everyone knew they were inefficiently administered.

"I don't think anyone cares much about it, really," Carson told me, wearily.

*The *Telegraph-Journal,* Saint John, N.B., Jan. 10, 1950.

**Ibid. To help him draft his reply, the Premier had Ned Hughes, then a legal officer in the N.B. Attorney General's office, later an executive officer of Shell Oil (Canada) Ltd. I was my own lawyer.

I knew he was wrong. The Grits cared; they hated it, despised the publicity, the controversy, and "that son-of-a-bitch Camp" landing on the doorstep of the unsuspecting returning officer. It made them be what they did not want to be–cautious, careful about doing things, so that things should not only be done right, but *appear* to be done right. It was an unaccustomed consideration.

Atkinson thought the protest had a day's good press and took some of the edge off McNair's victory. "But forget it," he advised.

"Ewart," I told him angrily, "you will never know all the things they are doing to us. (Probably he knew more than I!) The only way for us to fight is to put the fear of God in them–about the Act, about the law, and about our intentions to be tough about it."

The Charlotte County by-election seemed instructive on two counts: the greater the prospects for intimidation, as could be seen from some of the poll results, the heavier the Liberal vote (Blacks Harbour); while the more secure, self-sufficient, and independent the people were, the lighter the Liberal vote (St. Andrews). Many people could not, I suspected, ever be convinced of their rights and freedoms. But the Liberal machine could be persuaded, perhaps, of the dangerous risks it was running. If the machine could intimidate people, we had to intimidate the machine. You must, I concluded, fight fear with fear.

5

*No man should enter politics unless he is either independently rich
or independently poor.*

Robert Manion

IN 1950, THE NEW BRUNSWICK LEGISLATURE CONVENED, AS WAS ITS
custom, in February: forty-six Liberal members and the Speaker, five
Conservatives, and a couple of ghost-writers. The opposition leader,
Hugh Mackay, came to Fredericton, bringing with him Ken Carson,
and they settled into the suite of offices allocated them in the Legislative
Building.

Carson had a passion, born of painful necessity, for doing everything himself; he not only wrote all the speeches for the opposition
members, but prepared their Notices of Inquiry, in pursuit of information which oozed out of government departments like sugar dripping
from maple trees. Some Inquiries went unnoticed; others were summarily dismissed as unanswerable.

The opposition caucused frequently, and Atkinson would sometimes attend, as party president. He plainly wearied Mackay as he
annoyed Carson.

"Look here, Ken, all you have to do is just ask the question–'What
is the secret deal between John McNair and K. C. Irving?'–just ask
that question and you'll have these fellows in an uproar."

"What deal are you talking about, Ewart?"

"Never mind what deal. I know what I'm talking about. Just ask
the question."

"Ewart, you can't just ask a question like that."

"Goddamnit, Ken, why can't you?"

"They aren't going to answer it."

"Of course they aren't, Ken, but everybody in New Brunswick is
going to be asking themselves, 'What *is* the secret deal between John
McNair and K. C. Irving?' See what I mean?"

Rumours of the sales tax persisted and flourished. And when it
came, it was, for Mackay, vindication of sorts, while for the others it
provided an anvil upon which to hammer the government. But none
were prepared for the fierce opposition of an aroused merchant class
which, sensing a threat to its interest, was suddenly mobilized to action.

The protest broke like a summer storm over the government. On
the day of the vote on second reading, the merchants gathered in the

park across the street from the legislature and, armed with spokesmen and a petition, vented their opposition to the tax. Somewhere, perhaps, were the evocative lessons of the Boston Tea Party; for here were the descendants of the Loyalists who had been driven from the New England Colonies by a revolt against "taxation without represen- tation." Now surprisingly defiant, they were standing before McNair's legislature, respectable, orderly, yet unmistakably hostile.

McNair was tempted to read the Riot Act; the Tories hoped he would. But the storm passed, as did the legislation, and the session quickly resumed its serene and leisurely progress towards prorogation.

The timing seemed shrewdly arranged. The tax had been introduced in mid-term of the government's mandate. Hopefully, the issue would soon be a dead one, with the tax accepted by the next election. Anyway, there was no swift ascendancy in Tory fortunes or even rising optimism. If anything, matters were somewhat worse.

Atkinson thought it would be a good idea to summon the Young Progressive Conservatives to Fredericton, and Aulder Gerow sent out the call. I was anxious to find out how many there were. The press dutifully reported the news of the impending conclave of Tory youth, enriched by the announcement that John Diefenbaker would address the closing banquet.

On Saturday, perhaps a dozen YPC's arrived, all of them English-speaking, and none of them very cheerful about the party's prospects. We met in one of the smaller function rooms on the mezzanine floor of the Lord Beaverbrook Hotel, sitting in chairs scattered about the room. It was a dull, formless meeting, like the day outside. In the contempla-tion of an uncertain future, there was a good deal of criticism of Mackay, expressed in spiritless, despairing voices, devoid of heat or feeling of any kind. Conditioned to Liberal mores, I listened with fascination to these unfamiliar sounds of dissent. As the day faded at the windows and the room darkened, a distant, disembodied voice suggested the YPC's "do something" about the leadership, perhaps go to Mr. Mackay and suggest he find a successor.

Gordon Fairweather, whom I was seeing for the first time, quietly and firmly talked down the proposal in a mature and reasonable speech, given while he remained seated. When he finished, the room was in nearly total darkness and we adjourned; there was nothing left to say.

Immediately, Gerow and I confronted a serious problem. Mr. Diefenbaker had called from Nova Scotia to tell me he could not speak in Fredericton. He was in Nova Scotia, he said, and there was no means by which he could reach the city in time. He had not been aware of the distance involved, and he was sorry for the inconvenience, but he would have to cancel his appearance. I proposed that we charter a plane and fly him to Fredericton. He declined, repeated his regrets and hung up, sounding annoyed at my persistence.

We were left without a speaker and with a number of townspeople about to descend upon the hotel, having paid two dollars in the prospect of hearing Mr. Diefenbaker. The sale of tickets had been reasonably good, but now, reluctantly, we refunded the tickets on request. (Some came and, on finding Diefenbaker absent, simply left without claiming their refund.)

There was yet another problem–the press. Two of them, in fact, now waited upon Gerow and myself, notebooks in hand.

"Where's Diefenbaker?"

"He's not coming. Brooks will be the dinner speaker."

"There don't seem to be very many YPC's here," one of them said discerningly.

"Oh no," Gerow replied, bravely, "there are a lot here."

"Where the hell are they?"

"Well," Gerow said, "we split them up into discussion groups–four groups–they're meeting all over the hotel."

There was an odour of fish about it. "Are you going to get them together?"

Aulder said, putting a friendly hand on his questioner's shoulder, "Why don't you come to my room for a drink?"

"Fine, but we got to have a story."

"You'll get your story. But all these meetings are closed and as soon as the chairmen have their reports we'll be meeting in a general session. Meanwhile, let's go up to my room and have a drink."

Torn between suspicion, duty, and thirst, the press yielded to the last.

"For God's sake," Gerow whispered to me, "don't leave me now."

We paraded through the ominously quiet lobby, deep in its weekend calm, rode an empty elevator, and walked a silent corridor to Gerow's room. With much ceremony and deliberation, the YPC president poured generous glasses of white rum, topped with Sussex Golden ginger ale, for the press. The first quick round was followed by another, then others, as Aulder began a highly fanciful briefing on the day's activities, producing verbal accounts of "interim reports" from non-existent committee chairmen, elaborate detailed description of policy debates, climaxed by a brilliant summary of the activities of the organization committee, which he said he had chaired himself.

An hour later, one had fallen ill and lay motionless and silent on the bed. The other, glass in hand, stood in the centre of the room, rocking to and fro on uncertain legs. He had a sudden twinge of conscience.

"Jesus, Aulder," he said, "I better get to your goddam meetin'. Got to get somethin' for the paper."

Aulder studiously examined his wristwatch. "Oh migawd," he said convincingly, "I've missed my own meeting. It's over."

"Over?" asked the reporter, blinking at the news.

"I'm afraid," Aulder said, "a lot of the delegates had to leave for home early. It's 6:30 now and I'm sure at least half of them have already left."

"Well, what the hell," he said philosophically, "guess we might as well have another drink."

Only the sternest sense of duty drove Mackay to attend the legislature, where he sat, restlessly squirming but resolutely enduring, throughout endless repetition of litany, distinguishable only by its tonal quality as to whether it was coming from the back or front benches.

Upstairs, Ken Carson sat at his desk, scribbling pages of foolscap which were passed on to the stenographer who typed them out, then to be passed on to the caucus spokesmen of the day.

The youngest man in the caucus was Hugh John Flemming, fifty. He did not rely entirely on Carson but sometimes brought matters to the attention of the legislature which reflected the views of his wife, such as urging expanded library services. In the manner of all heirs apparent, Flemming had adopted his own tactics and style—bland and likable.

John Wood, seventy-three, a farmer from Kings County, white-maned and moustached, short of stature and slow of foot, could read reasonably well, but he would annoy Carson when, on days he was scheduled to speak, he would say, "Haven't you finished my speech yet, Kenneth?"

But he could be depended upon not to wander too far from his text, which could not be said of Gladstone Perry, sixty-nine, now the veteran of the caucus, who had a self-deprecating wit and an unfounded suspicion that he could contain McNair by flattery. Often in the legislature he went on his own:

I want to discuss for a moment now the Hon. Minister of Health in connection with education. The province has free clinics and vaccination but I think it is a crime to have free school books issued each year instead of having the old ones fumigated. There doesn't seem to be much sense in having vaccination when the kids pick up germs by licking the pages of old school books.

McNair enjoyed Perry, as Mackay did not, and occasionally, when the Premier sought a few minutes' sport, he would remind Perry of the letter he had written (back in the days of Tory government) to the Minister of Agriculture, who was then embarking upon a government program of buying seed potatoes for export. Wrote Perry, according to McNair, "Don't buy no Liberal potatoes."

45

For Mackay such moments–and they were frequent–were agony. Late in the session, Carson and I followed him back to his hotel room after another day in the chamber. Exhausted, he fell on the bed, pushed his glasses back on his forehead while a thin stream of blood trickled from one nostril. He was sixty-two years old, plainly exhausted, but doggedly persistent. Prompted by some dutiful inner mechanism, he would not quit. He had less than five years of life remaining; half of it he would give to politics.

With the coming of spring, Ewart Atkinson's compulsive efforts to bestir New Brunswick's Tories had been finally chained and bound by intransigence and apathy. The party was lifeless.

When the legislative session ended, the five Tory members returned to their ordinary tasks–Dr. Kennedy to his practice, John Woods and Glad Perry to their farms, Hugh John Flemming to his mill, while Hugh Mackay resumed his happier rounds in Saint John and Montreal, busying himself in the marketplace.

Carson, still a remote, inscrutable figure to me, returned to Saint John, as well. His large, high-domed head overlooking a permanently quizzical expression, his slow, wheezing voice emitting from a lanquid, bulky frame draped in coarse, dull-grey tweed, Carson seemed either impervious to despair or totally immersed in it. Atkinson had been the first and only Conservative I had met who was in any way seized with a sense of urgency. By contrast, Carson seemed gripped by some massive, numbing sense of patience, like a prisoner facing years of sentence he cannot bear to count but is determined to survive.

If Atkinson had believed my returning to New Brunswick to enter the ranks of the Progressive Conservative Party would give new impetus to political affairs in the province, he must have been sadly disappointed. But he concealed it well; what he could not hide was the dismal condition of the party. His inventive, inexhaustible optimism began to wear on me, as it plainly did on his party confreres. And not only was the party broke; so was I.

To leave New Brunswick was, to me, an admission of ultimate defeat. To stay, in the present circumstances, was sheer irresponsibility. I was slowly seized by the realization that the cause was lost. There was no hope for it.

I met Flemming in the lobby of the hotel and asked him his advice. Well, he said, in that absent, semi-detached manner which would later madden his cabinet colleagues, he was sorry things hadn't worked out, but they hadn't, had they? And while Ewart had not consulted him about it in the first place, had he done so he would have advised against the party opening an office at this time. He hoped I would stay in New Brunswick, though; had I ever thought of selling insurance?

Ruefully, I told Gerow, "The sap is running. And so am I."

At a mere twenty-eight years of age, you do not like to admit defeat. But Don Quixote had broken his lance on the impenetrable armour of New Brunswick Liberalism. Or was it Toryism? I reflected on the sullen, shrunken ranks of the Conservative Party, and their wearied, aging band of spokesmen in the legislature; on Ken Carson, but for whose prolific pen they would be all but speechless; and upon New Brunswick itself, the stolid, uncomplaining people now sensing another spring, the sun beginning to stir the land, new hopes rising in wintered spirits–and, with the legislature prorogued, politics, like the snows, receding for another year.

New York City seemed good again, the familiar, dramatic skyline, a half-forgotten pace and zest. My daughter had grown since Christmas. My wife, Linda, was relieved the New Brunswick ordeal had ended; we did not talk about it. Instead, I explored job prospects.

First to *Time* magazine, up high in Rockefeller Center, filling out application forms, producing samples of my written work and certificates of academic bona fides. A young man in a Brooks Brothers suit, with Ivy League tie, haircut, and smile, asks me about myself. When I mention the Progressive Conservative Party, he blinks, unable to comprehend the apparent contradiction in the two words. Then he says, "Let's go downstairs and have a drink."

Over a highball he looks at me and asks, "How do you think you would like it, working for *Time*?"

I tell him I think I might like it a lot. "How do you like it?" I ask. "Oh, I like it."

"What is it like?" I ask him.

"Well," he says, thoughtfully, "it's like working in the world's finest whorehouse."

Maritime emigrés have unlimited choice; if they do not like New York or Boston, there is always Montreal or Toronto. Since they all seem more or less alike, the choice does not matter much, although some are in Canada and some are not.

Anyway, jobs are not scarce; only five years after the last one, another war is beginning, this time in Korea. Canada, even Toronto, is comfortable and calm and complacent. And the people all seem to be wealthy, secure, and impressed with themselves and with one another.

J. Walter Thompson is a famous name in advertising; here one finds grown men, swathed in soft grey flannel suits, wearing foulard ties and pocket handkerchiefs, agonizing over the right phrase to describe the delectable flavour of Wrigley's Chewing Gum. But, as someone says, it is a good place to apprentice, "the best shop in the world to come from," and there is a vacancy for a junior copywriter.

In a pine-panelled office, furnished in beige and cocoa and dominated by a monstrous dieffenbachia plant, growing like algae in the corner, an imposing man with a British accent looks at me with just a slight air of indifference:

"We pay people here," he says, "just what it costs to replace them."

In my case, it was two hundred dollars a month.

"That's fifty dollars a week," I say aloud, and too hastily.

"No," he says, allowing himself a smile, "that's two hundred dollars a month."

Well, it was a start, which is all a Maritime boy needs from life.

6

IN MID-JUNE, 1952, ATKINSON WROTE ME, HIS FAMILIAR EBULLIENCE unchanged:

My feeling is that we will not have either a Provincial or Dominion election this year unless Eisenhower secures the Republican nomination, in which case it would be practically assured of a Republican victory. If, on the other hand, Taft secures the nomination, Trueman [sic] will likely be drafted by the Democratic party, and if he is the Democratic party will be returned. . . .

It is, therefore, my opinion that if Eisenhower gets the Republican nomination, we will have an election in the Province in August or September and a Dominion before the United States Election because it would be apparent that if we had a change of government in the United States, it would have a strong tendency to create a change of government here. . . .

His letter concluded with an indication that politics was still his elixir:

In the meantime, I am not working too hard, and my health is good, and I expect to be around for many years yet, and may yet be foolish enough to return to Public Life. People tell me that if I will accept the nomination for York-Sunbury, in the next federal election, I will win, hands down, and now that they are passing legislation to give Members in Parliament over ten years a Pension, I might be willing to spend ten years in the House of Commons and go to the Senate, and I would then be ready for the world beyond.*

A part of his Eisenhower hypothesis proved to be true; the General was nominated by the Republican Party, after which McNair did call a general election. In his reasoning, however, there was nothing so subtle as the effect of a Republican victory in the United States upon the electoral mood in New Brunswick. It was simply that his government had been in office four years; to wait the full five-year term would indicate lack of confidence, a feeling far removed from McNair's mood.

In 1951 the Tories had chosen a new provincial leader; not surprisingly, it was Hugh John Flemming. His candidacy was contested by a Moncton barrister, J. Babbit Parlee, but the choice was never in doubt, and opposition to Flemming was impersonal, a token expression

*In 1953, he opposed Milton Gregg in York-Sunbury, and lost, but reduced the Liberal majority to a mere 1,000 votes.

by the Moncton wing of its sense of alienation from the Fredericton and Saint John factions.

On assuming the leadership, Flemming retired to Juniper, and the flurry of energy and enthusiasm within the party subsided, so much so that Tory National Headquarters in Ottawa, sensing the possibility of the provincial organization's becoming extinct, began to prod Flemming to act.

Finally, William L. Rowe, a sometime party trouble-shooter and son of Hon. Earl Rowe, was sent to New Brunswick to see the new leader and to investigate the causes of his reluctance. Rowe travelled to Juniper and found a man of inestimable calm and shrewdness awaiting him. Their conversation, at first discursive, inevitably came to the central, single problem: party finances.

With Mackay gone, the party had lost its chief source of subsistance. Flemming was neither willing nor able to emulate Mackay's example of personally financing the provincial organization. With an election imminent, candidates to be unearthed, and a nucleus of organization to be mustered, Flemming made it plain to Rowe that nothing could be attempted without tangible assistance from Ottawa.

Rowe arranged for a $10,000 contribution to the bankrupt provincial party, and soon after there were fitful stirrings among New Brunswick Tories.

McNair, meanwhile, was beginning his search for an election issue. The sales tax was now two years old, and the rage of the merchants had settled into sullenness. ("And four cents for McNair," they would sourly remind their customers, adding the tax.) There were difficulties, on the North Shore particularly, in collecting the tax from some merchants who failed to keep proper records and defied government threats to prosecute.

But there was nothing on the horizon, including the new Conservative leader, to disturb McNair's sublime confidence. He had beaten his opponents often, and with increasing ease, not only with a better argument, but with a preponderance of conventional political resources –organizers, publicity experts, a friendly disinterested press, and money.

When men in power lose their touch, their facility in determining the political climate, the tragedy is always that they are the last to know it is gone. For a while, their power and reputation will sustain them, or the gift of their opponent's folly may rescue them, but when decay in judgement sets in, it permeates the bones of the public man and he has not long to last. It is a terminal condition and no amount of luck may save him.

And so it was with McNair. Increasingly isolated from his colleagues, increasingly lonely in his personal life, drawing more and more upon his private judgement, he enjoyed the company of fewer men and sought the advice of none. He drank a little more, not too much, his friends say, but more than had been his habit, betraying his loneliness, perhaps his boredom, and the invisible relaxation of the coils of a fiercely disciplined mind.

There were other changes. Tweedie, for fifteen years the mainstay of the Premier's office, had voluntarily left McNair in 1951 and entered the civil service as director of the New Brunswick Travel Bureau. McNair did not ask him to stay, and while the two men remained friends, they seldom saw each other.

When he left the Premier's office, Tweedie had been asked by McNair if he would occasionally provide advice and be available for consultation in the forthcoming election. Tweedie agreed; he did better than that, writing twice to McNair, as a longtime friend and personal aide, to make suggestions. But the response had been silence and, from other sources, Tweedie was soon made aware that his advice was no longer needed.

His successor in the Premier's office was Charles McElman, drawn from the provincial Liquor Commission where he had been secretary to the commissioner. McElman was a militant partisan and a man of abundant self-confidence. Once in the office adjacent to power, he introduced a new style into the business of serving the Premier and, as he became more familiar with his new employer, he developed into an aggressive advisor. He was soon to become a self-trained expert in advertising and would instruct Larry Jones, from the Toronto office of Walsh Advertising, on how to respond to the Tory election campaign.

In the spring session of the legislature, McNair had measured his new adversary. Flemming was a different man from Mackay. He was younger, a less obvious target, more cautious in strategy, less impulsive in speech. Throughout the session, McNair stalked Flemming, seeking, as he had with Mackay in his first years as opposition leader, the opportunity to discredit him with one massive blow.

When Flemming criticized the expenditures on the Broad Road highway contract, which were greater than the estimates, McNair pounced. While Flemming was merely complaining of the cost, McNair chose to interpret the criticism as a charge of corruption. He appointed a Royal Commission to investigate Flemming's "charges," confident that, as a result, he could prove Flemming irresponsible.

Only McNair seemed to understand this strategy. As for Flemming, he was mystified. Far graver and more specific charges had been made before, in other matters. No one on the Tory side of the House could have anticipated McNair's response. But as Tweedie was to say later, there had never been a highway project in history that could withstand the thorough audit of an official enquiry without something being found to justify its search. "When you turn over all that gravel," he would say, "you are bound to find something underneath."

Anyway, the public sees the smoke and suspects fire. The Broad

Road Inquiry sat during the spring, raking over gravel contracts and examining cost-plus details and other minutiae of the project. Daily news reports of the proceedings served as deadly counterpoint to the steady pounding of the opposition on the sales tax issue.

The New Brunswick trade unions had been outspoken in their criticism of the new tax, and McNair's almost Victorian wariness of the labour movement hardened into enmity. So that when organized labour infiltrated the New Brunswick Electric Power Commission, a hitherto impregnable bastion of patronage, with Donald Cochrane as its senior political officer, McNair declared war on yet another front.

Seeking a diversion from the sales tax issue, the Premier created a highly dramatized portrayal of the union which was seeking to gain bargaining rights in the Power Commission, claiming that it represented "sinister interests in Washington, D.C." and that union certification would transfer control of the publicly owned commission to "foreign hands." It was a bizarre, curiously inept, yet deliberate strategy which led to war on two fronts, one against the Tories and another against the trade unions, an involvement as dangerous in politics as in war.

As McNair manoeuvred the government into a collision course with the union, it became evident what he wished to achieve. Given a crisis in the Power Commission, an interruption of service through a strike, followed by a court order, and a swift restoration of service, McNair could use the chaos and near-disaster as an election issue. Few in New Brunswick would deny him a mandate if he could show himself to be guarding the public interest against the forces of darkness.

Early in the summer of 1952, it seemed certain that the Power Commission employees would be driven to a strike. McNair obviously would do nothing to deter them.

In mid-July, the union organizer issued a strike order. Flemming was at his home in Juniper, minding his business, but amid the scent of pine and fresh-hewn lumber he caught the unmistakable whiff of an election in the air. On July 16, after consulting with Carson, he sent a telegram to the union leader, Mr. Tracey:

GREATLY DISTURBED AT PROSPECT OF STRIKE OF POWER
COMMISSION EMPLOYEES . . . THE PROJECTION OF THIS MATTER
OF INTERNAL ADMINISTRATION INTO AN ISSUE IN THE COMING
ELECTION CANNOT HELP BUT BE CONFUSING TO THE GENERAL
PUBLIC STOP I APPEAL TO YOU TO RECOMMEND THAT THE STRIKE
ORDER BE RESCINDED . . . THAT NO MISLEADING ISSUE BE
CREATED . . . .

Tracey obliged. The meat having been removed from the issue, McNair still would not give up the bone. He demanded that Flemming explain his "motives" for sending the telegram, hinting at deep conspiracies and secret agreements. He would have preferred a strike, but, committed to the issue, he was not to be diverted from it. Not yet, anyway.

Blandly, Flemming replied to McNair's charges, addressing himself to the public:

The Premier seems to infer that I deserve censure for sending this telegram which many people consider averted the strike. My own opinion is that I acted in accordance with my responsibility and your best interests. I feel sure that you will agree with me.

The summer of 1952, for all its mellow warmth, was a cruel one in New Brunswick, bringing the last crippling epidemic of polio before the discovery of Dr. Salk's miraculous vaccine. The disease was common enough in the best of times in the province, but this summer the numbers of stricken children increased by the week, and the facilities in the Fredericton clinic were sadly inadequate.

Now the lines were drawn, and they would soon converge. But it seemed clear, in the languid weeks of summer, that politics in New Brunswick would resume its accustomed course. McNair, sitting in his quietly efficient, tree-shaded office, Flemming, in the woods at Juniper, each enjoying the seeming tranquillity of the summer, neither could measure the restless unease beneath the placid surface of everyday life.

Few noticed that, in August, the writs were issued for a general election on Monday, September 22.

As the parties turned to confront each other, there were few secrets between them, only the possibilities of surprises. Each believed to know what the other would attempt to do, and McNair, who had so often bent the opposition to his will, proposed to campaign on his record, as illustrated and illuminated by Walsh Advertising, and on the "sinister" efforts of an international union to capture the Power Commission.

His opposition was resolved to campaign on more familiar issues—taxes, waste, inefficiency, poor roads, and "too long in office." The Broad Road Inquiry hung in the air, awaiting the report of Mr. Justice Bridges. The Tories suspected it would be a "whitewash," thus probably embarrassing to Flemming.*

There was always an anxious fear of McNair as an adversary, a profound respect for his political skills, for the awesome power of the Liberal machine; and there was a widespread belief among the Tories that, at some critical time in the campaign, the Premier would issue a

*When the report did appear, in the midst of the campaign, both sides claimed vindication. The issue was, by then, of peripheral concern, but the disadvantage was clearly to McNair. The damage had been done to the government long before the report was made. And Tweedie was right; there were faults to be discovered under all that gravel.

proclamation of such drama and magnitude as to exalt his position among the electorate. Whenever the Premier spoke on radio, Tories would hear him to the end, then rising from their chairs as men who have escaped divine retribution, say, with relief on their faces, "Well, he didn't make the announcement!"

McNair was always the general with the divine strategy, the coach with the prize play, the boxer with the secret punch and, besides, as Liberals gathered on street corners would remark, confidently, "You don't expect a Rhodes Scholar to get licked by some fellow from the backwoods, do you?"

In early August, I had the intriguing notion that it might be done.

There was not much there, in Juniper, except Hugh John Flemming's mill, a company store, the homes of the owners and managers, and the cabins, one of which I would live in for the summer of 1940.

The road which turned off the pavement near Andover ran back over rolling farm country and then through the woods, the dust lying so thick on the roadside that the branches of the trees and bushes were coated a powdery white. The road ended at Juniper, and there was nothing but silent forest, screaming saws, and men at work.

Men were not so plentiful as they had been; so many of them had already joined the Carleton-Yorks, or the 89th Battery, or the RCAF. The army, they would tell you, sure beats hell out of working, and there was no comparing the wages, and they fed you for nothing.

At Flemming & Gibson's mill, we worked a ten-hour day, for twenty cents an hour, although some got a bit more than that. It was a six-day week; Saturday was only a nine-hour day, to give the men time to get into town, if they wanted, for Saturday night shopping.

I worked on a chair-seat saw, which trims bark and removes knots from odd sizes of lumber You have to be damned careful with the saw, which is steam-powered and has the teeth of a shark. Once, working overtime, I was careless with a piece of wood and the unforgiving saw wrenched it out of my hand and sliced through the sleeve of my leather jacket, all in a split second, before it jammed.

Flemming had agreed to give me a job for the summer, perhaps as a favour for the son of a man he had known and liked. I needed the money for college and, as important, I thought it a good way to get in shape for football, which it was.

Hugh John had run for office once, in 1935, in a federal election, and lost. So, at the time, he was not active in party politics, although everyone in Carleton County knew that a man of his means and good looks, a man whose father had been Premier of New Brunswick, was bound to be a politician sometime.

I saw Flemming occasionally, striding purposefully through the mill. He seemed a pleasant, friendly man and everyone seemed to like him. One afternoon he stopped by my saw and watched me trimming wood, the edgings piled around my feet.

Hugh John leaned down and picked up a piece of edging, then looked at me. "You left a lot of good wood on that, son," he said, smiling a little.

Near the end of my two weeks' holiday, I drove to Fredericton to meet Flemming and volunteer my services for the campaign by providing the advertising through my agency, Locke Johnson.

The new Tory leader was unshakably firm in certain basic opinions, equally determined to be uncertain in others. Campaign publicity was something he was determined to be uncertain about; he did not value it much, knew next to nothing about it, and would have preferred, as of this time in his political career, to get along without it. As often as I pressed him in conversation, I would find he had changed the subject.

Flemming possessed a highly developed skill for evasiveness, and when he did not want to make a decision, he was a hell of a man to talk to:

"Hugh John," I told him, "we're running out of time. I have to go back to Toronto in two days."

"A fellow could always come back, I suppose," he said, philosophically, "if he had to."

"Look," I said urgently, "you're going to have advertising and someone has to do it, and there's not much time left."

"It won't be much. Not much money, you know."

"I don't care about the money. There will be money spent, and I'm only interested in how well it's spent."

"That's right."

"What's right, Hugh John?"

"It depends on how well it's spent."

"I think we can win if you have a good campaign."

"It's a powerful waste of money, in my opinion."

"Well, it shouldn't be."

"The Liberals spend too much money for publicity," he said. "Where do you suppose it comes from?"

"They have it to spend."

"That's right, my boy. They have it to spend."

And so on. But no decision. I came to the conclusion that Flemming must have made other plans, or he simply wanted no part of me. I guessed I had left too much good wood on the floor, under the saw, twelve years ago in Juniper.

I drove back to the lake, my mind made up to leave for Toronto on the weekend, conceding the election to McNair. With less than eight weeks until polling day, the Tories had yet to begin to create a campaign. By August, the Liberal Party was ready, as only a diligent, practised, and powerful organization knows how to be. Soon enough the cannonading would begin. The Tories, as they had before, would break and run by mid-September.

I left the lake on Friday morning, giving myself ample time to reach Toronto by Sunday. Leaving my family at the cottage to enjoy the summer to the last, I drove through Fredericton without stopping.

Along the river road, high up on the hydro poles, were the faded posters proclaiming Gen. Ernie Sansom as the Progressive Conservative candidate in the 1947 by-election against Milton Gregg. Some resourceful campaign adjutant had put them well beyond harm's reach, a precaution vindicated by their stubborn, faded presence. The General's face was ravaged by five years of weather, the letters that spelled his name reduced to suggestive hieroglyphics. But he was still there, a ghost of elections past, beyond the reach of vandals or marauding partisans, a part of the landscape.

The road was rough and familiar; this was the turn leading to the cool, shaded brook, where you lay on your stomach to look down where the currents had carved darkened pools beneath the bank, where fat trout could be seen turning slowly in the shadows. And this was the way to Lindsay's farm where, with Buddy Chase, now dead and buried in France, you stalked groundhogs and drove the horses, hauling off hay into the barn, and slept out at night in the orchard, in the sweet, deep grass, beneath the stars, hearing the cars on the Houlton Road throwing gravel into the ditches as they sped by.

At Lindsay's, I stopped the car, got out to look at the gnarled, coruscated trees in the orchard, the greying barns behind them, and the sun-faded farmhouse standing empty and hushed in the afternoon light. Nostalgia receded when I thought again of Hugh John Flemming and the Tory Party, of a hundred wasted days in New Brunswick spent searching for a sign of life.

No one knew McNair as I did, and no one knew the vulnerability of his party as I did. If you leave New Brunswick now, I told myself, you have quit, for the last time. And New Brunswick will never be the same to you. Before you leave, you must make Flemming say no, and go, or you must make him say yes, and stay.

It was sixty-seven miles back to Fredericton, down the river, the day dazed with sunshine, the heat rising in waves from the highway. I did not know where Flemming was; perhaps he was back in Juniper, or gone off to the North Shore. God knows. I rehearsed my speech all the way down river.

I parked the car by the Beaverbrook Hotel, walked into the lobby and immediately saw Flemming. Destiny's child!

"Hugh John," I said, "I was on my way home and changed my mind and drove back to look for you. You can win this thing, Hugh John, and I want to help."

56

He seemed, suddenly, receptive. "Maybe you'd better speak to Mr. Mackay," he said.

"Mackay?"

"It seems to me you should see him about this. He knows about these things and you should talk to him about it."

"Where is he?"

"I don't know," Flemming said, the voice becoming distant again, "in Saint John, I expect."

"I'll go to Saint John and find him."

"Look now," Flemming said, "you tell him I thought you should see him. See what he thinks."

I rejoined the river and followed it another sixty miles to Saint John. Mackay could not be found, but I discovered Carson in a nearby office, and told him of my difficulties with Flemming and of his suggestion that I see Mackay.

"Hugh John is a very strange fellow," Carson said, more to himself than to me.

But two days later Mackay came to Fredericton, and we met at the Beaverbrook. He seemed in better health, in good humour, relieved of his sense of duty and enjoying his role as an emeritus leader.

He had not thought much of the efforts of the party's previous advertising agency, he said, adding, "But they cost just as much whether they're good or bad." He asked me to outline my approach to the campaign, which I did in general terms, assuring him that an effective campaign need not be expensive. We could not, in any event, out-advertise the Grits.

He took it all in, approvingly. "Now to the big question. How much?"

"I want a budget of twenty-five thousand dollars," I told him.

"My God," he said, "you can't do much with that, can you?"

"All that needs to be done."

"Is that all you'll want?"

"Yes," I said.

"You have it," he said.

7

AND SO IT BEGAN. FIRST, CARSON AND I AGREED UPON THE DIVISION OF responsibility in the campaign. He would attend Flemming as principal advisor and speechwriter, and work out of his office in Saint John. I thought of going to Saint John with him, but finally I decided to move into the Beaverbrook Hotel and work from there.

I had one reason for the decision—McNair was in Fredericton and, I thought, the campaign in southern New Brunswick would be crucial to the result. There was a powerful radio station in the capital, a daily newspaper, and also a number of party supporters whose advice would be helpful. To do battle with McNair, I believed, you must enter his lair, and the struggle must be renewed each day. If McNair was the lock to Liberal power, York County was the key.

I resolved not to discuss advertising with Flemming. Instead, I would telephone Carson in Saint John and discuss plans with him, not only to have his opinion but corroboration of the facts as well. His memory was encyclopedic, and his sense of total recall was a prime resource. As our conversations proceeded, mutual understanding and confidence grew. Unlike most Tories I had known, Carson was inordinately careful about his citations. Both of us knew how devastating McNair could be with an opponent who did not have things straight.

I planned a three-week campaign, all that a stringent budget would allow, but it was enough. It had always seemed that the opposition began its campaign too early, so that both its supporters and their arguments were exhausted by the final week. It was common belief that the last week of an election campaign "belongs to the government." By that time, it had absorbed the full force of criticism and it had reconnoitred its ground and found breaches to be repaired. If the opposition is ahead, or running even with the government, with only a week to go, it must endure the closing rush of powerful forces fiercely applying the full weight of prestige, promise, and patronage.

So, I thought to myself, we must finish strong. It was easier to say than do, but I reserved budget for the final week's contingency. Something, by that time, would turn up.

The trouble with most political advertising is that most of it is unread, unheard, and unnoticed. I recalled Mark Napier's comment: advertising must "lend verisimilitude to an otherwise bland and unassuming statement."

Yet political advertising is not the same as advertising which only promotes the sale of products or services. At least, when it is, it

58

is a failure. What political advertising must do is create a sense of immediacy, of urgency and participation. Soap and cereal and insurance can be bought anyday, as everyone knows. Elections occur infrequently. Everybody has a vote–but only occasionally the opportunity to use it. September 22 in New Brunswick was one of those rare occasions.

Tories were invariably dull campaigners, spending half their time reacting to Liberal attacks on them, and showing themselves overly sensitive. Their rebuttals were filled with injured airs and declarations of wounds to pride. Tories had their piety, their sense of the fitness of things–a horror of debt, a dislike of taxes–and they were heard every four years to say, in effect, that things were as bad as they had last predicted they would be. They sounded plaintive, as though used to not being heeded, and they were no fun at all. Why not attack? Was ever a Liberal government or party more vulnerable?

Liberals appeared as men of conscience and compassion. McNair's sales tax, for example, was not to arrest insolvency, but to educate children, help widowed mothers, and provide free tuberculosis treatment. Of course. But Liberals avoided sanctimony by turning on the Tories with the condensation of generations of invective, produced by the great depression and the residue of history. Their speech was so earnest, their tone so emphatic, that the words unfailingly rekindled the passions of their audiences.

We could, I thought, give them some of their own back.

The daily press in New Brunswick was a passive one. Taking no editorial sides, it tended to favour the government. (On the last Friday of the campaign, the *Daily Gleaner* carried three editorials of equal length. The first dealt with "Back to School" and the need to instruct children in safety rules; the second welcomed the announcement of increased federal assistance in "the war against the spruce budworm," while the last welcomed the resumption of "Sunday train service between Fredericton and Fredericton Junction." It was soon to undergo a dramatic change in temper, but in the campaign of 1952, the Tory party had no allies among the media.)

There was, it seemed, a conspiracy of silence on the subject of provincial politics. Lack of opinion suggested lack of issues; the editorial calm daily proclaimed a general state of tranquillity. All forms of news, radio or newspaper, gave minimal attention to politics but reported on meetings as would the secretary's reading of the minutes, a bloodless accounting of events.

After brooding on this, trying to reconcile the various requirements into a single strategic plan, I decided to write my own editorial comments on the election and publish them daily in the six provincial newspapers. This would give continuity to the campaign. It would also supply argument and ammunition to the troops in the field, while offering a nearly immediate opportunity for comment. Furthermore, as daily columns, they might even build a reader audience of growing size—after all, there wasn't much else to read.

Someone had suggested a slogan for the Tory campaign, "Let's Clean House." I decided to sign the editorials "L. C. House."

I wrote seventeen of these editorial commentaries, typing them late at night and sending them by telegraph at night press rate direct to the newspapers. The agency supplied each paper with a border of question marks, for identification purposes, and the signature of "L. C. House," written in large, bold hand by my art director, Bill Kettlewell. I supplied both the daily copy and headline, which I tried to make as alluring as possible, all of which was set by the publication.

The columns appeared in random position throughout the papers, readily visible with the border of question marks, the type cast in bold face, as easily seen as read. The typesetters were dutiful in their labours, permitting only one minor error throughout the series. (Perhaps they were interested?) The columns were surprisingly well read, talked about, and quoted from. Within a week, L. C. House had become an established critic of the McNair regime.

Indeed, on one of his early visits to my hotel room, Flemming said he thought he should sign the columns himself and that they should carry his picture. I told him I disagreed; he was waging a statesmanlike campaign on a high level, and "L. C. House" was not. I telephoned Carson and we conspired, successfully, to dissuade Flemming from his idea.

On only one other occasion did Flemming involve himself in the advertising campaign, and that was at the outset. After the candidates had been assembled in Fredericton to discuss the party's platform, Carson and I returned to Saint John to put the resolutions in statement form, assembling the planks in some order of priority and preparing a preamble, which Carson drafted and read to Flemming over the telephone. We spent the night on it, had it retyped, and then rushed it to the press for publication as an advertisement. We were anxious that it appear on the following day, when Flemming was to also discuss his policies in a broadcast.

When the platform advertisement appeared, a forbidding, formidable wall of type, Flemming was on the phone immediately—first to Carson in Saint John, and then to me. His photograph, he said, should have been in the ad. My first reaction was a pang of remorse for not thinking of it, and the second was to invent a reason for not doing so. There wasn't room for it with all those words I told him. He was not consoled, and went on to complain about his picture when it had appeared elsewhere; it was an old and unflattering one. But that could be remedied, I assured him, by sending out new material to the papers and requesting them to remove the undesirable picture from their files.

Diverted from his original complaint, he rang off and I did not see him again until the election was over.

Yet Flemming was made of stern stuff. Beneath his seeming vanity, the courtly manner, bemused smile, and his amiable discursiveness there was an iron will, reinforced by stubborn principle.

When all the candidates met to draft the platform, there was a heated debate over the party's position on the sales tax issue. The majority wanted an unequivocal pledge to abolish it. There were few who urged caution.

Flemming had already made up his mind and, sitting placidly at the front of the room, beside the chairman, he let the debate wear on until all had exhausted their arguments. Then he spoke, without rising from his chair: "Well now look, boys," he said in a light voice, with neither heat nor menace, "if you want to promise to remove the sales tax, then I just think you'll have to get another leader, and that's about all there is to it."

And so the Tory plank on the sales tax declared, "We strongly favour the abolition of the Provincial Sales Tax. We pledge ourselves to direct our efforts to that end."

It even puzzled McNair, who said it could mean anything, or nothing.

Later, gathered in an upstairs room of the hotel with Mackay, Carson, and a few others, Flemming asked me what I would have done. I told him that if promising to remove the sales tax would promise victory in the election, the Liberal Party would not hesitate, were the circumstances reversed. Flemming insisted that it would be irresponsible, and victory should not be purchased by irresponsibility.

Flemming's example was instructive. Honesty and scruple plague Conservative leaders, as though they bear a private burden of atonement for the past, or are determined that others must not do so, in their behalf, in the future. However ambiguous the Tory resolution on the sales tax, had it meant to be precise—and dishonest—it could easily have been so. For all his shrewdness and despite his lack of sophistication, Flemming possessed a rough-hewn, rural sense of virtue, and although he could be evasive, circumlocutious, and ambivalent, he could also be firm and inflexible in matters where principle had gripped his mind.

Even so, as a factor in the campaign, I found it difficult to assess him. On the platform, he tended to verbosity; his speeches were invariably too long, giving one the impression, when he was finished, that he had said everything he could think of and had sat down only because there was nothing left in his mind to say. Carson, drafting his radio addresses which were disciplined by the limitations of time, would complain that Flemming would seldom take anything out, but would add page after page. So that when one listened to him on radio, one heard an astonishingly rapid delivery, a flood of words, a deluge of issues and subject material centrifuged in a torrent of breathless oratory.

There were occasional notes of evangelism in Flemming's delivery which, on radio, sounded strident. Yet, it was no worse than McNair's radio style, only different. The Premier was pontifical, his phrasing that of the pastor reading aloud the first verse of the next hymn, his tone suggesting the cadence of the liturgy. McNair's irony was somehow lost on radio, being reduced, by the disembodied voice, to querulousness.

Hearing the "radio McNair" with the hint of brogue, one imagined the voice coming from the altar, the candles dipping before his cold breath, the words sparse, the sentences neat, the thought concise. He was, it was said, the Oxford "double-blue"–the skilled debater, the diligent scholar, full of confidence and pride and a soulful sense of righteousness. By contrast, Flemming's idiom was that of the countryside, acquired in the bare, dim Orange halls, where speakers were judged by their fervour and stamina, and listeners came not for persuasion but for reassurance.

In late August, Flemming announced his party's platform. It was a half-hour speech of breakneck delivery, a race against the clock, but as Carson said afterwards, admiringly, "Well, Hugh John made it."

Listening, I could tell where Carson left off and Flemming began– somewhere in the middle of the address. Only Flemming himself could have said, commenting on education:

"Good qualified teachers, at any price we can afford to pay, are an excellent investment for any community. The teacher is the maker of history. To a very great extent in his or her hands lies the future of our democratic form of government."

Or, following on with a promise to extend library services: "We have no right to deny our young people entrance through books into this 'universe of light.' We need trained minds. We must spend the comparatively few dollars it will cost to make books easily available to all through regional library service."

And at the end, accelerating the pace of his delivery, Flemming concluded:

You will note that in this broadcast, I have made no mention of world conditions. This is not because I am unmindful of them. I give you my word that a Conservative administration will co-operate with the Federal Government, the British Commonwealth of Nations and the United Nations in every effort to keep peace in the world . . . .

And a final peroration:

62

The winds of heaven never fanned
The circling sunlight never spanned
The borders of a better land
Than our own beloved New Brunswick.
On September 22nd next I ask you to give the Conservative candidates
your loyalty and full support. In return we will give you our loyal
and faithful service.

It is not easy to believe that, in those days before the television era,
a radio address was an event, especially a half-hour address by a party
leader "through the facilities of the CBC, on a network of New Brunswick stations." Invariably, the speaker received several telephone calls
after his broadcast and heard comments on his performance for days
afterward.

Flemming's speech of August 29 was no exception; both substance
and delivery were praised. The breathless style created, for some, the
image of a vigorous, determined man, speaking with a sense of urgency.
All of which was true.

But there was, combined with the profligacy of words and variety
of subject matter, a consistent tone of frugality and caution; good
teachers "at any price we can afford to pay"; on schools he would say,
"I believe we must have new schools," adding hastily "but that does
not mean that I believe in extravagance and waste on the construction
of school buildings. An adequate school building is all we want or
need." Even the expanded library services would require the expenditures of "comparatively few dollars."

It was not merely the reiteration of the virtues of thrift, which
"being a business man," Flemming represented in New Brunswick
politics, but more than that, he was avoiding the snare set by McNair:
the inconsistency of arguing for reduced taxation and increased expenditures. The fifteen-point Tory platform was full of good intentions,
but they all turned on improved efficiency and an end to "waste and
extravagance," for which a credible case could be made.

On the sales tax issue, Flemming demonstrated his exemplary
caution, walking wide of McNair's trapline:

Now, ladies and gentlemen, it is impossible for me to give you
my word that on September 23rd next, when your votes have put the
Conservative Party in charge of your affairs, we shall immediately
abolish the Sales Tax .... We shall find out exactly where we
stand financially. I have an uncomfortable suspicion that we are much
worse off in this regard than the government has seen fit to tell us.

After determining our position, we shall immediately take steps
to put the Province on a sound, business footing so that we may

without any diminution of existing health, social and educational services, proceed toward the abolition of the Sales Tax at the earliest possible moment, and in the meantime, to give you what immediate relief from taxation it is humanly in our power to do.

A battery of lawyers, aided by a galaxy of ghost-writers, could do no better. There was a promise and satisfaction for everyone—except McNair—including the disclaimer, made necessary by the Tory past, that there would be "no diminution of existing health, social and educational services." But Flemming had added to the virtue of frugality another of consistency.

As September began, party advertisements blossomed in the newspapers and a chorus of alien voices began their frequent interruptions of standard radio programming. The Liberal campaign, breathing confidence and unction, fired its early salvoes. "Keep Going Ahead with McNair!" was the slogan, which Tories promptly rebutted by saying, "Keep going in debt with McNair."

It was not long before the Tory slogan of "Let's Clean House!" reached McNair's eye and the fertile, combative mind pondered it. In his next radio address he retorted, "Let's Keep Our House Clean!" It was noted by some of us, listening in disbelief, that the Liberals were responding to the Tory campaign. No one could remember McNair being so quickly defensive.

He appeared stung and surprised. Flemming had proven more ingenious than he had expected and, while the Tory campaign was not extensive, it was forebodingly sharp. For the first time in his career, McNair heard his own words being used against him. In much his own style, using material from the past, history was now being summoned to ridicule a hitherto impregnable public man. The public seemed at first startled, then amused, then fascinated:

TAX "With a Vengeance and Without Mercy"
WHO SAID IT?
MR. MCNAIR!

Mr. McNair likes to go to "the record"—into history—to dress up his political speeches. During this election campaign he has gone back as far as 1908. He may have to go back even further in order to avoid the real issues in this election.

But we only have to go back to 1944 to find Mr. McNair's true opinion of the Sales Tax. He delivered it in the Legislature, while his Liberal back-benchers cheered him to the echo. Here is what Mr. McNair said then about the Sales Tax:

64

"But we told them that there would be no personal income tax and NO SALES TAX. That was the rock upon which we would split.

"The Sales tax would have hit every old age pensioner, every widow, every person in the Province of New Brunswick. We hear much criticism from our friends opposite about direct taxation. There, Sir, WAS A PROPOSAL FOR DIRECT TAXATION WITH A VENGEANCE AND WITHOUT MERCY."

Six years later, it was a different story. While his Liberal back-benchers cheered him to the echo, he enforced upon every old age pensioner, every widow, every person in the Province of New Brunswick a tax "with a vengeance and without mercy"–the 4% Sales Tax!
WHY DID MR. McNAIR CHANGE HIS MIND?

Yours truly,
L. C. House

The Liberal campaign reflected a perfunctory slickness. Prepared well in advance, it soon became resolutely irrelevant. A campaign without flexibility can easily be planned by men with supreme confidence in the result and mere contempt for their opposition. And when it is obviously failing in purpose, pride will not let them change it, until it is too late, and their impulses have become governed by the sour desperation of men who know only that something has gone wrong.

Ridicule is the deadliest weapon in politics. Politicians are as vulnerable to it as children are to measles. As office, title, and prominence elevate the public man, as he grows accustomed to the deference of others, the ego becomes a swollen bladder for which there is no relieving orifice. Pride and self-righteousness shield him from simple criticism and partisan scorn. But no one likes to be ridiculed, politicians least of all, for theirs is an occupation demanding sober conviction and sincerity, and they know no holiday from it. A politician is a politician all the time, living with the image of himself as a public man, an image he covets and nurtures with a zealousness known only to other politicians. Which is why ridicule is seldom employed by one of them against another; they are not good at it, because it pains both the donor and the recipient, and few politicians are masochists.

The art of ridicule is left to cartoonists, columnists, and commentators. It requires a sense of madness, and since politicians are primordial men of sanity, it is another reason why they have so little talent for it. Men who persuade themselves that, given a mandate, they can govern others and make their lives more bearable cannot have a sense of the ridiculous They may have wit, grace, and style, yet if they were not politicians, they would not seem nearly so witty, graceful, or stylish.

If two men tell the same story equally well, the anecdotal politician will get the greater response, even applause, not because his story is funny (sometimes it isn't), nor because his audience wishes only to be indulgent, ingratiating, or polite, but also because all are struck by the incongruity of a public man–who must take everything seriously–taking anything lightly, especially himself. Politicians can often dissolve an audience by telling the most pedestrian anecdote, if it is about themselves.

Nonetheless, they are not prepared to be taken lightly. Throughout their careers, they guard themselves against so devastating a prospect. They know there is no defence against ridicule. Some politicians, a Dwight Eisenhower or a Louis St. Laurent, have a rare immunity to ridicule which may be put down to the essential blandness of their public personalities, the lack of eccentricity, or simply that they have been spared by fate; others are susceptible early in their careers, a Richard Nixon or a Winston Churchill, but develop a later immunity, largely through a stoic refusal to succumb. Still others who enjoy an early immunity to ridicule later become exposed, and in the twilight of their careers, are suddenly struck down, as though ridicule afflicted the oldest in the most devastating way–politicians such as Diefenbaker or de Gaulle. Or John McNair.

Slowly, McNair became, to me, a ridiculous figure. Isolated in his citadel of power, creating nebulous issues and spectral enemies with which to dismay the electorate, perpetuating a political mythology long after its relevance had passed–he was a politician arrived at the conjunction of comedy and tragedy. While my Tory associates continued to be earnestly apprehensive about McNair, still suspecting his magic powers in the tribe, I began to see him otherwise.

I called my art director, Bill Kettlewell.

"Bill, who did those Prestone Anti-Freeze cartoons for us last fall?"

They had been good, strong cartoons with a special quality of their own, an originality of style, I thought, far more significant than the commercial situations the cartoonist had been obliged to render.

"That was Duncan MacPherson," Kettlewell said.

"Do you think he could do some political cartoons for me?"

"He will if you pay for them."

"Find out where he is and let me know. I want to talk to him."

The first published political cartoons by Duncan MacPherson were done for the Tory Party of New Brunswick. They were primitive, but MacPherson's savage brush of ridicule was in every line. He had the satirist's gift of madness, a bold sense of the ridiculous, the quick sureness of an overall impression. Obviously, there was no virtue he could not profane and no politician's ego he could not explode, as we have all since learned to our sorrow and amusement.

We discussed possible situations for the cartoons and I urged upon him the importance of time. To assist him, I mailed him the standard photograph of McNair. Because I also wanted to use Gaspard Boucher, the Secretary-Treasurer of the government, in a subsidiary role, I had to describe his appearance to MacPherson over the telephone.

Within a week, he had produced an assortment of drawings, all devastating. I showed them to Flemming, who winced. He was particularly sensitive to one of Boucher; he suspected it would be considered anti-French. Only the enthusiasm of others present dissuaded him from preventing their being used in the campaign.

When the first of MacPherson's cartoons appeared in a Tory advertisement, McNair took his anger to the radio station with him. In an audible rage, he referred to the "Tory cartoons," mispronouncing the word as "cortooms" in his fury. And then, so that I would know that his intelligence apparatus was working, he referred to "the Camp-following York County Tory machine." The campaign was warming up, and McNair was the warmest of all.

8

AS THE PROVINCIAL CAMPAIGN ASSUMED ITS SHAPE, I GREW CLOSER TO
the concerns of York County, where four seats were at stake. McNair
headed the Liberal ticket, representing the city of Fredericton; Cochrane, the Power Commission vice-chairman, came from the neighbouring cotton-mill town of Marysville; Harry Corey, a prosperous lumber
dealer, and Harry Greenlaw, a potato merchant, came from the county
towns of Harvey Station and Millville. I knew each of them personally
and had to concede that the York County Liberals were experienced
and resourceful campaigners.

Opposing them were the Tory nominees: Dr. F. J. McInerney, a
Fredericton medical doctor and the only Roman Catholic candidate
in York; W. J. West, Q.C., a prominent Fredericton lawyer; Harry
Ames, a farmer from the Nashwaak; and Eldon Lawrence, the youngest
in the race, a shy, ruddy-complexioned farmer from "up river."

While McNair harped on his adamant opposition to union recognition for hydro employees, his advertising agency extolled the achievements of his seventeen-year reign. One advertisement listed 146
"Liberal achievements," including the modest claim (No. 145) of
"bringing prosperity to New Brunswick." But each day, in the press,
"L. C. House" excoriated the Grits, exposing waste and extravagance
and treating McNair with increasing irreverence.

On the local radio station, Jack Fenetey delivered daily five-minute
commentaries, immediately after his reading of the mid-day news. His
was a familiar voice on CFNB, and the recital of the five-minute phil-
ippics which I prepared for him carried the added authority of a familiar personality.

Radio listeners were assaulted by the dissonance of amateur voices
as well; as many as eight private citizens a day aided the Tory cause
by expressing their criticisms of the McNair government. The scripts
for these I vetted, alert to the laws of libel, fair comment, and the party
line, but by and large it was better to allow people to speak for themselves (certainly it was easier), which they did with awkward delivery
but ringing conviction.

The Liberals employed an unknown professional commentator
who sounded like a door-to-door salesman, oozing homilies on the
benefits of Liberal legislation addressed to "you mothers" and those
"older folks" in the listening audience. Like a bath in treacle. Otherwise, the Liberal air was reserved for the candidates who gave faithful
utterance to agency scripts, written by someone on the moon with a
goose-feather quill.

"My God," Ralph Hay said to me, "I'm beginning to think this is an unfair fight."

I had a less sanguine feeling about the campaign. Granted, we were scoring points, unsettling the Grits, and there could be no doubt the Tories were, for the first time in their lives, tasting blood that was not their own. But I brooded over the continuing public apathy. The campaign was a play as yet without an audience conscious of its drama. And when I asked myself the ultimate question—could Weldon Lawrence from "up river" defeat John McNair?—the answer was no.

Ralph Hay, like myself, was a Liberal renegade. Crippled by polio as a child, he had early turned to politics as an outlet for a combative spirit. His father had been an ardent McNair supporter, and as Hay recalled, on election day he would carry "the bag" from poll to poll in the city of Fredericton. But the son, introduced to Liberalism early, began to have his doubts, although loyalty to family voting tradition was hard to put aside.

By 1952, his father dead and his mother an invalid, Hay had developed a strong friendship with the family physician, Dr. Jack McInerney. When the doctor became a Tory candidate and asked Hay if he would assist in the campaign by writing his speeches, the conversion became complete. Hay became a crusading Conservative.

Short and swarthy, and overweight as are most to whom normal physical exercise is denied, Hay had an indefatigable spirit, combined with an alarming capacity for self-abuse. He smoked incessantly, the fingers of his right hand dyed indelibly with the stain of nicotine; he drank Coca-Cola with all his meals, whatever the time of day and whatever the food. Coca-Cola, strawberry shortcake, black rum, and MacDonald's Export cigarettes were the staples of his diet. But with his infectious laughter, boisterous partisanship, and impulsive, affectionate nature, it was impossible not to enjoy his company, even while remaining in awe of his habits.

The seminal thought of the issue which was to prove mortal to the York County Liberals originated with Hay. He came to my hotel room one evening in early September, dragging a useless foot, and settled his broad frame into one of the day couches.

I guarded my room, treasuring privacy as essential to work and contemplation. For these reasons, I did not invite company, and as insurance against it, kept the premises dry. All I offered was coffee, supplied by an almost constant procession of bellboys running between my quarters and the hotel kitchen.

Complaints over the austerity of my hospitality out of the way, Hay reflected on the campaign:

"Ever seen the polio clinic?"

"No, Ralph, I don't even know where it is."

"It's up there back of the hospital." An almost totally expended cigarette hung between his lips, the smoke rising directly to his nostrils. He coughed, removed it, and lit a fresh one. "My God, I feel sorry for those kids in there. It really is a terrible place." Cough.

Watching Hay smoke could be madly distracting. The first half of the cigarette was smoked while held between stained fingers, then as it burned to the last inch, it was transferred to his lips, at the near-centre of his mouth. There it was turned occasionally by the tongue, ash falling on his shirt front; smoke emitted from mouth and nose, accompanied by explosive fits of coughing. Gerow once described Hay as looking like a smouldering mattress.

"Fine," I said, "I'll drive up tomorrow and see it. What am I supposed to look for?"

"Better than that," he said, "I think you should talk to McInerney. There's been a hell of a row about it and the doctors are all mad at McNair."

"Where do I find McInerney?"

"He's out speaking tonight, but tell you what I'll do. Let me invite a bunch of them in and you can talk to them about it."

"I'd just as soon not have them here, Ralph. Can't we meet somewhere else?"

Hay rented a room in the Beaverbrook. The following night, when the candidate had returned from the hustings, I went upstairs to meet him. I found Hay, Dr. McInerney, and Horace Hanson, a local Tory activist and a nephew of R. B. Hanson, late wartime House Leader of the federal party.

McInerney and Hanson had come from meetings in the country and were now released from their duties. The rum began to flow, ice clinked in glasses, and the conversation swirled about the subject of the campaign. I had come to talk to McInerney, who turned out to be a shy, seemingly diffident man, with a perfunctory, limp handshake, and a breathless, off-hand manner of speaking. Like many doctors, he was a poor advertisement for his professional advice; like Hay, he was overweight and a chain-smoker. Every movement drew from him a gasp of exertion; protruding eyes indicated high blood pressure.

Hay thought him superb on the platform. My first reaction was anxiety, lest his breath suddenly fail him and the huge frame collapse on the floor; all I knew was that he would win more votes on election day, so Hay had predicted, than any Tory in the past twenty years. Everyone liked "Mac"–he would take much of the Liberal Catholic vote away from McNair. Provided he survived the campaign, I told myself.

The talk skirted the issue of the polio clinic. As with any other candidate–as I would later understand–Mac was primarily interested in his own prospects, and he talked to Hay about his speeches, the reaction to them, the lines that drew response and those that didn't. And like any other party activist, Hanson wanted to talk about the advertising strategy which, after praising the "L. C. House" columns and the MacPherson cartoons, he proceeded to disassemble and reconstruct. He was doubtful that Flemming was running strongly enough, or that we were hitting McNair hard enough. Hanson represented that generation of Tories who had known victory only in childhood, and as each election came, familiar hopes would be stirred again, bringing with them the nagging memories of past defeats.

All this earnest talk was interrupted with the arrival of a stranger, a physician-colleague of McInerney's, Dr. Everett Chalmers. He was impressive on sight, exuding confidence, his tanned face radiating cheer. Clothed in an impeccable white suit, Chalmers looked to me like Clark Gable about to meet Carole Lombard at the Ritz, as though the world were his oyster and he could win at anyone's game.

He was a surgeon, described as the ablest practitioner in New Brunswick. He looked it. Trim, wiry, graceful in movement, direct and brusque in his manner, Chalmers was a doctor's doctor and a man's man. Profanity was with him a compulsion; four-letter words were the punctuation in his speech, employed as adverbs, adjectives, nouns, and working verbs. He swore before his wife and children, nurses, patients, and colleagues, who listened enthralled at this striking exhibition of the electrifying versatility of the lesser words in the English language.

I was impressed, as the son of a Baptist minister would likely be. Chalmers was a Tory, and the courage of his conviction shone through the execrable language. He feared no one, least of all McNair, making him the rarest of Tories.

He carried a massive brief against the government's record in health services; with much profanity, but with a redeeming simplicity, Chalmers presented a convincing, expert critique which involved conditions at the polio clinic, government indifference to pleadings by the medical profession, its frequent derelictions and defaults of promise. More impressive to me, as Chalmers talked and as we all sat spellbound, were the lights of his compassion, which aroused the conscience and ignited the concern of his listeners.

"I'll tell you about the goddam Liberal health program. A woman comes to me, see, she's half out of her fucking mind, with this Christless lump in her breast. So I take a section, see, because she probably has cancer but no way in God's world I can operate on her until I damn well know what's wrong with her.

"Well, Jesus, I have to ship the goddam tissue to Saint John, on the fucking bus, see, and wait, Christ, three days to a goddam week while this poor woman is half out of her mind—maybe she's a mother, see, or has to work for a goddam living—but I can't tell her whether she has cancer or whether I have to remove the goddam breast or what the hell I'm going to do to her because the fucking Grits refuse to give us a clinic in this Christless city. And I've told those bastards a hundred times: for Christ's sake stop building fucking liquor stores and give your goddam doctors a decent chance to practise medicine and save a few fucking lives."

There followed a long, well-documented description of the frequent appeals the doctors had made to the Minister of Health and to the Premier. Finally, Chalmers came to the culmination of his narrative:

"So one evening I'm going home, see, and when I drive up in front of the house I see this big Buick parked there. I take a look and it's Smiler McFadgen. So I figure he's heard about the racket I've been making and maybe he has some message for me from the Big Boss himself. So I go over to his car, see, and he gets out and says, 'Doc, you sure are causing a lot of trouble at the hospital.' 'Fucking right,' I says. Then he looks at me and says, 'What d'ya want, Doc?'

"I says to him, "I'll goddam well tell you what I want. I want to see those goddam friends of yours thrown out of the government! That's what I want.' And I walk into the house and slam the fucking door."

"Dr. Chalmers," I said, trying to disguise the eagerness in my voice, swallowing the pulse in my throat, "would you make that speech on the radio here in Fredericton?"

"Sure. Why not?"

"I'd like to help write it for you. I think that's one hell of a strong case."

"Well, I wish to God you would. You put it down. I'll say it."

"Can you come down to the hotel tomorrow?"

"I operate in the morning," he said, glancing at his watch. "Jesus, it's late and I got to go. I have this guy tomorrow, see, and I have to take his fucking stomach out. Then I have to make my goddam hospital rounds. But I'll see you about eleven o'clock."

The campaign sprang sharply into focus. A hundred possibilities raced through the mind, fueled with the possibilities presented by this man's commanding presence, his terrible candour, and the personal authority and prestige that buttressed his argument.

Could Weldon Lawrence and Harry Ames defeat Jack McNair?
You're ——ing right they could!

McNair's Minister of Health was a peppery, middle-aged country practitioner, Dr. F. A. McGrand, one of two members from the neighbouring county of Sunbury. He had held his portfolio since 1944, and as the medical profession in Fredericton expanded in numbers, skills, and diversity of services, relations between the country doctor and the younger, more sophisticated doctors in the city grew increasingly hostile.

The government was becoming active in the health field, accepting larger responsibilities and an always greater share of the costs. Fredericton, as the medical centre for southern New Brunswick, found its services taxed to the limits of its modest plant, and McGrand found the Fredericton doctors on his doorstep often, confronting him with advice and proposals. Governments of that day were not used to being told what they must do; McGrand's reaction to this was characteristic of his nature and his age—he believed it was political.

As often as he could, he sought to avoid the doctors. When they went instead to McNair, he angrily accused them of attempting to go over his head. He declined invitations to meetings of the York-Sunbury-Queens Medical Society and ignored communications from its members. As a result, the doctors took to writing to the Minister of Health by registered mail. And in the end, they recognized his resentment of them as he felt their hostility to him.

The five-man Tory opposition in the legislature had known nothing of the intensive struggle developing between McGrand and his medical peers. Instead, they listened to the Minister's homilies in the House, and both Mackay and Flemming generously praised him, although Flemming, ever cautious, added to his commendation of McGrand the compensating afterthought that "unfortunately our honourable friend possesses a mind sharply divided between the requirements of his humanitarian duties and the demands of fiercely partisan politics." He knew the Minister of Health better than most.

In April, 1951, the York-Sunbury-Queens Medical Society unanimously passed a lengthy resolution cataloguing their criticisms of government health policies. McGrand had been invited to the meeting, but he stayed away, as was his habit.

The resolution dealt with "inadequacies," as the doctors saw them, in government programs in various fields—tuberculosis, poliomyelitis, cancer, and pediatrics—and concluded by urging "that extension of Government health services should be improved and extended."

This was one communication McGrand would answer. Stung, he replied to his detractors, addressing himself to the society's secretary-treasurer, Dr. J. A. Williamson:

Just received your letter of April 12, 1951, accompanied by an undated Resolution, reported to be passed by the York-Sunbury-Queens Medical Society.

Resolutions passed at a meeting are moved and seconded by their sponsors and passed by a vote of the meeting. My information is that this Resolution as forwarded to me was not passed at a meeting of the York-Sunbury-Queens Medical Society. Will the sponsors of this "so-called Resolution" be more specific in their grievances regarding government policies in the treatment of cancer, poliomyelitis and tuberculosis.

As it stands now this undated, unsponsored document is vague, indefinite, vacillating and meaningless.

May I have your reply as soon as possible.

The doctors, perplexed by this lecture on parliamentary procedure, merely repeated the dose. In July, they sent further resolutions to McGrand, with a copy to the Premier, and added:

We feel that our criticisms of April, 1951, were justified for the reason that the Executive of the New Brunswick society later in the month sent a committee to meet the Minister of Health to attempt to clarify the obscurities of the cancer administration plan. The results of this meeting have not been released to either the general profession or the public so far.

The syntax was that of men who do not write much more than prescriptions, but the sense of their message was plain. They did not trust the Minister in the new and complex relationships between government and the medical profession. And they wanted a medical laboratory in Fredericton and a new polio clinic.

To emphasize the demand for the new clinic, the society passed a resolution condemning the present facilities for the treatment of polio victims.

McNair watched all this with a wary interest, occasionally intervening himself, bringing his dour and business-like presence to reassure the doctors and settle minor grievances. He suspected the medical profession in Fredericton of Tory leanings, but he had friends and supporters among them, such as Dr. J. A. M. Bell. Although Bell had warned him of McGrand's unpopularity among the doctors, McNair put it down to petty professional pique.

In 1941, New Brunswick had suffered its worst epidemic of polio; Ralph Hay was one of those crippled by the disease. Now, eleven years later, another epidemic struck; although it was not so virulent as the previous one, it was serious enough to oblige the government to take clumsy steps to describe it as "an outbreak" rather than an epidemic. McNair did not need to be reminded that, in 1949, his government had promised to build a new, modern polio clinic, and to realize that since then, no site had been found, nor a sod turned.

Chalmers was to remind everyone else. It was a joy to draft a speech for someone who had not only an opinion, but facts at his disposal. He came to the hotel at noon; we did not stop for lunch. I had scheduled fifteen minutes of radio time for his speech, Friday evening, September 5. It would give the Grits something to ponder on the weekend. I proposed to publish the speech in the daily press the following Monday.

For too long the Liberal Party had been the exclusive custodians of the public welfare. The Tories were left to grumble as to the expense; it made no sense to me. Nor was I convinced, knowing the Liberal Party in New Brunswick, that their present concern for the welfare of the citizenry was much more than perfunctory, sufficient to allow them their pieties and to preach on Tory heartlessness. Flemming's reassurance that there would be no "diminution" in the social services should his party be elected appalled me for the need he felt to say it.

At this juncture, with Chalmers pacing the floor of my hotel room, a dead cigar in his hand, I welcomed the opportunity for audacity–an attack upon the Liberals, at their strong point.

The text finished, I listened to Chalmers read it through, relieved to discover that he could speak for fifteen minutes without lapsing into profanity. His delivery was remarkably good, there being an unexpected element of the theatrical in him, and I was further reassured by his courage and confidence. A man who spent his days in surgery, excising human frailty, using a precise scalpel with cutting edges so sharp they could not be seen, was not likely to shake before a microphone. Not this man, at any rate.

He had never made a radio speech before, he said, but off he went to the studio, manuscript stuffed in the pocket of his natty gabardine jacket, "without even a goddam drink of rum to warm me up."

Hay and I sat in the lingering daylight, before the radio in my room, to hear the speech "on behalf of the York County Progressive Conservative Association." Chalmers launched immediately into his attack on McGrand's policies and the consequences flowing from the fatally abandoned promise to build a new polio clinic. Describing the present building, where he had been for ten years the attending physician, he said:

It has been condemned by the Provincial Fire Marshal; it has been condemned by the Provincial Health Officer; it has been condemned by the Victoria Public Hospital; it has been condemned by the York-Queens-Sunbury Medical Society. It has been infested by cockroaches. It has been overrun by rats. It is the worst public building in New Brunswick.

And he recalled the confrontation with Smiler McFadgen repeating his question, "What do you want, Doc?" He spoke of the needless anxiety endured by patients, waiting for the long-delayed diagnoses to come from the laboratory in Saint John. He described the deterioration in the relationships between McGrand and his fellow doctors.

It was powerful stuff; eviscerating to Liberal morale, a knife turned in the vitals of their pride. And one could not forget that the speaker was a man worshipped by legions of patients who had been saved by his skills, a man celebrated for his compassion for the poor, who possessed a shelf of ledgers containing the accounts of unpaid bills.

The Tories of York County were elated; they had never had an ally like Chalmers. And the doctor could not conceal the fact that he was pleased with himself.

"I never knew so goddam many people listened to the fucking radio," he said buoyantly. "Christ, I can't even eat my meals for answering the telephone."

On Saturday night, the hotel still holding the heat of the day, I walked down to the edge of the river and bought a Coke at the outdoor food stand. Looking up, I saw the familiar shape of Smiler McFadgen at my side. Gingerly, we shook hands.

"That was some speech by the doctor," he said.

"I thought it was."

"He's got quite a mouth."

"He speaks his mind."

"I'll give you some advice, my friend. Don't waste any more of your time around here. I'll tell you why. On election day, you're gonna be the most disappointed feller in the world."

"I doubt that."

"Wait and see. Speeches are one thing, elections are another."

He smiled and was gone.

9

LARRY JONES, REPRESENTING THE LIBERAL PARTY'S ADVERTISING agency, occupied a suite on one of the upper floors of the Beaverbrook. Occasionally we would meet in the lobby and pause to make awkward conversation about the weather, the amenities of the hotel, or the lack of them.

I searched his face for signs of tension or anxiety but found none. He remained as cheerful and cordial as a YMCA games director. But I knew that his was a different life, as his role in the campaign was different, and that his attitude was more professional than mine. The Liberal campaign had been prepared long ago, suited to the strategies and calculations of men who were used to winning. His advertising budget was three times that of mine, and could easily be more, if need be.

Downstairs, in room 326, my own quarters became more cramped, confining, and chaotic as the days passed. A litter of newspapers, agency forms, varied correspondence, copies of speeches, *Synoptic Reports,* departmental estimates, first drafts of rough copy, and pencilled layouts covered the surface of the room, the floor, tables, chairs and adhered to the walls. Only the ceiling was bare. Atop this ocean of confusion, flotillas of coffee cups, ashtrays, and pop bottles held their stations, offering counterweight to gusts of air blowing through the open windows.

I began each day with the CFNB morning news, bracketed by Liberal spots; then breakfast (often the only meal of the day) and the morning paper, brought by a sleepy-eyed bellboy in his grimy hotel uniform, who slid the tray precariously on the coffee table, waited for me to sign the meal check and for his tip, his face reflecting wonder at this dazed man, surrounded by a sea of paper, who ate scrambled eggs every morning of life and drank black coffee as thick as pitchblende all day long.

Like a general rising to breakfast in his tent, my first hour would be one of surmise, gleanings of scarce intelligence, reflections on the opposition's intentions, countervailing forces, considering the tactical deployment of agate lines and radio flashes. There would be little hard news on the election in either media, so one studied the Liberal advertisements and government press releases, like enemy communiqués, seeing others only as others hoped to be seen.

Governments are full of guile and ponderous resourcefulness during elections. Elections spawn ingratiating departmental advertising in the daily and weekly press, proclaiming forest-fire control week, proferring advice to housewives on nutrition, calling for tenders.

Bureaucratic propaganda infests the news: the Department of Agriculture announces a new limestone subsidy policy (which is really the old one dressed up in a new press release); the Department of Mines and Resources announces a record increase in timber leases, or a reduction in budworm infestation; the Department of Industry reports the greatest tourist season on record; the Department of Health declares the beginning of its free chest X-ray program among the school children.

One imagines the grey, anonymous civil service spending its days responding to ministerial frenzy, searching branches of departments for signs of measurable progress and poring over statistics to find tomorrow's newsworthy indices.

The press burbled with self-indulgent Liberal advertisements, each from the same mould, cast-iron in its dullness, as though any sound would make a symphony, any statement win a vote. Sometimes, reading the stuff, I wondered if Liberals any longer cared; their advertising seemed possessed by an awesome, compulsive arrogance; a propaganda machine which, once started, could not be stopped from its volcanic regurgitations, soiling every page, intruding into every radio program, in every paper, on every station:

MOTHERS' ALLOWANCES
The Mother's Allowance Act was put into effect by the Liberal Government on November 1, 1943. It is an outstanding example of the great triumphs of social security that the present administration has achieved for the people of New Brunswick.

The Conservatives passed a Mothers' Allowance Act in 1930, but like their Old Age Pensions Act, it was never proclaimed nor put into effect.

In contrast, the Liberals brought in their plan, and have since proceeded, by amendments and improvements to the Act, to increase the benefits until now the annual payments will run over a million dollars.

Yes, well over five million dollars has been paid out by the Liberals in order that mothers in New Brunswick . . . .

There was no end to their benevolence, beneficence, and banality:

TREMENDOUS GROWTH IN FISHING—INDUSTRY JUMPS
FROM $7,000,000 in 1942 TO OVER $22,000,000 in 1952
. . . the cod catch averaged in the vicinity of 25,000,000 pounds per year. Flounders, which in the early forties averaged a mere one-quarter of a million pounds per year, reached 5,000,000 pounds in 1950

and in 1951 exceeded 6,000,000 pounds. . . . The Liberal Government is still proceeding with its programme for building up the industry. An increase of over 8,000,000 pounds in fish production is expected in 1952.

NBT28R

Keep going ahead with McNAIR

But it was formidable if only for its density. So many advertisements they must be coded and numbered. Good old NBT28R! I concluded sorrowfully that I might be the only one who would ever read them except the Walsh copywriter, his copy chief, the account executive, and the Premier of New Brunswick.

The morning newspaper was interesting for the news it printed, and did not print. There was a chronic scarcity of news about the election, all carried on the provincial page inside the paper. No mention had been made of Chalmers' speech, which was not surprising; it was the policy of newspapers, still envious of the intimacy and immediacy of radio, not to report on speeches given on radio, especially those given during paid time. (In Fredericton, the *Daily Gleaner* refused for years to list program schedules of the radio station.)

The *Telegraph-Journal,* the morning paper for southern New Brunswick, covered all nominating conventions. Throughout the campaign, it ran a series of photographs, picturing the candidates of each party in the various counties.

This day, the *Journal* featured the Tory candidates from Northumberland, a "fish dealer and mink rancher" from Millerton; an Upper Blackville man; a Rogersville insurance salesman; and a salesman from Chatham. The caption beneath their photographs gave further emphasis to the importance of digits to political reportage:

The Progressive Conservative Party is contesting all 52 seats in New Brunswick's 15th Legislature in the provincial election which will be held Monday, Sept. 22. There are 123 candidates, including members of the Liberal and C.C.F. parties, from whom electors will choose the government and its opposition. In Northumberland County these four men will be contesting the constituency's four seats . . . .

Like all the rest, these four men appeared suitably grave and responsible, jacketed in their best, wearing white shirts and thick-knotted neckties, their hair trimmed close to the sides of their heads, the unblinking eyes meeting yours.

Ralph Hay had become my sounding board, my ear to the ground, my reconnoitring cavalry. Working closely with McInerney, he supplied daily reports on conditions on the hustings as the York County candidates journeyed out to the small halls in the countryside.

79

It was the first election campaign for both of us as Tories.

"How will we do in Northumberland?" I asked him.

"We could win one of the four," he said.

I relegated Northumberland to the outer limits of possibility; I had known one such split in Carleton, which was enough to know how rare it was.

But in York, Hay's optimism struggled with his doubts that McNair could be beaten. We waited, almost hourly, for the Premier to make his move, to cease maundering on about the union issue at the Power Commission and suddenly, in a flash of revelation, exploit some dazzling issue of universal pertinence, something we ourselves had overlooked. But the days passed in their swift precision as the Liberal campaign laboured in its turgid irrelevance, while the Tory campaign, bristling with challenge, became increasingly impertinent and rousing in its confidence. We might, Hay said, win two out of four in York, but we would have to fight like hell to do it.

Election campaigns are to a large extent a clash between part-time partisans, casual recruits to a transient cause. Throughout, the lawyers continue their practices, the doctors go their rounds, the merchants attend their counters–even McNair busied himself each day with office chores, while Flemming touched base in Juniper as often as he could.

But as polling day draws nearer, men give more and more of their time to politics, leaving the office earlier, attending more frequent luncheon meetings, yielding some of their evenings and weekends while their wives complain that they see so little of their husbands because of "politics."

For the candidates, their managers and supporters, an election is superimposed upon the routine of their lives, and they endure this insurgent political duty while continuing their regular tasks, greeting their families, taking their meals and sleeping in their own beds.

In the Lord Beaverbrook Hotel, I saw it all differently. Beaverbrook was right when he had said the first attribute of the politician must be good health. Certainly the first demand of politics is for stamina; an election is an endurance contest, a struggle of wills between men in which some will falter and weaken as others persevere.

Fatigue breeds despair, engenders carelessness, numbs the will, fosters apathy, and clouds judgement; it is then that mistakes are made, and they may be fatal, especially when one is trying to bring down a government.

My summer vacation had been "training" for the ordeal. Throughout the campaign, while others slept, I worked. For during the day, there were only interruptions–an endless parade of partisans, each man with his own urgency, and incessant telephone conversations, until the ear was reddened from the deluge of words poured into it by Tories

80

calling to express their individual dismay, exhilaration, anger, pleasure, to ask advice or give it, report information and gather it. And one sat in the eye of the storm, besieged by daylight, cursing the routine habits of men who could only visit, or call, on their way to the office, or coming from it, or during lunch, or after supper, or before going to bed.

Then, finally, late at night and in the dark hours of early morning, when the Progressive Conservative Party of New Brunswick, all of it, had gone to bed, the urgent tasks of advertising began, and the typewriter clattered into the dawn, while empty galleys in the composing room of tomorrow's newspaper, and the silent microphones in darkened studios, awaited the words: a five-minute radio script for Fenety; a column by "L. C. House"; the copy for Monday's ad; announcements of Flemming's future broadcasts and public meetings.

A generation of New Brunswick voters had been raised in the Liberal arts, so to speak: history, as recorded in the seventeen years of Liberal administrations, was measured from the base years of the Tory depression by the simple arithmetic of comparing anything in 1952 with anything in 1935. Infant mortality, automobiles, shipments of potatoes, miles of asphalt, fish landings, old age pensions, children in school, annual rainfall and hours of sunshine everything was up, better, more abundant, less binding, sometimes by as much as 3,000 per cent.

But do people measure their lives by such tables? Do they really see themselves parading amidst armies of statistics, marching in column of route across the landscape, joining on the horizon's line to form millions of dollars, tons, or pounds: cyphers marching to make symbols of mystical meaning to the politicians? Liberalism was the guarantor of progress–never another depression while Liberals ruled and the fertility of their policies spawned their endless zeroes–$4,000,000, 9,000,000 pounds, 500,000 souls, stretching beyond the limits of the mind's eye–and human happiness reached into infinity.

A generation of defeat had deprived the Tories of the weapons of statistics in seven figures; they worked in fractions and in more homely equations.

Six Fredericton doctors signed McInerney's nomination papers. One of them was Dr. J. A. M. Bell, a lifetime Liberal. The Tories published a photograph of the scene–"DOCTORS ENTER CAMPAIGN"–showing McInerney seated at a desk, his colleagues standing behind him, sombre, unsmiling, wearing the suitable expressions of men who would "back the vigorous opening attack on the McNair-McGrand health policies launched by Dr. McInerney and Dr. Chalmers." The caption added that Dr. Bell would be making a radio address in support of the Tory ticket in York County. I told Hay it was the best advertisement of the campaign. A picture of six doctors was worth a thousand words, or even 25,000,000 pounds of codfish.

Bell prepared his own radio speech. He was the oldest of the practising doctors, a short, bulky figure with pale blue eyes, white thatch of hair, and pink complexion. He looked not unlike Santa Claus. He had been, along with Chalmers, responsible for the care of the government's patients at the polio clinic. But he was not a politician, and his speech bristled with earnest bombast. As difficult as it was for him to give it, it proved impossible for the Liberals to receive it in silence.

There had been no reply to Chalmers, no indication of response to his attack on the government's health policies. This had been disappointing to me and, with only a week remaining in the campaign, momentum was becoming difficult to sustain. In the contest of wills, neither side would yet yield.

Tweedie, watching the struggle from the remove of the civil service, concluded that the government would survive. It did not seem that the Tories had enough time. A Liberal friend asked him what he thought about his "young friends, Camp and Hay," now leading the Tory charge in York County.

"I feel like a father toward his children," Tweedie said. "I may not always approve of what they're doing, but I love them all the same."

But Tweedie was not in McNair's office, and McElman was. The new secretary to the Premier consulted McGrand, urging him to strike back at his detractors. There had been some errors of fact in Bell's criticisms and, besides, as McGrand had told him, there was another side to the story. Larry Jones advised against it, but McElman, feeling his new powers, and aware of the Grits' outrage and dismay following Chalmers' opening assault, helped McGrand prepare his reply and instructed the agency to arrange for radio time and space in the press for its publication.

The New Brunswick election campaign was instructive as a primer of Canadian politics, if not all politics. One of the lessons it taught was the wisdom of choosing your ground on which to fight and refusing to abandon it. Election campaigns are simultaneous monologues, separate views expressed by irreconcilable forces. Men, and their parties, have not for a long time joined together to debate, because debating is merely a technique at which some are skilled and others are not. Besides, who is to determine the questions for debate?

No, an election is like war at sea, where forces manoeuvre with deadly intent, each beyond the other's view, seeking to draw the enemy into his arc of fire. McElman, who would know better days as a tactician, now blundered into Tory waters. After the smoke had cleared, McNair and McGrand would lose their seats and he his job.

The lesson was learned and remembered: Never fight your opponent's war, never answer or explain, unless it be in the form of massive, total, unanswerable retaliation.

McGrand's rebuttal was defensive, sour, and self-demeaning, and while his argument was incomprehensible, he proved the case of the doctors against him. He was a politician with a penchant for malice, at least as McElman represented him in the version given of his speech published as a Liberal advertisement in the provincial press:

McGrand Hits Back
Reveals Personal Motives Behind Attacks on Him
"What do you want, Doc?"
Dr. Chalmers $10,000
Dr. Bell $5,000–
Honourable Dr. McGrand NO
Dr. Chalmers $7,000
Dr. Bell $3,000
HONOURABLE DR. MCGRAND PAID THEM OFF!

The insinuation was clear–the attacks on McGrand's policies were made by men who had demanded payment from him for medical services rendered to government patients. Receiving less than they had demanded, they resorted to public criticisms in a spirit of revenge.

McGrand's speech was delivered on Monday, appeared in the press, in full, on Tuesday. The printed version was only worse than the speech itself.

I met Larry Jones in the lobby.

"You surprise me, Larry," I told him.

He knew immediately what I meant, and for the first time his voice betrayed his unease. "I want you to know I had nothing to do with it," he said. "They wouldn't listen to me."

But they had delivered themselves into our hands. McGrand's widely publicized speech, published in full-page advertisements under McElman's glaringly offensive headlines, brought Chalmers and Bell to my door. In the war between the parties, the twin monologues had suddenly been joined, the partisans on both sides were now in close, hand to hand, and on ground of our own choosing.

Chalmers' anger was betrayed only by the fresh orchestration given his litany of profanity. When he spoke, his shoulders twitched and his head tossed from side to side, like a boxer feinting his opponent in the ring.

Bell was more subdued, pale with shock. Unused to the ruthlessness of politics, full of apology for the mistakes in his earlier address which McGrand had used as debating points against him, he wanted to redeem himself, he said sorrowfully. If someone would help him, he would make another speech. But he had been hurt, the wounds showed in the sag of his body and the quaver in his voice, while anger and remorse wrestled for his spirit.

Doctors Chalmers and Bell, the records showed, had provided, at the request of the provincial Department of Health, medical and surgical care for all polio patients at the hospital, serving from 1941 to 1948 without remuneration. After that, a doctor in the Department had submitted a brief to his Minister proposing that a schedule of fees be established to cover medical services in the polio program.

In 1951, a lump settlement had been made to both doctors, and the Department engaged another doctor, on an honorarium basis, to attend the polio patients. The payments to Bell and Chalmers, negotiated in part by McNair in an agreeable meeting with the two, averaged out to forty-five dollars a month. The Premier confessed himself "astounded" that the doctors had served for so long without once raising the matter of fees. There was no evidence that either doctor had pressed for payment, disputed the settlement, or ever discussed the matter with McGrand.

Hay volunteered to help Bell in the preparation of the fifteen-minute radio address, scheduled for Wednesday evening.

On Thursday, Chalmers was to speak for one-half hour on the Fredericton station and a further fifteen minutes on a province-wide radio network. Announcements of this marathon performance were prepared for all dailies. Carson, who confessed himself perplexed by the heat of the York County campaign, counselled caution in preparing Chalmers' network speech. Flemming, perhaps feeling the campaign was slipping from his hands, called Chalmers to suggest he drop the issue. Chalmers was not to be denied his say.

All day Wednesday, throughout the night, and Thursday morning, I laboured over the two texts, one for York and the other for a wider provincial audience, now fully caught up in the fury of the Tory assault on McNair's bastion in York County. Chalmers visited the room between his office appointments and hospital duties, bringing in a gallon of black coffee from a neighbourhood restaurant and leaving me, late Wednesday night, with two pills—"one to put you to sleep and the other to wake you up—now for Jesus' sake don't get them mixed up."

When it was done, we had thirty pages of script.

"Once more into the breach, dear friend," I said to him, the taste of a hundred cigarettes and the gallon of coffee in my mouth, exhausted, exuberant, and yet apprehensive. All the campaign, the days and nights of writing, planning, phoning, talking, scheming, fighting, now centred on this remarkably fearless, combative man whom I hardly knew.

"Don't worry about me," he said cheerfully. "I'll give it all I've got."

And to his everlasting credit, and to the glory of the Tory Party, to the dawn of the Diefenbaker years, and toward the myth of my own reputation, he did.

Now it was done: the last speech written, the final column by "L. C. House" telegraphed to the papers (closing on a note of sweet reason), the final advertisement prepared, bearing a huge photograph of a smiling Hugh John Flemming, listing his candidates beneath; at Friday midnight the radio mercifully would close down on political broadcasts, after the party leaders had made their penultimate appeals.

Late Thursday evening, McNair delivered a special broadcast to the voters of York and Sunbury counties. Incredulously, I listened to him defending himself on the polio clinic issue. I was alone in my room, delirious with fatigue; the familiar voice and the unfamiliar words were like adrenalin, or a shot of rum to a man taken spent from the sea, or cavalry coming to the relief of the surrounded garrison—no, like a white flag of surrender raised from the highest minaret, seen finally by attacking troops, their casualties intolerable, their ammunition spent, the sun falling in the sky:

Personally, I do not doubt that, in the event of their victory next Monday, Mr. Flemming and Mr. Tracy will, as their first move, clean out the Civil Service [McNair begging for votes in his own city, in his own administration] ... room must be found for the bevies of ward heelers, gravel salesmen and all other rag-tag and bob-tail of camp-following Toryism—particularly those who have been taking part in this election campaign. [More particularly the Dalton Camp-following Tories!]

I have scanned all the Tory advertisements. No one can detect in them any formal assurance that the Conservative Polio Clinic will be built in Fredericton .... Incidentally, I would point out that the Provincial Laboratory is in Saint John.

Vintage McNair! Jealous for Fredericton, contemptuous of Saint John!

This followed by a defence of the present polio clinic:

... while the exterior may not appeal to the aesthetic tastes of some, the interior is tidy, sanitary and comfortable. The beds are modern, the linen clean .... [It was hard to believe, the voice of desperation, a man clutching handfuls of air, falling into darkness.]

Then a complicated explanation of the reasons for not proceeding with the construction of a new clinic:

Shortly however difficulties loomed up. The Minister of Health became concerned. [Which way now was the buck passing?] The province was paying a per diem rate applicable to patients in a general hospital ... this rate was not applicable to the Polio Clinic where many of the services provided in a general hospital would

never be used. . . . It took time . . . to arrive at a new formula to be
used in fixing a proper per diem rate for polio patients. Last year,
the matter was finally settled and the way opened for construction
of the new Provincial Building.

The Government had however to reconcile this project with its
general construction programme. Some months ago [a tellingly vague
phrase], we settled on construction in 1953. [After that plea for
understanding, the voice turned to scorn, and to Chalmers.]

In a frenzied effort to transfuse some glimmer of life into the dry bones
of the moribund Tory Machine in York County he made his
sensational exposé. . . . Now don't misunderstand me, my friends.
I regard Dr. Chalmers highly as a good neighbour, a good citizen [an
oblique apology for the crudeness of McGrand and McElman], a
good doctor and a good surgeon. . . .

"Jackson," back to the wall, falling in space, cornered in the round-
house, plainly trapped; I listened to his dissertation on the doctors'
revolt against his Minister of Health, as he summoned all his ingenuity,
his voice all its unction, his leadership all its authority:

I hold in the highest regard all doctors, wherever located. We must
all do that. And when the present little unpleasantness is over,
we must combine to put the medical profession in this city back
on its pedestal.

We must not lose faith in our doctors because of any temporary
aberrations. They are our mainstay through life—from the cradle to
the grave. [Irony or sarcasm? The edge to irony.]

But, my friends, the one I hold in special high regard is the country
doctor—the one who answers every call, in good weather or in bad,
in season and out of season—the doctor who goes to his patient and
does not require his patient to come to him. [A needle for the
"city doctors."]

You have all noticed the recent invasion of Sunbury by the
Fredericton Medical Clinic. They are on a peculiar quest. . . . They
are saying to the people of Sunbury—"Surrender to us McGrand
that York may have his portfolio."

For eight years Sunbury has had representation in the Cabinet.
Why give it up?

May I tender to the people of that county some advice? It is this—
whatever else may happen next Monday, stick to your guns in
Sunbury . . . Vote for McGrand and Lawson.

In the long-drawn struggle of wills, McNair had yielded to the
pressure of his enemy and to the panic of his troops. What I knew of
politics, the crude, brawling struggle of the partisans, I had learned
from him. And still I learned from him, in this test of stamina and will.

But there was for me a twinge of sorrow, furtive stirrings of sympathy. Even if he were to win, I thought, he will not fight another
election, and the Liberal Party, without McNair, will not be a party
at all.

Flemming, now storming the hustings exuding confidence, goodwill, and cheerfulness, finished the Tory campaign in Minto, broadcasting live from a crowded meeting hall, his strong, strident voice once
more racing through his text. He had an apt and telling aside for
McNair:

Just four years ago, with the greatest mandate ever given a New
Brunswick Premier, he had all of New Brunswick with him. Now
he has all of New Brunswick against him.

It had a ring of truth.

On this last day of the campaign there had been *thirteen* Liberal
advertisements in the *Gleaner*. The rout was complete.

10

THE PEOPLE ARE SECRETIVE, HUSHED, AND GUARDED AS THEY COME TO vote. The Court House poll, across the street, under my window, presented a view of subdued, deliberate activity. When I awoke late in the morning on election day, the morning sun lighting the disorder of the room, I could hear footsteps below and the gentle closing of car doors; they were coming out to vote.

The maxim is: get your own vote out first! While the inside scrutineers check off the names as they appear at the polls, they look for the reluctant voters who, according to the canvass or local intelligence, are theirs, and the calls go out to bring them in. But the civil servants are left alone in their impartiality. They vote, nonetheless, and on this day they voted the government out, late in the afternoon, after clearing the papers from their desks, closing their files, sighting the clock to confirm the hour had come, the extra hour allowed them by statute on election days. Then they came out to vote against McNair.

Elsewhere, fleets of cars roamed the roads—more than were needed, because the drivers were paid and it was impolite to refuse a proffered car and driver. As the day wore on, they concentrated on the "purchasable vote"—where two dollars, or more, or a pair of nylons, or a pint of rum, or a drink of it, would bring a vote out, to be driven to the poll, given a party ballot and sent into the booth.

In New Brunswick, each party printed ballots, showing only the names of its own candidates.* These were kept in the polling booths, in good supply; it was the duty of the inside scrutineer to keep them so and, if possible, remove the opposition's ballots, or bury them under his own. (Or, sometimes, mutilate them by running a pin through them so they would be considered "spoiled" in the counting.)

The voter could, if he wished, scratch out names on the ballot and write in others, or simply cast a single "plump" vote (militant Catholics were alleged to practise this when one of their faith was running), or he could use the blank ballots provided by the election authorities and write down the names of his choosing. It was a system that invited malpractice and only rarely, in the "better" polls, was the invitation declined.

At the hospital in Fredericton, Chalmers canvassed the nurses' residence personally, escorting scores of nurses to the polls. When one

*But not always. In Carleton County in 1948, for example, the Liberals printed ballots with the names of two Tories and only one Liberal. Some unsuspecting Tories mistook the ballot as being the Tory one, thus casting the first Liberal vote in their lives.

of the matrons sought to contain his ardour, the Chief Surgeon addressed her in language she had not even heard from him in the operating theatre.

On this day, the Liberal machine purchased votes which went to the Tories, Liberal cars ferried Tory voters to the polls, and all a drink of "Liberal liquor" seemed able to do was embolden voters to cast their ballot against the government. It was not a good day for organization, except that the Tories worked harder than they ever had, the scent of victory now in their nostrils. They could tell, from the way the vote came pouring out, and from the anxiety reflected in the faces of their opponents, that things were going well.

When the polls had closed, Jack Fenety, the "voice" of the York County Tories, reverted to his role as CFNB's principal newscaster to read the returns as they began coming into the station. Hay and I, taut with anxiety, drove aimlessly about the streets of Fredericton, listening to Fenety on the car radio.

The Tories took an immediate lead in Fredericton, building on it in the county; Queens, Sunbury, Charlotte, Carleton, Saint John, Kings, and Victoria began reporting; Tories leading throughout southern New Brunswick. Then, incredibly, Madawaska reported from the north and the Conservatives were winning there.

I recalled a mid-campaign telephone conversation–at the time, only one of many–with Edgar Fournier, strongest of the three candidates in Madawaska.

"How are things down there?" he had asked.

"Great," I had told him. "How are things up there?"

"Madawaska," Fournier had replied emphatically, "is in the bag."

"Really?"

"Forget about Madawaska," he had said. "We have it. We are speaking to thousands, the Liberals are speaking to empty halls. Madawaska is in the bag."

When I told this to Hay, he had remarked, "He's crazy."

But we were sweeping Madawaska, and winning Restigouche, breaking the Liberal hegemony on the North Shore. And then we heard Fenety, his voice vibrant with excitement:

"The Progressive Conservative Party has now won the general election. Hugh John Flemming is the Premier-elect of New Brunswick!"

In York County, the Conservatives had elected three and were leading in the fourth race, but it was still close, a struggle between McNair and Harry Ames for last place. Weldon Lawrence, West, and McInerney were elected.

Meanwhile, the victorious Hugh John Flemming, his beaming wife at his side, was beginning his journey down the river, from his home in Juniper to the radio station in Fredericton.

The victor was God-blessed for ninety miles, the incantations rising to their climax when he arrived in Fredericton to park in front of the radio station, where he had to use his strength to press his way through the crowd, up the stairs, and into the studio.

I met him there, with Fenety and the station's owner-manager, Malcom Neill, summoned from his home for this auspicious occasion. They greeted him with unaccustomed awkward deference, recognizing in him a new presence, different from the Hugh John Flemming who had come, only a week before, to broadcast from their facilities.

"Congratulations," I said to him.

"Well," he said, still beaming, "congratulations to *you*, young man."

Whereupon I promptly gave him some bad advice. Both of us were tired, but he was sustained by the exclusive properties of his victory; for me, the reaction was already setting in, an aching weariness, nausea fluttering in the stomach, a persistent tightness in the chest. Flemming drew from his pocket two statements, badly typed on yellow sheets of paper, one marked "LOSE" and the other "WIN."

He put one back in his coat, saying, "I guess we won't be needing that one." He read out to me the statement marked "WIN." It was remarkably brief, and characteristically tolerant. It began by extending congratulations to "Premier McNair" on his hard-fought campaign.

"He's not the Premier anymore," I told him, erroneously, "You are."

Obligingly, Flemming stroked out the word "Premier" and substituted "Mr."

"I guess that's right, isn't it?" he said.

While Flemming was on air, McNair appeared in the station with Donald Cochrane and was led quickly to the privacy of an empty office. Cochrane and I shook hands, our lips moving in feeble greeting, stronger thoughts concealed in distant removes of the mind.

The radio ceremony done, I climbed in Flemming's car, and we were driven to the Lord Beaverbrook Hotel, there to confront an interesting scene illustrative of the uneasy, if brief, hiatus that lies between the fall of an old order and the rise of a new one.

We were met in the lobby by the hotel manager, plainly distraught. The ballroom, he said excitedly, had been reserved by the local Liberal organization for the evening and he could not allow anyone else to use it. It was clear the purpose for which it had been hired had been now voided by events and, unhappily for the manager, the room was presently jammed with boisterous Tories who, having seen the "Liberal victory celebration" advertised in the press, had come, by some mysterious common signal, to the ballroom to witness it. Their tumult could be clearly heard in the lobby.

"I have to advise you," said the manager, his voice quavering, "that I cannot allow that room to be used by anyone other than the Liberals."

90

Flemming hesitated, pondering the novelty of his position.

I knew the manager, having been a longtime boarder. "I think I should warn you," I said, "that if you try to do anything about it you'll have a riot on your hands."

He looked imploringly at Flemming. "Will you please try and get them out of there as soon as you can?"

It was the first Tory meeting I have attended in a "Liberal hall," so to speak, but Flemming was as true to his word as he could be. He made his way to the platform through a storm of cheers. The two triumphant city candidates, McInerney and West, spoke briefly, followed by Flemming. But the loudest cheers came when Ev Chalmers was brought to the microphone. After that, "L. C. House" was introduced and asked to speak.

I said something, in reference to the aborted Liberal victory dinner, about Balthazar's feast, adding a few more bellicose remarks which were well received. It was not a night for speeches, but only for applause, and after the winners had taken their bows and the celebrities their turns, the impromptu celebrations were adjourned. As we regrouped in the lobby, we met the manager again. He was appropriately grateful to Flemming and relieved to have the ballroom vacant. While he spoke, an empty rum bottle, tossed from the balcony by an invisible hand, crashed at our feet, scattering shards of glass across the floor.

Hay and I walked up the main street, drawn by the din of horns and shouting.

Queen Street was littered with surplus ballots, thrown from windows like confetti. Traffic was at a standstill, the streets and sidewalks a congealed mass of humanity. Many were inebriated, or pretending to be; all were noisy, amiable and curiously expectant, anticipating still some other phenomena to occur in this long day of miracles.

Tweedie had gone to see McNair, finding him alone in his study at home, dazed and shaken, unable to realize his defeat. On the last weekend before the voting, Tweedie had revised his earlier estimate of the election result and predicted the Tories would win. Now, McNair had not much to say, nor Tweedie much to tell him, other than to offer the consoling opinion that his defeat was a blessing since it would add years to his life and that his political record would stand for many years. He did not stay long, but withdrew and spoke to McNair's youngest daughter; he had warned her a week ago that this might be a hard and disappointing evening. When he returned to his home, Tweedie found his younger son, Alison, in tears. He asked his father, "Does this mean you will lose your job?"

By midnight the crowds had left the streets and the city fell silent, as though exhausted. I telephoned my wife at home, hearing, in the distant voice, the accents of incredulity. Asked to explain it all, I could not.

Only a few polls in the country remained to be counted in York and hopes still remained alive for McNair, at least until morning. But the government had fallen; a dynasty had ended in New Brunswick. The dawn would only bring confirmation of personal defeat for McNair and herald the beginnings of a Tory renaissance everywhere.

Before leaving Fredericton for a brief holiday, Flemming came to the hotel to see me, generous in his expressions of appreciation for my part in the campaign. I greeted him by addressing him as "Mr. Premier."

"Come now," he said affably, "Hugh John will do."

He took some pains to tell me of his plans, that he proposed to bring Carson into the Premier's office as his secretary and asked my opinion. I had a fleeting thought that he might have suspected I had aspirations for the job. If so, he was mistaken; I told him Carson was the ideal and only choice.

I then said I had two requests to make of him which he anxiously agreed to hear. The first, I said, was to reform the Elections Act (which he did not attempt in the ensuing eight years of his administration); the second was that he protect Bob Tweedie's job in the Travel Bureau. There would be, I knew, a few headhunters in the triumphant Tory party and Tweedie was foremost among their selected victims. Flemming was quick and convincing in his assurances. (Indeed, he was better than that. Soon after, he telephoned Tweedie personally, to reassure him of his value to the new government.)

In fact, despite McNair's dire election eve forecast of depredations against the civil service, and despite the belligerent hopes of some of his party, Flemming left that institution undisturbed. Even McElman, who was not a protected employee of the government, was offered an appointment in the public service, but he declined and became instead the Liberal Party's provincial organizer.

Before leaving Fredericton, I heard from Tweedie and, for the first time in five years, I felt relaxed and easy in conversation with him. Amity restored, I eagerly accepted his invitation to dinner. We dined alone, in what for me was unaccustomed style in New Brunswick, in the vice-regal suite of the Beaverbrook. For hours, we regaled one another with anecdotes and opinions on the election, my ebullience reinforced by good wine provided by the abstemious Tweedie, and by a friendship refreshed by renewed understanding.

As the evening wore on, he asked me if my agency had any interest in the advertising account of the Travel Bureau. The budget was small, he said, but the account was now serviced by Walsh, the Liberal agency, and while they had served the bureau well, he had every confidence that if I were to assume the account I could do as well, or better.

I had to tell him that the matter had never occurred to me and I wished I had mentioned it to Flemming earlier in the day. The prospect of having some continuing association with the new government, and with Tweedie in the bargain, was irresistible.

Weeks later, at Tweedie's urging (it was coming near to the time for agency-client decisions as to the next year's advertising program), I returned to Fredericton somewhat disappointed that Flemming had not voluntarily invited me to become the bureau's agency. I was in for a surprise.

Always difficult to talk to, Flemming, as Premier, was now nearly impossible. He sat in the old Premier's office, at McNair's familiar desk, papers of state surrounding him, and while I sought to engage him in conversation, he carried on an endless series of telephone conversations, with deputies, aides, friends, and his wife. While speaking on the phone, and listening to me, he held the receiver approximately eight inches from his ear, so as to listen to both voices, I gathered. Such divided attention was distracting.

Finally, we appeared to be coming to grips with the subject of the Travel Bureau account. Flemming's opinion of the value of the tourist industry was not high. "Most of them are people driving through to Nova Scotia," he said matter-of-factly. He added that he thought there was some waste in the bureau's budget and he wanted to have a good look at it. (He had taken the Travel Bureau under his own wing, primarily, it was believed, so that he could have ready access to Tweedie's overall expertise in government procedures.)

He cast about on his desk, fished out a letter from beneath one of the piles, and handed it to me. It was from the president of Walsh Advertising, on fine embossed letterhead, beginning by congratulating Flemming on his victory, leading gracefully to the statement that Walsh had been privileged to service the Travel Bureau account since 1948, concluding with the assurance that the agency stood ready and eager to continue this relationship in the years to come.

"Seems like a nice fellow," Flemming said, placing yet another call.

"Two months ago they were down here telling people you weren't good enough to be Premier of New Brunswick," I said, somewhat more heatedly than intended.

Flemming looked puzzled. "What's that?" he asked.

"They're the Liberal agency," I said, my irritability barely contained.

He put down the phone, the light of revelation in his eyes, a smile playing on the corners of his mouth.

"Well," he said, softly, reflectively, almost to himself, "we can't have that, can we?"

And so it came to pass that Locke, Johnson & Company Ltd. became the agency for the New Brunswick Travel Bureau, replacing Walsh Advertising Ltd., Montreal. Billings on the account for the first year were $46,993.31. (The account now bills $350,000.) And the agency's copy chief, myself, also became an account executive, a promotion of sorts, but more important, the account was to provide an enhanced sense of independence, a first-hand experience in the travel industry and in North American media, both Canadian and American. Thus it was even more important than I had realized at the time, when I had briefly lost my temper in the Premier's office.

But apart from that, when the dust had settled, life was unchanged. Occasionally, when I came to New Brunswick on bureau business, I would meet Flemming, or Carson, or perhaps one of the new Ministers, few of whom I had previously known. Politics, other than in the most general sense, was never discussed and the meetings were invariably brief.

As Flemming became more confident of his powers, which does not take anyone very long, he saw less of Tweedie. Besides, Carson and Tweedie proved to be incompatible, and although I tried for a while to reconcile their mutual hostility, I had little success. Later the Travel Bureau moved from the Premier's Office to that of the Provincial Secretary-Treasurer, Donald Patterson, an amiable and diligent man who had, unlike Flemming, a keen interest in tourism.

But as for politics, I gave no advice, nor was I asked for any. It was as though I were the new account executive from Walsh Advertising.

At the close of 1952, the Canadian Press rated the New Brunswick election as the second biggest news story of the year. I have forgotten what the first one was.

11

THE NERVE CENTRE OF THE PROGRESSIVE CONSERVATIVE PARTY OF
Canada was an aging, creaking, two-storey house on Laurier Avenue
West, Ottawa. The party had purchased the property during the
Bracken years and for that reason it was officially known as "Bracken
House," but commonly referred to as National Headquarters.

The story was that it had once been "a whorehouse for gentlemen,"
but now it was the central office of a national political party struggling
to survive on the avails of slender hopes and thin resources. Early in
the spring of 1953 I found myself invited to Ottawa to give advice on
advertising strategy for the inevitable general election, which all felt
would come in the spring or fall. (Instead, it came mid-summer.)

New patterns of life and new political fields were now open–some of
them appealing, others not. I became a commuter on the overnight
train between Toronto and Ottawa, a frequent guest of the Chateau
Laurier Hotel, and I came to have a permanent second-floor office in
Bracken House, a room overflowing with the unsorted accumulation
of passing events, piles of newspapers, correspondence, memoranda,
aborted plans, and stillborn programs–the residue of years of struggle
dating back to the war years, symbolic of the forgotten resolves and
abandoned aspirations of men who had once been quartered in the
airless, barren room and had then passed on to resume a normal life.

I found it somewhat depressing, and the struggle to find some
defined, effective role was a constant frustration. Obviously, I had a
lot to learn, but I was also convinced *they* had a lot to learn from me.

Here for the first time I met Richard A. Bell, a restless, distracted
man with a commanding presence and voice to match. There could be
nothing new in politics for Bell; he had seen it all during a career
which embraced the consecutive leadership reigns of Bennett, Manion,
Meighen, Bracken, and Drew. He was a product of disappointment and
defeat, with extensive experience in the follies and misadventures of
politics.

As the party's national director, Bell gave the impression of a
superior wisdom, which he no doubt possessed, but which struck lesser
men in the organization as mere arrogance. And whereas the retention
of loyalty to Conservatism required an act of faith, Bell's loyalty seemed
rooted more in the stubbornness of an iron will.

A distant second in command to Bell was Cappé Kidd, a lean,
languid-looking British Columbian with an unexplained British accent,
who was officially designated as the party's executive secretary. Kidd's

95

role seemed to be in headquarters administration, acting for Bell, then in the process of disengagement from the headquarters and returning to his law practice. Kidd possessed the only sense of humour in the national office; I felt a sense of humour to be an essential grace, but Kidd's past association with British Columbia politics had styled his wit to a mocking irreverence and cynicism.

At the heart of almost every political organization is a woman, and whoever walked into Bracken House and entered the dark, narrow reception hall would find the switchboard operator-receptionist on the left, the office of the national director on the right, the door always shut, while directly ahead, a long, dimly lit hall led to what had been a kitchen and was now a general utility room. But half-right, through an open door, sat Miss Kathleen Kearns, a small, compact, white-haired woman, behind a desk bristling with papers, periodicals, correspondence, and the daily input of all the activity of the national office.

Almost every incoming call came to Miss Kearns; each piece of mail crossed her desk; every visitor to the headquarters confronted her alert, penetrating gaze. Kay Kearns supervised the staff, signed the cheques, screened calls and callers, edited pamphlets, vetted outgoing letters, and cast a pervasive influence over headquarters activity, communications with the leader's office, and liaison with the Members of Parliament on the Hill.

She was a lady of indomitable spirit and ferocious loyalty. She began her political career working as a secretary to Sir Robert Borden, was attached as a clerk to the Rowell-Sirois Commission, coming later to the party's organization, where she soon became its conscience and continuity. Intensely loyal to George Drew, her attitude towards his wife, Fiorenza, was closer to worship. As a result, she formed her opinions of others according to her evaluation of their loyalty to George Drew and his wife. Thus she "adored" Donald Fleming, J. M. Macdonnell, or Clair Casselman; she was less sure of others, and when Diefenbaker's name was mentioned, a frown would mount her brow and she would purse her lips in silent disapproval.

None of this, of course, was immediately clear. But it became so as headquarters life grew familiar and as one overheard the daily conversations and the sometimes explosive reactions after telephone conversations had been completed, or when either the caucus or Parliament was in a crisis condition. Kay Kearns, it was clear, was the Tory organization's only indispensable member. Yet for all her encyclopedic knowledge, her resourcefulness and tireless ardour, not all of her influence was constructive or helpful; some of it, I thought, must be damaging.

For example, some queries from outlying parts of the country, addressed to the national director, would never reach his desk. "The fellow's a fool," Miss Kearns would say, referring to the writer. Her manner of dealing with enquiries from the press gallery would depend on the caller and the views of his newspaper.

But this was none of my business. I had been invited to Ottawa to prepare an advertising campaign for the next election, whenever it might come. For this purpose, a committee had been struck, comprising Bell, Kidd, Miss Kearns, Grattan O'Leary, J. M. Macdonnell, and George Nowlan, the party's national president.

After my arrival, another addition was made to the committee— Allister Grosart. I had not met Grosart before, but his name had been mentioned often in association with political campaigns which had previously been developed for Drew and for Leslie Frost in Ontario provincial elections. His agency was McKim's, his relationships within the Ontario Tory Party were believed to be extensive, and he was the only other advertising expert in Conservative circles, apart from myself, who could be said to have managed a winning campaign.

I met the members of this committee at one of its first meetings, gathered incongruously in a private dining room behind the bandstand of the Chateau Laurier Grill. I had arrived in Ottawa by train, wearing a new grey flannel suit purchased for this first, auspicious meeting with the brass of the Tory Party. For me it was an occasion full of mystery and ceremony. Here were faces attached to names I had only seen before in the press. In a setting of almost baronial style, a tuxedoed maitre d' commanded silent, efficient waiters, as we dined by flickering candles, liquor flowing into long glasses, wine pouring from bottomless bottles. The talk was assertive, incomprehensible, sometimes terse as a telegram, other times discursive, richly embroidered by historic anecdote and analogy, with a style of order and precedence that was like some internal secret, shared by all save myself, the newcomer, the stranger in the midst of this warm, intimate, mellow group of men, laughter rumbling in their throats, ritual smiles on their lips as their conversation played over the political scene, as the candles played upon the ceiling, creating both light and shadow.

All deferred to Grattan O'Leary, the man with the greatest charm, the superior eloquence, and the longest history. He had known Laurier, C. D. Howe was a friend, but he was closest to Drew.

"I said to George, only this morning, 'For God's sake, George . . .' " and it would be a stirring plea to do this, or not do that. When O'Leary spoke, the air crackled with opinion, caustic wit, and rueful humour. Next came Macdonnell, a gaunt, imperious, sombre man who ate little and drank less, making gentle persistent efforts to keep the subject matter relevant to the committee's interest, lapsing into long silences when rebuffed.

Nowlan was irreverent and the most gregarious, the easiest to like. As a recent entrant into the House after a fiercely contested by-election, his spurs jangled when he talked.

So this was the Tory inner circle, the party's president, the national director, the executive secretary, the man closest to George Drew, and Allister Grosart, who had managed winning campaigns for Drew and Frost in Ontario.

They were good company, interesting to listen to, and they were polite to strangers. I was there, I supposed, because they suspected I might have some magical properties–a talisman of better luck, an augury of a renascent political party which they spoke of convincingly, with affection and respect. Flemming had won New Brunswick and I had been a part of his victory; thus, I might be a part of a larger enterprise. It was as simple as that.

Yet, to the uninitiated, they seemed a strange lot. They had in common their filial feelings for one another, their likableness, their mutual tolerance for each opinion, however varied, so that as their conversation wore on, all seemed to agree even though each offered a different view. But the differences, really, were illusory, as though each looked upon the many-sided facets of politics and saw something different, in different light, which all agreed was there, whether it could be seen or not by anyone else.

How was New Brunswick won, I was asked. My answer was that it was won because Conservatives attacked Liberals on Liberal grounds, on welfare issues, and because Conservatives did not talk incessantly about taxes, government spending, and "what-was-the-world-coming-to," which Liberals always expected Tories would talk about. I told them I hoped the party, in the next election, would talk to people about issues that mattered to them, rather than issues that mattered only to the vestigial interests of the Conservative Party. They smiled and nodded agreeably, someone remarking that Flemming was helped by the sales tax issue, and then resumed their discourse, hazarding guesses as to the date of the next federal election.

Planning for the election proceeded slowly. Without a writ, there was no urgency. Besides, I found it impossible, as yet, to understand the shorthand of their speech, the half-finished sentences, mentioned names accompanied by raised eyebrows, veiled references to past events –it was like trying to learn another language, or break a code. But there was some progress.

Memorandum to: W. H. Kidd
From: Dalton K. Camp
Subject: Mr. Kettlewell

Following verbal approval from yourself and Mr. Bell, I have asked Mr. Kettlewell to contribute his services in creating layouts for the publicity campaign . . . .

Mr. Kettlewell has my complete confidence. He is the former Art Director of J. Walter Thompson and has recently retired from that company to devote his time to freelance endeavours. I think it could be said that he can give us the best professional advice available, that he is original and that he will give all our assignments complete attention. I also think that at this stage, such an arrangement is preferable to our using the services of the art department in an advertising agency, not only from the point of view of the quality of the work but at the moment I have no desire to have our layouts lying around in agencies' art departments.

I was determined to assume control of the advertising campaign for the next election, believing this to be my purpose for being in Ottawa. Thus, I sought to create my own cadre and to keep planning out of the hands of any single advertising agency, including my own. In this connection, I became increasingly wary of Grosart.

Kay Kearns had told me of the debacle of the 1949 campaign. The blame for it had been settled on McKim's, which had mounted an extravagant and ineffective campaign, climaxed by a full-page advertisement of solid, illegible type. The national director, Dick Bell, saw it for the first time published in the press; he had, Miss Kearns told me, broken down and wept.

On the briefest experience, I had come to the conclusion that advertising agencies in politics were wasteful, their judgement often atrocious, and that many of their decisions were likely to be based on their interest in a profitable campaign, rather than on an effective one. So that while it was natural there would be a sense of rivalry between myself and Grosart, representing competing agencies, much of the attitude was shaped by the stories told me by Kay Kearns, Bell, Kidd, and others about the previous federal campaign, in which McKim Advertising was felt to be responsible, even though Grosart himself did not appear to be blamed.

There were other seeds of conflict being sown. Grosart was determined that the issue in the election would be taxes; I was resolved that it should not be. Frequently we were drawn into debate, and each of us pressed our point of view privately to others as well. I appeared to have little success.

Finally Grosart informed me of his intention to make a survey of public opinion. I could hardly disagree with that, even while I suspected that parties, not the public, created issues. In addition, I had a low opinion of political polls and a healthy respect for their cost. But Grosart assured me that before the survey was taken he would consult with me as to the organization to be employed and also let me see the questionnaire.

In the event, he did neither. The survey was taken, through McKim's, and the questionnaire, I thought, was as preposterous as its findings. The poll had been taken just prior to the 1953 budget, when public interest in taxation was heightened by expectation and curiosity. When asked by the pollsters if they thought taxes were "too high," an enormously high percentage of the public indicated that they were.

Grosart was pleased with this result. I was indignant, suspecting that primitive research was being employed to advance poor strategy. When Grosart produced the survey results before the committee, I had an ominous feeling that its members were being treated to a sleight-of-hand demonstration by a deft, professional artist:

Are Taxes to Blame for High Prices?
Yes 66%
No 23%
Undecided 11%

Thus was the committee's view strengthened that taxation was the issue. But more than that, the survey confirmed the wisdom of the Tory Party's stance in Parliament and ratified its headquarters' propaganda:

What Keeps Taxes Up? (Spontaneous)
Waste and Extravagance	57%
Defence Spending	52%
Too Many Civil Servants	42%
Increased Costs	31%
Surplus Budgeting	30%
Added Social Services	27%
Farm Price Support	11%

Marvelous! "Waste and Extravagance" had been the party's war-cry since the end of the war. Kay Kearns, the author of the party's best political pamphlets ("Pocket Politics"–a precise imitation of a British Tory Party publication), had bulging files of material on the issue of government waste. Members' speeches were profusely illustrated with examples. The Currie Report on Defence Department spending irregularities (among them, the discovery of "horses on the payroll" at Camp Petawawa) had brought the item of "defence spending" readily to the minds of those interviewed.

Now Allister produced this document, reeking of the newest science and technique, all of which confirmed the wisdom, judgement, and practices of all present. Self-satisfaction flooded the meeting.

When asked in the survey, "What is your chief criticism of the P.C. Party?" sixty-five per cent of the respondents were classified as "Don't Know and No Criticism."

Of those who could think of anything to criticize in the Tory Party,

"Big Business" was the complaint of 4.5%; "Policies not Constructive" the complaint of 4.2%, and only 4.1% were found who mentioned the unmentionable–"The Leader." (The survey, with characteristic thoroughness if not valid sampling technique, broke this down as follows: "8% in Ontario, 2% in Quebec, 1.7% in British Columbia, 2.2% in Prairies.")

Voting trends were broken down into an infinity of fragments. The survey reported that 1.4% "refused to say how they will vote in 1953"; feverish analysis broke this down further, claiming that 82.6% of the 1.4% "say they voted in 1949" and that 21.7% of *them* voted Liberal and only 2.2% "say they voted P.C."

It was difficult to determine how large the sample had been and how representative. (Grosart had earlier mentioned 3,000 and that Newfoundland had been excluded.) But the fact that "82.6%" of the "1.4%" voted in 1949 suggested a poll of a substantial number of people. I was sceptical and said so.

Grosart was the master of diplomacy and of committee-management, an art for which I lacked both experience and potential. As the meetings followed in their ordered sequence, I became increasingly silent; it could be said, and probably was, that I sulked. There could be no doubt that Grosart was fully in charge, that the committee regarded me as a novice, and quite properly so. And since they were all men of vast experience themselves, they were convinced that experience was the most valuable of all requisites for politicians.

Paper proposals proliferated; a "Draft Work Plan for 1953 General Election (Confidential. Not to be Communicated)" was submitted to the committee by Grosart. It demonstrated his consummate knowledge of the men with whom he was working, laying heavy stress on the importance of meticulous planning, of committee surveillance of all advertising, of the significant role of the caucus, of maximum assistance to the constituency organization, and budget control. The committee was impressed by this exact reflection of its own opinions.

As for the advertising, I read, with a sense of despair, the following:

II CONSIDERATIONS
In respect to the 2 main objectives, some basic considerations are:
Objective 1. The Overall Appeal to the voters:
The function of Advertising and Public Relations is less to change public attitudes than is sometimes supposed. It is rather:
(1) *to analyse, evaluate and interpret* public attitudes in terms of basic wants, needs and desires–to find out what people are thinking as an essential factor in determining what we are going to ask them to believe, and how we are going to get them to buy.
(2) *to communicate this information* to the party campaign planners and advise how it can best be used to make the presentation

of Party policy conform to known factors in the market it is intended to influence.

(3) *to use this information* as a basic guide for developing an advertising and public relations appeal which will be realistic in terms of what people are thinking and what they want as an alternative to what they now have. Basically, public attitudes must be congruent to Party's overall policy. Party can't adopt "Liberal" attitudes merely because majority public attitude is Liberal.

This may be explained in terms of product merchandising whose principles are *partially* applicable.

Assuming that we have a product which has, we believe, a natural market and is superior to other products in that market, we develop a merchandising plan as follows:

(1) *We survey the market* to find out what qualities people are looking for or will recognize as desirable in the product. It is not enough to have a superior product. We must be able to convince people that it is superior, and that it has benefits for them they cannot get elsewhere. This applies not only to the product itself but also to how it is presented or packaged. Often, in fact, the proper package is a more important market determinant than the product itself.

(2) Knowing what people want, we then *examine our product* to see how it fits these requirements. We make sure that it has the essential qualities known to be desirable in the market, and we analyse it item by item to determine the advantages and disadvantages it may be faced with in relation to our competitors.

(3) *We develop a merchandising plan* (of which Advertising is an important part) to draw attention with the greatest possible skill to the superiority of our product in those qualities or aspects in which people are most interested.

The commercial product analogy must not, however, be carried too far. Experience proves that many of the successful techniques of product merchandising are not applicable in the political field. We have for example a much larger margin of error in interpreting the results of our market analysis (e.g. opinion attitude polls vs. product attitude polls). We do not have the endless "second chances" which are heavily relied on in a long-term product campaign. We have less control over our field force and no reliable daily "sales" reports to guide our market tactics. We are denied most of the "shock" techniques of commercial advertising (L.S.M.F.T. may eventually irritate people into buying Lucky Strikes, but we cannot afford to irritate voters. The memory of the irritation lingers much longer than the commercial).

We must therefore pick and choose carefully between product techniques, but we cannot afford to ignore the vast store of knowledge of how public attitudes react to believable quality claims and can be motivated to the desired mass action. As we pick and choose we remember, for example, that we do not sell the benefits of a correspondence course or the Encyclopeadia Britannica as we would detergents or cigarettes.

Elsewhere in the thirty-page document, Grosart had discoursed on "alternative methods" for the use of advertising and public relations which, the report read, were based on "a study of previous election campaigns of the two major parties." This "study" suggested three alternatives which were, in brief:

"METHOD I: The national responsibility is minimal, the candidate's maximal."

"METHOD II: National responsibility is maximal, the candidate's minimal."

"METHOD III: National headquarters assumes responsibility for the production of most of the advertising, radio, print and special material which will have more or less uniform application and use in all ridings."

After an extensive analysis of each of these options, weighing so-called "advantages" and "disadvantages," the report proposed "in broad terms" a recommended Plan. (Great care was always taken by Grosart to lead the committee to the proper conclusion, but to leave the illusion that the decision lay in the hands of its members.) The Plan was set down in summary form:

(1) The functions of Advertising and Public Relations as outlined in Considerations effecting Objective I–the *Overall Appeal to Voters;*
(2) Method III as to Objective 2–*Maximum assistance to Candidates.*

Grosart also stressed the need for opinion surveys–not one, but three:

We must decide whether to direct our appeal to all voters on a universal basis or to specific groups . . . in order of relative potential returns in terms of Conservative votes. The attempt to "be all things to all men" tends to degenerate into the "Me-tooism" which proved so disastrous to Messrs. Wilkie [sic] and Dewey. It tends also to spread the essential quality of our product too thinly over the whole, and to lose impact in relation to the body of voters who may be reasonably expected to be receptive to us. Our objective is not to convince *all* the voters. It would appear, therefore, to make sense to find out what part of the market we can realize and to concentrate all our efforts there. . . .

This was followed by a pitch for the "surveys":

We need to know not only to whom we should appeal, but also to what we should appeal. We assume that there are enough voters desirous of a change of government to achieve our objective. Our first requirement is to check this assumption.

Sitting in airless, smoke-filled rooms in the company of grown men, hearing them pondering these words, chewing over each phrase, holding sentences of almost total vacuity up to the light of serious consideration, all conspired to make me physically ill. I found myself palpitating with suppressed rage, gripped by massive, throbbing headaches, stuttering and incoherent in speech, and I would again and again lapse into truculent silence.

It was possible, of course, that these men possessed wisdom I did not share; that the Tory Party was fighting to survive, and not to win, because victory was impossible in any imaginable circumstance. And so they were content to sit in endless conference, absorbing themselves in considerations of meaningless profundity, out of a sense of desperation and duty, there being nowhere else to turn, nor anyone else to turn to.

The weakest point of my outrage was in my own futility. I did not know what I would have done myself; I was a critic without a constructive plan of my own.

And I did not know George Drew, other than as the Liberal caricature. But one detected, in the elliptical references of others, an uneasiness about the national leader which admitted to a lack of conviction as to his political prospects. Furthermore, the organization was obsessed with Ontario; it was the dead centre of its universe, with the Maritimes and the West loosely flapping hinges. As for Quebec, it was discussed only as an eternally unresolved problem.

Kettlewell and I continued, however, to plan advertisements, despite my growing feelings that our efforts were futile. I was all for giving the Grits hell, a bellicosity which glowed more feverishly the longer I remained at the headquarters of the Progressive Conservative Party.

Kettlewell produced a version of our mutual labours which faithfully reflected my mood:

"Don't take yourself too seriously.
If we wanted to get away with it

Who would stop us?"

C. D. Howe

A Study of Arrogance as seen from the Front Bench

We suspect Mr. Howe's bark is worse than his bite, (just as the taxpayer knows Mr. Abbott's bite to be worse than his bark). Mr. Howe is not, we suspect, an arrogant man. He is, however, an arrogant Minister. And he has company on the Government front benches in the House of Commons.

Herewith we submit a few "Howe-isms"–and a few "Liberal-isms"– which, we suggest, seem to show a rather alarming lack of humility, of propriety and even of responsibility on behalf of a Government which, after all, is supposedly a servant of Parliament and the people.

Our Mr. Fulton once asked the Government when it would see fit to answer a question he had properly asked in Parliament. He had, Mr. Fulton explained, been waiting over a month. "May I ask when I will get an answer?"

"When we get around to it," replied Mr. Howe.

On another occasion, the Leader of the Opposition made mention of the contribution made by a Conservative Government toward the development of a trans-Canada airline.

Said Mr. Howe: "Nuts."

When the Opposition submitted a proposal which would save the taxpayers a million dollars, the Minister of Defence Production brushed it aside, saying, "A million dollars is not a very important matter."

When the Leader of the Opposition rose to speak on a question of privilege he was greeted by the Minister of Transport.

"Who," asked the Minister, "wants to hear you?"

When a member of the Opposition rose to speak on a resolution moved by the Liberal Leader, he was told, "The Prime Minister has other things to do than listen to the hon. gentleman."

And when the Official Opposition asked the McNabb Report (prepared at the taxpayers' expense, therefore in the public domain) be made public, the Government at first denied the Report existed.

When finally forced to admit it was about somewhere, the Government refused to make it public on the original grounds that "the majority" (i.e. the Liberal Party) in Parliament did not want to make it public.

Is this Government too big for its britches? Is it arrogant? Arbitrary?

A political party which has held power going on to a quarter of a century might well come to the conclusion that its appeal to the electorate was somehow irresistible. It might feel–as Mr. Howe once put it–that it could get away with anything–"Who would stop us?"

That's for you to decide.

It would appear to us that the reasonable citizen might well have doubts about granting yet another term of office to a Government so steeped in the rich juices of its own self-importance that its best rebuttal is "Nuts" and its attitude towards the duly elected Opposition is–"Who wants to hear you?"

This Party, even to its most steadfast critic, remains nevertheless the only Party capable of displacing the present regime. At this time we solicit your earnest and thoughtful consideration of our point of view.

No. 2 in a series of pre-campaign advertisements presented for your consideration by the Progressive Conservative Party of Canada.

And here, all of Howe's words were given their appropriate citations in Hansard.

If nothing else, it was a portent of the Diefenbaker campaign to come. But the committee did not think much of it, and Grosart, adroitly steering his peers towards his own strategy, introduced a second report, described as "Work Plan Number Two (Private and Confidential)":

We are beginning to process material this week. It will be well if preliminary general agreement can be reached on the overall approach it is intended to make to the voters.

It is not enough to say that we have a good case. We have had a good case many times before and have lost elections. Many factors are involved and some essential ingredients of the election campaign are still not known. However, we are starting our campaign right now. Candidates are in the field. Public attitudes are already being influenced.

This is Stage #1 of our campaign

The time objective is Writ Day. The tactical objective is a running start on the final phase. The strategy objective is an operational plan already in gear, operating smoothly, and designed for quick change-over to the post-Writ-day strategy.

Merely to "gather material" between now and Writ day is no plan at all. A plan worthy of the objective will include the following

(1) A firm (but not necessarily final) decision about our method of approach. (APPROACH)
(2) Definite overall work objectives to be reached on or before writ day. (OBJECTIVES)
(3) A list of projects which will achieve these objectives. (PROJECTS)
(4) Assignment and acceptance of work tasks and responsibilities. (WORK TASKS)
(5) A time-table and the necessary checks and controls to make sure that the objectives are reached on schedule. (CONTROL)
(6) The necessary supplies, i.e. budget, personnel, research, etc. (SUPPLIES)

To achieve the above, the following suggestions are made for approval at to-night's meeting:–

1–APPROACH
There are many alternatives.
(a) All-out attack. "Turn out the rascals" (New Brunswick).
(b) A combination of attack and mild alternative action (the traditional Opposition approach).
(c) A "promise" campaign consisting of many general vote-catching specifics directed at various groups.
(d) A single issue campaign (such as King's Constitutional issue or Walter Thompson's health insurance issue in Ontario).
(e) A positive platform along the line of the 22 points in Ontario in 1943.
(f) A "switch" campaign, starting with one of these and switching to another at a strategic time.
(g) A "goodwill" campaign based on the assumption that people will vote for us if we don't irritate them into voting against us.

Suggested is a combination of the applicable features of (d), (e) and (g) above.

It might be described as follows:–

The single (d) issue is lower taxes. The Budget does not go far enough. The election hand-outs are based on higher national product not on cutting waste and wild spending. (The Currie Report and waste are used not as issues in themselves but as proof only that taxes can be reduced).

Work Plan Two proposed a pre-election advertising campaign. Hopefully, the committee had come to the conclusion that the election would not come until the fall. Thus Grosart called for "a low-pressure, institutionalized campaign," designed to remind voters of such elemental political facts as:

The Conservative Party is an historical institution in Canada and the only one other than the Liberals which has ever assumed the responsibility of office; it has traditional policies and approach to national problems; it has among its Members of Parliament a fund of extensive experience in the functioning of government; it is not merely "one of the other parties"; its membership extends to all parts of the country; its appeal is national and to all groups–racial, religious, income, age and particularly to women voters.

Magazines used would be confined to the national consumer group– Time, Maclean's and Readers' Digest, with possible occasional use of the week-end mass circulation papers in French and English, depending on budget.

12

GEORGE NOWLAN CALLED TO SUGGEST THAT I GO TO NOVA SCOTIA AND
meet Bob Stanfield. A provincial election was on its way and perhaps
I could help.

"Old man," he said, in that thick, hoarse voice, with its slight, undetermined impediment, "this is not going to be like New Brunswick.
Nobody's going to beat Angus L. and Stanfield is no Hugh John Flemming. But I think you should go down, at least, and look around."

"I don't know, George," I said. "I'm not much interested in any
more lost causes."

"Well, you and Bill [Rowe] go down and look around. There are
some seats I think we can win there [some of them were in George's
huge federal riding of Digby-Annapolis-Kings] and I'd like our boys
to have some help."

"I'll see what I can do."

"I know you will. If anyone can do anything down there, it would
be you."

"Thanks, George."

"God bless, old man."

I flew to Halifax, checked into the Lord Nelson Hotel, and called
Stanfield for an appointment. We had never met before, and I did not
even know what he looked like. But I had few illusions–he was, by
common opinion, a dull, dour man.

The offices of McInnes and Stanfield were at 156½ Hollis Street.
A flight of wooden steps led to the office, and there I found myself
standing opposite Stanfield in an austere, undistinguished room, the
afternoon sun pouring through a curtainless window and falling on the
plain, bare table between us.

Well, I thought, at least he's not pretty. Long-headed, with shrewd,
heavily lidded eyes (a slight cast in one, like the Shaws on my mother's
side), a long nose, and full mouth. All else was elbows and knees. He
invited me to sit down and for a while there was an uneasy silence.

"Some of our fellows think we could use a little help down here in
the election," he said finally.

The voice had depth and resonance and was almost without accent.
Dalhousie and Harvard, merged with Truro. (Good for radio?)

"How does the election look to you?" I asked him.

"Oh, I don't know. We don't expect to win, but we expect to do
better." (Pause) "Somewhat."

I had never talked to anyone like this before, at least not about politics. Farmers and their crops, yes. But not politicians; with them it was either blue ruin or certain victory–Armageddon or the Resurrection. Stanfield looked directly at you, a fractional smile, and when he swallowed, you noticed his Adam's apple.

I said, "I looked at the last election returns and you could have won if less than two thousand votes had gone the other way."

"That's a lot of votes in Nova Scotia." Smiling.

"You're a lot closer than we were in New Brunswick, last year."

"That may be true, but this is not New Brunswick. The Grits are pretty strong here."

"I don't see any reason why you can't win."

"Well, I do." Smiling again.

"I don't see any sense in running to lose."

"We'll do the best we can, that's all. It's not a matter of running to lose." No smile.

It was clear to me that we were getting on each other's nerves. If I sounded belligerent, it was because, I thought, I am so damned sick and tired of meeting Tories who can't win, don't want to win, never will win. And Stanfield, I suspected, thought I had a lot of gall telling him about his chances when all I had done was read the 1949 provincial election returns.

"Anyway," he said politely, trying to retrieve the subject of our meeting, "we thought perhaps you and Bill Rowe might lend us a hand. We've got a few problems–candidates, and that kind of thing. Then there's the publicity. We have a fellow here who has helped us in the past. I don't know how good he is, really, but you might be able to help us there."

The meeting concluded with the ceremonial handshake, a minimum of formality, and I was back in my hotel room. God knows he needed help; I don't believe I ever saw anyone who needed more of it. I took a DC-3 on the long, fluttering journey back to Toronto.

Stanfield's diffidence was puzzling, if not alarming. Our first encounter had been less than inspiring, and when I returned to Toronto I put Nova Scotia out of my mind, half hoping I would hear no more of it. Perhaps I had so appalled Stanfield he would look for campaign assistance elsewhere.

Ruefully, I told Nowlan that I had made some assessment of the situation in his province and concluded that I would only get on Stanfield's nerves.

"That's just what he needs, old boy," George said cheerfully.

I was not so sure. On April 15, Stanfield wired me:

Election announced May twenty-sixth. Anxious see you before end this week. Conventions take me out of Halifax most of next week. Perhaps you will phone me.

110

To which I replied:

Am conferring with Nowlan immediately. My committee meets
tonight. Am personally anxious to accommodate you in every
way. Will try to get clearance from all concerned today and try to
reach you by telephone tomorrow morning 10 a.m. Best regards.

There was no reluctance in Ottawa to have me go; perhaps they
expected another miracle, as in New Brunswick, or perhaps they felt
easier with my energies transported to other lands. Whatever it was,
I left for Halifax, somewhat low in spirit, yet hopeful that at least I
might be helpful in an area that was more familiar and where my
responsibilities would be better defined.

Resignedly, but cheerfully, I surrendered my federal campaign concerns to Grosart, confident that he would take them up. My campaign
theme of Liberal arrogance receded into limbo while the "single issue"
of high taxes came to dominate the minds of the party's strategists, if
not the electorate.

My second meeting with Stanfield was not much better than the
first.

"Where in hell have you been?" he asked icily.

But the confrontation was brief and then he was gone about the
province to attend nominating conventions while I moved into the
Lord Nelson Hotel, in a room overlooking a vacant lot and the backs
of ancient frame houses. Once more I began to address myself to a
familiar problem—how to fight an election everyone believed lost even
before the campaign had begun.

Nova Scotia in 1953 was a formidable Liberal fortress. To assault
it, I naturally sought to assemble the same weapons and tactical support I had used in New Brunswick. But the circumstances were not the
same. To begin with, as someone remarked, "Macdonald is not
McNair."

Premier Angus L. Macdonald was a living legend in Nova Scotia;
he "had the Gaelic," and with it, a reputation for integrity remarkably
unsullied—despite twenty years of unrivalled power, a government of
marked mediocrity, and a party seething with corruption. Scandal hung
about the government like a pall of smoke, but Macdonald towered
above it, aloof, imperious, disdainful, and invulnerable. In preparing
campaign strategy, I was repeatedly warned not to attack Macdonald,
indeed, not even to mention his name.

So, if the bishops were bunglers and the priests corrupt, the Pope
was sacrosanct, leaving the Tories in eternal purgatory. Yet there were
analogies to the New Brunswick situation, though not all of them were
encouraging:

McNair's strength had been in his hold on the Acadian vote, embracing all of the North Shore of New Brunswick. Macdonald's lay in his firm grasp on the loyalties of the Irish and Scotch Catholics which produced massive Liberal majorities in Halifax and on Cape Breton Island.

McNair's cabinet had been weak, as was Macdonald's, and the party organizations of both were dominated by a few powerful, acquisitive men. However, resentment of this clique seemed less in Nova Scotia than in New Brunswick. In Halifax, at least, the Liberal organization was admired by its supporters and simply envied by its opponents.

Tory strength, and prospects, in each province seemed to be in the non-urban areas, where the majority of the voters were Protestant. In Nova Scotia, urban Halifax seemed positively forbidding to Conservative prospects.

As in New Brunswick, the newspapers and radio stations of Nova Scotia were largely apolitical. The media made little effort to enliven public interest in elections. The Cape Breton *Post,* however, was an exception, with its fiercely partisan, pro-Tory editorial policy that was frequently reflected in its news coverage. It did not appear to influence the voters in its circulation area.

I was given a "publicity committee" to advise me. I sensed that Stanfield suspected I might be impulsive and headstrong. The committee was intended to be a restraining influence, or at least reassurance to the leader that the campaign would not run away without him. Its members were Richard A. Donahoe, the Mayor of Halifax, Leonard Fraser, the party's former leader, and Roland Ritchie, a prominent Halifax lawyer.

Oddly enough, the committee, none of whom were candidates in the election, proved to be at least as belligerent as I, and gave me much cooperation and encouragement.

Fraser became, in the few years remaining in his life, a warm friend. He had endured a brief, bitter term of leadership, climaxed by the provincial election of 1945, when his party failed to win a single seat; the CCF formed the official opposition, with its two members from industrial Cape Breton. Although a man of immense charm and cordiality, Fraser could never entirely conceal the wounds left by his defeat. But he was intensely loyal to Stanfield, who was his neighbour on Gorsebrook. Stanfield, however, had earlier warned me of Fraser's ardent partisanship, which could on occasion become excessive.

The Mayor of Halifax, in the judgement of a number of Tories, was the one man who could inevitably lead the party to victory. He was a formidable personality, with a rich, resonant voice, robust Irish wit, and a man who had survived, despite his Tory leanings, the strenuous infighting for which the politics of Halifax was renowned. In 1953 he

112

preferred to sit on the periphery of the struggle, puffing reflectively on hand-rolled cigarettes, offering modest counsel, and disseminating cheerful words of encouragement upon my efforts.

Rollie Ritchie, with his quiet caution and unemotive appraisal of events, personified the Halifax establishment. On Stanfield's "committee to watch Camp," he was its balance wheel, a third opinion which more often than not helped achieve consensus.

As matters developed, the publicity committee became important to me in my confrontations, which began almost immediately and raged daily, with the Halifax *Chronicle-Herald,* the only newspaper in Nova Scotia with province-wide circulation. The *Herald* was an institution, representing a merger of two papers. The Liberal *Chronicle* and the Conservative *Herald,* each of them fiercely partisan, had been joined in one powerful, prosperous enterprise, dedicated to the interests of Nova Scotia, as it saw them, and which on reading the paper I took to be overwhelmingly Liberal.

The Tory organization would be no match for its Liberal opponents in terms of numbers, resources, or skills. The habits of defeat were always a heavy burden, made more so by the tacit acceptance of other defeats still to come. To fire an organization into a combative mood seemed to be the first task of the advertising campaign, but confronted by a leader who knew his party could not win, and by a party that feared to mention the name of its principal adversary, this did not seem an easy task.

The Liberal Party treated Stanfield with casual contempt. Its first advertisement proclaimed "Wrong-Way Stanfield Again!" taking out of context one of his pre-election comments, accompanied by copy heavy with derision and mocking disdain.

Nearly everyone, in those earlier days of Stanfield's leadership, apologized for him. While admiring his pluck and perseverance, they mourned his essential drabness, his uninspiring platform manner, his lack of rhetoric. He was, in the eyes of most, a satisfactory interim leader, serving out Macdonald's time, as it were, until the Liberal leadership would change, after which Tory fortunes might be renewed under more promising and inspired direction.

In Nova Scotia, visiting Liberals put up at the Nova Scotian, a link in the CNR chain referred to as "the government hotel," while Tories were encouraged to stop at the Lord Nelson, an independently owned and operated establishment, with a kitchen which produced superb seafood and a staff that was openly Tory. Elderly gentlefolk sat out their retirement in comfortable chairs lining the walls of the lobby; the atmosphere was one of genteel, musty discretion, dark, comfortable, and hospitable.

113

Here I brought my typewriter and other paraphernalia, including a baseless though sustaining optimism, and settled in to challenge the twenty-year reign of Angus L. Macdonald and his Liberal Party. The problems, after New Brunswick and Ottawa, were familiar enough, even in this unfamiliar hotel and in a city I had known only briefly when a student at Acadia University.

But it was not, of course, New Brunswick, nor Ottawa, but something in between. There was no Carson, nor Hay, nor Chalmers on hand, although I was determined to find their counterparts. The budget for advertising was correspondingly modest, but adequate. And Stanfield was a man of different nature and habit than Flemming, more methodical, less self-assured, more intent on organization and procedure.

If the Halifax *Herald* was a familiar problem for me, I was a new one for them. As in New Brunswick, I began my own series of editorial-style advertisements in the press, and they were no less provocative. The *Herald* was nothing if not dignified and austere, and the Tory ads almost immediately caught the eye of management. A series of alarms was triggered throughout the advertising department and among the paper's legal advisors.

In this first campaign in Nova Scotia, it was difficult to find the enemy. Unlike New Brunswick, the Liberals in Nova Scotia put forward an astonishingly modest, seemingly amateur campaign. They used the media sparingly and their efforts gave the impression of being casual and impromptu; there was neither consistency, theme, nor pattern. Macdonald himself, in the early days of the campaign, was all but invisible.

The enemy was less a political party or persons in it, than an attitude of mind. A genteel civility and caution permeated all activity, creating a mist of impenetrable complacency. Behind it all, however, the Liberal organization purred with familiar efficiency, employing the acquired skills of two decades in power, combining public works and private charity to fashion its massive victories.

In the face of necessity, my own responsibilities broadened in scope. Bill Rowe and I journeyed to the Annapolis Valley in an effort to persuade a prosperous apple grower to stand as a candidate. We lunched with our prospect in Kentville, at the Cornwallis Inn. George Boggs, a retired gentleman farmer, arranged the confrontation and was our host.

Despite all our urgings, we were unsuccessful and we departed the luncheon without a candidate for Kings. But both Rowe and I had been even more impressed by Boggs, and after a whispered conference in the hotel lobby, we followed him to his home to persuade him to run. Boggs, to our immense relief, agreed to do so (and was elected).

Rowe toured the South Shore and provided sensible reports on the party's prospects, along with astute assessments of the candidates and the mood of the electorate. He had the rarest of qualities as a political organizer–he was a good listener. Best of all, he was a tonic for morale, always cheerful, encouraging, and practical. Maritimers were pleasantly surprised that anyone of such pleasing demeanour would be a representative of "headquarters" in Ottawa.

But as the campaign wore on, I became increasingly frustrated by the media. The *Herald* served notice that it would not publish my copy unless it were placed in their hands forty-eight hours in advance of publication. This fiat would prevent the editorial columns from being effective, if they could ever be, in their sense of immediacy. It also suggested censorship, and allowed the possibility of the columns being seen by the opposition before publication.

I descended upon the offices of that great journal, armed in defiance and outrage, to be ushered into the inner sanctum of the publisher, Mr. Daley, a calm, self-possessed gentleman of unmistakable authority and presence.* His office was pine-panelled, broadloomed, acoustically pure, and tastefully furnished. His desk was impressively tidy, his manner benign and fatherly. I received his undivided attention.

The paper, he told me, had a responsibility to all its readers, Liberal, Conservative, and otherwise, to see that political commentary which appeared in its pages was fair and reasonable in nature. He advised me that my comments were perhaps somewhat heated and intemperate, and while this was no affair of his, he would caution against it, since they might well have the effect of offending readers rather than persuading them.

I told him, briskly, that his paper had no right to make such a judgement. I had written nothing that was libellous, and as for fair comment, that would be my responsibility. Anyway, I argued, the Halifax *Chronicle-Herald* had no right to govern the tone and temper of the election campaign.

It was not much of an argument. I had my angry indignation, Mr. Daley had his newspaper. He was unmoved by my words. He picked up his telephone and summoned his editor, Frank Doyle, who appeared almost instantly, like a genie from a bottle.

Daley reviewed my complaint with Doyle, who smiled and said the paper's regulations about advertising copy applied as much to the Liberals as to the Tories. When I replied that this worked no hardship on the Liberals, but was a disadvantage to the Conservatives, Doyle continued to smile, commenting that the Liberals always seemed better organized than the Tories.

I had no doubt that I appeared to them a brash and presumptuous young man who was tilting at windmills. Both told me, sympathetically,

---

*I was not the first to make complaint. Long before this visit, Angus L. Macdonald had declaimed against Daley in the Nova Scotia legislature, categorizing him as "Public Enemy number one."

115

that they had known my father. They seemed distressed that he had had such a difficult son.

Finally Doyle and his perpetual smile withdrew, and Daley summarized the position. He said that he, personally, was a lifelong Conservative. But the paper had an obligation to its readers, the majority of whom supported the Liberal governments in Ottawa and Halifax. The paper sought to reflect this fact, although without conspicuous bias. It would remain fair to both sides. As a final warning, he did not think the Conservative campaign, as to date, would be very productive. But for the necessary business of submitting advertising copy two days in advance, he hoped I would not find it too difficult to adjust to this essential policy, since, as Mr. Doyle had pointed out, the Liberals had done so.

There was no other choice. The policy was a constant irritant, and it did destroy the concept of immediacy which I valued. But as for the foreboding possibility of censorship, it was never exercised by the paper, although it influenced me as I prepared the copy; I could visualize every sentence being examined by the *Herald's* legal advisors, by Frank Doyle, and, possibly, by interested Liberals.

As a result, the columns were sometimes more strident than pertinent and contained a good deal more bark than bite:

The closed eye and the loose tongue. . . .

There is a time when Governments who have held power for long
periods–like twenty years–collapse of their own weight. They
are voted into office, in the beginning, to breathe a little fresh air into
public offices, to clean out the dusty corners, empty the waste
baskets and give strict attention to the people's business.

This is Bob Stanfield's chore at this time. We have a Government
that is staggering under the burdens of accumulated errors, oversights
and blunderings of its own making. It can't get untracked. Its best
friends are its worst enemies.

Cabinet Ministers tend to become potentates. They move out of their
constituencies, lose touch with their electors and lose sight of
their real importance. In Nova Scotia, they have gone so far as to
provide pensions for themselves–they have talked themselves into the
belief that they deserve a lifetime reward.

Their thinking becomes confined–they hate to make decisions.
Their eyesight gets poor–they can't see problems. And yet, their
tongues get looser.

116

Something wrong at the Inverness Mine? The Premier writes a clever poem about it. His supporters are amused.

A Minister returns from Europe, his mission a failure. He makes a joke about it. The most important personage he met, he said wittily, was Rita Hayworth. He can't understand why the coal miners, for example, do not think this is funny.

A Liberal chairman gets caught short of a majority–the Opposition wins the vote in the Public Accounts Committee. What to do? The chairman votes twice–once to tie the vote, once to win the vote.

In power for twenty years, they are filled with their own importance. The Opposition asks them to investigate the responsibility, if any, of the Government's Security Department in the National Thrift case. It is voted down. The Opposition asks them to investigate the alleged illegal activities of liquor agents. It is voted down.

The signs are clear that this twenty year old Government will no longer use its majority as an instrument for progressive legislation.

These are only a few of the reasons why the voters of this province are inclined to agree that Twenty's Plenty.

NOVA SCOTIA NEEDS A

STANFIELD GOVERNMENT NOW!

(Inserted by the Progressive Conservative Association of Nova Scotia)

The Liberals responded to this, with some discomfort to me, through one of the cabinet, who observed that the Tories were proposing that Bob Stanfield be elected so that he could empty the wastepaper baskets in the government offices.

However irritating were my relations with the *Herald,* they were of minor significance compared to my struggles with CHNS, the *Herald's* radio station.

The ghost of Mackenzie King attended all considerations relating to political broadcasting. In earlier days, King had believed himself victimized by a Tory election campaign "soap-opera" which broadcast a dramatized version of the life and times of a Canadian family whose politics were anti-King and pro-Bennett. These programs, "Mr. Sage," intrigued listeners and may possibly have influenced some of them to vote against the Liberal Party. They also provoked Mackenzie King who, when elected to power, made certain that he and his party would never be so victimized again.

117

Thus, broadcasting regulations guaranteed for more than a generation that political broadcasting would be as dull, unimaginative, and sterile as possible. Impromptu conversation or dialogue was forbidden. All broadcasts had to be scripted and texts submitted in advance. For CBC free-time broadcasts, provincial or federal, scripts were required to be in the hands of the originating station two days prior to broadcast. Spokesmen for political parties, appearing on local stations, were obliged to leave a copy of their remarks in the hands of the station. All political voices were obliged to be identified by name, and all broadcasts, however brief, were obliged to carry the sponsor's identity both before and after the political message had been aired. Music or other sound effects were forbidden.

All this was done to purge the dread curse of political "dramatization." Station managers vigilantly monitored political broadcasting as though their lives, or their licences, depended upon it. They dwelt in constant fear of libel (or was it slander?), or profanity, or some other political vulgarity being unleashed upon their audiences. The most pedestrian criticism of government by opposition politicians filled station managers with unease. And while the private stations enjoyed the revenues which political campaigns were now producing in increasing volume, they did not enjoy the onerous responsibilities of acting as monitors and censors. The network-affiliated stations were fast becoming a central file for hundreds of inconsequential political announcements, partisan talks, and perorations, all of which the CBC obliged them to carry in its faithful obedience to Mackenzie King, in death as in life.

Innocence leads one to innovation, as well as into trouble.

Since Jack Fenety's daily radio broadcasts had been successful in New Brunswick, I cast about for a similar voice for the Nova Scotia campaign. This turned out to be John Funston, a personable, popular young sports announcer at CHNS, whose baseball broadcasts had made him familiar throughout the province.

When I asked Funston if he would serve as the voice of the Nova Scotia Tories, he was interested. Apart from the fee it would earn, Funston was a latent Conservative. But as an employee of CHNS, he said, he would be obliged to seek management permission.

Gerald Redmond was the station manager. A brisk, engaging man with a resonant radio voice of his own, Redmond invited me to his office to discuss the terms by which Funston's name might be associated with the Conservative cause. It was a simple matter of station policy, he told me, that its announcers were available to clients–all clients–for commercial duties. He suggested that I ponder the significance of this.

In short, while Funston would be allowed to broadcast for the Nova Scotia Conservatives, he would also be available to broadcast for the

Nova Scotia Liberals, should he be invited to do so. I asked Redmond if this station "policy" would apply in a hypothetical circumstance wherein the Ford Motor Company promoted its wares through the voice of John Funston. Would the station allow him to promote Chevrolet at the same time?

Redmond replied that he doubted that Chevrolet would be so unwise. Nor, he thought, would the Liberals. But he thought I should be aware of the possibility, and of the fact that the station would not be able to deny Funston's services to the Liberal Party, should they request them.

I was prepared to court such an unlikely risk, and Funston began broadcasting daily five-minute commercials, scripted by me, on all Nova Scotia radio stations.

The Nova Scotia Liberal Party was not accustomed to opposition, and that its opponents should mount a province-wide newspaper and radio campaign was a discomfiting novelty. As the campaign progressed, the Grits began to stir themselves. Macdonald himself took to the hustings, commenting sourly on "Mr. Stanfield and his Toronto advertising writer." And the Liberal organization, astonished by the discovery that Nova Scotia's most prominent sports announcer, John Funston, was a Tory, descended upon Redmond.

They were not long in learning the "policy" at CHNS, and Funston was promptly commissioned for a series of Liberal commercials. By this time, he represented a substantial investment to the Conservative Party; our own supporters, and presumably others, were hearing him daily, and they were cheered by his words and encouraged that such a provincial celebrity would be supporting the Tory cause. But then, one week before the election, some heard the voice of John Funston declaiming against the Conservative Party and supporting the Liberal cause.

Outrage and astonishment! After hearing the injured voices of incredulous Conservatives, who had first protested to party headquarters and were quickly referred to me in the Lord Nelson Hotel, I called Redmond.

My cold fury disconcerted the station manager, but he had a telling rejoinder—I had been warned of the station's policy and made aware of precisely such a possibility. Overnight Funston had become the station's most prized commercial property. There was, Redmond said, nothing he could do, other than regret my feelings, which I conveyed to him in eloquent, heartfelt, and unprintable terms.

For the Liberal Party, it was all in the game. But not everyone, mercifully, was willing to play. While CHNS might have a policy to permit Funston to broadcast in support of two competing parties, other stations' policies forbade it.

A gentleman named John Hirtle, manager of a radio station on the

119

South Shore of the province, telephoned Redmond to ask for clarification of the bizarre circumstances in which his station had received two sets of tapes bearing the voice of John Funston, both supplied by CHNS, speaking on behalf of two political parties. He told Redmond his station would not carry the Liberal voice of Funston, but would return the tapes to Halifax. Hirtle also informed Liberal headquarters of his action and expressed his displeasure at the lack of ethics in such enterprise. It was not only bad politics, he said, but bad radio.

Other stations followed suit, and one of them simply "lost" the Funston tapes supplied by the Liberal Party. In a single day, John Funston's seeming conversion from Tory to Grit was reversed. Redmond telephoned before leaving his office that evening to tell me he had discussed the matter further with the Liberal Party officials, and they had agreed to withdraw their request for Funston's services. I counted it a victory for the ordinary decency of private radio station management over the stratagems of an arrogant political organization.

Such incidents nonetheless escalated hostilities between the competing organizations and, so far as I was concerned, against those who were, for whatever reason, attempting to limit and frustrate opposition efforts to defeat the Macdonald government. The campaign in Nova Scotia came to be a war on more than one front.

The fifteen-minute free-time network radio broadcasts provided by the CBC were considered valuable opportunities for major party spokesmen to air their views. The broadcasts were well advertised, and considerable time and effort went into preparing the scripts. In the Nova Scotia campaign, these broadcasts originated through CHNS, which assumed the responsibility for having the text in advance. It was no surprise to me that CHNS bore its responsibility heavily.

Toward the close of the campaign, one of the prized network periods was assigned to Stanfield's running mate in Colchester County, G. I. "Ike" Smith. I knew Smith then only by reputation, which was an impressive one. He was known as a combative, resourceful, and relentless debater in the legislature—"Bob Stanfield's hatchet man," he was called—but Smith was also a responsible and reliable man. And he wrote his own speeches.

Smith dutifully drove to Halifax from Truro to bring the draft of his network address to me three days before it was to be delivered. A part of it dealt with the Royal Commission investigation into irregularities among government employees at the Inverness Mine, a fading, doomed industry in a poverty-stricken Cape Breton county which had fallen on hard times, at least partly through mismanagement. Most of Smith's comments, taken directly from the transcript of evidence given at the enquiry, were effective enough in condemnation of the government without enlargement from him. I had the draft retyped at party headquarters and then took it to CHNS to comply with the onerous regulations requiring scripts to be submitted in advance.

On the following day, I heard Redmond's now familiar brisk and authoritative voice on the telephone inviting me to visit his office. It was about Mr. Smith's network address, he said. What about it? Well, there were one or two matters the station wished to discuss.

At the station I was led to Redmond's office, treated something like a suspected arsonist in a munitions factory. I sat down across from his desk after being introduced to a Mr. Laurie Daley, son of the publisher of the Halifax *Herald,* who was legal counsel for the station. The air was heavy with foreboding.

Substantial portions of Ike Smith's text, Redmond informed me, were not suitable for broadcast. Mr. Daley had read it and suggested these be excised. The objections were to the references to the Inverness Mine. The station not only had its own responsibilities, Mr. Redmond said, but responsibilities to the CBC, to other stations on the network, and to the radio audience as well.

"It's a good speech," Redmond said, "but it would be even better if Mr. Smith would just omit a few paragraphs."

I looked at Mr. Daley with as firm and hard an eye as I could muster. "I have no right to agree to any changes in the speech," I said. "I have no intention of advising Mr. Smith to make any changes. And I don't think you have any right to act as censor for the CBC, other stations, or the people of Nova Scotia."

Mr. Daley replied that the station held that right in regard to anything proposed for delivery through its facilities.

"I think it's preposterous that a radio station can tell a politician what he can say, or can't say. That's his responsibility, not yours."

It was the same argument over again, first with the Halifax *Herald,* now with its radio station. Redmond and Daley were cordial, but they were unyielding. No changes, no speech.

"Then there will be no damned speech," I said.

Perhaps, they said, I should discuss it with Mr. Smith.

It seemed to me to be a giant conspiracy, a powerful, effortless corporate policy to muffle the opposition and to protect the government. I said so, among other things, before leaving Redmond's office, and I walked back to the Lord Nelson, shaking with anger and calling down curses upon the spectral ghost of Mackenzie King and Liberals everywhere.

Ike Smith was incredulous. "It's all on record," he said. "Everything about the Inverness Mine is a matter of public record."

"No changes, no broadcast," I told him.

"To hell with the silly buggers," he said.

But Smith himself went to the station to discuss their objections to his speech. They were as adamant with him as with me. In the end, he yielded to the station's demands and deleted the offending paragraphs.

There were two private stations in Halifax, CHNS and CJCH. The former was owned by the Halifax *Herald,* the latter by Pearson

McCurdy, son of Liberal Senator F. B. McCurdy, and owner of the Halifax *Chronicle* before the merger with the *Herald*. McCurdy's station had its offices on the top floor of the Lord Nelson Hotel.

In my long, despairing walk back from the meeting at CHNS, I had concluded resignedly that the Tory Party was friendless in the media world of Halifax. Indeed, if anything, my own stubbornness might only have earned the party added enmity.

Early in the campaign, I had made enquiries about the management of CJCH. The station, I was told, was managed by a young Cape Bretoner, Finlay MacDonald, son of a former Tory Member of Parliament. When I seized on that, I was told that the station's owner, Pearson McCurdy, was an unreconstructed Grit and that Finlay MacDonald, far from following the politics of his father, was both friend and supporter of Angus L. Macdonald. To confirm this fact, Finlay had signed the nomination papers for Angus L.'s candidacy in Halifax South.

Despondent and desperate, I decided to seek the advice of Finlay MacDonald, whose office was only a floor above mine in the hotel. He was instantly hospitable, and I sat in his office and poured forth my troubles with CHNS, recounting the bitter meeting I had just left after refusing to submit to censorship of Ike Smith's speech.

Young, boyish, prematurely grey, with a mischievous smile and an impulsive nature (which some would say was in fact a rapidly calculating one), MacDonald heard my tale of woe. In the background, I could hear the music and voices of the station's program.

"Wait a minute," MacDonald said, getting out of his chair. I watched him leave the office, stride down the hall, and enter the studio. He flicked the switch, opening the microphone in front of him.

On behalf of CJCH, MacDonald announced to the station's audience, he wanted to inform all politicians and all political parties that they could come to the studios of this station and say whatever they had to say, without any interference, direction, or censorship from the management. The air was free, MacDonald said, and any representative of the political parties was free to use it at CJCH.

When he came back to the office, to sit at his desk again, he said to me, "Now, what else can we do?"

It was the beginning of a beautiful friendship. Finlay MacDonald became a formidable political ally: decisive, resourceful, fearless, and intelligent. I would not have wanted him as an adversary. In the politics of Nova Scotia, he had been an undeveloped resource.

13

FINLAY MACDONALD PROVED TO BE BOTH INNOVATOR AND ACTIVIST, qualities desperately needed by Stanfield's party, whose organization possessed an admirably methodical thoroughness in conventional political activity, but lacked inspiration and spirit. He mounted the testimonial dinners, mass rallies, network radio and television productions, and brashly pioneered in many novel aspects of the new politics.

But MacDonald was not an organization man. He knew little of politics as seen at the polling subdivision, in the wards, or in the elaborate ritual of the committee decision-making process. He preferred to improvise and to act, to be given specific responsibility and see it through himself. Because of this, his party valued his contribution, respected his expertise, but liked him only a little.

Articulate, sophisticated, and self-sufficient, Finlay MacDonald and men like him make politicians uneasy. Such men are likely to be held suspect, since the simple family traditions of Toryism and the familiar tribal loyalties of politics are plainly not much a part of them. Furthermore, such men are as complex, in themselves, as the system in which they operate. Their life-styles are different, as are their values. Often their personal independence makes them seem unreliable, while at other times their catholicity of outlook makes them appear indifferent.

I was not much impressed with Stanfield's organization. It was largely composed of a number of genial, well-intentioned people who were not without experience, as survivors at least, in previous campaigns. But they moved at a deadly pace; urgency was unknown to them. Politics had become a part of their lives, like the weather, and, elections, like the weather, came and went, with varying results. Nothing was predictable except defeat, nothing certain but that another election would follow in due course.

In Halifax South, where Angus L. was the Liberal candidate, the Tories had a surprisingly aggressive, youthful organization, and a bright, attractive, young candidate. John Milledge, all agreed, was not going to defeat Angus L., but the young men supporting him seemed to lust for the battle anyway.

Their leader, Rod Black, had uncommon gifts as an organizer: an elaborate concern for detail together with a capacity to delegate responsibility with precise instructions; an unsurpassed patience as a listener, enjoying your jokes, treasuring your wisdom, begging your advice; and finally, Black knew politics where the votes were counted—in the polls.

The son of Hon. Percy Black, a former Highways Minister in the Rhodes-Harrington government and federal member for Cumberland, Black had seen enough of election-day activity to be wise to the ways of machine politics. In Halifax, genteel Tories remained aloof from the lower wards, where the poor lived and where the enormous Liberal majorities were produced. Black knew about false enumeration, impersonation, telegraphing, bribery, and intimidation, and all the arts and practices of party machines; but unlike his Tory contemporaries, he was not afraid to meet the practices of machine politics head on.

The constituency of Halifax South contained both rich and poor—the comfortable, warm homes of the Halifax elite and the grim, desolate slums of the economically depressed. Black left the fashionable "uptown" wards to others; he worked the downtown and waterfront wards and emboldened others to follow him there.

He disdained such fancy and amorphous political activity as campaign advertising and radio broadcasts. For him elections were fought in the boarding houses and tenements, by the enumerators at the doors, party agents in the courts of revision, and by alert, hard-nosed scrutineers in the polls on election day. Otherwise, it was up to the candidate to "get the hell out of the committee rooms and bang on doors until he drops."

Milledge was a green candidate, but learning in a fast class. Black demanded that he canvass every waking hour of his day, preferably in the lower wards. Milledge enjoyed making radio speeches because he liked attacking the government. Black believed it a waste of time and resented my helping Milledge prepare his radio material.

When the election was over and Macdonald had won, I congratulated Black on the respectable showing of his candidate. "He would have done a helluva lot better if he hadn't wasted so much time with you," grumped the organizer.

Despite our disagreement, I was much impressed by Black's courage and his total commitment to a cause that was obviously hopeless. But Black and those close to him were building for the future, which was to come much sooner than any of us could have believed.

I saw little of Stanfield in the campaign. He toured the province, speaking each night at constituency rallies, employing his own sparse, simple prose to spell out his party's platform—better roads, more effort to create new industry, and consideration for the municipal ratepayer groaning under the mounting burden of education costs.

As a source of information on the campaign, Stanfield was hopeless. It was not that he held anything back, but that he found nothing significant to report. His party would do better, he knew that, but it would not win as he had said from the start. And when he was asked the invariable question, "How did your meeting go last night?" he would as invariably reply, "Oh, all right, I think." Every audience he

124

met was "a fair crowd," and each candidate's prospects he considered as "not bad."

He seldom commented on the advertising. "Some of our people are worried that you might be too hard on Angus L.," he once said. Then I asked if we should be saying anything about the rising out-migration of young people from the province. "The hell with that," he said. "It sounds too much like 'Let's bring the boys back home.'" I gathered the reference was to a Tory campaign cry of days past, and best forgotten.

Leonard Fraser travelled to Pictou to address a public meeting in support of the Tory candidate. The speech was to be broadcast, and for days Fraser laboured over his text. It was to be his only intervention in the campaign, and he was eager to make it significant. He returned with glowing accounts of the meeting and the size and enthusiasm of the audience, and to claim the seat for the party. As well, he brought back a recording of his speech, and one Sunday we sat in his living room to listen to it.

The speech was a bitter, forceful attack on the sitting Liberal member, linking him to a trust company bankruptcy. Sitting there, hearing it, I was shaken by both its eloquence and its ferocity. Hearing the partisan crowd roar its approval, seeing Leonard beam with reflected satisfaction, I had fears for the seat in Pictou, but my heart went out to this aging, handsome man who had once led his party to disastrous defeat and was now, I suspected, close to death. And I could not blame him for his last, vociferous hurrah.

In the closing week, one felt the tightening grip of the government on the electorate. It is a sixth sense, like that of bats flying in darkness, the invisible echoes in the air, that tells you that they are winning and you are losing.

Angus L. was in full strength and majesty, now touring the Valley and the South Shore where many of our hopes were lodged. He was commanding, confident, disdainful, and effective. People were still saying "All's well with Angus L."

And we made mistakes. Rowe returned from a meeting in Shelburne where young Jim Harding had attacked his opponent, the Minister of Industry, but had gone too far. Rowe reported that even the Tories did not like it. Then there were criticisms of Fraser's Pictou speech. And persistent complaints among the Halifax Tories that Stanfield was not forceful enough—an almost certain harbinger of the government's re-election.

The campaign was coming to an end. Ultimately, there was only one more thing to do. On the night before the forty-eight-hour ban on radio broadcasting was to begin, Stanfield was to speak at a public meeting in Dartmouth. Our last chance.

I was asked to prepare a draft. Everyone was tired, including the publicity committee, but we discussed the leader's closing campaign address and explored suitable themes. In such circumstances, one looks for illuminating example. Finlay MacDonald suggested one when I had invited his thoughts.

Fresh in all minds then was the victory of General Eisenhower in the 1952 election in the United States. Fresh in MacDonald's mind was that Eisenhower had climaxed his campaign by promising if he were elected to the presidency that "I will go to Korea." The question, said MacDonald, is what can Stanfield promise, if elected, that *he* will do? MacDonald was right; it was now a time for Stanfield to personalize his appeal, to commit himself to some direct action. But what?

The chronic failure of the Macdonald government had been in its efforts to attract new industry to Nova Scotia. Even the most modest attempts–a fish-packing enterprise and an Angora rabbit ranch–had led to failure, as well as to some ripe partisan humour. (When Angus L. had addressed the Cumberland convention, someone had tossed a rabbit in the hall.) There had been a parade of undistinguished ministers in the Industry portfolio. The Department itself was lethargic and unimaginative. All this had been uppermost in Stanfield's criticism of the government.

Speeches which open and close campaigns are taken to be of special significance, especially those that wind things up. They may raise the morale of the party on the eve of battle at the polls; they may consolidate support and attract the last, lagging numbers of undecided voters to the cause; they may unnerve opponents at an hour when it is most difficult for them to reply or recover. It is a masterful accomplishment to achieve all three in a single speech. But in Stanfield's case, it was a matter of making a dim prospect somewhat brighter, and of giving the appearance of finishing strong in the face of a stronger finish by Angus L. Macdonald.

While it was not so dramatic as a promise to go to Korea to end a long, stalemated war, it satisfied some of us, anyway, to propose that Stanfield say that, if elected, he would himself take over the Department of Industry and give it the leadership and direction required. "Better than nothing," Finlay MacDonald commented, when I told him. "But for God's sake," he added, "have him say it with conviction."

Given this assurance, he made provision for a live broadcast of the speech on CJCH. But I had another matter in mind to add to the "I'll go to Korea" portion of the text.

A young Halifax broker had told me of a transaction he had observed passing through his firm. It was simple enough: a number of shares of distiller's stock had been forwarded from the distillery to the account of a cabinet minister. There could be no doubt, my informant said, that it was a gift.

I discussed this information with the publicity committee, all of

126

them lawyers and two of them with extensive experience in public life. At the outset, I argued that, while I thought Stanfield should raise the matter, I would not propose this move, or even tell him of the incident, unless all the committee were in agreement that he should make use of it. We spent two days debating it.

Finally there was agreement that Stanfield should reveal the information in his Dartmouth speech. He agreed to do so, but wanted the subject broadened to include the general question of conflict of interest, and his own view that no minister of the Crown should possess shares in any company doing business with the government of Nova Scotia.

As for the commitment, if elected, to assume the Industry portfolio, Stanfield thought it rather dramatic, which is precisely what his advisors had in mind. But he agreed to our suggestion in the face of unanimous urging.

Politicians lead lives of their own, subject to the peculiar demands of their profession, one of which decrees that while they must make daily decisions which affect the lives of others, it must never appear that these affect their own. Any government policy, however laudable or sensible, which appears to bring some personal benefit, however oblique, will be the subject of suspicion, cynicism, or contempt. The prudent politician, especially if he is in a position to influence or determine decisions of policy, will bear in mind the risk to his own reputation, and that of his colleagues, should he expose himself to suspicion of conflicts of interest between his private life and his public duties.

Real estate holdings, common stocks, bonds or debentures, family associations with private enterprise, and company directorships are all danger areas, and it is the greater part of discretion not only that there be no conflict of interest, but that there be no possibility of it.

The Nova Scotia government, as with all provincial governments, is the sole agent for the sale and distribution of beer, wine, and spirits in that province. If a minister of the government in a position to influence or to determine purchasing policies is trading in such stocks or, worse, is in receipt of shares as a gift, then a question exists regarding conflict of interest.

The minister involved was Harold Connolly; the donor was an Ontario distillery. The motives may well have been innocent. But the possibility of risk to the public interest should have been obvious.

Connolly was a gregarious, likable man, a politician's politician, skilled in party organization and well endowed with the gift of rhetoric. Because he was such a successful politician at the polls, it was perhaps easier for his opponents to suspect him. But it was not as simple as that.

The Conservatives had been building a case against the general practice of liquor agents in the province, most of whom were easily identified as Liberal partisans. The Tories had attempted to press the issue in the public accounts committee during the legislative session by asking that some of the agents be called to give testimony. But their motion had been defeated through a uniquely expedient means; the chairman of the committee, naturally a Liberal member, had voted twice on the motion–his first vote creating the tie and his second vote breaking it.

The Tories were further enraged by the operations of a Halifax bottle exchange, managed by prominent members of the Liberal organization. The exchange functioned as a government-created monopoly. As the only agency which could trade in beer bottles, it bought used bottles from the general public and resold them to the Nova Scotia Liquor Commission. The Tories believed the bottle exchange to be merely a means for raising party funds.

Unlike alcohol and gasoline, alcohol and politics do mix. Politics must be, to begin with, the hardest-drinking profession in the world; nearly all its ceremony begins or ends in drink. In the Maritimes, pints of rum are traditional legal tender for vote-buying, or "treating," as the practice is euphemistically called. Provincial governments are deeply involved as buyers, dispensers, distributors, regulators, and profiteers in spirits. Hence, relationships and contacts between distilleries and political parties are natural and inevitable.

Party funds rely heavily upon contributions from the distillers and brewers. And since the provinces themselves determine which brands will be stocked and sold in their stores, and in what quantities, none of the producers of the products has been known to withhold support.

These relationships, sometimes hazardous and often dubious, are the product of good intentions. After Prohibition was repealed, various provincial administrations responded to the renewed legitimacy of liquor sales with varying degrees of permissiveness. It is not logical to censure the liquor industry when all it has done is attempt to live, not only according to the politicians' laws, but according to their practices as well.

As a lobby, and an adjunct to political activity, the industry is as lively a force as its product, and exerts influence in much the same ways as do other interest groups, including the financial, transportation, oil and gas, and construction industries. But in no other example is there such immediacy, and day-to-day proximity, as in the business of alcohol and politics.

Stanfield, when he came to power, sought to make the relationship less binding. He abolished the monopolistic bottle exchange (saving the taxpayer a modest $40,000 annually), passed legislation forbidding the employment of local agents by brewers and distillers, and implemented, as nearly as possible, an "open door" purchasing policy, by which any and all might sell their product to the Liquor Commission, leaving the quantity to be determined by consumer demand. And he immediately put the commission under the political authority of his trusted friend, Ike Smith, who had become convinced of the wisdom of allowing all producers ready access to the commission. Previously when certain distillers, or brands, had been excluded, Smith feared the influence of the larger distilleries. In the new policy which accepted everyone, it was a case of the more the merrier–and the safer.

Stanfield made his final campaign speech in Dartmouth, before a satisfactory gathering of some two hundred, and broadcast by radio station CJCH. In delivering it, he provided early insight into his nature.

Finlay MacDonald and I went to the meeting, standing at the back of the hall, watching the effect of the speech on the rain-dampened crowd. The first section of the text dealt with general issues, a resumé of the campaign, followed by the declaration that Stanfield would himself assume direct responsibility for industrial development if he were chosen to form a government. The last section dealt with Harold Connolly, and as Stanfield turned the page and came to the subject, I saw him hesitate, look up at the audience, and then heard him say:

"Now, they told me to say this . . . ."

I could scarcely believe my ears. Then Stanfield was quickly into his text, reading it in a flat, unemotive, half-audible voice. Obviously, he was reluctant. When it was over, the meeting ended abruptly, as though someone had turned out the lights. Many in the hall had not heard the last portion of his speech, and others who heard it had not understood it.

What most remembered about it was that Stanfield, with his typical unprepossessing platform manner, had said something about Harold Connolly and then, in a somewhat stronger voice, had said that should he, Stanfield, become Premier he would not allow any minister to hold either interest or shares in any enterprise doing business with the government of Nova Scotia.

The Halifax *Herald* did not mention the matter in its morning paper, which had province-wide circulation. (Perhaps the speech was delivered after the paper had gone to press.) But in its evening edition, largely limited to circulation in Halifax, it carried Stanfield's charge on the front page, together with a comment from Harold Connolly: "Beneath comment."

The Dartmouth speech had no measurable effect on the election; no one ever mentioned the Connolly affair again. The Nova Scotia campaign ended in fog, drizzle, and hush.

Rowe and I were invited for dinner at Harry MacKeen's handsome home on the Halifax Arm on election night, to dine and listen to the returns. We had our meal in tense, worried silence, relieved only by MacKeen's reminiscences of past elections.

Mrs. MacKeen pressed me for a prediction. Defiantly, I said,

129

"We're going to sweep the province."

After dinner, we sat with cups of coffee and stared at the radio. The returns were not long in portending the results.

Immediately, the five Halifax seats fell to the Liberals. Milledge trailed Angus L. by nearly two thousand votes. In Cape Breton's industrial areas, the Tories were running third in most of the contests.

"That's some sweep, Mr. Camp," Mrs. MacKeen said sourly.

Rowe and I left early, convinced that the election had been a ruinous rout.

Angus L. Macdonald's government was re-elected for its sixth term on May 26, 1953. But the next day, with the published results before us, the defeat began to take on more of the semblance of a moral victory.

Stanfield and Smith had carried Colchester, though narrowly. On the South Shore, Ken Jones had defeated a cabinet minister. Also defeated were the Speaker of the Legislature and the Chief Government Whip. While the party had again been shut out in Halifax and on Cape Breton Island, it had done well in the Annapolis Valley (Nowlan would be pleased), on the South Shore, and in western Nova Scotia. It had increased its representation in the legislature from eight members to thirteen, even while losing three of the seats it had held at the time of dissolution.

It had also lost Pictou West by only five votes and Pictou East by ninety-eight; Harding had lost in Shelburne by 129 votes, and Digby had been lost by 252 votes. Working my own permutations, I told Rowe that but for a mere 487 votes Macdonald would have had a minority government. It was close enough; indeed, out of 343,000 ballots cast, Stanfield's party had received only 20,000 fewer votes than the Liberals.

But the party was woefully weak in Halifax; almost one-half of the overall Liberal plurality in popular vote was in the city. Connolly had carried Halifax North by over 3,550 votes, the largest majority in the province. In Cape Breton the CCF had clung stubbornly to its two seats, but the rest belonged to Macdonald. Everywhere else, the Tories had held the Grits at least even and results could be assessed by the quality of the candidates, or the organization, or perhaps in the campaign itself.

There was one further campaign curiosity which was to affect the final result. The Tory candidate, Ernest Ettinger, had won Hants East by a single vote, 2,249 to 2,248. After the votes had been counted and the result announced, another ballot box had been "found" in the shed of a Liberal poll chairman, the seal already broken on the box, and a number of ballots inside. When these were counted, the Liberal candidate was declared the winner in Hants East, reducing the Conservative representation in the new legislature to twelve. (The election was later voided by the courts and a by-election called. Incredibly, this time Ettinger lost by a single vote–cast by the returning officer. "We're pretty evenly divided down here," Ettinger commented to the Toronto press.)

Stanfield told the press he was "naturally encouraged by the increased representation and higher proportion of the popular vote" and said he found the campaign "more vigorous and more exciting" than his first one, in 1949.

There was no doubt that he meant it. He returned to Halifax from Truro the day after the election and drove Rowe and me to the airport.

En route home, Rowe and I persuaded ourselves that Stanfield could win the next election and that we would somehow help him do it. We were met at Malton by our wives, who commented on our backroom pallor and expressed sympathy that we had not won. On the contrary, we assured them, it had been a very great victory.

The Halifax *Chronicle-Herald* commented on Macdonald's "fresh mandate." Some of its words, I felt, had been written for me:

. . . But governments are not necessarily bad because they have matured with the years; and while nothing is permanent except change, the change could be worked in public policies as well as in the complexion of ministries.

A long time ago, a party leader in this province said this about an Administration in Ottawa: "We have a Government in power which has held office for nearly eighteen years, so long, indeed, that they have got it into their heads that they own the country. . . . Long holding of office has brought about its inevitable consequences–corruption and jobbery in every branch of the public service."

It was a harsh and intemperate indictment and one which no one but a graceless partisan would level against any Government in Canada in these times. Such are not the inevitable consequences of a long term of office. . . .

It was, on the whole, a cleanly conducted campaign, reflecting credit upon workers and candidates alike. . . .

Let yesterday's verdict be accepted by everyone, irrespective of political persuasion, and let examination of public policies be fair, reasonable and constructive.

Writing on letterhead from the mayor's office, Donahoe had more encouraging words:

As a lifelong resident of this province, I was happy that we made such a good showing, and I attribute it in large measure to your work on the publicity end of the campaign. Like you, I believe there is every possibility now that Bob Stanfield will be the next Premier of Nova Scotia. . . .

It was quite unnecessary for you to thank me for the very little time I was able to spend with you. I found it both entertaining and instructive. . . .

I hope that the fortunes of the political world will throw us together again and that we will have the benefit of your assistance in future campaigns.

Angus L. Macdonald was more stung by the decline in his political dominance than any of us realized. For the first time, the Liberal popular vote fell below 50 per cent, while the Tory popular vote rose to 43.4 per cent, an increase of ten per cent since Stanfield had assumed the leadership of his party.

Puzzled by the loss of votes and seats, Macdonald could only suspect religious prejudice. He polled his cabinet but found none who shared his view. Henry Hicks was especially emphatic; what he and others did notice was that their leader was aging and his powers, like his popularity, were now on the ebb of the tide.

If the Tories were unaware of the depth of dismay among their opponents after the 1953 election, the Liberals seemed oblivious to the changes within the Tory organization. In the city wards and rural polls, Black and others were fighting fire with fire, prepared to be as ruthless as their opposition had for so long been known to be. And the Tories were no longer so easy to silence; modern campaign techniques had come to the aid of partisan politics and offered antidote for an otherwise bland and indifferent medium which for too long had seemed determined to maintain the status quo.

14

DALTON K. CAMP
CARE NATIONAL HEADQUARTERS PROGRESSIVE CONSERVATIVE PARTY
OTTAWA
ARE YOU DEAD OR ALIVE PLEASE REPLY

RALPH HAY

WE WERE DEAD.

The Progressive Conservative Party of Canada was in a state of ruin. It lacked coherent purpose, organizational thrust, poise and self-confidence. It was as though it were doubtful of its mission. In the party's national office, while everyone knew an election would come in 1953, sooner or later, all hoped it would be later. Time was its only ally and St. Laurent conscripted that to his own cause by dissolving Parliament and issuing writs for a general election to fall on Monday, August 10.

Thus, tomorrow's leisurely considerations had now become today's pressing decisions. Fatalism infected action, and the managers and their advisors reached out to grasp only that which was familiar to them, and near. The prospect of an August election appalled them; as someone said, the Tory vote would be secluded in summer cottages; the cities would be insufferable; campaign audiences would be small and distracted by the heat; the farmers would be tending their crops. All of which was true.

Kay Kearns had prepared an exhaustive survey of the 1949 general election results; it read like a Domesday Book. In Drew's first campaign as his party's national leader, the Conservatives received twenty-six per cent of the total votes cast in British Columbia, trailing the Liberal and Socialist parties; seventeen per cent in Alberta, behind the Socreds and the Liberals; fourteen per cent in Saskatchewan, against forty-three for the Liberals and forty-one for the CCF; twenty-four per cent in Manitoba, again third to the Liberal and CCF parties; twenty-five per cent in Quebec, against sixty-one for the Liberals; and twenty-eight per cent in Newfoundland, as compared to seventy-two for the Liberal Party.

Only in Ontario and the three Maritime provinces were the Tories within striking distance of the Liberal Party, and even there the gap between was an awesome one.

During the Nova Scotia provincial campaign, Abbott had brought down his budget, dispensing tax reductions and heralding the election

("... the cynical coincidence," wrote Scott Young in *Maclean's* magazine, "by which in election years we are always given our most striking tax cuts, as if they'd been saved for that purpose"). Notwithstanding, the strategists at Tory national headquarters were preparing themselves to go Abbott one better—or $500,000,000 better—in tax reductions. I had never liked the idea of promised tax cuts, and I liked it even less after Abbott's budget.

The strategy lacked appeal for a number of reasons, not the least being that it would be unpopular in the Maritimes. The less the federal government took in, the less it paid out in tax-sharing arrangements among the provinces. But more than that, I disliked the image of the Tory Party as a frugal bookkeeper. Instead, I longed for an appeal that would recognize the problems of disparity and the numberless outsiders in the Canadian society.

Some of this feeling infiltrated the "pre-campaign" magazine advertisements published in *Maclean's* and *Chatelaine* and which, much to our surprise, appeared in the middle of the campaign. The first of these two full-page advertisements dealt with the history of the party, the second with a theme closer to my heart:

You have only to read the statement of one Government Minister—
a Minister who does much of the "shopping" for his Government—
to prove it.

This is the Minister who said to Parliament: "What's a million? I daresay my Hon. friend could cut a million dollars from this amount—but a million dollars is not a very important matter."

A million dollars would buy shoes for 200,000 children. A million dollars would put five million quarts of milk on family tables. A million dollars would provide the down payment on 400 homes for families now living in crowded apartments or in slums. What's a million—indeed!

But you have more than the Minister's word or that of the Progressive Conservative Party to indicate the extent of waste and extravagance in Ottawa. You have the Currie Report, the McNab Report, the Auditor General's Report—and an almost endless list of items drawn from the Government accounts that prove how needless has been the Government's policy of high taxation.

As an attempt to reconcile my own views with Grosart's, it was a satisfactory compromise. But in the time between the production of the advertisement and its publication, with the Nova Scotia election intervening, much transpired at national headquarters to shift the balance of campaign strategy to the issue of taxation and to remove my own concepts from the centre of the decision process. And anyway, we were all caught up in events, the campaign was on, candidates were crying for material, and new priorities dominated activity at headquarters.

From Nova Scotia, after recuperation leave in Toronto, I returned to Ottawa and to the headquarters, airless and stifling in the heat of an Ottawa summer afternoon. Upstairs, I was told, the campaign committee was deliberating on the party platform. I joined the meeting, finding Dick Bell in the chair, with Grattan O'Leary, J. M. Macdonnell, Cappé Kidd, Grosart, and Miss Kearns present.

The plank under discussion was a promise to cut taxes by a further $500,000,000. The figure shimmered in my mind, like heat waves rising from Laurier Avenue below. A half-billion dollars? There was no scale by which I could measure it.

A decision was necessary. Drew was to open the campaign in London within days. O'Leary, obviously, was preparing the speech; he was enthusiastic about the proposal–it was something people wanted (Grosart's polls had "proved" that), and it would be something everyone would understand–a bold, clear-cut, decisive stand.

When I rejoined the committee, they had adjourned their deliberations to commend me warmly for my efforts in Nova Scotia. I lacked the nerve to be argumentative so soon. They knew my views from past arguments and, anyway, I was the new boy in the class. I adopted a disapproving, despondent visage and sat in silence.

J. M. Macdonnell, his long, ascetic face a mask of disciplined civility, his lean frame folded upright in his chair, intervened in one of the silences following O'Leary's eloquent advocacies. As the party's financial critic in the house, his opinion was critical.

"It occurs to me, Grattan," he said, in his quiet, high-pitched, thin voice, "that if George Drew were called upon to form a government, I might have the responsibility of serving as his Minister of Finance. And if we are committed to reducing taxation by a half a billion dollars –well, I don't think I could do it."

Uneasy laughter and shifting about in chairs.

"Oh, for God's sake, Jim!" said O'Leary, turning to him with the disarming, impish smile and beguiling tenor of voice. "The first thing to do is to get *in*. When we get in, you'll find a way. And if you can't, you can think of something to say."

"I hope no one will ask me how it can be done," Macdonnell replied. "I don't think I could tell them."

Then talk of Abbott's surpluses, of waste and extravagance, of economic forecasts–and of the need to be bold. Macdonnell would not retreat from his view, but left the decision to his leader, George Drew. He would rather remain in opposition than come to power with a dubious mandate. He was not suited to strategies of this kind, anymore than he understood Allister's surveys and the hustling talk about advertising.

George Drew went to London to open his campaign and proclaim the party's platform. The press rightly seized upon the pledge to reduce taxes a further half billion dollars as the major plank, and so reported it.

The effect on the Tory Party and upon its candidates and workers was instant consternation. In the Liberal Party, as it reacted intuitively and almost immediately, the effect was satisfaction enhanced by incredulity. Two hundred and forty-eight Tory candidates, the leader included, had cast away their election prospects, and any chance of flexibility and manoeuvrability, on a single issue.

Liberals were quick to point out that such a promise, while denying the possibility of such an achievement, would mean less money for the have-not provinces, would negate any prospect for increases in welfare and pension payments, or salary increases for the armed forces and the public service, or expanded federal activity in public works. Tory candidates willing to promise action on specific local needs—a new post office, wharf, or subsidy—found themselves trapped in their leader's bold promise. As their Liberal opposition gleefully pointed out, not even George Drew could spend more money and cut taxes at the same time. The Tory platform became a scaffold for every candidate who did not have the luck to be running in a traditional Tory riding.

And there had not been, of course, either consultation or warning. Drew's election manifesto was intended to be a bombshell, and it was, bursting over the heads of the unsuspecting party candidates and organization. No more than a half-dozen men had made the fateful decision.

John Diefenbaker, running as the party's single sitting member in Saskatchewan, informed headquarters that no advertising would be either seen or heard in Saskatchewan without his prior approval. What he meant to say was that he and his supporters wanted to disassociate themselves from the party's platform.

From the outset, then, the federal election campaign of 1953 was an experience in futility. The result was never in doubt. Everyone worked hard and without complaint; it was only that the effort seems much harder when it is known to be futile.

15

IT WAS IN 1953 THAT AN AUSTERE PATRICIAN CORPORATE LAWYER OF great dignity and bearing was converted to the image of "Uncle Louis," an achievement of public relations and advertising prowess already documented by others. Mr. St. Laurent, with his graceful facility in both the French and English languages, would have carried the electorate had he been made up as Scrooge, or had the essential severity of his character and personality remained unaltered. ("He's a Bourbon aristocrat," John Bassett, Sr., had once told me.) As the 1953 campaign grew to full dimension, the transfiguration of Canada's Prime Minister was achieved by the modern techniques of advertising and publicity, and the process accommodated and confirmed by a willingly helpful press.

The Liberal Party seized the new instruments of communication and used them confidently, deliberately, and effectively. Where the former leader, Mr. King, had been a man of mystique, mystery, and, some said, intrigue, his successor, thrust into an age of growing media sophistication, became a man of a familially common mould, everyone's handsomely aging uncle, doting on the children, whimsical, a little patronizing and a whole lot more visible. The image was vague, somewhat fuzzy, seen through filters of sentiment, layers of gauze woven by exuberant flacks and romantic commentators. But the evidence, as presented in assiduously retouched, richly-coloured photographs, was testimony enough to convince Canadians that, after a long period of spinster rule by a man essentially drab and determinedly colourless, they were now led by another who could have been the head of the house of "One Man's Family."

On reflection I am struck by the fact that, while this was happening in the campaign of 1953, none of us at Tory headquarters seemed aware of it. While the advisors and strategists pored over every published word uttered by the Prime Minister and his cabinet, no one looked up to see that the Liberal leader had changed his clothes. I recall no one saying, for example, how devilishly clever it was to take this man, a wealthy corporation lawyer, and convert him into some Gladstonian version of "The People's William," so as to magnify the contrast with Mr. Drew, who had unwillingly acquired the image of a harsh, malevolent partisan—and a stuffed shirt to boot.

The Liberal Party, like the administrations it produced, had the reputation for managerial competence. Always, it seemed—at least until the Pearson years—they were superior in strategy, execution, and technique. For all the Tory criticism of them as being, by nature, wasteful,

137

extravagant, and inefficient, the Liberals were in fact competent. Men like Howe and Abbott must have looked at the opposition benches and marvelled, first at their own luck, but also at the frequent manifestations of administrative incompetence—the lack of skills, the disdain for technique, the waste of manpower—reassuring evidence of Tory inefficiency, like a genetic flaw.

George Drew was very nearly a modern politician. He sensed the value of media, the latent power of advertising, and he explored, as best he could, ways by which they could be used. But his councils were dominated by men who were lawyers, who saw the electorate as a jury, as Meighen had seen it, and election campaigns as great debates, where the logic, persuasion, and forensic skills of trained advocates, such as themselves, were the real tools of victory. That they were wrong is regrettable, and poignantly touching to one who knew and liked them and sensed the strength of their faith.

One grieved for the Tory Party: not only that it would lose the election, but that it was so hopelessly outmanned, outmanoeuvred, and outclassed. Drew's personal campaign in the country was conducted in seemingly lonely isolation from the party's headquarters; the central guidance of the campaign rested in the hands of men who, however diligent and tireless their efforts, lacked any sense of innovation. As for the party at large, it was almost completely out of touch with the leader, the party office, and the electorate.

All this may seem like a harsh judgement on an organization of a party that, incredibly, would form a government after the very next election. (But only two of those present at national headquarters for the 1953 campaign would have effective roles in 1957—Grosart and myself.) It is obvious that while I was appalled by the campaign strategy, I had none better to advance. Instead, I had only a generalized complaint as to what had been done and how it was done, even though I had the responsibility for some newspaper advertisements and pamphlets which, to me, seemed woefully ineffective.

But politics is a wasteland of aborted intentions and rusting, failed enterprise. It is a grand design, fashioned by amateurs and novices, as well as by experienced professionals. In its circuitry is the complex imprint of many minds and judgements, and a good deal of caprice and luck. Somehow men are drawn to working on it with love, hate, and tireless fascination and, if they are wise, they come to see it as a life process of trial and error, triumph and defeat, elation and despair, and faith and experience, and it is unwise not to recognize its ongoing, epic impersonality.

A fortnight before election day I slipped out of Ottawa, uneasy and disconsolate, nursing a profound sense of personal failure, made more soulful by a feeling of inadequacy. I left Grosart, shirt-sleeves rolled above his elbows, freely perspiring and resolutely cheerful, to cope with the balance of the campaign. He impressed me by his continued methodical, calm efficiency, his seeming indifference to the dark clouds of disaster which had hung over the campaign from the beginning. He was now fully in command and he would, I thought, be the last to leave the bridge.

I said goodbye to Kidd, finding him slouched in a deep leather chair, his feet on the desk of the national director, the window behind him shuttered against the heat, the room close, humid, and dark. "Well, old boy," he said languidly, "I guess we can congratulate ourselves on all the good ideas we didn't have." With that he exploded in hysterical laughter.

On election day, in New Brunswick, a sombre sky brought rain which began in the morning and continued into the night. My wife and I packed the car and drove off for Nova Scotia. Along the way, we listened to the returns on radio. At the outset, cheerful news came of the election of Tom Bell in Saint John-Albert, a gain from the Liberals, and for the Tories the addition of a youthful, promising new man in the federal caucus. But from then on it was disaster, relieved only by occasional announcements of the survival of a few familiar names–Brooks, Nowlan, Casselman, Drew, Adamson, Rowe, Macdonnell. In the end, only fifty-two Conservative members were elected.

"Uncle Louis" had swept the country: the Grits would have 171 members in the next Parliament. Ominously, the CCF elected almost half as many members as the Conservatives, twenty-three. One hundred and ninety-six Tory candidates had gone down to defeat.

The next day, I drove up the Annapolis Valley to see George Nowlan, the only Tory to win in Nova Scotia. He was weary from the campaign and rueful about the results across the country.

"Dear God," he said, "where did we ever get that platform?"

I professed surprise that he did not know. He was, after all, the party's national president.

16

IT WAS A SURPRISE TO ME TO HAVE SO QUICKLY FOUND A PLACE IN THE Tory party, astonishing to have been given so much responsibility and to find myself so soon at the centre of things. It was even more astonishing, once there, to discover how much need there was for people who, by some peculiar process, had acquired political judgement and could offer advice and inspire confidence in others.

The party's hierarchy seemed to have evolved principally on the basis of survival, so that the elite was essentially made up of amiable and elderly mediocrities. I had come to realize how few men–a very few at the centre–determined party policy and strategy, and how few of those had any genuine gift of political judgement. Influenced by the opinions of others, as well as my own, I began to suspect that I might be one of them.

And I was glad to be a Tory. Whatever its frustrations, such as those I had experienced in Ottawa, I found myself among kindred spirits, disarming in their innocence of power, uncorrupted by arrogance or cynicism, endearing in their stoic perseverance and uncomplicated in their loyalty to that mysterious meaning of Conservatism.

My employers treated me with some additional, if guarded, respect. The firm's active principals were Liberal in their politics, but impressed and not at all chagrined that one of their employees had once overstayed his summer leave in New Brunswick and returned with the scalp of a Liberal government–and an advertising account. For a while, I was introduced to other clients as the resident copy chief and giant killer, a personification of the power of the agency's advertising.

In the spring of 1954, William L. Rowe called me. I had not seen him since his occasional visits to Tory headquarters during the 1953 federal election.

Lunching at Simpson's Arcadian Court, Rowe furthered my knowledge of the internal politics of the national Tory party and asked my advice–as though I had overnight acquired some special wisdom–about a dilemma confronting the party establishment and involving himself. He had been asked to become national director of the party; the invitation had come from J. M. Macdonnell, on George Drew's urging, and further pressed by Earl Rowe, his father, and Clair Casselman, a member of the caucus and his brother-in-law.

He would fill the position left vacant by Richard A. Bell, who had returned to law practice. More important, he was to fill the position before it became occupied by someone sponsored by George Hees, the party's national president, whose popularity in the party was coming to be resented and whose ambitions were suspected by a few who were in positions to feel threatened.

Hees had won the party's presidency against Gordon Churchill, although Churchill had been the favourite of the party's inner circle, including Drew. Once installed, Hees became both a peripatetic and public president, surpassing any of his successors in his contacts with the party's grass-roots and in his skills in dealing with the press. He had become a powerful and independent influence in the party. Such men are instinctively feared.

I did not know Hees, other than through the pages of the Toronto *Telegram,* which exalted his every public word, but I did not like him either. In later years, I found myself frequently in opposition to him, and while there has never been personal enmity, there has never been friendship either. It is always easier to judge harshly men you do not know.

Rowe was reluctant to accept the post of national director. He disliked Ottawa and much preferred to remain on his farm, north of Toronto, sallying forth occasionally to assist the party when asked, and when convenient. He had a young family, a stable of trotting horses, and private business interests. All these took priority over politics. Besides, he added, he did not know enough about the party, or about politics, and he did not want to go to Ottawa merely "to stop Hees."

I found myself urging him to accept. On the briefest acquaintance, I had been impressed by Rowe, a handsome, trim, engagingly modest young man who appeared on sight to be the least arrogant of all "headquarters" emissaries I had ever met, in either party. His farm background served him well in contacts with rural supporters, and his lack of self-interest and political ambition was obvious. As well, Rowe was a gentleman, soft-spoken, civil, and tolerant. I could not imagine a better man to represent the national party.

But Rowe had more in mind. He turned the conversation around me, saying he would accept the position of national director only if I would agree to accompany him to Ottawa and become the party's public relations advisor.

I replied that it would be impossible. I would not leave my present situation for Ottawa; I had only grim memories of the place and, like him, I did not think I would enjoy living there. Further, I knew few members of the parliamentary party. I added, however, that I would be willing to help where I could, but it simply could not be a full-time occupation.

In the end, Rowe agreed to become the full-time national director, and I agreed to serve as his part-time advisor. How this would be done we left to later exploration. Neither of us was convinced we had made the right decision, nor did we have the least idea how we would work it out with our families, employers, and the Conservative Party.

When the announcement was made of the appointment of the new national director, by Rowe himself at a press conference in Ottawa, its import was unmistakable to the national president, George Hees. He came the next day to see Kathleen Kearns, sat across from her desk, and, according to Miss Kearns, "wept like a child," saying, "Why have they done this to me?"

I moved back into my old office at the head of the creaking stairs in national headquarters, finding there the dusty memorabilia of the 1953 campaign, my own.

Dick Bell, Cappé Kidd, and Grosart were gone, leaving only Kay Kearns among the senior personnel. Rowe and I moved in to convert this dreary building into the bustling centre of party activity.

At the outset, Rowe was determined to run things his way, even though it meant making his own mistakes. I drafted a memorandum which he sent to Miss Kearns, instructing her on procedures regarding headquarters' mail and telephone calls: all mail addressed to the national director was to come unopened to his desk; all incoming calls for him would be relayed directly from the switchboard.

Miss Kearns was annoyed by this challenge to her dominance and suspected that I was to blame for it. She was right. For some weeks afterwards, she was cool towards me, but more cordial relations were ultimately restored after frequent luncheons at La Touraine, during which Rowe and I reassured her of her indispensability.

It was soon clear to us that national headquarters functioned primarily for members of the caucus, occasionally for the leader (who had his own staff on the Hill), and only rarely for the party at large. Communications were minimal. The preoccupation of the national office seemed to be to oblige the members who demanded overnight servicing of their mailing lists so that they could send out Hansard copies of their speeches to their constituents. It seemed like a legitimate function, but still it did not seem right that the national office should be consumed in this work and little else.

If the Tory Party was indeed the party of Big Business, it had very little to show for it. The headquarters' budget was barely enough for subsistence. Rowe and I pored over the operating budget, searching for economies which would liberate funds for more productive organizational activity. None seemed obvious.

We set out to find ways by which we could improve the morale, performance, and prospects of the Progressive Conservative Party's moribund organization. The disordered, malfunctioning central office we repossessed offered only one encouragement–things could not be worse. It was a familiar starting point to me.

I found it shocking that a party with such a noble history, with so many achievements, with identifiable national heroes–Macdonald, Tupper, Borden, Bennett–which had managed, despite its more recent defeats, to maintain the allegiance of a third of the Canadian electorate, should be reduced to its present feeble condition. It was no one's fault. But now it was the responsibility of everyone within the party, as Rowe and I agreed, "to do something."

A major problem was party finance. It was a mystery to me, and for reasons best described as intuitive, I preferred that it remain so. During the ensuing twenty-one months of formal association with the party's national office, I spent a good deal of money and Rowe saw that it was forthcoming. While he frequently recounted his difficulties with the finance committee, I provided only a detached sympathy.

Nevertheless, organizational efforts of the Tory Party were, to a significant degree, hobbled by chronic poverty. The larger Canadian corporations, the prime source for support, were not sufficiently impressed by Drew's leadership or the party's prospects to make more than token contributions. They seemed more impressed–or perhaps inhibited–by the massive managerial competence of C. D. Howe.

Tory fund-raisers, hats in hand, visited the captains of finance to solicit their support, arguing that, unless the Conservative Party survived, the inevitable alternative to Liberalism would be "socialism." It produced sufficient response for survival. J. M. Macdonnell, a dutiful, determined man, brooked insult and indifference, often sitting for hours in the reception rooms of the great corporations, refusing to be turned away until he had been given an audience. Many of us gave him the credit for keeping the party alive.

There is a difficulty in this business of party contributions. It could never be suggested that donations to the Conservative Party bound the recipient to the interests of the contributor. Generally, it was enough to assume a community of interest, in that the party and its supporters both admired the free enterprise system, however loosely that system may be defined.

Greater problems are created by the collectors–or the finance committee–who often presume to judge as to how the funds can best be spent, a judgement based on their business experience, which has little or nothing to do with politics. What seems to them to be an extravagant expenditure by the party managers is, in view of the party, a necessary one. And so the problems are compounded; there is never enough money, and the allocations of the party funds are incessantly questioned by the fund-raisers. No one in my experience weathered these harassments as well as Rowe during his brief tenure as national director. But even he was compelled to live with the second thoughts and personal judgements of those who held the purse strings.

My arrival at national headquarters was signalled by the finance committee and became an avenue for solicitation:

MEMORANDUM FOR FRIENDS OF THE TWO-PARTY SYSTEM
Two Key Appointments

The efforts being made by the Finance Committee have already made possible two key appointments in the Progressive Conservative Party's National Headquarters, Ottawa.

The appointments, announced February 1, are Dalton K. Camp as Director of Publicity, and Donald Eldon, Director of Research.

Director of Publicity
The new Publicity Director is a 34-year old Toronto Advertising Executive (lately made head of his Company's public relations department) with considerable experience in political activity. He managed the publicity campaign for the New Brunswick Conservatives in their successful bid for office in 1952 and for Nova Scotia's Opposition party in 1953, where the Conservatives recorded strong gains; and again, in 1954, he was Campaign Manager for the first Conservative candidate to be elected in Halifax since 1933.

Camp is a graduate of the University of New Brunswick, received an M.Sc. Degree from Columbia University and was awarded a Beaverbrook Overseas Scholarship in Political Science, at the London (England) School of Economics.

His new responsibilities at National Headquarters include the publication of a new party magazine–"Progress Report"–which will appear for the first time in April. He is also developing a publicity program suitable for national Daily and Weekly newspapers . . . ."

If party finance was a constant problem, it was no more so than that of headquarters' relations with the parliamentary party. By nature, the caucus is sensitive, jealous, and domineering. To a significant degree, it *is* the party and as such demands constant attention, recognition, and praise. Within it are the inevitable factions, cliques, and rugged individuals. Each and all require delicate handling, for while some hide their ego better than others, it is a mistake to assume any public man to be without one.

There were fifty-one members in the Tory caucus after the 1953 election, thirty-three coming from Ontario and the remainder a scattered representation of the country–only four from Quebec, six from the Prairies, five from the Maritimes, three from British Columbia, none from Newfoundland or the Territories.

Rowe began his assignment with Drew's confidence, but better than that, he had family connections in the caucus; his father and a brother-in-law, A. C. Casselman, and personal friends–Monte Monteith, J. M. Macdonnell, Ellen Fairclough, Clayt Hodgson, and Bob Mitchell–the hard core of Drew loyalists. Most of them met together almost daily, after hours on the Hill, exchanging cordial opinions over drinks. But the national director also had enemies, or at least detractors. Hees, of course, was assumed to be one of them.

144

John Diefenbaker was an enigma. Popular with the press, presumably admired by Liberals ("Now, if only *he* were your leader instead of Drew," they would say), greatly in demand as a platform orator, Diefenbaker maintained a distance from his parliamentary colleagues. He rarely attended caucus, was not usually available to the Whip's Office when it was attempting to organize the schedule of opposition speakers, and beyond the call of the duty roster for attendance in the House.

It was assumed, in that busy corner of the politician's mind where future probabilities are stored, that Diefenbaker had lost his opportunity for the leadership. First elected to Parliament in 1940, he had sought the leadership of his party at the Winnipeg convention two years later, receiving just 79 out of 872 votes on the second ballot that elected Bracken. In 1948, he had tried again, and was crushed by the forces in support of George Drew, receiving 311 votes out of a total of 1,242.

Now he enjoyed a life of splendid isolation, watched warily but at a distance by his colleagues. His acquaintances in the party probably were more numerous than any, but his friends fewer. Among the organizational staff, only Mel Jack, a wandering member of Drew's personal staff, was close to him. Whenever we sought a reaction or opinion from Diefenbaker on organization matters, we would send Davie Fulton to inquire. Diefenbaker believed the headquarters staff to be opposed to him, and the feeling was therefore reciprocal.

"If only," Hugh John Flemming had once told me, "you could get Mr. Drew and John Diefenbaker to campaign together on the same platform in an election, you would carry the country. Mr. Drew is a very able man, but Diefenbaker is popular." Such seemingly sensible stratagems had no chance of becoming reality. Diefenbaker was, as his associates described him, "a loner."

Of all the Tory members of caucus, I knew and understood George Nowlan best. He was to me the least puzzling and complicated of men. Only rarely will public men reveal their personal interest; Nowlan had the habit of doing so. For that reason, misunderstandings with him were few. He had a limitless capacity for friendship. He gave advice freely, and with utter candour. Through Nowlan, more than any other, I came to know the intricate internal machinations of the parliamentary party—which members were loyal to Drew and which were not; the fever chart of the caucus; the complex relations with the press gallery; how rumour was launched and news was leaked.

Like Diefenbaker, Nowlan had the distinction in 1953 of being the only Conservative elected in his province and, like his Saskatchewan colleague, Nowlan had managed to survive in a province where the Liberal Party enjoyed an historic dominance. He also was something of a loner, but he was much too gregarious a man, too fond of companionship and eager for argument, to remain aloof or estranged for long from his associates and colleagues.

In many ways Diefenbaker and Nowlan were much alike. Each conducted his own press relations, each enjoyed harmonious relationships with the Ottawa establishment (it may have been that the civil service responded to men of their individual stamp), each of them projected an independent attitude on matters of policy, and each was believed to be more liberal than conservative. And both of them privately disliked Drew.

Nowlan would recall the humiliating experience at Acadia University, in his hometown of Wolfville, when George Drew and M. J. Coldwell had met in joint debate. The confrontation became so heated that Drew had aimed physical blows at Coldwell. It was the climax of a by-election campaign in which Nowlan would be defeated. The incident at Acadia was judged to be the reason. (After the affair one of Nowlan's children, in tears of rage, rushed up to Drew, saying, "You have just defeated my father.") In defence of the Tory leader, Nowlan later explained that Drew had been suffering from a cold, for which he had taken one of the new sulpha drugs plus some alcohol. As a result, his attack on Coldwell had been launched from a fevered mind.

Although George Nowlan was frank about nearly everything political, he concealed his deepest thoughts on the subject of the Tory leadership. But there can be no question that, as with Diefenbaker, the personal ambition was there, a stubborn flame flickering in the depths of a restless, indefatigable spirit. There would come a moment in time when the leadership lay almost within his grasp, and only Diefenbaker's unrivalled shrewdness and cunning would keep the prize from him and quench the flame at last.

It was Drew's party, and it was not. When Tories talked of successors, all assumed a normal transition and forecast it for some time in the 1960's. By then, it was reckoned, Diefenbaker's opportunity would have passed, as perhaps also would Donald Fleming's. The men most mentioned as successors, in these early appraisals, were Fulton, George Hees or, just possibly, Leslie Frost, Ontario Tory Premiers being automatically considered leadership possibilities.

Drew's power was precariously based. When he was chosen in 1948, fresh from his triumphant provincial campaign, the conventional wisdom had been that he would carry Ontario. Instead, while Bracken's bucolic campaign of 1945 had harvested forty-eight of the eighty-two seats in Ontario, Drew could win only twenty-five in 1949. Now he held only thirty-three seats in his native province. Far more significant, however, was the uneasy knowledge that the powerful provincial organization of Leslie Frost, managed by his lieutenant Alex McKenzie, remained studiously aloof from the national party. The Ontario Tory *bonne entente* all had hoped for under Drew's leadership had become, instead, a deep, unfathomable estrangement. No one understood it, and no one could repair it either. Without it, Drew's authority in his own party was tenuous and limited.

In Western Canada, he was either anathema or a stranger, as he was in Quebec. In the Maritimes, the elders in the party respected him and remained puzzled by his electoral failures. But the younger Tories, the new men rising in the ranks of the party throughout the country, spoke of him with restrained enthusiasm, if at all.

You could not, Rowe and I agreed, organize the Progressive Conservative Party of Canada in the name of George Drew. Yet we greatly admired him and, for my part, I came to feel increasing sympathy for him. He was something of a tragic figure to me, a man who had saved a province from what would have been a damaging experiment with socialism, who was, as I observed him, as able a man as could be found in the House of Commons, and, surprisingly, a man with a curious self-conscious shyness, as though he had been rebuffed so often he feared further hurt and humiliation.

Drew had a deformed left hand, injured in war, which he habitually concealed, perhaps unconsciously, in the pocket of his suit coat. When he was standing to speak, the damaged hand thrust in his pocket, he gestured only with his right hand, his large, square body erect, shoulders back, the athletic chest and slightly protruding stomach thrust forward, all lending his figure an exaggerated corpulence, giving his physical mannerisms an unnatural stiffness, and creating a general impression of stuffiness.

When I came to know him, late in his career, he had learned to contain his temper and subdue the bombast which had flowered so effectively in his early days when his rival had been Mitch Hepburn. Politicians, deliberately or not, are shaped as much by the personalities and characteristics of their adversaries as by their own; Hepburn had left his mark on Drew, as, no doubt, had Mackenzie King and C. D. Howe. But George Drew engendered in me a sense of sadness, almost of pity. Throughout his long career, he had been ringed by hostile forces beyond his control and outside the range of his understanding. He had been hated, ridiculed, demeaned, and defeated, his true nature distorted, his destiny denied. He was a political Job.

In repose the muscles twitched in his cheek and occasionally, when he blinked, his eyes would close like a boxer anticipating a blow, almost a flinch. When he was listening, his tongue would play against the cheek inside his mouth, as he measured his pauses, censoring his thoughts. This impression was further confirmed by his manner of speaking, which included a frequent stammer and numerous audible hems and haws. I thought him a hard man to hate.

Yet people hated him.

There is a coarse, cruel strain in the politics of Canada which one

147

discovers soon enough after becoming involved in its processes. It is necessary, it seems, to foment the passions of fear and suspicion, so that popular leaders may ride to power on their tides. Thus it was seemingly not possible to make St. Laurent an object of affection without making Mr. Drew an object of hatred. However fiercely I had opposed McNair, I had known and respected his personal qualities; I had only been surprised, on leaving his cause, to find his adversary, Hugh Mackay, not at all the plutocratic, selfish man McNair had painted, but instead a civil, compassionate, baffled soul, like Drew, who had come to politics to contribute something to it. But such men found their careers more like a sentence to obloquy, and served out their years in personal bafflement and private sorrow.

Feeling all this, and frequently discussing it, Rowe and I wore the armour of defiance when we encountered George Drew's many detractors.

17

OF ALL THESE YEARS, 1954 WAS THE MOST FATEFUL. ANGUS L. MAC-
donald died in April; in September, Henry Hicks succeeded him in
office; in November, Richard A. Donahoe won the Halifax South by-
election–a Tory elected to Macdonald's old seat, the first Conservative
to represent any Halifax constituency since 1933.

Robert Stanfield's wife had died in a tragic highway accident; now a
widower with four young children, he decided only after anxious soul-
searching to remain in politics. Nova Scotians, moved by his private
sorrow, looked again at this gaunt, homely, soft-spoken man and discovered in him the qualities they most admired in public men. He
became, for the first time, set apart from other politicians and, as
Macdonald had been, above public rebuke and partisan scorn.

Angus L. had died suddenly, a legend in death even as in life. An
apocryphal story had sprung from the period of mourning and it became
truth for its frequent telling.

It was that he had walked from the legislature one evening with
some of his colleagues, and one of them had made a coarse, jesting
remark about Stanfield. Whereupon Macdonald silenced the laughter
that followed by saying, "Bob Stanfield will never do wrong by Nova
Scotia."

The story spread through Halifax and the mainland into Cape
Breton, recounted affectionately by Liberals and Conservatives alike,
creating a mystical bond between Macdonald and Stanfield. Indeed,
the more people came to think about it, the more apparent the resem-
blances between the two men seemed to be.

Macdonald had left no successor. He had led his party for so long,
with such imperious ease, that he loomed above his colleagues, all of
them standing in his shadow, all alike in their adherence to him, as
convinced of his permanence as of their own expendability. Even after
his death, they were a long time rediscovering their long-concealed
ambitions.

When cabinet met after the funeral, Harold Connolly seemed
a logical choice to be acting Premier until Macdonald's successor could
be chosen in convention. The logic had merit because of Connolly's
seniority and because, like Macdonald, he was a Catholic and a member
for a Halifax constituency; it seemed likely, at least to a number seated
around the table, that the next leader and Premier would be neither
of these.

And Harold was an amiable, cheerful colleague, knowledgeable about matters of organization, which would be useful in maintaining party stability and continuity in the weeks ahead. If Harold had any ambitions beyond this present, temporary position of acting Premier, they were not clear to his colleagues, although some of them did say, when the matter was being settled in cabinet, that they would like a commitment from Connolly that he would not stand for the leadership.

Ironically, before Connolly could answer, Henry Hicks opposed the suggestion, remarking that everyone should be free to make his own decision, including the acting Premier, and the matter ended there.

As for Hicks, some thought he should run and some thought he shouldn't, and when a survey was made of his prospects, it was not sufficiently encouraging. Hicks went off for some spring salmon fishing in New Brunswick, his mind made up that he was out of it.

Connolly's mind was far from made up; given his preference, he would have been happy to go to the Senate, but when he raised the matter with Robert Winters, the party's federal authority in the province was vague and not especially reassuring. And when Connolly suggested that if he were not appointed to the Senate he would run for the leadership and win, Winters coolly told him to do what he liked.

Winters was accountable for much of the damage to be inflicted upon the party in Nova Scotia. But then, as Hicks would say, Winters was not much of a politician, and as everyone knew, the federal cabinet was above such small matters as applications to the Senate and rarely felt the need to act upon them any sooner than seemed essential.

Connolly enjoyed the role of acting Premier, so much so that he began to consider the possibility of being confirmed in the task. The Halifax Liberals, so long in central positions of authority in the party, deeply entrenched in the preferential dispensation of patronage, were the first to urge him to become a candidate. And Catholics, who knew well the vital importance of the Catholic vote to the Liberal Party, thought it bigoted to suggest that Protestants might want their turn at the leadership. Such thinking was not only bigoted, they argued, but a threat to continued Liberal rule.

The Premier's office was in Halifax, of course, where the engine of the Liberal machine was also housed. Naturally, Connolly heard a disproportionate clamour urging him to run and, even though his enemies alleged he had it in mind all along, he was given encouragement from all those he encountered in the familiar neighbourhood of his political domain.

So he declared his candidacy, proclaiming himself the legitimate heir to Angus L. Macdonald, accompanied by the modest confession that, in fact, Angus L., on his deathbed, had more or less ordained that the mantle of his leadership should fall upon him.

Others knew better. Connolly had been appointed to the cabinet by A. S. MacMillan, who had served as Premier while Angus L. was absent in the service of Mackenzie King's wartime administration. Had it been

Macdonald's decision, it was told, Harold would not have been chosen, but when the leader returned from Ottawa to sweep the province in the election of 1945, he kept Connolly in his cabinet only because he could think of no way of being rid of him. Or so they said.

Malcolm Patterson, Henry Fielding, Henry Hicks, Arthur Mac-Kenzie, and Hector Hill were the other candidates for the leadership. All, except Hill, were cabinet ministers, and all were Protestants. When Connolly declared his candidacy, most of the Catholic vote rallied naturally to him, while the Protestant vote remained dispersed among the five other contenders.

Gradually, imperceptibly at the beginning, and then more openly and with increasing virulence, the contest for the Liberal leadership became a matter of religion. In the predominantly Protestant areas, it seemed more than coincidental that the constituency delegations were overwhelmingly Protestant. While in Halifax, constituencies chose delegates who were predominantly Catholic. The Liberal Party was slowly being brought to boil under the steady heat of religious strife.

The convention, held on Labour Day weekend in the Halifax Forum, was a debacle. On the day of balloting, Acting Premier Connolly attended a pleasant ceremonial function to honour the visiting Duchess of York, and when it was over, Connolly and Mayor Donahoe and their wives drove home together.

"How do you feel about your chances today?" Donahoe asked the candidate.

Connolly told him, "I'll win on the first ballot, or the second one."

On the first ballot, Connolly was within fifty-eight votes of winning a majority, and on the second, he was only forty-one votes short. Henry Hicks was a distant third, then only a poor second. But the resolve to deny Connolly the leadership grew among the delegates like a physical presence, and as candidates were eliminated ballot after ballot, their support went to Hicks. In the growing tension, tempers were lost and hard words exchanged among the Liberal brethren. No longer was leadership the central issue of the convention. Instead, it was the matter of religion.

Henry Hicks was all that Connolly was not–from the Annapolis Valley in rural Nova Scotia, a Protestant, a Rhodes Scholar, a lawyer, Macdonald's chosen Minister of Education, and demonstrably abler than any of his colleagues in matters of administration. As the afternoon wore on and the tensions in the Forum worked their chemistry, Hicks emerged as the chosen instrument to repel the challenge of Harold Connolly. The Protestant votes came to him ballot by ballot as other Protestants dropped from the race while Harold Connolly's vote hung suspended, tantalizingly near success yet increasingly far from it as the Protestant tide rose around him until, finally, on the fifth ballot he was engulfed by it.

Hicks had 312 votes for his victory and Connolly 229, which was just thirteen more votes than he had received on the first ballot.*

Afterwards, Connolly was driven to Yarmouth where, as head of the government, he had been scheduled for the second of the day's pleasurable affairs of state, that of addressing the annual dinner following the International Tuna Cup Match. It was to have been a victory celebration, held among people for whom Connolly had a natural affinity—the press, sportsmen, American businessmen, and assorted gentlemen of the public relations industry. A suite had long been reserved for the Premier, well stocked with cases of liquor, and the evening had promised to be memorably cheerful until the results of the final ballot had become known.

When the Acting Premier arrived, now serving the last few hours of his brief time in office, he went to his room, his face dark with anger. The door of his suite closed and there he remained in the company of a few friends for the balance of the long, despairing evening. Down below, the saltwater fishermen and their sporting companions dined well, idly pondering the mysteries of politics in this peculiar little province, feeling it incomprehensible that such a nice fellow as Harold Connolly could be Premier one day and a stranger the next as the result of a decision by his own party.

Henry Hicks became the unwitting catalyst in the Conservative Party's struggle to be reborn in Nova Scotia. Because Hicks was a man of decisive habit, of quick and sometimes caustic phrase, and a public man whose administrative abilities far exceeded his political judgement, he was to hasten the restoration of the two-party system in his province, if not in Canada, to burnish the image of Robert Stanfield, and to shatter, perhaps forever, the nearly monolithic support of Nova Scotia Catholics for the Liberal Party.

In all these matters, he was both architect and victim, unwitting, unwilling, innocent yet blameworthy. From the hour he succeeded to the Premiership, he was to preside over a government in swift decline of its powers and over a party in ruinous disarray. Of those who were present at his victory, almost half cursed the moment of his triumph and bitterly regretted it forever after. No amount of time could heal the wounds left by this furious assault on a long-enshrined Liberal ecumenicism.

By nature, Henry Hicks was neither prudent nor cautious. He was, rather, something of a plunger. A short, stocky, balding man, with a brief moustache and a vague oriental cast about the eyes, he had the small man's suggestion of vanity and aggressive confidence. He rushed his fences as though they were not there.

And he inherited a party that was not his, but had been shaped by another man, in other times. Many of those around him disliked him

*	1st Ballot	2nd Ballot	3rd Ballot	4th Ballot	5th Ballot
Connolly	216	232	229	224	229
Hicks	83	108	178	263	312

152

and, what is worse, said so. The fact that he was a respecter of good wines, something of a gourmet, a bit of an intellectual, and took snuff, all served to deepen the suspicions of those who looked upon him, with dismay, as the unlikely successor to Angus L. Macdonald.

Fresh from his convention triumph, the new Premier reformed his cabinet (Connolly had resigned, refusing to serve beneath him),* and issued writs for three by-elections–in East Hants, where the 1953 result had been voided by the courts; in the dual riding of Inverness, where a bench appointment had opened a seat; and in Halifax South, left vacant by Macdonald's death.

Of the three, only Halifax South was critical. Should Henry Hicks carry Halifax South, he could establish his leadership over the fractious, rebellious Halifax Liberals. The seat was traditionally Liberal and predominantly Catholic; since 1935 Macdonald had held it easily.

In this crucial test for Hicks, it is possible to fault his judgement for plunging so soon into such a contest. But he might have been the last to know, and to know the least, of the deep divisions created by his convention. Halifax South was to measure it more precisely, and for all to see.

The by-election was also crucial for Stanfield. It would be a certain augury of his political future, a test by which his potential could be calculated in the new circumstances in Nova Scotia. There were now six seats in Halifax, all of them Liberal. No Tory leader could be credible as a potential Premier unless, or until, his party was in contention in Halifax. No Tory leader had been so since the collapse of the Harrington government in 1933.

In the politics of Halifax, religion was a pervasive factor. Halifax South, North, and Northwest were considered Catholic, while Halifax Centre and West were considered Protestant. The federal seat of Halifax City and County was a dual riding, one of only two in Canada, where tradition dictated that the parties would nominate one Catholic and one Protestant. The city alternated between Catholic and non-Catholic mayors, each limited to two terms of office. Such considerations were respected by all parties, and these had application throughout the political system, from the appointment of judges and senators down through the election of aldermen in the wards. Protestants might, if they liked, nominate Jews in their stead, but the traditional position of the Catholic in the rhythmic process was held inviolate.

Thus, Richard A. Donahoe had succeeded a Protestant as Mayor of Halifax, and subsequently been re-elected by acclamation for his second term. At this conjunction in the careers of Stanfield and Hicks, the Mayor of Halifax was supremely, ideally suited for his role as the Conservative candidate for the prestigious seat in Halifax South.

Those who revere the history of politics come to value the men whose careers illuminate events, such as Richard Donahoe, whose life

*Connolly was appointed to the Senate, July, 1955.

153

and times span four decades of the politics of Nova Scotia, whose rich and vivid speech articulated the Tory cause from the days of R. B. Bennett to those of Robert Stanfield, and who was, all the while, that most rare of a Conservative spokesmen–an Irish Catholic in the city of Halifax–whose lot it was always to be significant to others, to lend his name to their cause, and bearing, all the while, slights and oversights and aimless injuries to pride and, in the end, to see his own deeper interests and ambitions finally disappointed.

One half of Halifax is Catholic, and eighty per cent of that half is Liberal. Among the Irish, Donahoe was a rarity for his stubborn Conservatism. Rarer still, it was the legitimate inheritance of his family, on his father's side. A great aunt Moriah had come to Halifax from Ireland and financed, from her own savings, the passage of two of her brothers, named O'Donoghue. This dutiful, diligent lady was housekeeper for Sir Edward Kenney, a merchant prince of the day.

The Irish who came to Halifax in that period of history arrived predisposed to Liberalism and with an earned antipathy to the word "Tory." But one of the O'Donoghue brothers arrived in Canada with an open mind toward the new world and its politicians. As he took up life in Halifax, he was impressed by one politician–Charles Tupper– whom he heard advocating free education. It was the beginning of a Tory strain that would run through generations, delivering Richard Donahoe to the Tory party at a time when all might have been merely another failure without him.

The present-day Donahoe family has a rich political history, most of it Liberal. In July, 1867, the provincial election and the first federal election were held on the same date. The Liberal slogan of that bitterly anti-confederate campaign was "Sold for the price of a sheepskin," and on that busy day, the city of Halifax elected three provincial and two federal members. Among them were the great-grandfathers of both Richard Donahoe and his wife. Both of the victors were anti-confederate Liberals.

Part of the O'Donoghue family remained Conservative. The surname was changed to Donahoe when the partnership of "O'Donaghue and O'Donaghue," grocers and vinters, was dissolved. The partners were not related, and the forebear of Richard Donahoe changed the family name in the process of establishing his own business in Halifax.

He did, however, keep his Tory political faith, however rare it was among the Halifax Irish and among his own kin. In the provincial election of 1928, for example, only two Liberals were elected in Halifax, and one of them was Edward Cragg, husband to Donahoe's sister. The Craggs, during the campaign, lived with Richard's aunt, an elderly woman of Tory persuasion. One day while Richard was visiting, she asked him how the election was going, saying mournfully, "I can't get a word of truth in this house."

In the 1930 general election, while Donahoe was a student at Dalhousie, "Uncle Ted" Cragg informed him that he was to be one of the Liberal candidates for Halifax and proposed that Richard be his driver. But after the nominating convention, Uncle Ted informed his nephew that "the organization" had vetoed his choice of driver in preference for an older man whose family was of unquestioned and undiluted loyalty to the Liberal cause.

Donahoe reported his disappointment to his father, who commented wisely that unkept promises were to be expected of Liberals. He advised his son to seek employment at Conservative headquarters.

Donahoe was welcomed at Tory headquarters by a young lawyer and organizer, prominent in provincial politics, who promptly appointed him a driver and headquarters handyman. It was one of the smaller coincidences of politics that Leonard Fraser, ten years later, would be nominated for the leadership of the provincial party by the youth whom he had just taken on for casual employment and pocket money in a federal election campaign.

Before the campaign was over, Donahoe had caught the eye of the party. His job was to drive speakers from platform to platform during the evening "double-headers" scheduled by the organization. In this performance, speakers would begin the evening at one meeting and, having given their addresses, be driven to another, exchanging places with platform performers at the second meeting.

One evening Donahoe delivered the first of the evening's orators, who completed their duties, but their replacements did not arrive. The chairman, in desperation, asked young Donahoe to fill in, which he did with obvious relish, and when he had finished his peroration both he and many in the audience felt they had heard the best speech of the evening. For the balance of the campaign, Donahoe became a platform orator as well as a headquarters driver.

"Uncle Ted" Cragg and his Liberal running mate lost the election in Halifax, swept away by the Bennett tide. The Tory ticket was successful, even though one of the candidates was decrepit with age and had conducted a speechless campaign, being merely led onto the platforms and introduced to the crowds. To Donahoe the result was vindication of sorts, and it was a start in politics.

It was a rare time in the political history of Nova Scotia, with Tory governments in office in both Halifax and Ottawa. But it was not to last. Economics and ineptitude were to conspire against the Conservative Party, and the consequences would be devastating.

For forty-three years, from 1882 until 1925, the Liberal Party had governed Nova Scotia; for twenty-six of those years, George Murray had been Premier and party leader. His successor was Ernest Armstrong, whose luck it was to lead his party to overwhelming defeat.

The Tories, enfeebled by this long travail, were leaderless in 1925, although, in a titular sense, their chief was Laurie Hall, father of a daughter who would become the second wife of Robert Stanfield. On the eve of the election, the Tories met in convention, but they did not elect Hall their leader. Instead, they chose Edgar Rhodes.

The election of 1925 was a Tory sweep; Rhodes' reconstructed party won forty of the forty-three seats; among his members were George Nowlan, Percy Black, and Gordon Harrington. The Liberal debacle was nearly total.

Three years later, in 1928, for reasons none could explain, Rhodes called a "snap" election, jettisoning his overwhelming majority in the legislature to seek a fresh mandate. Perhaps he had foreseen the crash and the depression to come, or anticipated the election of R. B. Bennett in 1930 which would bring him a federal cabinet post; whatever the reason, it could be no less plausible. To this day, the survivors shake their heads in disbelief.

There was no mystery in the result. The government barely escaped defeat, its majority reduced to three. The fortunes of the Liberal Party miraculously and quickly revived. To make matters worse for the provincial party, the depression did come, Rhodes did go to Ottawa to become Bennett's Minister of Finance, and Harrington, his successor, clung to office for the full five-year term of the government.

While this brief Tory interregnum was coming to its close, Donahoe and Ike Smith were classmates at Dalhousie Law School. One of their law professors was Angus L. Macdonald, in whom Donahoe found both personal friendship and political promise. Macdonald had "a streak of mysticism," Donahoe recalls, and could be "either mundane or lyrical." Sometimes one could not be sure of the difference.

Macdonald had run as the Liberal candidate in Inverness, in the 1930 federal election, and was soundly trounced by Isaac Macdougall, a leather-lunged hustings spellbinder. Returning to the Law School after the campaign, chastened and broke, Macdonald was forced to sell his second-hand car. Donahoe recalls that the sale was made to an Antigonish farmer who was as yet unable to drive; Donahoe obliged Macdonald by delivering the car to its new owner and, en route, paying court to a girlfriend.

In 1931 the Liberals convened in Truro to choose a leader. There was little enthusiasm for either of two declared candidates. Then Lauchie Currie, in a fiery peroration, nominated a relatively unknown Angus L. Macdonald. His speech stampeded the convention. After that, the youthful new Liberal leader energetically campaigned throughout the province, returning exhausted to his lecturing duties at Dalhousie. (Harrington, the Tory Premier, proudly said to Donahoe, "Macdonald has to do that and I don't. The people know me.")

The Nova Scotia legislature had reformed the Elections Act, introducing the modern practice of enumeration. In 1933, the mandate

156

of the Harrington government exhausted, the new legislation underwent its first, fateful test. The result was "the franchise scandal" which helped Macdonald to his first victory and the restoration of a Liberal government.

The government's partisan supporters took some pains, in the process of enumeration, to omit the names of Liberals from the voting lists. When the lists did appear, they were sometimes posted late at night and so high on the telephone poles that citizens were obliged to climb them to search for their names. The result was confusion, dismay, and legitimate public indignation.

Long lines formed before the revising officers. A demonstration marched on Province House; all but one of government's ministers were absent, and that one refused to meet the demonstrators, but ducked out a back door. Donahoe, then serving as Deputy Provincial Secretary, recalls the conflict between the government's better intentions and the partisan stratagems of its supporters. He also recalls that the Grits made the most of it, taking pains to notify a select group of prominent citizens that their names were not on the lists, whether or not, in fact, they were.

F. B. McCurdy, a Privy Councillor, was one distinguished citizen whose name had been zealously omitted. When he appeared, outraged, before the registrar he was asked blandly, "Are you twenty-one years of age?" Dutiful administrators, clinging to the letter of the law, created the firm impression that they were conducting a deliberate slowdown.

But the queues which had formed before the Courts of Revision were no greater than those which formed at the polls on election day as Nova Scotians elected a new government, under a new Premier, who was to be unbeatable and unassailable for the remaining twenty-one years of his life.

In defeat the Tory Party lapsed into a long period of futility. Harrington led it again, in 1937, and lost. This time the margin of defeat was greater. The next year on Bastille Day, July 14, Harrington abruptly resigned as leader, but at a party convention later in the year he was re-elected. Within months, he again resigned and the party drifted leaderless as men turned to other, and graver, concerns. Canada was at war, and in no part of the country was there a greater response to the call to arms than in Nova Scotia.

When the Tories called a leadership convention, there was a strong movement within the party to cancel it. The argument was that the "phony war" would soon be over, Germany would be defeated, and the men would be home again, providing new prospects for the leadership. Perhaps one of these prospects would be a war hero.

The dispirited party gathered in Halifax, in the Masonic Hall, in early 1940, and the convention began only after a prolonged discussion as to whether to proceed. Finally, Donahoe nominated the convention's only candidate, Leonard Fraser, and a dispirited party at last, and at least, had a leader at the helm.

Fraser, a handsome man of great personal charm with an excellent platform manner, had all the attributes of a successful political leader but one–he could not convince enough people of his sincerity. He was almost too handsome, too bright, too persuasive.

When Fraser had first asked Donahoe to be his nominator, Donahoe had been uncertain. He told Fraser he would nominate him provided no one better appeared before the convention.

"Who, for instance?" Fraser asked.

"I don't mean George Nowlan," Donahoe replied.

Nowlan did not want Fraser, nor did he want Donahoe to move Fraser's nomination. But in the end, there was no alternative, and Donahoe made good his promise.

18

IN THE GENERAL ELECTION OF 1941, THE PARTY HAD FARED NO BETTER against Macdonald. Fraser had lost his own seat in Hants, but when Conservative Percy Black resigned in Cumberland to begin a career in federal politics, the Liberals allowed Fraser to take up the vacancy and re-enter the legislature unopposed.

Angus L. joined the wartime government of Mackenzie King, but returned to lead his party in the 1945 general election. The Liberal slogan had been "All's well with Angus L.," as indeed it was; not a single Tory was elected.

Once again personally defeated, in Queens, Leonard Fraser resigned. All the party could do, voiceless in the legislature and having sustained four consecutive defeats, was cling to survival's shelf. It found the man to help, if anyone could, in Robert Stanfield who, not without reluctance, accepted the presidency of the party.

Donahoe, along the way, had been blooded. He had opposed his friend and mentor, Angus L., in Halifax South in 1937, and he had represented the Catholic half of the Tory ticket in Halifax City and County in the federal election of 1940.

In 1946, a year after the Tory Party's debacle in the provincial election, Donahoe ran for Mayor of Halifax, losing by only 181 votes to Gee Ahearn. Even then he might have won, except that Harold Connolly "threw in his troops" in the north end, after earlier assuring Donahoe that he had no interest in the mayoralty race. Three years later, in the provincial election of 1949, Donahoe opposed Connolly in Halifax North, faring badly, but unwilling to see the seat go by acclamation.

In that contest, he ran for the first time under the leadership of Stanfield, who had assumed the thankless task of leading a winless party. There had been occasional gatherings in one of the small meeting rooms on the mezzanine floor of the Lord Nelson Hotel. Fraser, Nowlan, Stanfield, and a few others would meet to review the circumstances of their beleaguered, leaderless party. On a number of occasions, the leadership was offered around the table, but there were no takers. Finally, Stanfield agreed.

The convention was held in the autumn of 1948 in the Capital Theatre. Once again, Donahoe nominated the party's leader, and once again found himself opposed to Nowlan, who sponsored Stanfield's only opposition, J. Fred Fraser, a Halifax engineer, whose signal claim to political fame was to oppose Stanfield for the leadership.

159

The party had viewed Stanfield with little real enthusiasm. Some would have preferred Donahoe, still others Nowlan. Donahoe lays claim to being the first to state what has since become a popular truism. He said to his wife, returning home after the convention:

"Stanfield will be the hardest man to elect, but when he does win he will be the hardest man to defeat."

For most in the party, Stanfield had seemed the only man available with the stamina, the private means, and the patience for what everyone knew would be a long, hard pull.

As for Donahoe, he began to win in 1951, with his election as an alderman, then as Mayor of Halifax in 1952, followed by re-election by acclamation in 1953. Then within a year, Angus L. Macdonald was dead, Connolly had lost the leadership, and Henry Hicks called the by-elections in Halifax South, Hants East, and Inverness for November 16. Wisely, though not willingly, the Tories wrote off Inverness as a serious possibility. Isaac D. Macdougall was salvaged from the Halifax water-front and shipped back to the county where he had been its thrice-elected member in Ottawa and where he had once defeated Angus L. himself. The Liberals nominated an oft-defeated Tory, J. Clyde Nunn, an Antigonish radio station manager. Hants would simply be a re-run.

The by-election campaigns of 1954 found Stanfield a widower, responsible for four young children (the youngest less than a year old), and he had made it clear to his party, when he had decided to stay on in the leadership, that whatever the demands of politics, his family would come before them. He insisted on being home each night, however late, so as to begin each day with his children.

Despite this caveat, private grief and loneliness seemed to drive Stanfield to deeper involvement in the tasks of reconstructing his party. He needed the company of others and he became, as a result, more available and more accessible than most leaders. At party gatherings, he was often the first to arrive and the last to leave, and his supporters noticed, for the first time, his remarkable personal qualities, which included, to their surprise, a wry sense of humour, an unexpected egalitarianism, and–most surprising–a barely concealed streak of compassion.

Thus the man who had earlier earned their respect now held the affection of all his party and the fierce, unquestioning loyalty of the hard core of his supporters. They no longer discussed his weaknesses, but marvelled at his strength; they no longer doubted his capacities as a leader, but were fiercely determined not to let him down.

The Halifax South Liberals held their nominating convention in the ballroom of the Nova Scotian Hotel ("the government hotel"), the wounds of their leadership convention still unhealed. Premier Hicks was there, and so was Harold Connolly, his career in provincial politics plainly at an end but making an outward gesture to party unity. Connolly was on his way to the Senate.

The Liberals elected Alban Murphy, very nearly an ideal candidate in ordinary circumstances, and the best that could be found in any event. His only opponent had been Dr. Henry Reardon, a physician with a strident partisan tongue (who would later slander both Stanfield and myself from the privileged sanctuary of the legislature). Murphy's father had once been the member for Halifax South, and the candidate himself had served as chairman of the School Board, president of the Board of Trade, and at the head of a successful family clothing business.

A local, transient weekly–one of many which would appear and disappear in Halifax, especially during times of high political excitement–reported on the convention:

But to many, listening as speaker after speaker faltered through his
lines, appearing on sure ground only when paying tribute after tribute
to the memory of the great Angus L., Liberal leaders, candidates,
and delegates, had all the appearance of whistling past a graveyard.
Henry Hicks expressed confidence that Liberals would be returned in
all three constituencies in November 16's by-election, but . . .
It would take a good man to beat Donohue, [sic] and Angus L.
was gone.

The Haligonian correctly anticipated the candidacy of Mayor Donahoe, whose nomination was unopposed. After the candidates had been chosen, I returned to Halifax, to the Lord Nelson Hotel, to find the Tory Party in a fever of activity. Rod Black's training program for his organization in the lower wards of the constituency had not ended with the 1953 election. The troops were ready.

At the Lord Nelson I was given a room overlooking the Halifax Gardens, offering a striking overview of autumn's changing colours. One finds that hotel rooms improve with one's prospects.

This time there was no publicity committee. Instead, I met with Stanfield almost daily, and our discussions had little to do with the newspaper and radio campaign being mounted, but with his running verbal battle with the new adversary, Henry Hicks. In almost all respects, it was to be a preview of the next general election.

I had become by now, or so I believed, a student of political styles. I had studied St. Laurent, Drew, Hugh John Flemming, McNair, Stanfield, and Macdonald, learning from all of them, for all politicians are instructive. One finds personal strengths and weaknesses in each of them; the successful campaign is one that manages to pit the strengths of one protagonist against the weaknesses of his adversary. But to do so in Nova Scotia required the co-operation of both Stanfield and Hicks.

The new leader of the Liberal Party proved to be obliging. It had been impossible to engage Angus L. Macdonald in useful debate, since he appeared determined to remain above the campaign if not above

161

politics itself. Hicks, however, seemed eager to debate at the slightest provocation. We called the proclivity "rabbit ears," meaning that he heard all that was said by his critics and seemed compelled to react. It was, perhaps, not only part of his nature but part of his political circumstance. Anxious to demonstrate his qualities as a leader of men and of his party, Hicks adopted the worst of postures for the best of reasons. In the by-elections of 1954, he came out swinging.

Stanfield is a man of stubborn conviction and dogged persistence. In his simple, unadorned language he will argue an issue and remain with it long after most of his advisors and supporters have wearied of it; in this exhausting, wearing process he will, more often than not, tempt the most prudent adversary onto his own ground.

If patience was a virtue with Stanfield, it was an abomination to Hicks. When the Tory leader raised once more, at the outset of the campaign, his persistent complaint about the alleged improprieties of liquor agents, Hicks responded with his accustomed alacrity.

His reaction had been partly stimulated by the recent discovery of malpractice by liquor agents among employees in a Cape Breton retail outlet who, according to testimony, had been rewarded for "pushing" the brands of one distiller. This was generally assumed to be common practice, but the public revelations cemented Stanfield's case and encouraged his resolve to make it an issue in the by-elections. During the Cape Breton hearings, the names of a number of agents had been mentioned in testimony, but it was the issue, not the individuals, which now interested the Tories.

Henry Hicks began his campaign by announcing the names of seven men against whom charges had been laid by the Attorney General's department. As to Tory charges that these were, in fact, patronage appointments, Hicks said defensively, "Some are Liberals, and some are not."* Then, his voice brisk with bravado, he challenged Stanfield to give him the names of any others in the province who were liquor agents. Put up or shut up.

It was an inauspicious opening for the government's campaign, and it created renewed anxiety among Halifax Liberals. Not surprisingly, those whom Hicks had named were Haligonians, some were indeed Liberals, and some were Catholic. It occurred to the chieftains of the Halifax organization that their new leader would have no compunction in making any of them scapegoats merely to silence the opposition. This was not, in their experience, the way the game was played. To make matters worse, their leader had invited Stanfield to enlarge on the numbers of those who, unhappily, were now enjoying public notoriety as liquor agents. It seemed further evidence that they had been right all along in supporting Harold Connolly.

For a week following Hicks' announcement of the charges against seven men, and the challenge to Stanfield to produce the names of the

*At least one had been a known Tory supporter.

culprits, we debated the next move. While I could not admire Hicks' strategy, I was impressed by its audacity, not at all anxious that Stanfield respond by making himself an informant in the eyes of the Nova Scotia electorate. Nor was Stanfield. During the week, Hicks renewed his challenge and complained that, as yet, he had not heard from the Tory leader. Again, he was serving against his own cause. The Premier, and not Stanfield, had whetted public interest in the issue, and while it seemed clear enough to me that he wanted to divert the Leader of the Opposition from the issue and into an unacceptable role as a vengeful informant, it was also certain that he had guaranteed Stanfield a large audience and possibly the last word in the matter.

Seven days after Henry Hicks' speech, we inserted an advertisement in the Halifax *Herald,* bearing a portrait of Stanfield's calm, impassive face:

FRIDAY
Listen to Robert L. Stanfield
Leader of the Progressive Conservative Party of Nova Scotia
In reply to Premier Hicks' speech
on the subject of liquor agents
CJCH 10:15 p.m. to 10:30 p.m.

As the Lord Nelson was "the Tory hotel," so CJCH had become "the Tory station." Finlay MacDonald's liberality in matters of censorship and the inconvenience of submitting broadcast material in advance created new and improved circumstances in radio.

"Just tell your people," Finlay said, "to come into the station in time to make their talk. On the way out, we'd appreciate it if they'd leave a copy of their talk with the receptionist."

And sometimes, when speeches were painfully drafted by hand, not even that was done. The ghost of Mackenzie King had become a mere vapour.

MacDonald's new policy at the station, either by coincidence or by example, marked the end of the zeal for censorship among the Halifax media. Less than a year before the advent of television, radio was liberated for the use of politicians and their parties. Even while the CBC persisted, far into the television age, with efforts to restrict the use of the media by timid and crippling prohibitions, the new breed of politician, and his fresh corps of advisors from the advertising and public relations field, treated the regulations with increasing disregard and circumvented them with increasing impunity.

It would have been doubtful if, a year previous, the question of liquor agents could have enjoyed such public airing. Angus L. would not have deigned to discuss it, nor would the media have allowed such latitude to the opposition. For the first time, I could see how substantially the media had replaced the hustings as a political forum.

Stanfield and I discussed, throughout the week, the text for his radio speech and his reply to Hicks. Other advice had been sought, and it fell into two conflicting recommendations: that Stanfield must satisfy Hicks, and public opinion, by providing the names of those he knew to be liquor agents. ("Why not? They're all Grits!") But there was a strong dissenting view that Stanfield should not mention any names. Len Fraser was foremost among those who argued this point, saying that Stanfield shouldn't "tattle" on fellow Nova Scotians.

I was between the two opposing views. I proposed that Stanfield review the opposition's long fight to force the government to recognize the problem, but put the onus of revealing more names upon Hicks by sending him a letter, attaching a list of the names. Stanfield developed this further by proposing an official enquiry into the matter and providing Hicks with a list of "witnesses" who might shed light on the subject of liquor agents.

Stanfield set to work drafting the speech while I prepared a draft of the letter to Hicks. They turned out to be remarkably alike. We then met and exchanged copies of our work, improving on each other's labour. Now that our relationships were considerably easier, the differences in our habits and dispositions had been accepted and reconciled. (For example, I preferred to work late at night but not early in in the day, to my annoyance and his when his calls often would wake me. Now, whenever his first call of the day would come, usually near the noon hour, he would always begin by saying drily, "I hope I didn't get you out of bed.")

Further, there was a mutual trust and confidence. The "publicity committee" days were over; I needed to consult no one as to advertising. But at this stage, Stanfield wrote a first draft of his speeches after which, as the practice developed, I would polish. Still later, in future campaigns, the first draft was developed in conversation and the second draft was invariably the last. It reflected a genuine meeting of minds.

Stanfield had a horror of adjectives, adverbs, and emotive words. I had a passion for them, admiring the speeches of Winston Churchill more than any other. Stanfield's drafts, written in a sparse, brief hand reflective of the style, were full of fact but barren of feeling. I was inclined the other way; words, for me, conjured images, communicated with the senses, all of them, and formed impressions which facts alone could not create. Radio listeners especially, seeking food for thought, could be starved by a diet of facts and figures.

All this time, I was learning in a hard school. I was still new to politics, to the Conservative cause, to the quick convulsions of election campaigns, and to the direct use of media, so each day brought some kind of discovery. And in the process of discovery were better methods of communicating ideas, of condensing a multitude of issues and argu-

164

ments into their most cogent, effective form. Stanfield was, in his way, doing the same, and while I may have improved his rhetoric on occasion, he in turn improved my sense of proportion, and from him, as from a good editor, I learned something about the value of simplicity and the discipline of restraint.

19

PRIOR TO HIS BROADCAST, STANFIELD WROTE HICKS A LENGTHY LETTER
that we felt would satisfy those who felt the Tory leader must "put up or
shut up" on the subject of liquor agents, the crux of which read:

... Recent events, however, have disclosed to some extent the
existence of liquor agents and their activities. This information has
been widely publicized through the press and radio, and that,
I assume, is the chief reason why your Government was compelled
finally to investigate.
This cursory investigation has resulted in charges being laid against
seven individuals. These charges were laid on October 27th, but only
after you had divulged the extent and nature of them in the course
of a political radio address. In that same address you invited me, as
Leader of the Opposition, to furnish you with a further list of names of
liquor agents. You will forgive me, I am sure, for interpreting this
request as a purely political challenge. ...
We have now and have had for sometime, a list which includes the
names of liquor agents, some of whom no doubt have since withdrawn
their connections. This information was and is, to a large extent,
public knowledge. Some of these men have been and are well known,
indeed favourably known to the Liberal Party and to the Government.
I am sure that with a minimum of effort the Attorney General's
Department could duplicate such a list.
We still remain of the opinion, however, that the proper course of
action is not solely a series of charges against individuals, however proper that may be at this time, but the course of action most
consistent with the public interest is a complete and exhaustive
legislative inquiry into the entire matter.
The Government may, if it wishes, read for itself the names of those
men the Opposition originally requested appear before the
Legislative Committee three years ago. It may add to its knowledge
further by a careful reading of the evidence given during the
course of a recent trial in Cape Breton. It will find the names of others,
if it so wishes, simply by making the most meager of inquiries
elsewhere.

And in his subsequent radio address, Stanfield informed the public
of his action, which included his renewed demand for an official enquiry:

166

... to return to Mr. Hicks' request that I give him a list, I have today written a letter to Mr. Hicks, which contains a list of persons whom I have reason to believe are liquor agents; but let me give you this assurance, the names I have set forth on this list will come as no surprise to Mr. Hicks. He can read, and he has read these names before. Nor would they come as any surprise to you because, if you have followed recent events, these names would also be familiar to you.

... I have given Mr. Hicks a second list, which contains the names of some of the people whom I feel would be valuable witnesses before a Royal Commission. These names include the present Chief Commissioner of the Liquor Commission, together with the names of those gentlemen whom the Opposition requested be called before the Public Accounts Committee some three years ago. To paraphrase Mr. Hicks' own remark, some are liquor agents and some are not. Some of these are gentlemen against whom the Government has brought charges, but again some are not. It is perfectly clear that we are making no charges. We are simply requesting that their testimony be made available; and we are saying further that we believe such testimony would be pertinent and helpful to the public inquiry which is, we believe, the first essential in cleaning up this long neglected mess.

Hicks did not reply; Stanfield had the last word. Nor was anything further done about the issue until Stanfield took office. Of the seven who were later tried, six pleaded guilty.

The Liberal Party had its own advertising consultant, Jack Wilcox, a native of Halifax and a representative of a Toronto agency. (In 1967, Wilcox, then with Public and Industrial Relations Ltd., produced the newspaper circulated at the leadership convention in support of Stanfield's candidacy.) The Liberal Party's advertising seemed to reflect a conscious anxiety, an uncertainty as to which note to strike:

PERFORMANCE COUNTS:
New, Aggressive Leadership
Under Premier Henry Hicks:
"The Liberal Party of Nova Scotia, with an unmatched record of service in the past, stands united and confident, frankly facing the problems of the province, and determined to find effective solutions to these problems." (From recent speech of Premier Hicks)
The New Liberal Leader Has
Been Premier Less Than Two Months

Following this somewhat defensive declaration, the advertisement ventured seven "significant events" which, it proclaimed, showed "the new leader to be a man of action." Yet the glorious past was not to be forgotten:

Proud of its record, the Liberal Party stands for these great programs:
• Old Age Pensions
• Family Allowances
• Mothers' Allowances
• Old Age Assistance
• Pensions for the Blind
• Disabled Persons' Pensions

And the advertisement concluded on a rather irrelevant note:

Elect Three Practical Businessmen to the LIBERAL TEAM

There was indeed value, in Nova Scotia, in the word "Liberal." The Tories adjusted their speech and their strategy accordingly. They praised Macdonald–". . . the old government and the new are one of the same," Donahoe said, "different only in that the new suffers by the absence of that great Nova Scotian, Angus L. Macdonald." Such tributes seemed only elemental common sense. Conservatives took pains not to offend those of Liberal faith. In one of his handwritten drafts, Stanfield indicated how such pains were taken:

. . . Look at what was done to Ern Ettinger in Hants East at the last provincial election. Not only did the government party vote people who had no right to vote in the constituency. That would have been bad enough. But despite this, Ern Ettinger, the Conservative candidate, was elected when the votes were counted on election night. Thereafter, ballot boxes were improperly opened. When the ballots were counted on the recount–after the ballot boxes had been improperly opened–Ern Ettinger was counted out.
Now, my friends, it is all very well for members of the government to talk about the franchise scandal of 20 years ago. I am telling you something that happened a year ago.

It was as though organization Liberals were incapable of such behaviour as stuffing ballot boxes; instead, "the government party" would be the culprit.

The by-election in Halifax South was contested on a number of levels, and the dust and din of battle were remarkable. Politics is a passion with the Irish, and while they are formidable when standing together, they are even more so when pitted against one another. The fight between Alban Murphy and Richard Donahoe was waged in the Loyal Irish Society, into the wards, cutting party lines and straining family ties.

168

Rod Black, working almost around the clock, fought the Liberal machine hand-to-hand. Election lists were closely scrutinized for ineligible voters; aggressive young Tory lawyers monitored proceedings at the Courts of Revision, filling the air with challenges and the Tories added as many names to the lists as did their opponents. All this was new, and disheartening, to the Liberal organization.

Donahoe, over Black's objections, used radio frequently in his campaign. But he also canvassed, especially on rainy evenings. Once, when he visited my hotel room, drenched with rain but exuding cheerful confidence, I extended sympathy:

"You're soaking wet, Richard."

"I'm even wetter inside," he said. "Sixty cups of tea this evening."

The distant sounds of the struggle in Inverness were sometimes entertaining, but not encouraging. The Attorney General, campaigning there, charged that the Tory stand on the question of liquor agents was motivated by a desire "to stir up support of temperance people." (In fact, a fringe benefit we had not thought of.) Otherwise, the campaign seemed to be a noisy exchange of insults between Isaac Macdougall and Clyde Nunn:

Mr. Macdougall has claimed Liberals have no horse-sense or they wouldn't run a "Clyde" in a free-for-all.

Mr. Nunn says the Tories have the "race-horse" and "I am the Clyde." He says that "Clyde" is the kind the people of Inverness County need, and not "one in lily-clad silks winded and broken."

"That's the way it is down here," reported the Cape Breton correspondent for the Halifax *Herald*.

It seemed a long way from the campaign in Halifax. In any event, there did not seem to be anything any of us could do.

But in Hants East, where Ettinger had been declared the winner in 1953 by a single vote, before the "recount" and the discovery of ballot boxes mysteriously re-opened in the night, I expected a Conservative win.

The struggle between the Tory undertaker and the Liberal merchant had been joined by a CCF candidate, whose handful of votes would be significant on election day. It was generally assumed that the CCF would take support from Ettinger, since they were also anti-government votes. I was concerned when Alex Bryson, a Saskatchewan Member of Parliament, arrived in Hants East to assist in the CCF campaign and, like it or not, to assist the Liberal Government as well.

Still, I found it difficult to imagine myself making much of a contribution to Ettinger's campaign. Politics in that precisely divided rural community turned on issues that were unfamiliar and bewildering:

dust control on country roads, alternate paving programs, and internal rivalries having nothing to do with politics. There was also, in the belief of the organization, a highly purchasable vote, but in that practice I had neither experience nor faith.

I spent one Sunday afternoon with Ettinger, assisted by Finlay MacDonald, painfully contriving a radio address for the candidate who was, however genial and well-intentioned a man, one of the least articulate office-seekers I would ever meet. I reduced the text to the barest minimum of words, shortening sentences to the simplest construction, but Ettinger was neither a speaker nor a reader. He might better, Black would have been quick to say, have spent the day canvassing.

The Liberals mounted a strikingly audacious campaign against Ettinger, demanding that the Tories "run a clean election." In the local press of Truro and Windsor, party advertisements proclaimed, with ineluctable piety, that the Liberal candidate "accepted the nomination in the by-election now pending, on condition that there would be no illegal influencing of voters on his behalf."

Both parties, depending upon their circumstances, had between them perpetuated the common practice of bribery. It is impossible to discover when these practices began, other than to know they became traditional. But, in logic, they seem so easily a product of a liberal democracy in which the franchise became universal while standards of literacy varied enormously, as did individual interest and involvement in the political process.

Obviously, the poor come to feel they have little at stake in an election; they have learned from long experience that they are as poor after one election as before the next, and that they remain as disadvantaged under the government of one party as another. They have also learned that their vote has only fleeting value–on election days–and that it can be auctioned between contesting parties, or sold to one party so long as there is another party to whom it could presumably go. As well, the poor have the right not to vote, which has been, as often as not, the possibility against which the political parties apply their persuasion.

There were some 5,000 voters in Hants East, thinly spread among twenty-five polls over the countryside. The poll captains knew, often with unerring precision, how many of the voters in their poll were Grit or Tory, and how many had votes for sale. In both Hants and neighbouring Colchester there were numbers of Negroes, Indians, and others who were simply poor, living in small, isolated communities, in flimsy shacks along the roadside or in collapsing farm houses on marginal, unproductive land.

The price of a vote was not great; for some, the practice of being rewarded for one's vote was a matter of stubborn principle. Entire families would refuse to visit the polls until they had been "treated" by one party or another or, as was sometimes the case, until they had been

170

rewarded by the party of their choice. Boxes of chocolates and stockings for the women, pints of rum for the men, and frequently candy for the children were standard "treats." On occasion, especially when the contest was believed to be close, two- and five-dollar bills were considered more effective. Voters were thus visited by busy agents of the parties who offered bribes for their votes or bribes not to vote; it became one of the more sophisticated extensions of this practice to locate the hostile proportion of the purchasable vote and bribe it to stay home.

The practice was by no means limited to the countryside, but was as vigorously applied in the cities. There were fewer difficulties and less uncertainty in the rural areas, because the intelligence was better. Rural poll organizers knew their neighbours; they knew who was poor and what their politics and their price were.

On election day clouds of dust hung over the country roads as the cars of competing political parties hustled from house to house, hauling out their vote, bargaining, bartering, and buying the poor and recalcitrant. These men, consumed by their partisan pride and fervour, compulsively rendered meaningless the fundamental purpose of their restless energy, which was to maintain a party system by allowing the free choice of free men as to who should govern them.

What struck me about it was not only the general public indifference. After all, it confirmed the widespread cynical view that politics was corrupt anyway. But the press was also indifferent; in all the years that common bribery flourished in the Maritimes, and elsewhere, no one can recall a newspaper crusade against it. There seemed to be tacit agreement that nothing could be done about it, or that it was endemic to the system.

So the practices persisted, and the practitioners grew more skilful, until one could not safely say that free elections did exist, or that governments were freely chosen. Parties in power, given opportunities to create enormous campaign funds, had an incalculable advantage over their opponents. Perhaps it is why so many of them could endure in office for so long, not because they were mandated by the electorate, but because they had purchased their majorities from the poor, the Negroes, the Indians, and the dispossessed.

Corrupt practices and their effects are now less significant. The press has yet, other than in some fitful partisan convulsion, to expose it to the light of public opinion. But, paradoxically, the use of media by the parties and the advent of radio and television have greatly reduced its significance, while the mounting demands on party funds made by the new instruments of election campaigning—advertising and promotion—have made substantial inroads into funds traditionally allocated for "poll organization."

In addition, political organizations fell into the hands of younger men, many of whom had a contempt for the customs of their elders and

171

who stubbornly refused to consent to the corruption of the poor, if for no other reason than they themselves felt corrupted.

As well, of course, many of the illiterate poor were dying off, and a new literacy with a more general affluence helped reprieve the party system from continued crimes against itself.

In Hants East, in 1954, each side exchanged dark threats, as each proclaimed its purity of purpose. The Tory candidate sent a personal message, by householder mail, to his constituents.

Please make your choice next Tuesday without fear. The ballot is secret. The Liberal organizers have tried to coerce some of our people by asking them to sign a statement that they will support Alfred Reid. I know that you will resent such an attempt to destroy the secrecy of the ballot. The ballot is secret. The Liberal Committee won't know how you vote; *they have no right to know.*

I asked Ettinger's organizer if, on election day, the Liberal Party would conduct a "clean" election.

"Like hell they will," he said convincingly.

	BY-ELECTION RESULTS	
Halifax South	P.C.–Donahoe	5,876
	Liberal–Murphy	4,585
		(1,291)
Hants East	Liberal–Reid	2,257
	P.C.–Ettinger	2,256
		(1)
Inverness	Liberal–Nunn	4,825
	P.C.–Macdougall	3,205
		(1,620)

On November 16, the "Angus L. Tories" in Halifax South returned to the Conservative Party, while the Irish vote split among the two candidates as it had never done before. Stanfield, as a party leader, was acceptable and Hicks was not. These factors, according to Donahoe, gave him his majority. It should also be said that he was the ideal candidate, probably the only Conservative who could have won.

Ettinger lost in Hants East, the vote count on election night ending in a perfect tie. The Returning Officer then exercised his prerogative and cast the decisive ballot for the Liberal candidate. I considered the result a mistake in strategy; while the Tory organization had concentrated on Halifax South, the Liberals had done the same in Hants, where Hicks was less controversial and where his organizers were made more welcome.

Inverness, Rod Black had once said, would be the last Liberal seat to fall to the Conservative Party. (He would later be proved nearly right.) Nunn, thrice-defeated as a Tory candidate, finally found his way into the legislature, as a Grit. It was the last sad hurrah for Isaac Macdougall.

But the Tories were jubilant. They could now demand that Hicks call a general election, claiming the result in Halifax demonstrated that he could not continue in office with Macdonald's mandate.

As a result of the by-election campaign, Black emerged as the acknowledged leader of a gathering force of Tory volunteers throughout the province, all of them devoted to Stanfield and growing in conviction that he would form the next government.

And my own relationships with Stanfield were vastly improved.

Someone asked Stanfield what he thought of Dalton Camp. "Well," he said, with typical caution, "I'd just as soon not go into a campaign without him."

20

THROUGHOUT 1955 ROWE AND I TRAVELLED THE COUNTRY, STRUG-
gling to re-establish mutually productive relationships among Conservative partisans, discovering in the process how painful and awkward
were many of our problems. Some decisions were both obvious and
easy to make; others were no less obvious but much more difficult. We
did not always get our way and, of course, we were not always right.

Early in the year, on March 18, the Prince Edward Island legislature was dissolved and we faced a severe test of our policy to involve
the national organization in provincial elections. We knew nothing of
Island politics, which has many unique features; our assumption that
Tory prospects could be measurably enhanced by the provision of
reasonable funds and an aggressive publicity campaign was not to be
proven in the Island's general election. If anything, it seemed to suggest that things might have been better had we left them alone.

In the beginning, it did not appear so. The Island media, for advertising purposes, were of a sublime simplicity. There were two daily
newspapers, the larger one being the Charlottetown *Guardian* ("Covers
Prince Edward Island like the dew!"), which appeared to be of a
somewhat Conservative inclination, since many of its editorials were
lifted from the pages of the Upper Canadian Tory papers. The evening
paper, *The Patriot,* was fiercely Liberal–an incontestable fact that was
rationalized by the explanation that its circulation was smaller than
that of the *Guardian.* Apart from a few weekly newspapers of little consequence, the remaining media consideration was the Charlottetown
radio station, which was scrupulously neutral.

The newspapers were modest in size–they could be read in their
entirety in less than ten minutes–but were therefore eminently satisfactory for use in the campaign. And happily, the radio station was
immediately next door to the Charlottetown Hotel, so that the media
were concentrated both figuratively and literally.

The *Guardian* possessed a unique advertising buy; a front page,
banner headline at either top or bottom of the page (or both) could
be purchased daily. These seemed an ideal means of publishing slogans,
simple adjurations, and clever partisan ripostes.* Again I resorted to

---

* Some examples: Stop Family Compacts, Family Contracts–Vote Conservative
One Good Term Deserves Another–Vote Matheson
Government For The Few Is Just About Through–Vote Conservative
Smear Not–Fear Not–Vote Liberal
"We Stand On Our Record" (Matheson)–Vote Conservative
Keep the Garden of the Gulf Growing–Vote Liberal
Things Go Wrong When They're In Too Long–Vote Conservative
Hitch Your Wagon To the Matheson Star (Liberal)
For A List Of Broken Liberal Promises, See Page 5
For Conservative Platform, See Page 20. (This latter, published by the
Liberals, referred to a blank page.)

the editorial column as the prime element in the advertising campaign. Its effect on the reader, and voter, was dubious.

Eugene Spicer, a family friend and then manager of a bank in Summerside, visited me at my hotel. "I can tell you this," he said, chuckling, "those columns are the first thing everyone looks for in the paper. They've never seen anything like it around here."

Indeed, they had not–and as I later concluded, they never would again. Not, at least, from my typewriter. As the campaign wore on, and the signs of defeat loomed more certain, the columns became increasingly crude and acidulous. My control over party publicity was absolute and, as a result, I allowed a personal sense of frustration to overcome a better judgement; the columns increased in vehemence even though I suspected they were damaging to the campaign.

We could not, in any circumstances, have won. But, as I later confessed to Rowe, the party might have done better. It was the first time that a campaign I had been involved in could be said to have actually weakened the party's position. It was also my first and only adventure in political nihilism, and when it was over and I had recovered my normal disposition and poise, I determined it would be my last.

As simple as it seemed to reach the Island voter, the campaign proved to be of elaborate complexity. There were, after all, less than 40,000 voters, nearly all of them accessible to the uncomplicated media structure, and there were no third parties in the contest. Nevertheless, no election in North America was quite like it: the 40,000 voters held, among them, the power of nearly 100,000 votes. This phenomenon is best explained in the *Parliamentary Guide:*

P.E.I. Legislative Assembly
Consists of 30 members: 15 elected as Councillors and 15 as
Assemblymen. Each Electoral District in the Province has
two Representatives, namely, a Councillor and an Assemblyman.
A Property Holder can vote for both Councillor and Assemblyman,
but a Non-Property Holder can only vote for the Assemblyman.*

Islanders lived with this anachronism without complaint; only the Tory Party proposed reform, but there was no significant public opinion to support it. In theory, a single voter in a general election could have as many as thirty votes. It was a common experience to meet people who had a half-dozen or more. A man who owned a home, a place of business, and a summer cottage, each located in a different constituency, could cast six ballots, while those without property, and the poor, would have but one vote to cast. As a consequence, since the

*The universal franchise has since been introduced to Prince Edward Island as the result of legislation introduced by the Conservative administration of Walter Shaw.

175

party vote in the constituencies was generally close, defeat or victory could turn on the disposition and mobility of absentee property owners.

The principle seemed to me indefensible, but most Islanders supported the practice. Farmers and merchants valued their extended rights of franchise as a means of maintaining property taxes at reasonable levels and restraining the demands of other groups in the society–the poor, for example–upon the public treasury. That the Liberal Party had remained in power for twenty years and had not seen fit to reform the franchise act was further evidence of the political wisdom in perpetuating it.*

So that when one thought of election day organization, the mind was seized by the need for abundant transportation. Logistics seemed all-important. But, in fact, the vital factor was intelligence–knowing the names of the so-called property owners from outside the constituency and expediting their progress to the various polls. In this, the Tory organization proved no match for its opposition.

Political talent was not abundant on the Island, and the most talented to be found among the Tories were not candidates. In proportion to its modest population, Prince Edward Island may well have a remarkable number of able politicians, but the demands of modern politics were greater, in 1955, than the numbers available. And on the Island, politics was almost entirely an avocation for the men, with a premium attached to age and experience.

In other ways, however, the Island conformed to the Maritime pattern. The Tory Party had been out of office since the depression, its last administration going down to defeat in 1935, when the Liberals swept the polls, carrying all thirty seats in the legislature.

J. David Stewart was Mayor of Charlottetown and the party's treasurer, which meant that it was he who visited the financial centres of Upper Canada to seek funds for the party machine. He was, as of this moment in time, the only one with the talent and, some would say, the nerve to do it.

His father had been the last Tory Premier to be elected on the Island; politics was for him a familiar activity, and he had for it an almost evenly measured respect and disdain. He appeared to be a popular mayor and to enjoy the office, even though he was an unusual politician–blunt, terse, and tough talking–and he was an unusual Islander–worldly, prosperous, and cynical.

I had not met anyone like him. He was rare in that he had been urged to lead the party and refused, as he had refused to run for provincial office. His qualities of leadership were evident; he was successful, self-sufficient and generally liked. Where he was not liked, he was

*Substantially the same voting system, maintained for similar purposes, still exists in Northern Ireland.

respected. But Stewart preferred the mayor's office–"I get a kick out of it," he would say. He was the first under-achiever I encountered in Canadian politics.

Islanders could be proud of Stewart; he had won the D.S.O. in World War II and had been the first, perhaps only, Maritimer to command an Ontario regiment. (When he came up the line to take over the Argyle and Sutherlands, the legend ran, he greeted the officers saying, "My name is Stewart. I'm taking over.")

He warned me of the disaster impending for the Tory Party at the polls. "We're going nowhere," he said, smiling. "Don't get your hopes up."

On the final weekend before election day, Stewart and I drove to his club. While he went inside, I waited in the car, listening to the news on the radio. Another car drew alongside and I watched, with growing curiosity, while a man laboured in the darkness, filling his trunk with cases of liquor.

When I stepped out to take a closer look, the man walked around from behind his car to peer into my face. "Hello," he said cheerfully. "I know who you are. You're that fellow Camp."

"That's right," I said. "Who are you?"

"It doesn't matter," he said easily. "But I know all about you. You're a bright fellow, Mr. Camp. Heard all about you."

"Well, not really," I said.

He took my hand and shook it.

"I like you, Mr. Camp," he said.

I decided he was sober, nonetheless, and also that he was a Liberal.

"See that stuff?" He pointed to the trunk, stuffed with booze.

"That's election ammunition," he said, pride in his voice. "And because I like you, Mr. Camp, I want to say to you that I'm sorry for what we're going to do to your Tory friends on election day. I really am. I'm sorry for you because I like you, Mr. Camp."

He closed the trunk, entered his car and drove away.

I told Dave Stewart about it.

"He's right," he said, chuckling.

On election night I went to Stewart's home to hear the early returns, sitting in his study, the shades down, glass in hand, braced for defeat, defiantly optimistic nonetheless.

The results, poll by poll, began in a trickle, then quickly became a flood of Liberal majorities. Twenty-seven Liberals elected, only three Conservatives. Rossiter, a maverick, had won, along with Dewar, a country doctor, and the party's hapless leader, Reg Bell. Walter Shaw was defeated, as were the younger men in whom I had seen promise for the future.

There was not a crumb of consolation in it; the party had suffered a devastating defeat. For that matter, so had I.

177

Stewart, reading my thoughts, said, "Don't take it personally. Have another drink."

I had several—at the party's gloomy headquarters, at Reg Bell's house, at the hotel—and I telephoned some of the losing candidates to express my regrets. I also called Rowe at National Headquarters.

"Don't worry about it," he said. "You did the best you could."

I was not so sure I had.

I felt just sorry enough for myself to assume all the responsibility for the debacle. One was, after all, prepared to take a good deal of the credit when the results were otherwise.

Still I was genuinely puzzled. What did people want, expect, or demand from their public men? The evidence gathered from the Island campaign seemed to suggest that, no matter what the circumstances, Islanders would never elect a majority from one party while the other party was in power in Ottawa. Never in their history, I was told, had they done so and, I was to learn, neither would they do so in future.

I held to my stubborn conviction that I had written some of the best, and toughest political advertisements of a growing career. They might as well have been written on the wind:

The Happy Liberal Family
Tracing the family tree of the Liberal Party is easy. The big limbs
are plain enough and the twigs and sprouts don't matter.
The biggest branch in the Liberal Family Tree is the contractor's
branch. Then there's the Legal Branch.
The Premier is part of the Legal Branch of the Liberal Family Tree.
His law firm is part of the Happy Liberal Family.
One member of the firm is also a member of the Government
Temperance Commission. A brother of a member of the firm is a
representative of a liquor firm.
Now the fellow who is on the Temperance Commission is also Pensions
Advocate for the Department of Veterans' Affairs. Another member
of the Premier's law firm is Crown Prosecutor for Queens County
(and it's rumored soon to be for Kings too). The Premier is also
Attorney General. The Premier's brother is not a member of the law
firm; he is one-half of a contracting business. Last year the
Government paid this contracting business more than $400,000
for services rendered. So . . .
If you want to see the Temperance Commission, you'll see a fellow
from the Premier's law firm.
If you want to see about a veteran's pension, you see a man from
the Premier's law firm.
If you're hailed into court, you'll be prosecuted by a fellow who's a
member of the Premier's law firm.
If you want to enjoy some Liberal patronage, you can see the Premier.

178

If you want to see the Attorney General, see the Premier.
If you want a job on a government contract, see the Premier's brother.
But if you want Good Government on Prince Edward Island,
you'd better come and see us.
Vote Conservative on May 25th!

21

*There would be a new house and new people to choose from, and our
aim should be to enlarge the bounds of our party so as to embrace
every person desirous of being counted as a "progressive Conservative,"
and who will join in a series of measures to put an end to the corruption
which has ruined the present Government and debauched all
its followers.*

John A. Macdonald
February 9, 1854

DESPITE THE BLUNTNESS OF THE DEFEAT IN PRINCE EDWARD ISLAND,
Rowe and I shared a mounting optimism for our general strategy
throughout 1955. We were becoming increasingly involved with provincial politics, and increasingly bold in the allocation of time and
resources towards building a national organization upon a firm provincial base.

We flew to Fredericton to discuss with Hugh John Flemming the
impending federal by-election in Restigouche-Madawaska. Flemming,
his shrewdness now buttressed by power, would have preferred that we
not contest the seat, vacant since the death of Gaspard Boucher. His
argument was not easily challenged; the federal seat was traditionally
Liberal, although Flemming had won the six provincial seats in the two
counties in 1952. Because of patronage problems and the usual dis-
appointments and disaffections which were the inevitable legacy of a
new government, he was reluctant to see a test at the polls by the federal
party with a provincial general election now only a year away.

Besides, by-elections cost money and Flemming was under no illusions that if Restigouche-Madawaska was contested by the Tories, his
own organization and its resources would have to be committed. Should
the Tories lose, which Flemming believed the likelier prospect, the
morale of his provincial party would be shaken. It was not a risk he
wanted to run.

But Rowe and I found an ally in one of Flemming's ministers, Roger
Pichette, a Restigouche County member. It was Pichette's view that the
seat could be won with the right candidate. And that was J. C. "Charlie"
Van Horne. Neither Rowe nor I knew Van Horne, but we were impressed by Pichette's description of him—young, attractive, dynamic,
and personally popular. It was enough to convince us that, despite Flemming's reluctance, we would fight for the seat.

The question was argued for two days, Rowe meeting with Pichette
while I met with Flemming and with Carson. It was clear to me that

both were reluctant to be identified with the federal party. More than once this attitude was justified as being the settled policy of Ontario's Premier Leslie Frost, which confirmed its wisdom.

Indeed, it was the conventional wisdom: that Frost disliked Drew and that the Ontario provincial party, which continued to be a conspicuous success, disdained the family ties with its federal cousin, which had been a conspicuous failure. Try as he might, Rowe could find no allies within Frost's provincial organization. He knew them all, and they greeted him warmly, exchanged opinions freely, and called one another by their Christian names. But it ended there.

If the Ontario Tory policy appealed to Flemming, the knack of it eluded him. Inevitably, he discovered that political neutrality in federal politics made no impression on the Liberal government at Ottawa, which had become the natural adversary of the provinces, whatever their political stripe. Some were more natural as adversaries than others, but none were friends. Such was the nature of Liberal federalism, even if it was not necessarily true of Tory provincialism.

Rowe and I dug in on Restigouche-Madawaska until grudgingly, reluctantly, Flemming acknowledged that the seat would be contested and agreed to Pichette's advice that Van Horne should be the candidate.

It was a triumph of sorts for the new headquarters' policy. But more than that, it confirmed the essential reality of politics, and the basic motivation of politicians. There were, indeed, a number of conflicting opinions on the by-election but, in the end, after exhaustive discussion and argument, there proved to be only one common interest.

Flemming could not forget the significant contribution Rowe had made to his fledgling leadership when, finding him buried in the winter snows of Juniper, Rowe had promised and delivered the funds necessary to allow Flemming to organize his party. And although Flemming did not entirely credit the praise bestowed on me for my part in his election campaign, he did not discredit it either. He was now nearing the end of his first mandate; in the final analysis, it would be better to risk the loss of a federal by-election than risk losing the confidence and liking of two Young Turks who had been helpful in the past and might well be again.

And Rowe and I knew that in this crucial test of our policy it would be impossible to explain how, in New Brunswick of all places, the provincial Tories had refused to fight. But we also knew that once Flemming was committed to the contest, there would be more than the meagre resources of the federal party at the disposal of the Tory candidate. Flemming could afford to let the seat go by acclamation, but he could not afford to let it go to the Grits in an election.

Van Horne was nominated and, with Pichette at his side and the power and presence of an anxious provincial administration in full support, he won the seat handily. For the first time in thirty-seven years, Restigouche-Madawaska returned a Conservative. In 1953, the Liberal majority had been 5,542; two years later, Van Horne's was a comfortable 2,737.

Flemming, looking ahead to a general election in the coming spring, took heart. Things were obviously better than many in the party, disappointed over patronage, had told him.

With Van Horne's election there had been two other contests, both of which the Tories lost, both in Quebec, though there had been a conspicuous improvement in the Tory vote.

That Quebec had been less disappointing than expected was a pleasant surprise. On many evenings, far into the night, Rowe and I talked about Quebec. Against us stood the intractable facts of history, the countless misadventures, petty conspiracies, and a confusion of personalities jostling and manoeuvring for titular positions in a paper organization. The obstacles seemed insurmountable; and they were.

But there was at least, as a result of all our talk, the resolve for innovation. The party desperately needed a Quebec leader, someone given rank and station in the national party who could then command prestige and credibility within his province.

Leon Balcer had first won his seat in Three Rivers in 1949, with a majority of 51, and been re-elected by a substantially increased majority in 1953. He had also served a term in office as President of the Young Progressive Conservatives.

He was the ideal of the English-speaking Tory of that day as a French-Canadian politician. First, he could win. As well, he was young, darkly handsome, personally engaging, soft-spoken, reasonably conversant in English, a lawyer, a family man (with connections on his wife's side with Duplessis), and a record of war service in the Canadian Navy to further endear him to Tory traditionalists.

He appeared to be, on acquaintance, a tolerant and unaffected man of immense goodwill, lacking any trace of self-interest or ambition; indeed, he sometimes appeared diffident to a fault.

Why not Balcer as president of the national association? Rowe and I explored this prospect with some members of the caucus. Gordon Churchill, whom Hees had defeated for the presidency, was enthusiastic. So was J. M. Macdonnell.

Hees had been an active president and, therefore, popular with the rank and file. He was less so with the members of caucus who were close to Drew.

There was, in all this, a quality of meanness, compounded by envy of Hees' style, his good press, and suspicions of his leadership ambitions. The bruising struggle against Gordon Churchill for the party presidency had left wounds that not even a man as ebullient as Hees could heal. Now, with another meeting of the national association at hand, Hees, like most office-holders and office-seekers, kept silent as to his intentions of running for re-election.

Rowe and I decided to exploit the circumstances, and the silence, of the national president. We met with Balcer to persuade him to run–there was not much reluctance–and then drafted a statement for him proclaiming his intentions. The rest we left to the press and Hees.

Balcer's declaration that he would seek the presidency came as a surprise. The press found Hees, off skiing on the weekend of Balcer's announcement, and asked the national president the obvious question.

In reply, Hees said he had not really made up his mind whether to re-offer or not, but he didn't think he would. Balcer was elected unanimously as Hees graciously stepped down, and the national association had its first French Canadian president; in fact, Balcer became the first French Canadian to be president of any national party organization.

With care and deliberation, the product of endless hours of private conversations, Rowe and I began building an organization modelled on our own concepts and reflecting our mutual judgements. Throughout the Maritimes, we had already developed personal relationships based not only on political realities and the twinning of federal and provincial resources, but as well upon a common outlook and attitude. In Ontario, Rowe was at least *persona grata;* with Balcer as President, we believed we had fresh possibilities in Quebec.

I was producing a regular monthly magazine, *Progress Report,* which was finding wide acceptance within the party, even while it had its inevitable critics in the caucus. (The chief complaint was that it carried too much material about provincial politics and did not do enough to extoll the role of the federal Members of Parliament.) A young French-Canadian assistant was appointed by Balcer, with Rowe's agreement, to the staff at headquarters. Richard Bedford Coates, a nephew of R. B. Bennett, was brought in to assist me, and to act for Rowe and myself when we were absent from the office, as we frequently were.

We seemed to be making progress with Drew, so that when I proposed a series of "Second Century Dinners," commemorating the formation of John A. Macdonald's party one hundred years ago, featuring the national leader as the principal speaker, and presenting a select group of his colleagues and provincial leaders in concert, the response from Drew was affirmative and enthusiastic.

The value of these dinners seemed obvious: to stimulate interest in the party among its supporters, the media, and the general public; to provide the national leader an ideal platform, an auspicious occasion, a friendly audience, and extensive media coverage; to indicate the national quality of the parliamentary party by bringing to the head tables prominent members from each of the provinces (except Newfoundland, where we had none); to identify Drew, and the national party, with the various provincial leaders, largely to Drew's advantage; to publicize the party's inarguable historic contribution to Canada; and, by doing all these, to emphasize the new condition of unity in the Tory Party.

The press, at any rate, could not cavil over the legitimacy of the Second Century Dinners; however partisan some of its members might be, they could not begrudge the party the distinction of its past even while they might dispute its future.

There were four dinners in all–at Winnipeg, London, Three Rivers (the only place in Quebec, Balcer advised us, where he could guarantee a crowd), and Charlottetown, this latter being a recognition of the beginnings of Confederation.

In October, 1955, Rowe and I advanced on Winnipeg to enlist the essential support of Duff Roblin. It was my introduction to Roblin and my first visit to Manitoba. Churchill was anxious that we establish, at the organizational level, better relationships with this energetic new leader of the provincial party than those which existed between Drew and Roblin. It was not difficult, for Roblin was brisk, earnest, intelligent, and to the point.

He immediately asked Rowe if he would have the same co-operation from us as we had given Flemming and Stanfield. He, too, was facing a provincial election and he thought he could win it. But he needed help, "and I want you guys to come out here and do a job for me."

That, we told him, was talking our language.

The national party maintained a Winnipeg office, most of which was occupied by Miss Hilda Hesson, the "national director" of the women's organization. She and the office were a legacy of the Bracken years. Roblin had been granted squatter's rights on the premises and enjoyed a small cubby-hole for himself and a secretary. To make matters worse, Drew had "his own man in Manitoba," whose advice he took on provincial organization matters, who was largely unknown to Roblin's organization and had, in fact, opposed Duff in the leadership convention.

Shortly after this first visit, Rowe arranged for Miss Hesson's retirement and the office was turned over to Roblin, with the national office sharing the cost of a provincial organizer.

With these improvements, Roblin was genuinely helpful in making the first of the Second Century Dinners a success. But the occasion was not without its problems–among them, deciding whom to invite from the caucus to represent the party at Winnipeg. The head table included Ellen Fairclough from Ontario; Leon Balcer from Quebec; Doug Harkness from Alberta; Howard Green representing British Columbia; Duff Roblin, with Churchill's agreement, for Manitoba; Cliff Levy, one of Stanfield's M.L.A.'s, for Nova Scotia; and George Hees, the national president, to represent the party's association.

The triumphant Charlie Van Horne, elected but not yet seated in

Parliament, would be displayed from New Brunswick; while P.E.I. and Saskatchewan, having only one member each in the House, provided obvious choices. Angus MacLean agreed to come, but Diefenbaker would not agree, nor would he decline. This, we were told, was "standard practice with John."

And then, to our dismay, Drew fell ill and was taken to hospital. Unsolicited, other than by Rowe, I began to prepare a speech for the ailing leader.

Diefenbaker had not arrived. Van Horne had.

Charlie came into our rooms, resplendent in a light grey double-breasted suit, radiant with a wide, brassy smile. He was our talisman, the symbol of past and future success, the evidence that Tories could win.

The ambitious format for the dinner was not without its logistical problems: how to get ten politicians—the spokesmen for nine provinces and the mayor—on their feet and sit them down again, leaving enough time for Drew to deliver his speech and not begin with an exhausted audience.

It had to be managed. The speeches must all be short, and they should not be redundant, other than in their prophetic echoes of victory and the underlying theme of party unity. As well, there must be safeguards against the political gaucheries to which politicians, out of their environment and fired by the size of the audience, are sometimes prone.

Rowe sent each of the speakers to me to discuss what they would say. Some, like Ellen Fairclough, were already suitably prepared. Others were not. Some asked me to "write something," which I did, cheerfully. Two secretaries from the national office took dictation, typed drafts, then prepared mimeographed texts for the press. By late afternoon prior to the dinner, all was working with controlled precision. With two exceptions.

I said to Van Horne, "What do you want to say, Charlie?"

"I don't know," he answered. "Whatever you want."

"I want you to tell them about your election—and the support of Hugh John Flemming. We're trying to stress party unity and co-operation out here."

"Sounds all right to me."

"I'll write it out for you, if you like."

"Sure," he said.

"Come back in half an hour," I told him, "and we'll have it ready for you."

He got up to go. "There *is* something I'm gonna tell them," he said.

"What's that, Charlie?"

"What I said in my election campaign: the Grits are spending too damned much money on a bunch of peasants in India and not enough for the poor people of Restigouche-Madawaska."

I got out of my chair, concealing a twinge of anxiety, putting on my public relations smile, searching for calm.

"I don't know about that, Charlie," I said, allowing myself a light chuckle, as though enjoying his astuteness.

"Oh?"

"I think you might save that for some time when you're speaking for Restigouche-Madawaska. In the House, or some place like that. But this is a kind of national forum tonight; it might be misunderstood."

"You wouldn't say that, eh?"

"No, Charlie, I really wouldn't."

"Okay," he said, smiling again. "I'll come back and get my speech. You write it out."

"Thanks, Charlie. Thanks for your help."

The telephone rang.

"Hello," I said cheerfully.

"Is Bill Rowe there?" a voice asked faintly.

I looked through the door into the next room to see Rowe talking with Churchill and Roblin.

"He's tied up for the moment," I said. "Who's calling?"

The voice grew stronger, full of a disdain edged in mournful sorrow: "Diefenbaker." There is room in that word for a lot of feeling.

My God, I said to myself, he's here!

"Just a minute," I said. "I'll see if I can get him."

It was not good enough.

"Never mind," the voice said, becoming more morose. "You tell Mr. Rowe when he is free perhaps he might call me."

"Sir," I began, trying again, "I'm Dalton Camp. Sorry I didn't recognize your voice. We're glad you're here."

Silence filled the pause.

"Bill is anxious to see you," I went on. "Could you come down?"

"Oh, no, I won't bother him. I know he's busy."

The fool now rushed in where no angel, or wise man, would have ventured.

"We'd like to have a text of your remarks," I said.

"Why?"

Strange, I thought, no one had asked that before.

"Well, sir," the public relations man said, "it's for the press, and also it helps us with the rest of those who will be speaking–so that everyone isn't saying the same thing."

Come to think of it, now, that *was* insulting–no one said things that Diefenbaker said, or said them so well.

"I never have a text," Diefenbaker said, the voice distant, disdainful.

Another pause. "Well," I said, groping for words to comfort the voice, to reconcile the injury, to effect some personal contact.

"There's only one thing to talk about," the voice resumed.

I laughed, filling another silence. "Well," I said again, waiting.

"There's only one thing to say here," said the voice of John Diefenbaker. "Wheat."

"Well, that's fine," I said.

"Is Drew going to talk about wheat?"

"I don't know," I said, feeling the answer was somehow inadequate.

The hopelessly dislocated conversation ended, I went immediately to Rowe and Churchill.

"Damn it," Churchill said, "let's not talk about wheat. People in Winnipeg have heard enough about it. They don't want to hear any more."

But the problem was, I told them, that we had no text, and would not have one, and I was concerned that Diefenbaker would take too much time, so that Drew would be restricted by what he said, or in the time he would have to say it.

"I'll speak to John," Churchill volunteered. "But I'm damned if I want to hear about wheat."

He went off to find the banquet's problem guest.

Drew returned from hospital to the hotel, fortified by drugs, his wife at his side and his own speech in hand. Rowe preferred mine, but the national leader stuck to his own, dictated from his bed of misery. Running a fever, heavily sedated, this remote, uncertain man drew on physical resources which were depleted more than any of us knew, to write his own speech for an audience, more than half of whom he knew were opposed to his leadership.

Experience had made him wary of the counsel of others, except for a very few—perhaps only his wife and Grattan O'Leary. He listened to advice with dutiful patience, but made his own way, by the lights of his own will and wisdom.

The head table was a logistical problem.

It seemed to stretch, literally, a mari usque ad mare: Augus MacLean, Cliff Levy, Van Horne, Leon Balcer, Ellen Fairclough, Roblin, Diefenbaker, Harkness, Howard Green, Stewart McLean, the provincial president, the mayor of Winnipeg and his wife, George and Fiorenza Drew, until it seemed we would need to breach the walls.

Had we added all the spouses, there would have been twenty. Instead, we seated the wives (and Ellen Fairclough's husband) together, immediately below the head table. When the head-table guests gathered before dinner, Rowe explained the seating arrangements. There seemed to be cheerful agreement from all concerned. Most of the wives were happy to escape the head table.

Rowe and I sat in the darkened far corner of the banquet room and watched and listened with apprehension as our carefully managed pageant unfolded before an audience that was not quite capacity. The mayor brought his brief greetings. Green, with a few sparse, laconic phrases, set an admirable precedent for the others. Ellen had something to say about Ontario. Harkness was also a man of dispatch. Levy read my brief text, word for word. So did Balcer.

Van Horne was the object of some curiosity, as we had anticipated. He had a strange presence, an aura of uncertainty about him, with his shrewd, cool gaze, and his intrepid smile, half hero, half rogue, a broad hint of the maverick and a touch of arrogance. He carried my text to the rostrum in one hand and, relieved, I heard the familiar words.

When he had finished reading, he folded the paper deliberately, putting it in the pocket of his coat.

"One more thing, Mr. Chairman," he said, "down in New Brunswick we don't see the sense of giving money to people all over the world—like India—when we have our own problems right here at home. Thank you."

Applause ushered him back to his seat. He sat down, nodding to his left and right, smiling, pleased with himself. The son of a bitch, I thought, and I recalled speaking to one of his organizers after the by-election.

"Your man might be a cabinet minister one day," I had said, after congratulating him on the campaign.

"Not Charlie," was the reply. "He'll be Prime Minister or he'll be nothing."

And then came Diefenbaker, to loud applause. The lean, taut figure stood poised at the lectern, head turning slowly as his eyes swept the room. They seemed to glisten from some deeply felt, private emotion. He began slowly, as though searching for his words.

He was anecdotal, entertaining, warm, and wonderfully relaxed. He gathered his audience around him, held their eyes on him, his voice rising to fill the room, leaving the impression of an instrument of infinite range and power, seeking just the right pitch and volume for this modest family occasion. They laughed with him, and when they were not laughing, they sat forward on their chairs to smile upon him, glowing in their approval and affection. They had no doubts that he understood them, as they understood him.

The room thus bathed in empathy, the speaker allowed a dramatic pause; the smile left his face, the eyes glowed with a sudden fierceness. The audience waited, breathless, expectant.

"You ask about wheat?" It was like a whip cracking in the hushed air.

Thunder clouds gathered on the brow of the speaker. He turned his body from the waist, one arm thrust out from the shoulder, the forefinger nearly on the head of Drew, as the lightning struck.

"George Drew was *right* about wheat!"

188

Applause, rising from the tables, chairs pushing back from the tables, men and women rising to their feet, faces reflecting an enraptured warmth, while Diefenbaker took his seat, unsmiling, his head down, a look of absent bemusement upon him.

Even after the audience was seated again, while the chairman rose to resume the program, it was a long time before the laughter and the hum of conversation had ebbed from the room.

"That was great," I said to Rowe.

"You noticed," he said, chuckling, "that the bugger got the wheat in."

Then Drew, doing his best, attempting the impossible, to sustain the charged atmosphere left him by Diefenbaker. He was good, sound, sincere, non-abrasive. Few of his audience knew he had come from hospital to make his speech. He was not too long about it and, because of that, they heard him out, the deep resonance of his voice holding them as the words marched forward to disappear in minds already sated with speech.

When it was over, the audience stood, awkwardly gathering themselves once more to rise from their chairs, clothing sticking to damp flesh, various discomforts felt, a few dry mouths yawning, but a standing ovation nevertheless. Perfunctory, ritualistic, lacking the emotion of the response to Diefenbaker.

Looking at Drew, numb with fatigue and dazed with relief, like a distance runner after the race, and at Fiorenza, barely suppressing her anxiety for him, I wondered if they too sensed the difference in the reaction of the crowd. I knew they must.

Politics is theatre, and occasions such as this, the first of the Second Century Dinners, are as opening nights in New Haven.

On balance, the press was good, a verdict of significant importance, since it would influence Drew's judgement of the dinners, his confidence in Rowe and myself, and the attitude of the financial people who must, of course, pay the bills. Nothing is so expensive in politics as failure.

Editorially, the Winnipeg *Free Press* was disapprovingly sour about Drew's speech. But the news coverage was extensive and fair. Surprisingly, neither the *Free Press* nor the *Tribune* mentioned Van Horne's attack on the Colombo Plan, for such it was, although they quoted him from his prepared text. The moral was obvious; politicians who depart from a prepared and pre-released text are often ignored.

There were new delights in this for the members of the national headquarters staff. We had at last involved the leader of the party in our activities and, with him, others in the caucus. As our lines of communication strengthened, mutual confidence grew between Parliament Hill and Bracken House. It was easier now to get through to Drew, and to lobby among the caucus for support and understanding.

189

The more we came to understand Drew, the more sympathetic a figure he appeared. When he finally summoned the courage to dismiss Mel Jack from his House of Commons staff–to the advantage of both of them–the press attacked him with savage criticism. Yet, in fact, the two men had long before ceased to speak to each other, and Jack spent most of his time with Diefenbaker. It had become an impossible situation and only Drew, timid and uncertain in direct personal relationships, would have endured it as long as he did.

He was chronically understaffed, and when his private secretary died suddenly of a heart seizure, more of the fateful tragedy of the Tory leader was revealed. Rowe and Dick Bell were given the task of removing the secretary's private effects from his office. They found a desk jammed full of correspondence which the leader had never seen, much less answered, including two letters from Arthur Meighen, the second of which enquired plaintively why there had been no reply to his first. As well, there were sessional indemnity cheques, dividend coupons, and other personal matters concerning Mrs. Drew and the management of the household, all hidden in the drawers of the desk, much of it unopened. It could only be assumed that this vital member of the leader's personal staff had suffered a nervous breakdown long before his fatal attack and for weeks and months had ceased to function in his responsibilities.

Bell and Rowe sorted out the mail and Drew, with painful exertion, dealt with it, though unable to bring himself to explain the reason for the protracted delay in his reply. All of us wondered, and none of us knew, how long this had gone on, and when still more correspondence was found in the deceased secretary's apartment, it became clear that for at least a year, through some aberrational judgement, Drew had been allowed to see no more than half of his mail.

Little wonder, then, that so many professed to have been offended by Drew, ignored or snubbed. As I said to Rowe, God only knew how many people were walking the streets of Canada under the impression that George Drew would not bother to acknowledge a friendly letter, respond to a reasonable request, or, for that matter, pay his bills.

Drew quickly found a replacement, recruiting Derek Bedson from External Affairs. When Bedson moved into the leader's office, an era of unprecedented efficiency was launched. Mail was answered with awesome dispatch, appointments were made and kept, and copies of relevant correspondence, determined by Bedson's far-ranging and astute interest in party organization, began filling the mail baskets at headquarters. At long last, communications between the leader's office and his headquarters had become fully established.

The parliamentary party now rallied to fight a familiar, formidable adversary, C. D. Howe. The issue was the renewal of the Defence Production Act, a measure originally enacted during the war, re-enacted for Korea, and now to be extended for a further five years.

Parliament balked. Drew, at last, had an issue in which his respect for the parliamentary system, his procedural skill, and his stubborn nature were all fully employed.

The debate dragged on through the summer of 1955 while the opposition resourcefully exploited the rules, finally manoeuvring the government into the position where Parliament could withhold Supply. But while the government was up against the need for money with which to maintain its operations, the Tory caucus was yielding to fatigue. Some of Drew's colleagues were urging that he abandon the fight.

On a Saturday, at Stornoway, Drew held a reception for the caucus and staff to introduce Derek Bedson, his new private secretary. Rowe and I, and our wives, attended, standing in the garden under a burning sun, drinking fruit punch while the members drifted from group to group, wondering aloud if the opposition should give in to C. D. Howe.

Later in the afternoon, when the crowd had thinned and the sun had mercifully receded behind the towering elms overhead, Drew, with Howard Green, J. M. Macdonnell, and George Nowlan, strolled the lawn in a slow, wide circle; their heads were bowed, hands clasped behind them, foreheads knit with frowns. Four more stubborn men could not have been found in Canada, and debating their resolve, they strengthened it. There could be no question, as they finished their stroll, that there would be any retreat from the issue.

That evening, St. Laurent telephoned Drew to suggest a compromise. But Drew remained stubbornly opposed to the principle and said so.

On Monday, St. Laurent withdrew the legislation and the Defence Production Act lapsed into history.

It was, in fact, Drew's first clear triumph in Parliament. Celebrating at La Touraine, Rowe and I toasted further victories to come, and it seemed that Drew fully shared our optimism. Earlier in the day he had said to us, his voice ripe with prophecy, "We haven't seen anything yet. Wait until they bring in their pipeline legislation."

22

THERE WERE PROBLEMS IN SASKATCHEWAN, WHERE ALVIN HAMILTON
was the party's organizer, his salary and office expenses financed out of
Rowe's headquarters' budget. He was, as well, the provincial leader
and, to complicate matters further, seeking the federal nomination in
Qu'Appelle.

But the problems were more immediate. The party had a single
member in the Saskatchewan legislature–Robert Kohaly, who by
some mysterious and unique combination of circumstances had been
elected in the constituency of Estevan. Reports began to appear in the
eastern press that Kohaly was being wooed by the Social Credit.

We flew to Regina to reconnoitre the ground. We went to Murdo
MacPherson's home for cocktails; the conversation was amiably discursive while Rowe fished for information, about Hamilton, about
Kohaly, about the prospects for a moribund provincial party dominated by one man–Diefenbaker. MacPherson was hospitable, but not
very helpful or encouraging.

I met two young lawyers, natives of Nova Scotia, who were
beginning practice in Regina. They were homesick and eager for news
of Stanfield.

The Saskatchewan Conservative Party, they said, was a joke. No
organization, no support, no funds, no future. "Why the hell shouldn't
Kohaly go Social Credit?"

Alvin came to our hotel, bringing Kohaly as well as the provincial
president, Bob Svoboda, and Herb Marsh, the party's finance man.
We went up to our room to talk.

There were not enough chairs for all of us, so Rowe and I
stretched out on the two beds. The meeting began about nine o'clock
as Alvin undertook to brief Rowe on the state of the organization in
Saskatchewan. At eleven, he was still talking. Glancing over at Rowe,
I could see that he was struggling to remain awake. Marsh, Svoboda,
and Kohaly sat mute in their chairs as Alvin plunged on, through
thickets of elaborate and infinite detail. His cigar smoke hung heavily
in the room.

It was new to me, whatever he was saying, but my mind struggled
in vain to find the essence of it, to relate it to the immediate circumstance, until, finally, the conscious will surrendered to the drone of his
voice and words surrounded and engulfed the senses. I felt myself
going under, as though anaesthetized.

In an effort to rediscover my voice, I said I wanted to go down-

192

stairs to the lobby and invited Kohaly to go with me. Relieved, he joined me and we left the room.

I walked with uncertain steps to the elevator, my head throbbing, my ears numbed from speech, my lungs filled with smoke from Alvin's cigars.

"Well," Kohaly said, breaking the silence between us. "Now you know my problem."

Alvin was his problem. Not the Social Credit overtures, which were real enough, but not welcomed. Alvin, his Pygmalion, was the problem.

"During the sessions," Kohaly said, lament in his voice, "Alvin does the research, writes my speeches, watches over me from the gallery, calls press conferences and answers the questions, issues statements to the papers."

Poor Kohaly. Anyway, now I understood. He was the lone member, a caucus of one, buried under the weight of the party's organizer, the party's leader, and an earnestly relentless tide of good intentions which were, in simple terms, driving him out of his mind.

I asked Kohaly for his solution. He thought it would be helpful if Alvin either resigned as provincial leader, or as organizer, or removed himself from federal politics. Or, at least, that responsibilities be reassigned so that Kohaly could act and speak for himself in the legislature.

I promised him that we would help clarify these matters. He promised that he would end any further speculation as to his joining another party. We returned to the room.

Rowe gave me a look of entrenched pain and sorrow while Alvin continued talking, like a man released from solitude, until his associates finally rose to their feet to insist that we conclude our meeting.

When they had left, I opened the window to fill the room with fresh, chill air. Outside, in the silent streets, the wind tossed random snowflakes against the lights.

"How did you make out with Kohaly?" Rowe asked me.

I told him.

"My God, I feel sorry for that poor son of a bitch," said Rowe. Then he was asleep.

Between us, we had reconnoitred nearly all of the Progressive Conservative Party, exploring a good deal of it together. Our view of it represented, in all probability, a broader perspective than anyone else could have, with a unique knowledge of its complex component parts and its strengths and weaknesses.

In Saskatchewan, our judgement was to let Alvin Hamilton go. There could be no wisdom in prolonging this kind of decision. The Regina office had become a drain on the resources of the national office; Hamilton had become a strain on Kohaly who, apart from

Diefenbaker, was all the party had to represent it in the province. And Hamilton, for all his compulsive talk, his files and index cards, charts, graphs, and vote projections, was a misallocated resource. If that relentless energy were applied to a single federal constituency–who knows? Perhaps Alvin could win Qu'Appelle.

Limp with fatigue, we arrived back in Ottawa determined to complete our mission. We found Drew at Stornoway, meeting with Macdonnell and Donald Fleming. When we raised the subject of Saskatchewan, Drew took us off into the privacy of another room. The three of us took turns pacing the floor, while Rowe reported on Kohaly. Drew was relieved to be told he would stick, but he seemed uneasy about our recommendation that Hamilton be removed as party organizer.

He listened, standing still in the middle of the room, blinking, his tongue playing on the inside of his cheek. "By God," he said, distantly, "I don't think you should do anything until you've talked to Diefenbaker."

When it was discussed with Macdonnell, he agreed with us, and with Drew. Macdonnell said he would speak to Davie Fulton, the best caucus communicant with Diefenbaker, who would then discuss the subject of Hamilton with him. We left it at that and, having done so, nothing was heard of it again.

Politics has its own peculiar hours–some public, some private. The hours for political business begin, feebly, at lunch and continue to midnight, or beyond. These are not the hours of party leaders or ministers, more largely engaged in public enterprise, but for those who toil for them.

Breakfast was simply coffee at the office, late in the morning, and with the coffee a glance at the morning mail. Most of it would consist of faint signals from the hinterlands, requests for speakers, literature, policy–"Dear Sir, Please send me a brochure telling me what the Conservative Party stands for." The reply would be a precise statement by Donald Fleming–announcements of constituency meetings, the elections of officers, copies of correspondence from the leader's office, and bills.

The principal means of political communication is not the mail, but the telephone. Pink slips from the switchboard collected in neat piles on Rowe's desk–Call Mr. Bedson, call Mr. Macdonnell, call the bank, call "Your Father," call Blair Fraser–and always there was a half-hour spent before lunch returning calls.

Then up the hill to the parliamentary dining room, or for sandwiches in a member's office, or a longer, more leisurely meal at La Touraine or the Chateau Grill. It is invariably liquid–martinis, or Rob Roys, or, if in members' offices, straight Scotch over ice, and "just a little water."

194

"The secret of success in politics," Beaverbrook said, "is good health." Politics makes demands on the constitution, all those compulsive cups of coffee, rich foods, lashings of booze, the enervating, debilitating, sedentary routines of sitting and talking, smoking, drinking, talking.

Some manage more ascetic lives, disdaining alcohol and tobacco, keeping to their parliamentary timetable, going to their beds when the House rises. But Parliament has a dozen drinking clubs which convene at noon, at six, after ten—while the messenger staff runs to and fro, fetching bottles in plain brown paper bags, to be stored in filing cabinets until they are drained by the anxious thirst of men in politics.

Rowe wore a medallion around his neck, inscribed with the words: "Allergic to Penicillin." There were politicians who should have worn legends reading: "Allergic to Seagram's V.O." or "Do not give me Dewar's." And yet, in this endless sequential routine of drink, dine, talk, and drink some more, how good it was to be young, strong, and endlessly fascinated.

The habits of politics must shorten many lives, as it breaks the careers of others, but there remains a hard core of survivors whose stamina is tribute to what the human constitution can endure.

In the winter of 1955-56, Rowe and I lived hard, bruising lives, preoccupied with the growing strength of the Tory Party and, of course, confident of our part and powers in it. The Second Century Dinners had been a success, Drew had enjoyed an encouraging tour of the Maritimes, almost everyone seemed satisfied. But, of course, not everyone.

One should always be prepared for that. I was concluding another productive week in Ottawa. It was Thursday and I had left Nowlan's office to go to the parliamentary cafeteria, fifth floor, Centre Block. It was during the afternoon coffee break, and when I came in I saw some of the gallery press sitting at the long table near the coffee urns and the cash register. I decided to take my coffee with them.

"Mr. Camp," a sweet voice called.

It was Olive Diefenbaker, smiling, with John; they were sitting alone, near the door. I returned the smile, saying hello, but I had seen Arthur Blakely and wanted to talk to him.

"Sit down," Diefenbaker said. "I want to tell you something."

Well, it had been a good week and perhaps he would make it even better.

I had not seen him since the dinner in Winnipeg, and never in my life before that, and when I sat down, it occurred to me that our last conversation had been ridiculous. Maybe he remembered it, and maybe we would do something to repair it.

"I don't want my wife to be insulted again, you understand?"

He was looking at me, or through me, but I was almost certain I

195

had heard him right. Frantically, the mind raced ahead of the tongue in search of clues to the insult to Olive Diefenbaker.

I looked at Olive who looked down into her teacup, half smiling.

"I don't understand," I said, and I could not have been more truthful.

"I don't blame you," Diefenbaker said. "I know how they do these things, but I want you to know."

"Yes, sir," I said, feeling myself slipping into an abyss of incomprehension.

"I want you to know that wherever I go, my wife goes." His voice was low, quavering, menacing.

"I don't understand," I said, looking at him.

Olive said, "Now, John, he doesn't understand."

"I mean Winnipeg," he said. "If I'm asked to sit at the head table, my wife sits with me. You see, that's the way it is with me. My wife does not sit below the salt."

Ah, the head table at Winnipeg! Relieved, I began to explain. "The trouble was," I said, "there were too many people for the head table. We had to ask all the wives to sit together at another table."

"I believe Mrs. Drew was at the head table," Diefenbaker said, a debater's note of triumph in his voice.

"She was the only exception," I said. "Except the mayor's wife."

"John," Mrs. Diefenbaker said, smiling at me, "Mr. Camp has explained it couldn't be helped. Let's not talk about it."

"Just a minute," he said. "I know how these things happen. But I want you to know, you see, there will never be a next time. That's all. If my wife can't be there, then I won't be there. Is that clear?"

"All right, John," his wife said.

"I'm sorry," I said.

"I just want you to know," he said.

"Nice to see you again," I lied to them, getting up from the table, going out the door.

What a strange man, I thought, recalling what I knew of him, which was not much, only that the press was now writing his political obituary. He had lost his chance, they were saying; he was drifting away from the centre of power in his party, his voice less frequently heard, and he was growing old (the damp of crocodile tears staining the pages), and younger men, like Donald Fleming, were moving to the fore.

How little it mattered, though–Diefenbaker's pique, the speculation as to successors–when all around us were the signs of progress, like a long spring, bringing fresh bloom to faded hopes. And I found myself inextricably caught up in the cause of the Conservative Party, as though it were my own, and hostage to its fortunes, good and bad. But I was certain they were good, and becoming better.

196

23

IN JUNE OF 1956 FLEMMING WON AGAIN IN NEW BRUNSWICK. AND once again I managed the publicity campaign from the Lord Beaverbrook Hotel. It was a unique experience; rather than attacking a government I was now defending one, and I came to know, for the first time, the perquisites of office, of having greater means, of the leverage of patronage and the other multitudinous advantages of power.

There was a deceptive ease about it. In York County, without McNair leading the Liberals, and with Dr. Chalmers now a candidate, the local Tory organization poured it on–a massive advertising budget, an extravagant poll organization, and on election day, a flood of rum and two-dollar bills.

Michael Wardell, publisher of the *Daily Gleaner*, proved to be a remorseless ally. His was a different newspaper from the *Gleaner* of four years ago, when it had been blandly Liberal. Now Wardell's editorial pages belched forth salvoes of praise for the Flemming government, and laid heavy fire on the Grits.

The campaign was fought on Flemming's decision to build a thirty-million-dollar dam on the upper Saint John River at Beechwood. Reluctantly, the Liberals had given the project their support in the legislature, conscripted to it by a government motion which demanded a simple "aye" or "nay"; the "ayes" had it, although one factious Liberal claimed the dam would be unproductive because "there's not enough water in the Saint John River to float a straw hat."

Governments seeking a second term are difficult to deny; their opposition is seldom reorganized after defeat; citizens are responsive to the plea that the new government "deserves a chance to show what it can do," the assumption being that one term is never enough; disaffected and disappointed partisans of the government party cease their grumbling over spoils and return to the cause and party discipline, impressed by the logic that the promise of future favour is better than none at all; the press is usually sympathetic, or at least passive; the impartial contributors to election campaigns lean with the wind, blowing in the government's favour.

In many instances the government, with only one term of office, tends to fight the campaign by repeating the grievances of the last one; having had an inside look at things during its term of office, it can castigate its opponents with more authority and unnerving accuracy.

Flemming had reached the peak of his political prowess, in robust health, supremely confident, enjoying widespread personal popularity. He had been judicious about the re-allocation of patronage, to the dismay of some, but generous enough to neutralize many Liberal supporters who, to their immense relief, found themselves with the new government still as a client. There was an expansive road-building program, Beechwood was underway, and there was a good deal of construction and building in the public sector. Times were good. Flemming's simple theme of "Power, progress, and prosperity" appealed to the merchants and entrepreneurs, and our slogan, "Carry On, Hugh John!" struck most as sensible. The government had even reduced the sales tax by one per cent.

At fifty-seven years of age, Flemming was possessed of seemingly limitless animal energy. A picture of relaxed, smiling strength and poise, he moved about the province fully in command, beaming upon his constituents, grasping every outstretched hand, exuding goodwill and optimism.

And when he had won handily a second time, a disgruntled Fredericton Grit had said to Ralph Hay, Flemming's executive assistant, "Now the son of a bitch will be in forever."

I, among many, had little doubt of it. The campaign had been surprisingly easy. For the first time, I was not alone in the Beaverbrook Hotel, but accompanied by Bill Kettlewell, who prepared the layouts and worried through the production details. The party also provided a secretary who took dictation, typed copy, and answered the frequent summons of the telephone.

In the common rooms of the Beaverbrook–the lobby and the dining room–we came to know our opposite numbers: Richard O'Hagen, a public relations expert from MacLaren's Advertising, and a tense, dour young man from Canadian Advertising, Montreal, who was the Liberal Party's copywriter, and author of a number of bitter personal attacks upon Flemming. Both of them worked under the direction of Charles McElman who had not, we reckoned, improved much in judgement since 1952.

Occasionally, when we found them seated in the dining room, we conspired with the hotel staff to be placed near them. Then we would enliven our meal with animated conversation and uproarious laughter, made more enjoyable by glimpses of their bleak, downcast faces. Psychological warfare, we liked to call it.

I was light years away from Ottawa so that when, near the end of the campaign, Ellen Fairclough telephoned me from her office in the Centre Block, I was only surprised by what I assumed was her interest in New Brunswick.

"What do you think about what's going on up here?" she asked.

My response had to be: "What's going on up there?"

It was, of course, the pipeline debate; Donald Fleming had been expelled from the House and Ellen had, at the next sitting, draped his vacant desk with the Canadian Ensign while Donald had flown back to Toronto to a hero's welcome and a tumultuous public meeting. The escalation of the debate, the absorbing interest in it in Upper Canada, and the thunderous disapproval of the government's handling of the issue expressed by the press had escaped notice in New Brunswick, where the local newspaper carried little of the debate and conveyed none of its significance.

"Win your election," Ellen said, endearingly, "and hurry back here. We've got these fellows on the run."

Flemming won thirty-seven seats. The Liberals clung to fifteen, among them one in Kent, which some Tories had hoped to carry because of an imagined split among the Liberals. Instead, the seat was won by a thirty-year old unknown, Louis J. Robichaud.

When the count was all in, after the victory toasts and after the special celebration of Chalmers' overwhelming triumph in York (the Liberals had also lost their deposits against Flemming and his colleagues in Carleton), as the night fell silent, those who won and those who lost made common cause in exhausted sleep.

In moments of great exhilaration, anxiety tugs at the sleeve of celebrants like myself.

Elections—the Grand Guignol of politics—in which I had come so unexpectedly to play so large a part (this was my eighth, including the early Liberal ones), were a fascination, a struggle of wits and skills, a clash of armies, a test of will and nerve, a challenge to ingenuity. So inviting to the tactician (and the rhetorician), a challenge to his judgement in a contest in which, unlike so much human activity, there was a clear, sharply defined conclusion, a result whereby those who triumphed and those who failed were, after counting the ballots, identified.

Below my window, silhouetted in the darkness, a warning navigation light glowed dully from a girder along the familiar span of the old CN railway bridge that hovered over the river. From there, below the light, Byron Priestman, having survived the war, had leapt to his death in another earlier spring, in a futile effort to rescue two youths from drowning.

He had been a promisingly brilliant physics professor and I remembered as a student seeing his serious, lean face, the trim, athletic frame, on the campus. Now I could only remember his name, and the heroic self-abandonment of his act, and their finding him deep in the fierce cold of the river, one of the boys held in his arms.

I am never able to look on the bridge without thinking of Priestman, whoever he was, and having thought of him again, the mind becomes reflective, turning to politics, and, on this occasion, the evening's celebration of the mindless, easy victory, the self-satisfaction

199

suddenly touched by introspection, the wine turning sour. Hugh John Flemming, thirty-seven, Austin Taylor, fifteen. Dalton Camp, thirty-seven, Richard O'Hagen, fifteen. New Brunswick, thirty-seven, New Brunswick, fifteen. Byron Priestman zero.

He had been walking for exercise on a weekend in the early spring. The ice had just gone from the river, leaving it to swell upon its banks, turbulent, black, and impenetrably cold. He started across the bridge, following two boys—perhaps he went to warn them—but reaching the centre span he heard and saw them in the water. And then he jumped from the bridge to join them in death.

In the bloodless wars of politics, the wounds are to pride and place. In such activity, men easily exaggerate their relevance to it. More than that, once caught up in it, the significance of politics becomes disproportionate to their lives. To many, I suspect, their importance to themselves, as to others, lies in their being politicians. One would wish it to be the other way round—that their importance as politicians lies in men being themselves, true to their best impulse and finest ideals, less concerned with the victory of a party as they are more concerned with the survival of their own personality and nature.

But party politics feeds and flourishes upon the blood of sublimation. Every man must serve another's larger cause, giving or lending himself in whole or in part to another judgement, a further condition, a greater good, a lesser will, a common motive and purpose, and these replace his own criteria, the immediacy of his own conscience, until his own moral nature becomes a mere accessory to the cause, which is no more his than his neighbour's, but the product of some ill-defined greater good and lesser evil.

In the trackless wastes of politics, men lose their purpose, and the stars by which they once steered vanish in the bottomless sky of other men's aspirations. They wander like nomads, from oasis to oasis, quenching their thirst from the wells of power and warming themselves by the abandoned fires of those who have come and gone before.

24

THROUGHOUT THE EARLY SPRING IN 1956, THE OPPOSITION LAY IN WAIT
for the government of Canada to introduce its legislation providing
financial assistance to the American builders of the trans-Canada pipeline. According to some assessments of the government's policy, it
meant that the promoters could finance a $200 million project with only
$8 million of their own money, but employing $80 million loaned by the
Canadian people. And at no risk.

As one letter-to-the-editor put it, "I wouldn't mind a piece of
that action myself."

Because of my involvement in other considerations, the issue
itself did not occupy my interest. Nevertheless, it demonstrated, even
to so distant an observer as myself, the magnificent personal qualities
of George Drew. While none of us knew it, it was the last decisive act
of his leadership, and fittingly, the most exemplary of his career.

Two months before C. D. Howe was to introduce the contentious
legislation in Parliament (introducing closure at the same time), Drew
had set forth his party's position in words which stand the test of time
better than most of Parliament's rhetoric:

First, refer the whole question immediately to a committee of this
house to obtain the facts and make appropriate recommendations.
Second, insist upon the reorganization of Trans-Canada Pipe Lines as
an all-Canadian company which can proceed immediately and under
Canadian control.
Third, if Trans-Canada cannot carry out its undertaking, then open
the whole matter and permit new interests to make their proposals
for an all-Canadian line, Canadian controlled.
Fourth, if it can be shown and I doubt that it is so, that part of the
pipeline must be built as the government asserts on this occasion,
then instead of building a part which could become an orphan
under certain circumstances in the future, let them build the whole
pipeline and lease it for operation under Canadian control.
By one of these methods, Mr. Chairman, Canada's main gas pipeline
can be returned to the control of Canadians as it should be. This is
our chance here in the House of Commons to mark a turning point in
the greater control by Canadians of their own resources.
Let this be a declaration not only in relation to natural gas but in
relation to our great resources generally, not in any spirit of selfishness,
not in any narrow approach but rather with the idea that as trustees

for future generations of Canadians, along with an export that may be carried out under wise and appropriate conservation and control, our main purpose will be the future welfare of Canadians themselves.*

Drew had been attempting to inspire his party to a national resources policy, while warning Canadians of the dwindling stock of their possessions. It was not yet so fashionable a view; the United States' ambassador, measuring the incidence of nationalism in Canada, found it so low that he felt no impunity in attacking the Conservative national leader as the principal carrier of it. His action would stand as a useful precedent for later and more dramatic incursions into Canadian politics.

Dealing with Drew's views with references so thinly veiled as to be transparent, the ambassador responded from a public (Canadian) platform:

A prominent Canadian in a speech of a few weeks ago reviewed the problem and expressed the belief that "Canadians should declare their economic independence of the United States." He warned, in a somewhat emotional appeal to his audience, that "... we are not going to be hewers of wood, drawers of water, and diggers of holes for any other country, no matter how friendly that country may be." In the same speech, however, he readily conceded that "Investment from the United States and elsewhere ... has been largely responsible for the pace of our–that is, Canadian–expansion within these past few years."
This Canadian also emphasized the danger to Canada of exports to the United States depleting Canadian raw material reserves.
In this connection he spoke about mounting Canadian exports of iron ore to the United States.
This type of problem arises frequently. It usually results in expressions of official concern or in diplomatic representation. Sometimes the cause of concern is eliminated; sometimes it cannot be.
In either case, there has been an exchange of views, every effort has been made to clear the air and, irrespective of final results, the fact that each country has studied and understands the position of the other is in itself exceedingly helpful.
Although in a free enterprise economy, capital is tireless in its efforts to find profitable fields of investment, it requires a congenial climate. To create the impression that foreign capital is not welcome in Canada ... would, I think you will agree, be contrary to the broad long-term interests of this country.

Apart from, and perhaps despite, Ambassador Stewart's intervention, when the Minister of Trade and Commerce introduced his Bill on May 14, he found the opposition fused as one in its determination to extract a terrible price for the government's policy and its procedure.

*Hansard, March 15, 1956, p. 2182

As for Drew, his love for Parliament and his nationalism were also joined and, though not many could have thought so at the time, it was as though history had shaped him for this hour, which he made his own, despite the diffidence of many of his party and the weariness of some of his colleagues.

The long, deep trough of calm into which the country had settled after the war was now coming to an end. For the first time in a decade or more, Parliament became central to politics, and many who had never valued its customs and traditions–indeed, knew little or nothing about them–now were persuaded to a sudden, solicitous concern, a sentiment urged upon them by press and radio which gave dramatic and extensive coverage to the tumultuous battle over a measure few lay observers could understand, in a forum which many had come to consider irrelevant.

The pipeline debate consumed no more than ten hours of Parliament's time and received final approval in the Senate by a vote of fifty to six, with one-third of the senators absent for the vote.

In the House the debate was terminated by closure, a rare device, in Canada's Parliaments at least, for resolving arguments. But before that, Donald Fleming had been expelled from the chamber, Mr. Speaker Beaudoin had mysteriously reversed his own ruling after allowing himself overnight consultations with government ministers, the opposition had expressed its complete lack of confidence in the impartiality of the Chair, and the government's image of competence and wise benevolence had evaporated, revealing, instead, a galling arrogance overlaid with a surprising maladroitness.

When it was over, the casualties included the myth of ministerial infallibility and the mystique of "Uncle Louis." The Prime Minister was now seen in a new and harsher light, with hints of irascibility, coloured by dotage, and the suspicion that he was not so much a father-figure as a figurehead. That Mr. Howe could be capable of intemperate and imprudent action was not surprising, but that Mr. St. Laurent could be so plainly impotent in the face of it came as an unmitigated disappointment.

One could not exaggerate the effect of all this upon the Conservative Party, which suddenly found itself, for once, allied with a majority of public opinion, where it could be said to exist, on a major issue. Roused from a lethargic fatalism, the party could see itself as a genuine alternative to the St. Laurent administration, even given the leadership of George Drew, whose original promise now seemed possible of fulfillment, for it appeared obvious that while the public might not, after the debate, have liked Drew more, it liked Mr. St. Laurent a good deal less. At the same time, Fleming, Fulton, Hees, Green, and Macdonnell had emerged as political figures of some national stature, as Diefenbaker could be said to have re-emerged.

And yet, it was possible to exaggerate the effect of the pipeline debate on the country. Public attitudes differed sharply between those who drew their political intelligence from the *Globe and Mail* and those who gathered it from the provincial papers, where the coverage was thinner, or from the feeble signals of local radio stations, where public controversy was smothered in the blandness of community enterprise and banal chatter set to music for working housewives.

In Quebec, the Maritimes, and on the Prairies, Ottawa was mysterious and remote, and the vagaries of parliamentary procedure, not to mention esoteric subjects such as pipelines and high finance, found a response, if any, more like indifference than indignation.

Returning to Ottawa after the New Brunswick victory and after the pipeline debate, I found the euphoric confidence in national headquarters and on the Hill both novel and puzzling.

Unfortunately, the entirely unique spectacle which would ultimately lead to the creation of an independent Speaker, some dozen years later, impressed the press even more than it did members of the House of Commons. Drew's motion of censure of the Speaker came to a vote on June 9, Friday, at four o'clock. Only 144 of the 263 members were present; about half of the Liberal and Social Credit members, a total of 109, upheld the Speaker. ("If $10,000 a year will not keep them at their posts–and will not keep them at their posts even in a major crisis–how much will?" fumed the *Globe and Mail*.) Only thirty-five members of the opposition supported Drew's motion. Half of the Tory caucus was absent.

If men residing at the fulcrum of events could respond to the climax of such a crisis by taking their weekend pleasures at home, why was it surprising that the country, and substantial numbers of the rank and file of the party, failed to recognize this valiant struggle for principle by a handful of the parliamentary caucus? By any standards Drew's leadership throughout the pipeline debate had been superb–courageous, resourceful, and relentless. Indeed, it inspired many, other than those who were close to him and whose duty it was to sustain and support him.

All this occurred to me after the event, during the summer, when leisure allowed me my own analysis of the debate. I had listened, respectfully, to caucus members who argued that this recent chaos in Parliament would be a crucial issue in the next election, and felt annoyance at my own doubts. A substantial element of the caucus had wanted to quit the debate over the Defence Production Bill, just as it was about to be won. Half the caucus would not lend its presence, on a Friday afternoon a year later, in support of an issue which went to the root and branch of the parliamentary system, at a time when the party's leader had reached the peak of his parliamentary prowess, and the zenith of his career of public service.

What, then, was the Conservative Party, whose cause so many were so anxious to advance? I could only conclude that it was not what I had thought it to be–the caucus–but something else, or somewhere else. Where I had found my allegiance was among the rank and file, a dogged, faithful, formless few who were to be found throughout the country, whose constancy deserved better reward than their elected members could give them.

The caucus, I then decided, was a part–and only a part–of a political party whose capacity for survival I had come to admire, whose dutiful, innocent loyalty I had come to love, and whose luckless course I was determined to help change.

Then, abruptly, Drew was gone. A good part of our activity in the past two years appeared wasted; once again, national headquarters seemed a doomed enterprise.

It should not have come as such a shock. Drew had been ill in Winnipeg; during the Maritime tour we had had to find a doctor to attend him; with increasing frequency, Rowe had been saying, worriedly, "Drew is not well."

When Rowe phoned me at headquarters in Ottawa to ask, urgency in his voice, that I meet him in Toronto at the Royal York Hotel as soon as possible, I did not ask a reason. Instead, I flew down immediately, finding Rowe in his room in the late afternoon of September 21.

Drew and his wife were elsewhere in the hotel, Grattan O'Leary with them, Rowe told me, as were Earl Rowe and Leon Balcer.

"He's been to see his doctor," Rowe said, "and he has to resign. If he carries on, it will kill him."

I turned away, masking my reactions with a simple four-letter word.

"It's a bugger, isn't it," Rowe said.

Indeed, it was.

It had been six years ago–in the summer of 1950–that I first met George Drew; I had come to Ottawa to see him, on the day Mackenzie King was buried, to volunteer my services.

I had not known then, as I do now, that politicians are besieged with such offers. I knew only that I had failed to help rally the party in New Brunswick, but the ego remained stubborn enough to persuade me that I could do something for the Tory Party if only it would give me the opportunity.

So, briefly, I met him in his office, ushered in by his private secretary. The funeral cortège had borne King to his final resting place that day, and now Drew was plainly of mixed emotions and mood. He had never heard of me, nor did he appear to know why I should be in his office and, for a time, neither did I. The funeral was a distraction, and so were the sudden developments in Korea which were now leading to Canada's involvement in war.

I sensed, on this most unlikely of days, the banality of my mission. As well, in the presence of this imposing, stolidly handsome figure, I found myself awaiting the resonance of the radio voice, searching for clues to the fierce controversy which marked his political career.

Minutes later, after awkward pauses and exchanges of unfinished sentences, I decided he was not, as I had read of him, a vain, posturing, cold, and bombastic man. He was shy, painfully shy, sensitivity showing in the uncertain smile. Behind the cautious, veiled gaze, I suspected, were clouds of personal doubt and anxiety.

"Well, see so-and-so," "Consideration will be given," "let us know where you are in the event that"—polite, platitudinous—"God knows they need help in New Brunswick and good luck to you."

But I liked the man, not for what he was, but for what he was not; he was not what I had feared, what I had heard he was.

Five years later, travelling with him through the Maritimes, I saw him as very few had: Drew among the people, prying away at the closed minds of his own party, unlocking the prejudices of bad publicity and a mean press.

"George Drew knew my fa-a-a-ther; Father knew George Drew . . . ." Sung to the tune of "Onward Christian Soldiers," it had been a popular form of mockery for a politician seemingly fashioned for ridicule. But on the Maritime tour, whistle-stopping by car, putting up in small towns, one saw something of the private man. In his underwear, sipping Scotch, the flaccid, pale skin of his arms reflecting the fatigue in his face, the speech more halting, Drew saying:

"What's the name of this place?"

"Where are we tomorrow?"

"I can never remember that fellow's name. What is it?"

"Oh, God, yes. I remember."

"Has anyone talked to Ottawa?"

Managers of politicians assume that their men are Titans, flawless in physique and indefatigable in strength. Or at least the managers plan itineraries as though it were so. I watched George Drew drive the roads from Amherst to Springhill to Parrsboro to Truro, wrenching himself in and out of various automobiles (local negotiations on who was to drive the party leader from point to point were matters of high diplomatic delicacy), gathering his mind to utter appropriate homilies in town halls, balancing teacups and shaking hundreds of eager hands, struggling to identify names and faces from the context of earlier briefings. Fatigue began to infect his posture, speech and manner.

When we had finally arrived in Halifax in the early dark, we deposited him in a suite in the Lord Nelson (the Tory hotel), ordered him his supper, and sent for a doctor. Neither Rowe nor I asked the nature of his complaint; it was enough that he said that he felt "shaky."

Rod Black had called me earlier in the day to offer advice as to Drew's visit.

"Now this time," he said, only a little belligerently, "when he comes to Halifax, have him meet the people that do the work. Every goddam time he comes here, he only sees Harry MacKeen. Well, let him meet some of the common folk for a change–the people who work their guts out for the son of a bitch."

When I found a moment to be alone with Drew, I passed on the advice. "They hope when you're in Halifax you'll meet as many of the organization people as possible. I gather there's some feeling that you see Harry MacKeen and no one else. It upsets them, I gather."

Drew, his tongue flickering in his cheek, pondered it. "Well, by God," he replied, "I think I ought to be able to see my friends."

The doctor prescribed rest, giving as his diagnosis that Drew was exhausted. But being a Tory, he remained in the suite until Stanfield arrived, making political small talk with Drew while Rowe and I fretted. Sometimes Drew responded and sometimes he did not seem to hear, and when Stanfield came in, we quickly ordered ice and opened a bottle of Scotch.

If Drew was incapable of small talk, Stanfield was worse. For two hours, over slowly sipped drinks, Rowe and I sat and watched the two men, frequently volunteering subjects for conversation ourselves when the dialogue of our principals faltered and flagged. We were like Boy Scouts rubbing two dry sticks together, seeking a spark.

Stanfield withdrew by ten o'clock and Drew said to us, as we tidied the room, "I'm going to bed."

We left him, standing coatless and tieless at the door of his bedroom, the weariness of the day etched upon his face. A half-hour later, I returned to the darkened suite to retrieve some documents Rowe and I had left behind us.

The connecting door to Drew's bedroom was open and, looking through, I could see the beds were empty. Drew was gone. I permitted myself a twinge of anxiety, but curiosity was stronger.

Down in the lobby, I asked Cliff, the doorman, "Have you seen Mr. Drew?"

"He just went out, Mr. Camp," Cliff said. "Mr. MacKeen came in his car to pick him up."

These were my thoughts, swiftly random recollections, as I sat in the Royal York with Rowe, both of us downcast and morose, reflecting on Drew's resignation.

It was punctiliously handled, without any advice from us, as though Drew had long since thought it through. The letter of resignation was drafted by O'Leary and addressed to Leon Balcer, the party's national president. I was to take this sorrowful correspondence to Ottawa and have headquarters make copies for distribution to the press. Until then, nothing would be said.

Rather than risk uncertain flying weather, I decided to take the night train while Rowe remained behind with Drew, whose personal plans were as yet unknown. While waiting for the correspondence to be prepared, and for the train departure, I sat with Rowe. Darkness filled the room, lit only by the dull glow of Union Station below us in the street. The hotel was eerily silent.

"What will you do, Bill?"

"I'll have to see the convention through."

"When will that be?"

"I don't know. Soon, I hope."

"It will be Diefenbaker."

"I don't really know," Rowe said. "It might be."

"Then what?"

"Back to the farm," he said.

"And back to the agency," I said.

"Don't say that. There's Nova Scotia. We can't let Robert L. down. We want to finish that."

"That's different," I told him. "But it has to be the last one for me."

Rowe went off to Drew's suite to pick up the letter of resignation. Before he returned, his telephone rang and I answered it. It was George Hees.

"I have to talk to Bill," he said.

"He's not here, George."

"You know about Drew?"

"What do you mean?"

"About the resignation," Hees said. "It's a terrible mistake. I'd like to talk to Rowe."

"He's not here, George, but I could tell him to call you."

"There's not much time. Has Bill talked to the doctor?"

"I don't think so."

"Well, my God, he should talk to the doctor. I just called him. He didn't tell me that Drew had to resign. I think it's important that Bill talk to the doctor."

"I will tell him that."

"Tell him I said the doctor didn't tell me that Drew had to quit. Look, he needs time, that's all. He needs a good rest. There's no reason why he should resign. I think he's making a terrible mistake and we shouldn't let him do it. Tell Bill that, will you?"

Hees gave me the doctor's number and his own, and said he would await Rowe's call.

Rowe returned to the room, bearing two envelopes containing copies of Drew's resignation. Puzzled by the Hees call, he dutifully telephoned the doctor.

Doctors seldom speak in absolutes, and they do not speak about the condition of their patients to strangers, but perhaps this was an exception. The advice was absolute enough, even though the condition of Drew's health was not elaborately described: If Drew carried on as leader of his party, he would seriously risk his health and possibly his

208

life. It was as simple as that. But the doctor would not say, pressed by Rowe as Hees had done, that he could not carry on–it was up to Drew, he said, and while he might survive it, the possibilities were not good.

"The trouble with Hees," Rowe said to me, "is that he's not quite ready for the leadership yet."

I left him as he began to call Hees, rode the elevator to the lobby, crossed the street to the station, and boarded the train, enveloped in a pall of gloom. Life had come unstuck.

The long, dark train journey to Ottawa seemed appropriate; I was in no hurry. An era was ending, a great design was to be abandoned, a chapter closed in many lives. "Politics is an uncertain science," someone had told me. But however uncertain, it was seldom unknown. Now it was. Propped against the wall of my bedroom compartment, the blinds raised, I studied the blackness rushing past the window.

George Drew knew my fa-a-a-ther,
Father knew George Drew;
George Drew knew my fa-ther,
Father knew George Drew!

Television was still a child; few Canadians had as yet seen it and some remained unaware of its existence. We had thought Drew looked appealing and convincing on television. His speech was too richly coloured for radio, and he was at his worst in print, where headlines consistently reported that Drew "Blasts" so and so, or Drew "Hurls Charges" or Drew "Attacks" such and such. In the linear age, as McLuhan would say, headline writers shaped political images, and opposition leaders, Drew especially, emerged as men who spoke entirely in pejoratives, living a life of unrelenting belligerence, sounding alarms and taking apocalyptic views.

The first reaction of politicians and their managers to television was to resist it. There were negotiations between Liberal and Conservative headquarters which led to an agreement that neither party would use television in American border cities for election campaign purposes. This left only the CBC, with its limited facilities, and it was generally felt that we would want to use as little of that as possible.

None of us clearly saw what was coming, which was a medium that would profoundly change politics, campaigning, reporting, and politicians themselves. Perhaps, had any of us realized its potential and its implications, we might have been frightened by it. Instead, we considered television a kind of extension of radio, which was important of course, but not nearly so important as the printed word.

Drew had been undone by print, just as St. Laurent had been created by it. Drew might have been recreated by television, just as St. Laurent was to be undone by it. Politicians, in the late hours, fingers curled around warm glasses of watery Scotch, like to ponder hypotheses impossible to prove; as old boxing buffs will argue whether Joe Louis could have beaten Jack Dempsey, politicians would argue if George Drew could have defeated Louis St. Laurent in the general election of 1957.

God only knows, they would say, but given the pipeline debate, the Harris budget with its meagre six-dollar increase for the pensioners, given C. D. Howe's half-jest to the complaining farmer in Minnedosa, "You look pretty well fed to me!", given Suez and the evocative passions it stirred among Canada's Anglophiles, given this harvest of campaign issues and, as well, the margin of superiority of Drew's television appearance over that of his opponent, the Tories might well have won in 1957 under Drew's leadership.

But I doubt it. The narrow victory achieved by Diefenbaker was fashioned not so much by the issues, or even by his superb handling of them, but by the fact that he had the enthusiastic support of provincial organizations, especially Ontario's, which Drew would have been unlikely to have enjoyed. Perhaps more important, the 1957 campaign marked only the dawn of television as an influence in election campaigns, while it signalled the twilight of the absolute predominance of the press. It is difficult to imagine the English-language dailies being as sympathetic to Drew as they were, in the event, to Diefenbaker.

With the news of Drew's retirement from the leadership and politics, the caucus named Earl Rowe as House Leader, on the understanding, some believed, that he would not himself be a candidate for the leadership and would remain neutral in the contest. While Diefenbaker and Fulton proclaimed their interest, George Hees journeyed west to explore his prospects and, finding none, returned home to announce his support of Diefenbaker. Donald Fleming's candidacy was soon to follow.

National headquarters gave itself over to the task of organizing the convention, directed by a convention committee whose principal members were Rowe, the national director, Balcer, the national president, and Dick Bell, who agreed to act as convention chairman. As the candidates declared themselves, they were invited to appoint one member to the committee.

Its early meetings were routine and outwardly cordial, but there was a suppressed sense of tension, and conversation consisted largely of awesomely perfunctory little speeches, as though all were filling in time while awaiting a mysterious explosion or a rock-fall. There was a deep, widespread suspicion that Diefenbaker mistrusted the committee; not even his genial nominee, Dr. Blair, the M.P. for Lanark, could dispel it.

At the outset, I had expressed to Rowe my conviction that Diefenbaker would win easily—on the first ballot—and while Rowe need not be partial to any candidate, including the obvious winner, he must not be "neutral against" any of them either, especially the winning one.

Leslie Frost had immediately thrown his support to Diefenbaker, urging him to place his leadership campaign in the hands of Allister Grosart. A clear majority of the caucus was pro-Diefenbaker. Intelligence from the provinces indicated a strong preference for Diefenbaker, with the exceptions of Quebec, Nova Scotia, and Prince Edward Island.

But none of us at headquarters nursed any illusions; the guard was changing, and though we would see our responsibilities for the convention through, mentally we had submitted our resignations. It was not the most inspiring place to spend one's time.

My interests were not in the leadership convention, which I considered predetermined, but in the general election in Nova Scotia. Hicks had decided to seek his own mandate, and called the election for October 30. Relieved to escape the oppressive environment in Ottawa, I cheerfully answered the call to come to Halifax once more and do battle with the Grits.

25

"WE CAN WIN NOVA SCOTIA," I HAD ASSURED DREW, IN A MEMORANDUM written in the spring, "but it will not just happen."

On September 15, the Tories held a "victory rally" in the Halifax Forum, busing their supporters from all over the province to fill the place and hear speeches by Stanfield, Nowlan, Ike Smith, and Donahoe, and songs sung by Joan Fairfax and Wally Koster, two imported stars of the Canadian Broadcasting Corporation. The impressive proceedings were broadcast. The rally was a roaring success, as it was almost certain to be, given the fact that Black had organized the delegates and Finlay MacDonald had organized the program.

"The Hicks Government," Stanfield said confidently, "will be removed on whatever day it chooses to be defeated at the polls." Hicks, as though acting on Stanfield's command, called the election promptly and named the date, October 30th. The new Premier had received conflicting advice from his colleagues, but in the end he decided he should not delay further, even though two years still remained of the government's term in office.

There had always been something of the new broom about Henry Hicks, and there was no doubting the need for a thorough house cleaning, both in the cabinet and in the caucus. Hicks complained of endemic drunkenness among the members (before, as he said, it became publicly acceptable), and the cabinet of Angus L. did not suit the post-convention political realities. So, even though there were strong arguments against an election, the frustrations of another year of making do with misfits and left-overs loomed even greater.

It was a strange election; Stanfield challenged Hicks to call it and, obligingly, Hicks did; Stanfield predicted his own victory, which was not characteristic of him, but this was to be an uncharacteristic campaign.

The Tories were ready as they had never been before. When the writ was issued, almost all the candidates had been chosen, nearly all the polls were manned, and almost all the policy had been written. In Stanfield, the party had the anti-politician, the least typical of leaders, a man who despised rhetoric, disdained pumping hands, slapping backs, and making small talk. To him politics was a service, as service was a duty, and as duty was a family tradition. The Stanfields had held nearly

212

all the public offices there were, but none had as yet been First Minister.*

In Nova Scotia, politicians are either looked up to or looked down upon, and it was clear that most Nova Scotians looked up to Robert Stanfield. They admired his calm, and they respected him for his presumed financial independence–for they felt that a man's honesty was assured if he was rich in the first place, and thus more likely beyond temptation. And they liked Stanfield's plain, unostentatious manner. The quality of the chieftain matters a good deal to Nova Scotians. Perhaps it was all that mattered, because local candidates were invariably selected by partisans with populist notions. In the same way that hockey players were beginning to make their way into politics, local candidates for the legislatures tended to be men of some reputation in the community, successful as merchants, or doctors, or do-gooders. Thus, the distinction between one party and another came down to differences in leadership. In Nova Scotia, people wanted to be led by a man they could look up to, who had about him the mystique and the manner of the chieftain.

But it was a strange campaign; the most persistent recollection is that it was seemingly endless, while the fortunes of the Tory Party and the future of many of its members seemed suspended, between transition and hiatus.

One remembers the breathless, early autumn days, as summer lingered on throughout September, and the trees in the Public Gardens, just beneath the penthouse windows, slowly turning to rust and brilliant yellow, while at night, the thick, quiet rains drifted in upon the city from the ocean, falling upon the dark streets, while the drenched leaves slipped soundlessly from their branches to blanket the ground and line the gutters.

The Canadian economy was still enjoying the momentum of the recent Korean War. We would be running against "never had it so good" Liberalism.

The Liberal Party had its advertising team of Cockfield Brown sequestered in the Nova Scotian Hotel. Cockfield was, as well, the agency for the federal Liberal Party, for a number of government departments, and, significantly enough, for the Trans Canada Pipeline people. One knew, therefore, what to expect: the campaign would be efficiently conducted, the material would bear the mark of professional skills, but it would also be bloodless, even somewhat alien.

*Frank Stanfield, the father, was four times elected to the Nova Scotia Legislature and later became Lieutenant Governor of the province; a brother, Frank, served two terms in the House of Commons; an uncle, John Stanfield, later a Senator, won a federal by-election in Colchester in 1907 to become the only Conservative among 17 Liberal members then representing Nova Scotia in Ottawa. The family had also held various municipal offices.

It takes time to feel out a campaign. The effectiveness of political strategy depends upon intelligence, upon information received of the enemy's intentions before he intends that you know of them. One of the early harbingers of victory is the presence of informants, eager to leak plans to the opposition.

Thus, late one evening, a stranger mounts the stairs of the penthouse, rings the bell, and stands in the shadows of the unlit entryway to hand me a thick roll of paper. I will, he says tonelessly, be interested in seeing this material. I thank the anonymous donor, and he disappears into the darkness on the stairs.

But he is right; it is interesting, this series of Liberal pamphlets on a range of subjects from agriculture to industrial development. They are all in first-proof stage, uncut, the ink still damp, with an extra-colour red. Each of them bears the campaign photograph of Henry Hicks on the cover.

The pamphlets expressed a state of mind: dull and perfunctory. But they contained a desperate cleverness–Henry Hicks, looking like a sombre general turned junta politician, wearing conspicuously in a lapel buttonhole his Second World War veteran's pin. The point this sought to make was that Hicks was a veteran and Stanfield was not. It privately amused me, imagining Cockfield Brown's task force seated about the hotel suite, turning over in their minds the advantages of their client's leader over his opponent. "Well," one of them might have said, finally, "he's a veteran." That's it, they assured one another. Put a pin on him–there must be one of them around somewhere–and remind the war generation of the service of Henry Hicks.

There is an assumption that the only politics of true significance is that within the boundaries of the West Block, the Chateau Laurier, and the Rideau Club. After all, that is where the senators, lawyers, and other thinly disguised lobbyists are seen to mingle. It is where the deputy ministers hold sway over their departmental dominions, and where just being there and knowing one's way about gives one so great a sense of self-importance as to be envied by others. But this activity is artifice–highly coloured, synthetic and like a plastic plant or a wax apple. And so it seemed to Nova Scotia's Tories, who were in the midst of a provincial election. To be nagged by the distant concerns of a national party moving to convention seemed to them an annoyance.

So when Davie Fulton came to town in search of support, he found that the delegates were not yet appointed and that no one in Halifax cared much about the convention, although Rollie Ritchie agreed to be his man in Nova Scotia.

As a courtesy, Rod Black invited some of his organizers to his home to meet Fulton and drink rum. Although the talk was almost entirely about provincial politics, toward the end of the evening Black asked

Fulton to say a few words. This he did, stressing his relative youth and the fact that there was a long rebuilding job ahead for the national party. He was heard in painful, polite silence.

Before that, George Nowlan had come to the penthouse, depressed and concerned because Sidney Smith had declined an offer, made him by Nowlan, Macdonnell, Fleming, and Balcer, to become a candidate for the leadership. Smith gave reasons of health and his doctor's advice. As a result, said Nowlan, there was no one who could stop Diefenbaker, which meant the party was in genuine danger.

Dick Coates, writing from National Headquarters, reported that "our friend, Gordon Churchill, has, in a somewhat shame-faced fashion when he looks at you, gone all out for John Diefenbaker."

Coates also submitted a memorandum outlining plans for further additions to the party's literature. He proposed that Drew's House of Commons speech on the subject of Canada's resources be made into a pamphlet. I replied:

I have the reservation that should we go ahead with such a pamphlet
it would be a presumption on our part that Mr. Drew's policies
as set out in that speech are continuing party policy. I am not sure
that it is our particular responsibility, at this time, to make such
an assumption. After all, most of us at headquarters are something
like lame duck senators.

I maintained a remote interest in the Ottawa scene, although occasionally I felt compelled to make contact with Rowe, reflecting uneasy wariness.

Memorandum to: W. L. Rowe   October 9, 1956
    from: D. K. Camp
... As I see it, we seem to be seeking speakers (for TV and radio
free-time broadcasts on the CBC) who are not committed to
Diefenbaker. Otherwise, there does not seem to be too much reason
for their selection. . . . I think we should avoid the impression
of going all the way down the line."

Rowe, like his father a great racing enthusiast, was sometimes torn between his love for racing and his duties at party headquarters. Coates reported on these conflicts with perception and good humour:

The convention is playing hell with the National Director's horse
racing at the moment. One of the most soul-searching decisions he has
had to make was his cancellation of the Thursday night race in
Montreal. This, I might say, precipitated a veritable crisis in the
affairs of the Rowe family. There were long distance calls to Toronto,

consultations with the Honourable Earl, telegrams, questions as to
who was to drive, whose car was to be used, where was Ola,
why was Butch driving his father's car and what car was his father
to drive, etc., etc. . . .

But the contest in Nova Scotia could not have been fought without
resources and, for the first time in a long time, because of Stanfield's
rising reputation and because of Rowe's unshakeable confidence in our
basic strategy, help was forthcoming that was of crucial importance.
One of the joys of working with Rowe was that he would keep his word
and honour his commitments. These are not common political
attributes.

As the campaign began to warm, he sent a brief, hand-written
message:

Dalton–
I have 'twenty-five' for you and Bob and if demands are made soon
and heavily I hope for another 'five'. Keep in mind the fact
I have to have 'fifty-five' for the middle of December for Convention
purposes. . . . I shall be down Thursday or Friday!
William

There were other signs of interest and concern with the campaign
in Nova Scotia, and my part in it. Writing from the Leader of the
Opposition's office in Ottawa, temporarily occupied by Earl Rowe,
Derek Bedson reported further on distant events:

I spoke to George Drew yesterday by telephone. He is very sad
and only regaining his strength by very slow stages.

Duff Roblin, the letter continued, had been in Ottawa to argue the
merits of Winnipeg as a convention site. He "accepted the choice of
Ottawa with good grace. He . . . prefers Diefenbaker as being best
from his point of view as a provincial leader . . . but he spoke to John
re the feelings of H.Q. D. said that there would be no firings at H.Q.
should he win. In view of Duff's concern about this, I was very relieved
to have so much re-assurance."

Two weeks later, Bedson wrote again and referred to Drew's
condition, but more encouragingly: "the chief [is] just beginning to
feel as he was last June. He seemed to feel that his resignation might
have been hasty but on the whole he was taking the blow in an admirable way. . . . So far he has not decided whether or not to sit for
Carleton next session."

Bedson's letter reached me in the critical stage of the long campaign, and I was touched by his references to my own thoughts and
feelings:

216

... I'm a bit worried over you and how you may feel on election night
if Stanfield does not win. Surely no one could have given more
time or effort than you in these past few weeks. Whatever result,
you have had the Grits running and–even at this distance–I'd say you
had an even chance of pulling off a stunning victory. I find it
frightening to see anyone giving as much of himself as you have
done for the Conservative Party. . . .

Even the New Brunswick Tories, who had renewed their mandate
only last June, demonstrated a surprising and gratifying interest in the
campaign in Nova Scotia. The genesis was the unfailing brusqueness
of Premier Hicks.

In the spring, St. Laurent had made a vague and general gesture to
the Maritime provinces, saying that his government would be prepared
"to consider sound and healthy projects" within the Maritime provinces, as submitted by the provinces and inviting federal participation.
It wasn't much, but Wardell's militantly alert *Daily Gleaner* grasped
the straw and Flemming, campaigning on the hustings, saw it as an
opportunity to advance his cause.

He proposed to the sister provinces in the Atlantic area that they
convene in Fredericton on July 2 and prepare the means and
machinery for responding to Mr. St. Laurent's "invitation." He sent
personal messages to the Premiers, each of whom replied tactfully and
gracefully, indicating a wish to co-operate. But not Hicks. He made no
reply to Flemming's telegram, and told an enquiring reporter that, "If
the Premier of New Brunswick, *whoever he may be after June 18th,*
wishes to advance certain proposals, we will be happy to listen. . . ."

The gratuitousness was not lost on Flemming, nor did it escape
Stanfield who gave a speech in which he described it as "a smart-alec
retort to a perfectly sincere suggestion" and complained that "the people
of Nova Scotia have been made to look small."

After his successful election, Flemming promptly renewed his
invitation. Hicks, with noticeable reluctance, was obliged to respond
this time, since the Premier of New Brunswick, "whoever he may be
after June 18th," turned out to be the same as the Premier of the month
previous. As a consequence, Flemming now could only consider Hicks
to be hostile to New Brunswick, to himself personally, and unsym-
pathetic to the general concept of Maritime co-operation. Certainly the
Premier of Nova Scotia could not be considered an ally in any confrontation with Ottawa which required Maritime solidarity.

Stanfield, Carson, and I, individually and collectively, observed all
this with disbelief. Before Stanfield made his speech attacking Hicks
for his obduracy, Carson had provided us with helpful background information. As well, the *Daily Gleaner* published the full Stanfield text,
since it helped Flemming in his own campaign, just as it furthered

Wardell's policy for which the co-operation of Maritime governments was essential. And it gave strength and credence to Stanfield's criticisms.

We found it difficult to understand Hicks, a man surrounded by troubles and enemies in his own party. Surely these were enough to satisfy the most voracious appetite for conflict. Why, then, would he go farther afield to seek powerful new enemies?

With the election campaign underway in Nova Scotia, Carson wrote in his own barely decipherable hand, informing me as to the thoughts of "a mutual friend who sometimes takes an interest in politics." Unquestionably, the "mutual friend" was Flemming, and this signal of his interest was a tonic to Stanfield and his campaign team, as was the sincerity of Carson's closing sentence: "I am following your efforts with prayerful interest."

Near the end of the campaign, an even more efficacious interest was to be shown. Flemming himself called to ask my assessment of the result; I expressed a guarded optimism, confessing that the view from the Lord Nelson Hotel rooftop was not the most advantageous to be found.

"How are they making out for other things?" Flemming asked.

"Other things?"

"Well," the voice answered languidly, "I mean for the things that are needed for a good campaign, and for election day."

"I don't really know," I said. "When you're fighting Grits you can never have enough of anything."

"Are you going to be there this evening?"

I replied that I was.

"Well, look now, you'll likely be getting a call from a friend of ours. I expect he may want to be of some help to you."

That would be wonderful, I said.

"I don't think we can get much done with that fellow who's over there now," Flemming said, referring to Hicks. "I suspect everyone would be better off if there was some change in things."

Of that I was certain.

Both Flemming and his party's finance chairman helped in Nova Scotia, and helped mightily, as much with their unmistakable interest as with the more tangible assistance they provided. I liked to believe these were the fruits of the national headquarters' policy of mutual co-operation, but I had also to admit that Henry Hicks had been a substantial help.

A Fredericton acquaintance, a self-proclaimed seasoned political observer, troubled himself to write a letter urging greater effort on my part:

My dear Dalton:
So sorry I could not have spent a moment with you whilst I was in

218

Halifax but I had no available time. My friend, I am afraid you
will have to get more pressure on there, I note that your opposition are
using CHNS and stealing the slogan you had here during the last
election "Go Forward With Hicks," I'd suggest that you throw caution
to the winds while there is still time which I am sure will bring you
the desired result. I can't understand why you don't feature the
one lane bridges since the roads are not bad–I'd even go so far as to
suggest that the Minister visit the N.B. Bridge Dept. All the best
Dalton–I just wanted to say how sorry I was not to have known you
were in Halifax until just before I left and to wish you luck–
lay it on heavy.

Anyway, the stands were packed with quarterbacks; some who
were helpful and some who were not; some who knew the score, as the
saying went, and some who did not. It was not always easy to dis-
tinguish the experts from the spectators.

"The following message is broadcast by the Nova Scotia Progressive
Conservative Party. This is Max Ferguson speaking. . . . The Liberal
Party has been in power in Nova Scotia for twenty-three years. Many
Nova Scotians feel that's long enough."
    The most familiar and best-liked voice in the Maritimes, the creator
of Rawhide and one of the nation's unique talents, opened the Tory
Party's provincial radio campaign with the first of a series of five-
minute political broadcasts. To Max Ferguson, it was a professional
undertaking and at a satisfactory figure; for myself, and for Finlay
MacDonald who had made the arrangements with Ferguson, it was a
coup of some significance. To the Grits, it was an outrage. But to
Ferguson's principal employers at the CBC it was enough to hasten network executives to Ferguson full of cries of alarm.
    When the regional vice-president of the Canadian Broadcasting
Corporation was made aware that the voice of his star performer was
limning Tory sentiment over every radio station in Nova Scotia (except
his own), his reaction was as to a crisis of epic magnitude, even for a
CBC vice-president.
    "You see," Max Ferguson had been heard to say, on the free air of
Nova Scotia, "after twenty-three years of one-party rule in this province, Nova Scotians find themselves slowly and steadily falling behind
the rest of Canada. . . . For example: the average weekly earnings
during the last full year–that would be 1955–are nearly thirteen dollars
lower than the weekly pay cheque for the average Canadian. As a
matter of fact . . . Nova Scotia's weekly pay cheque is even lower than
New Brunswick's."
    From the Yarmouth light to the Cape Breton highlands, listeners
were enthralled, especially Tory ones. But not for long. After just three

broadcasts, Ferguson was forced to yield to the pleas of his CBC employers. He came one evening to the Penthouse to explain his circumstances and express his regrets, aware that his withdrawal from the broadcasts would cause some difficulties. I felt a good deal of sympathy for him, reminded once more of the limits of personal freedom in the Canadian liberal democracy, and the deadly seriousness with which party politics was taken, especially by those who were alleged to have none, such as executives of the CBC.

However, three broadcasts by Ferguson were better than none at all. Finlay MacDonald took his place as the voice of the Tory campaign, and there was nothing but high praise for the enthusiasm and conviction with which he delivered my daily assaults upon the Liberal Party of Nova Scotia.

But the essence of the campaign, and its prospects for success, turned on Stanfield. Party leaders, like their parties, are an omnibus of the plans and promises of others. They are also the embodiment of the aspirations and avarice of hundreds, some of whom are personally unknown to them, but who see in the leader their own special opportunity. Victory in politics brings not only satisfaction to the winners, but also power and preferment, and ever since these were wrenched from kings and their divinities, the party leader has borne the burden of other men's hopes, their public ambitions, and their private dreams. It is not an easy load.

And now Stanfield, who on first acquaintance had seemed too frail and fragile a man for the ordeals that must be endured to succeed in politics, seemed suddenly to have acquired the mystique of success. There were few, if any, detractors. His supporters now looked on him to lead with the complete assurance that his way of doing things, his steady, unspectacular, and determined way, was the only one certain to bring victory. It was as though the leader had acquired a halo about him, which only those of true faith could see. There was no doubt that many claimed to see it.

The election campaign was scheduled to open at a nominating convention in Richmond County on September 25 and end on October 27, at a rally in Truro. For Stanfield, it meant twenty-nine days of continuous activity, twenty-five constituency rallies, six network radio broadcasts, and two television appearances. He began the campaign with characteristic calm and a quiet confidence, and finished in much the same condition, only a trifle weary of the sound of his voice, his right hand calloused, and his sparse wardrobe the worse for intensive wear. But from the start, he had thought he might win, given some luck, and he had anticipated that Hicks would help him, which, obliging to the last, Hicks did.

Most of us – the strategists and the more articulate candidates – thought industrial development would once more be the principal Tory issue. Although Stanfield had long ago taken deliberate pains to dis-associate himself from the family underwear business in Truro, he could not escape association with the name and reputation of a Maritime firm that had been stubbornly successful. The factory work force was not as yet unionized, a fact which brought charges from CCF spokesmen, none of whom seemed to be above invoking the principle of guilt-by-asso-ciation, that Stanfield was anti-labour. But there was also a general public belief that anyone named Stanfield must know more about in-dustry than a mere politician, and this belief did no harm to the credi-bility of the party's position on industrial development.

At the candidates' meeting, where the platform had been put to-gether, Ike Smith had submitted a plan calling for government sponsor-ship of a "Nova Scotia Industrial Development Organization," in which the public would be invited to subscribe. The government would, in turn, "match each subscription on a dollar for dollar basis," attaining a min-imum capital of ten million dollars. This, of course, was the forerunner of Industrial Estates Ltd. which became the most highly active, publi-cized, and criticized industrial promotion organization in the country.

It would be difficult to find evidence that this plan had any effect on the electorate. Hicks' Provincial Treasurer, Ron Fielding, said the pro-posal "went over with a dull thud." Perhaps he was right, although Stan-field retorted that "a dull thud is the noise that is made when a sound proposition comes in contact with an empty vessel."

It was Stanfield's opinion that the most sensitive issue in the province was the mundane one of roads. The leader, and his diligent adjutant, Smith, drafted a nine-point program described as "an essential part of the industrial and economic development of Nova Scotia." The first of these nine points called for "hardsurfacing, without delay, all roads in the province which are now ready or near ready for paving."

At this, incredibly, Hicks took instant issue, abandoning whatever strategy he may have had in order to debate a matter far too complex to be understood by the average voter. Instead, Hicks only seemed to be arguing against paved roads, which Stanfield appeared to favor. Worse, he appeared to be questioning Stanfield's honesty, an effort doomed to failure.

During election campaigns, provincial highways departments are customarily full of plans. Survey crews roam the roads, driving stakes along the roadside, leaving behind the clear promise of future improve-ments. Work is found for government supporters who possess gravel trucks; they haul their cargo from friendly pits to be piled on country roads where more men and machinery are employed in spreading and raking it. In many instances, roads are improved to the point where they are suitable for paving and, in almost as many instances, these are left to deteriorate until the next election, when they may again be im-proved, along with the expectations of the local residents.

Opposition candidates are seldom satisfied with the condition of the highways, while government candidates bear witness to the substantial progress already made and pledge even greater progress in the future. The politics of asphalt, gravel, and grading often have more effect on the results in rural areas than do the more esoteric issues preferred by the media, including taxation, education, and the personalities of the leaders.

Stanfield's first plank in his highways policy was shrewdly designed to match the politics of election "road building." When elected, he said, he would immediately pave all the roads the former government had brought up to, or near, paving standard during the campaign. Hicks airily dismissed such an undertaking, saying it would cost the province two hundred million dollars to pave all the roads "ready or near ready" for paving. Stanfield, he said, was being irresponsible. Given the issue he wanted, Stanfield made the most of it. To pave a mile of road that had been prepared for paving would cost, according to Stanfield's estimate, an average of $13,000. Hicks' figure of two hundred million dollars would pave all the dirt roads in the province – or at least some 15,000 miles of them.

For the next four days, Stanfield challenged Hicks from the hustings, asking him to support his charge with the facts. Was the Premier saying that there were 15,000 miles of dirt road now ready for paving?

When Hicks merely repeated his accusation, Stanfield sent a telegram to his adversary, releasing a copy to the press. It was dated October 1; the campaign had begun:

I am fully confident that to pave all roads ready or near ready to pave would cost only a fraction of the amount stated by yourself or of the amount stated by the Minister of Highways.

I have three times publicly asked that the details of your estimate including the designation of all roads ready or near ready to pave and the estimated cost of hard-surfacing such roads to the sum of $200,000,000 or $222,000,000 be made public.

I therefore again urge that you make public at the earliest moment, preferably within the next four days, a detailed statement certified correct by the Chief Engineer of the Department of Highways showing all roads in Nova Scotia which are according to the present standards of the Highways Department (a) ready for paving, (b) near-ready for paving. This statement should contain a description of each road sufficient to identify it together with the mileage under each of (a) and (b) and the estimated cost of paving each road.

The figures used by yourself and the Minister of Highways are inconsistent with information given previously by officials of the Highways Department and are unsupported by any data available from official reports of the Highways Department. The recent statements made both by yourself and the Minister are sufficient to create grave doubts in the minds of many as to the accuracy of official government publications and of statements of government officials. In fairness to both I submit that a detailed statement such as I have urged be made at the earliest possible instant.

The next day, the Liberal candidates in Stanfield's dual riding of Colchester sent their own telegram to the Tory leader:

In order to assist you in deciding that your proposal re paving is a financial and physical impossibility within the time you state, we would invite you to join with us this afternoon, when we could show you some of the roads in Colchester County ready or about ready for hard surface and which we are satisfied will receive such treatment within a reasonable time of our election.
To cover them all would be impossible with the limited time available. Please reply promptly care of 61 Inglis Street, Truro, giving place and hour you can meet us.

Margaret Norrie Hector Hill

Stanfield was entertained by this. Expressing the hope that the correspondence would be published in the local Truro press, he replied:

Thank you for your telegram. Unfortunately you do not appear to understand the issue in question . . . you imply that there is in our county extensive mileage ready or near ready for paving. This indicates some confusion in your minds between roads ready to pave and roads which need to be paved.

On October 3, Hicks replied to Stanfield's telegram by letter, sent by hand. We read it with keen interest, finding that it confirmed our suspicions and our hopes. Hicks' quick tongue had once more run him into difficulties, and he would have trouble getting out from under his charges that Stanfield had been "irresponsible" and "absurd and ridiculous."

Nonetheless, the Hicks' reply was the product of an agile mind; half of his argument was that he had not understood Stanfield correctly, while the other half reiterated his criticism of Stanfield's highway policy:

. . . Undoubtedly, the phrase "ready or near ready for paving" could mean different things to different persons, and the Department of Highways had no way of knowing which roads you referred to as being in this category. They therefore made a calculation based on the improved roads in the province which have been graded and gravel surfaced. At the end of this construction season there will be 7,786 miles of such roads.
It was, therefore, on this basis that the calculation referred to by the

Minister of Highways was made. This allowed the cost of paving in addition to some allowance for improving the base course of the roads in preparation for paving. Unfortunately, paving costs this year are running higher than the $13,000 or $15,000 per mile to which I believe you made reference in another speech.

Two days later, at a rally in Yarmouth, Stanfield devoted a major portion of his network radio speech to the issue. The campaign was now a week old, and the major issue had become highways (as Stanfield wanted it), and a public contest between himself and Henry Hicks as to who was the more responsible (which was the way I wanted it).

"In Mr. Hicks' letter to me," said Stanfield, in deadly earnest, "he admits the fact that he never had any estimate or any information from highway officials on the cost of paving those roads that are ready or near ready for paving. What he had done, he now says, was work out a rough calculation on the cost of preparing for paving – and paving – every gravel road in the province of Nova Scotia.

"Finally," Stanfield concluded, "let me say this. I don't propose to campaign for votes in Nova Scotia by being cute with the truth. We are going to talk sense and talk straight, and if we can't, then we shouldn't say anything at all. There is, after all, a clear distinction between a fact, a false impression and a falsehood. And no one can tell the difference any quicker than the people of Nova Scotia."

The general public must have been mystified by the precise subject of this debate; the phrase "ready or near ready for paving" is not one that contains either a ringing clarity or a memorable imagery. Some of our urban supporters confessed not to understand the issue and were anxious that Stanfield drop it. But it perfectly suited the strategy of the campaign that Stanfield directly confront Hicks over a matter of fact. In this kind of clash, Stanfield was at his best, and Hicks, inclined to be too clever and careless with his rhetoric, as are many politicians, was not. And in the rural areas of the province, the minimal understanding by the voters of the dispute was that Stanfield wanted to have more roads sooner, while Hicks was explaining, peevishly and rather defensively, that it could not be done.

"Talking sense and talking straight" became the sharp edge of Stanfield's solid, stolid image. Using Henry Hicks as the whetstone, the image of Robert Stanfield had become one of a man with an almost overwhelming regard for the truth and a no-nonsense approach to politics, a portrait of a politician who would not stoop to conquer and who would not employ rhetoric to hide the true nature of things.

There were other issues in the 1956 election, but none in my judgement so significant as this, or so instructive. One learned, if one needed the lesson, the value of simplicity and the dangers of carelessness. And one learned once again that the hardest battles to win are those fought on an opponent's chosen ground .

Henry Hicks was, in an opposite sense, as great a teacher as McNair. The Liberal Premier was no mean adversary; the confidence which he so manifestly exuded was sometimes discomforting, giving his opponents the impression that he had secret knowledge of the voting intentions of Nova Scotians denied to mortals. He was undeniably able, and very close to being self-sufficient – an important quality for a provincial premier. But Macdonald's fragmented, aging party was not a rich inheritance, and it was perhaps fortunate for the Tories that Henry Hicks had neither the opportunity nor the time to make the Liberal Party in Nova Scotia his own.

Stanfield, on the other hand, had built an organization with painstaking care and deliberation. The men closest to him, such as Smith and Donahoe, were politically gifted and completely loyal, while the organization – the crew in the engine room below – were young, strong, and enthusiastic. Of all the men around the Tory leader, George Isaac Smith, his friend and Colchester running mate, represented the supreme example of selfless loyalty.

Ike Smith was an ideal first lieutenant, equipped with many qualities which Stanfield lacked, including the highly articulate, combative, jugular-seeking sense of the trial lawyer. After its many years of docility, Smith's gifts served the Tory Party well in the Legislature. He was universally respected, as much by his adversaries as his allies, and he was also perhaps the only man in the party who could change Stanfield's mind once it had been made up.

But the quality all most admired in Ike Smith was his selflessness, a quality so rare as to be unique in politics. While Stanfield campaigned throughout the province, Smith dutifully canvassed every poll in Colchester. Perhaps because of this strenuous grass-roots exercise, he had an almost exact appreciation of the thoughts and attitudes of the average Nova Scotia voter. Almost daily, during the provincial campaigns, I would hear from Ike Smith as to his reflections – and those of his constituents – on the events and issues of the moment. These were distinguished by his remarkable detachment and self-effacement; his only concerns were for Stanfield and the party he led. Nothing else mattered.

Smith was also a crucial voice in policy matters, to which he contributed a practical, innovative, and informed judgement. His sense of the appropriateness of an idea to the time was unerring. For ideas whose time had come, Smith was an intelligent inspiration, while for notions whose time had passed, or had yet to come, Smith employed all the formidable powers of his advocacy, combined with his impressive capacity for obstinacy. (I tried, on several occasions and without success, to write into the party's platform a pledge to reduce the voting age; each time it was vetoed by Ike Smith. But as Premier of Nova Scotia, some years later, he introduced the measure himself which gave the vote to nineteen-year-olds.)

Short, slight, and deceptively frail in appearance – he was built something like a raindrop – with an inscrutable countenance and eyes that nearly disappeared when he smiled, Smith was a reminder of how deceptively nature may package the ablest, toughest politicians. He did not look like a leader, but men intuitively turned to him in crisis. He did not act like one either, forever deferring to Stanfield, content to be silent unless called upon, happy to serve in another's cause, and accepting without complaint the lesser, unspectacular tasks of politics.

The Tory campaign was further strengthened by Donahoe, whose resonant oratory was much in demand, and by George Nowlan, whose hustings humour was a formidable weapon. Wherever Nowlan travelled in the campaign, he made people laugh. Referring to a Liberal claim that Hicks had negotiated better fiscal arrangements with Ottawa, Nowlan told an audience:

To suggest that the Premier of Nova Scotia negotiated this new tax deal is to suggest that Sir Isaac Newton negotiated the law of gravity. The truth is that both of them were hit over the head.

As the campaign wore on, Liberal candidates began to edge away from their leader. More and more, their speeches and advertising evoked the name of Angus L. and references to Hicks all but vanished from the media, other than through the efforts of Cockfield Brown & Co. Ltd.

I monitored the Liberal advertising campaign with a baleful, militant interest. Indeed, I had a more belligerent attitude toward Cockfield Brown than I had for its present client. There were reasons. I recalled the statement made by John Hamilton, the Tory M.P. for York West, in the House of Commons during the pipeline debate:

I understand that the public relations director of Trans-Canada Pipe Lines is ensconced in Suite 514 of the Chateau Laurier Hotel, and he is the same man who was the public relations director of the Prime Minister in his last election campaign. I understand he is turning out some speeches . . . they may have been some of the speeches we have heard in this House.

The references were to the present agency of the Nova Scotia Liberal Party: the creators of the image of "Uncle Louis" and so powerful and influential a firm as to represent the Government of Canada, the Liberal Party, and Trans-Canada Pipe Lines all at the same time, when all were joined on the same issue.

Ensconced in the penthouse of the Lord Nelson, I considered it vitally important that life in Nova Scotia, where the politics was not quite so global as in Suite 514 of the Chateau Laurier, nonetheless be

226

made more trying for Cockfield Brown & Co. Ltd. When the Liberal television commercials first appeared, we immediately protested to Davidson Dunton, the CBC's president and the author of the regulations governing political commercials. In our view – and in fact – the commercials violated the regulations as they applied to restrictions against animation*; they were, for the period, slick and patronizing, which is to say they bore the unmistakable imprint of the agency's competence, as well as its opinion that they were being prepared for the eyes and ears of yokels.

Dunton, not at all to my surprise, dismissed our protest and allowed the commercials to be continued. But harassment has its own rewards; his decision further hardened the combative resolve of Stanfield's organization; and, for those who were aware of the controversy, the commercials themselves were seen in a different light, the mystery being how anything so trivial could, at the same time, be illicit.

But television was as yet too limited in its reach and too inhibited by regulation to allow the parties to make effective use of it. The media war was still fought in the press and over the radio. The battle reflected the strategies of both sides, and the state of mind of those who were the creators of the advertising.

On the last day of the campaign, each party produced large newspaper advertisements carrying personal appeals from their leaders, each prepared, undoubtedly, by the respective agencies. Cockfield Brown presented a huge, close-cropped picture of Henry Hicks, in his most authoritarian, junta general's pose, inscrutably, almost secretly, smiling, veteran's pin gleaming from his lapel, a neatly folded white pocket handkerchief protruding from his breast pocket, white cuffs flashing at the wrists. The first sentence of the Hicks' statement read:

It is my earnest and conscientious belief that a Liberal administration offers Nova Scotia greater opportunities in the future than does any administration which could be formed by any other political party.

Stanfield's photograph, square-cut, was far less prominent in the Tory advertisement. Unlike Hicks, Stanfield's pose allowed him to look directly at the reader. His first words were:

I believe the great majority of Nova Scotians have it in their hearts and minds that our Province needs a change in government.

At the conclusion of these appeals, each man's signature appeared. These, alone, offered a study of the two adversaries, and insight into

*"... film clips, film slides, music, animation, cartoons and still photographs may not be used," decreed the corporation, drawing down its skirts.

227

their distinct and contrasting personalities. I had no doubt this would occur to many others who saw the advertisements.

Elsewhere in the daily paper on that closing day of the campaign, another full-page advertisement carried the names and faces of the Tory candidates under the headline: "Nova Scotians Are Looking Here Today For The Leadership They Want Tomorrow!" As indeed they were. But, in truth, the advertisement was an attempt at conciliation. It was a gesture – and an expensive one – to appease one of the party's candidates who had claimed injury to pride and, he thought, to his prospects. The advertisement, when it had first appeared, described the candidate for Cumberland Centre, Stephen Pyke, as a "coal miner." Actually, the distressed Pyke, and his wife, told me by telephone, he was simply a clerk for the Springhill mining company. I confessed the error was mine, but this did not console the Pykes. To make amends, I repeated the advertisement in the next day's press, properly describing the candidate in Cumberland Centre as a "clerk." All seemed satisfied, and Pyke was elected, as he was certain to be anyway, even if he had been described as a draegerman.

Nova Scotians traditionally vote on Tuesdays, which means the final weekend of election campaigns is a test of endurance and a drain on already depleted resources of nervous energy. Fatigue and anxiety go together, and when there is nothing left to do, when all the deadlines have at last been met, in the sudden tranquillity emphasized by the silent telephone and the strangely tidy rooms, the spirit gives way to a nagging pessimism.

From Ottawa, Kay Kearns telegraphed encouragement: "On the eve of your great day please accept warm wishes for every success." Rowe and Coates sent similar messages, and a prep-school classmate wired from Charlottetown: "Good luck I'm with you." But these did nothing to decrease the tension which, by now, had settled in the chest, sending signals of pain whenever one thought of the morrow and the fact that the fateful decision was locked in the fathomless minds of three hundred thousand strangers.

Finally, when the polls have closed, interested parties gather before their radios, in groups, in pairs, or alone. And once again, the increasingly familiar feeling of dull weariness and apprehension – so many days, so much effort and intensity of feeling, so much at stake and so little left now to buffer disappointment. At this precise moment, winners and losers are alike in their isolation, equally vulnerable – and all stare at the radio, as though it had a mouth to speak, and eyes to see.

Alone in the penthouse, with darkness falling on the roof outside, a half-empty, cold cup of coffee at my elbow, I listen for the first returns from Halifax. Of the seven metropolitan Tory candidates, only Donahoe is leading. Even there, it is close. Elsewhere, all are losing. My God, we are going to lose, I instructed myself: Nova Scotia is Liberal, the same yesterday, today, and forever.

228

But of course, it was not. Halifax, yes, but narrowly so; in 1953, the Liberals had swept Halifax with an overall majority of 9,400 votes. Tonight, as the votes were counted, their overall majority had fallen to 2,000 – while across the province, where the majorities had been smaller, this marked decline in Liberal fortunes brought down the government.

Within the first hour, the issue was suddenly, surprisingly resolved. Industrial Cape Breton began to report astonishing gains in Conservative support. In the end, the margin of victory came from embattled coal miners, the steel men, and the hard-pressed merchants in the urban areas, all of whom had for years given their sentimental support to Angus L. They had no such feelings for Hicks. Instead, they turned to Stanfield, who looked to them like a man who might do something.

It is too simple an explanation, of course; it leaves out the personal pull of many of Stanfield's candidates – Pinky Gaum, a diminutive Jew who had been a Second World War prisoner in Germany and a genius in scrounging from the enemy; or Layton Fergusson, a legendary local baseball hero who was profoundly trusted by his peers; or Ned Manson (in whose drug store Nathan Cohen used to loiter and read movie magazines), who had carried on a one-man crusade against a corrupt and inefficient hospital administration. But, in the long run, the victory belonged to Stanfield, whose patient search had found the men who could win for him, and whose personal qualities commanded their loyalty and confidence.

It had been a big vote; almost eighty percent of those eligible had turned out, a crucial five percent more than in 1953. The Tories had polled forty-nine percent of the popular vote, the Liberals forty-eight percent, and the CCF, which held one seat, got the rest. And it was close. Ettinger had won Hants East with a "landslide" majority of fifty; the Liberals had won one seat by forty-five votes, another by just five; the Tories had thin majorities too – winning by three votes in Kings West, and by sixty-seven votes in Lunenberg Centre.

Over and over again, radio voices repeated the news – Progressive Conservatives twenty-three seats, Liberals nineteen, CCF one – the end of a twenty-three-year Liberal reign. Immediately, the clichés began to form – Stanfield, forty-two-years old, became "Canada's youngest Premier" (succeeding Hicks, who was a year younger); the result was acknowledged to be an "upset"; Upper Canadian Tories claimed it as a "national omen."

Finlay MacDonald called the penthouse, his voice enriched by a jubilant pride. "You better get out of there before you jump," he said. "Come on down and shake the hand of a man from Cape Breton." I went, taken in a cab driven by a Tory driver (we would all be Conservatives now, I thought), to find Finlay's living room full of employees of Cockfield Brown & Co. They were stunned, sitting morosely on the floor, injuries to pride being nursed by Nova Scotia rum.

"For God's sake," one of them said to me, "don't tell me you knew what was happening in Cape Breton."

"Why, of course," I told him, lying through smiling teeth.

Rod Black was only moderately happy; he sat on the floor in his bungalow, pulling reflectively on his drink, the house alive with the sounds of jubilant poll captains, scrutineers, inside agents, and drivers. He was not satisfied with Halifax.

"Imagine," he said, "those bastards winning the Northwest by 190 votes."

I suggested he return with me to MacDonald's and meet some of the genuinely disappointed, now in opposition. Black shook his head.

"Nope," he said, raising his glass and toasting the room at large. "When I win, I want to be with the people I win with, because when I lost, they were the only people around."

In Truro, they got out the fire engines and drove Bob Stanfield and Ike Smith around the town. Stanfield had the biggest personal majority of all in the election.

Before the long night of celebration was over, I had talked to my wife, to Bill Rowe, and to George Drew. As for the latter, I thought I could detect, even in the fulsomeness of his happiness over the result, a certain poignant tone of the sorrow of one who cannot fully savour the fruits of victory.

The morning after brought telegrams and long distance calls, effusive in their enthusiasm and praise. But it was a sad and strangely anti-climatic day: the red headline of the Halifax *Herald's* front page proclaimed the British invasion of Suez. Another headline signalled the Russians' brutal conquest of Hungary. Almost everywhere but on this narrow peninsular strip of land, men were mourning fallen hopes and ruined dreams. The victory in Nova Scotia barely made the front page, a news judgement with which I could have no quarrel. (And then, the following day, a "bump" at Springhill brought death, sorrow, and a profound anxiety to the mining community and to all Nova Scotians.)

Not long after returning home, I received a letter from Drew, written in his own hand:

My dear Dalton:
On the night of the historic election in Nova Scotia, I had the opportunity to congratulate you on your splendid contribution to that success. Since then I have been receiving letters in which the high esteem for your work has been expressed over and over again. Whether they have written to you personally or not I can assure you that the members do realize what a fine job you did.

I need not tell you how disappointed I am that I am not going to be actively associated with you in the months ahead. Whatever my

230

activities may be however, I do want you to know how much I
appreciate all that you did and the many kindnesses you have extended
to me personally. I hope we shall continue to see each other frequently
even though it will be in a different way. I confess I was looking
forward to 1957. I am convinced that the television is a decisive factor,
properly used, and I thought we would be working together devising
ways and means to make the best use of it. That is not to be but
I do wish you all success in that interesting and challenging adventure.

Again may I say "Well done in Nova Scotia." May the future
bring equal satisfaction and success.

26

THE CENTRE OF OTTAWA IS DOMINATED BY WHAT PEOPLE, INCLUDING
Mayor Charlotte Whitton, scornfully call Confusion Square, which is a
poor man's Trafalgar Square or Place de la Concorde. In the midst of
this chaos stands the National War Memorial with its cast-iron figures of
First World War soldiers, unveiled by King George VI on the very eve
of the Second World War. The most heroic building in this mid-capital
complex is not Parliament and its Peace Tower, which would be the
sentimental favourite, but the massive Canadian National hotel, the
Chateau Laurier. Its underground tunnel leads, like an umbilical cord,
to the railway station, and an alabaster likeness of its namesake, Sir
Wilfred himself, sits calmly in the lobby, a perpetual eyeless gaze fixed
upon the guests. Unless one is arriving by train, in order to reach the
Chateau it is necessary to first pass it and then return, as though the
hotel had its own gravity system; in a way it does.

In December, 1956, the Tory Party and John Diefenbaker are being
drawn together at long last, as 1,324 delegates and their alternates
descend upon the city to meet in convention.

Most of them have come by train, enjoying the economy of convention fares; it is to be, incidentally, the last political event of the year
1956, which is as well the last year of Canada's Railroad Age. And most
of them, stepping down from the sleeping cars to walk a little shakily
along the platform, are immediately apprehensive, secretly awed, and
aware they are entering enemy territory. In the sombre light of winter's
shortened days, amongst chill and indifferent strangers, their unease is
accentuated. Conservatives do not feel comfortable in Ottawa; Liberals
do.

People of lesser influence go to the Lord Elgin, while those of rank
and station put up at the Chateau. But in the higher interest of democracy, all of them will gather at the old coliseum on the Exhibition
Grounds where, as the climax to three days of ceremonial deliberation
and speech-making, they will ratify the choice of John Diefenbaker as
George Drew's successor.

Even though the result is certain, the achievement will not be graceful or painless. Such things seldom are. To begin with, when a new
chieftain is chosen, his lieutenants must ensure him of the value of their
support. To do so they will seek enemies to subdue, thrusts to parry, and
challenges to put down, even where none exist, even if they must invent
them. So Diefenbaker, living in the Chateau, surrounded by loyal,

thirsting supporters, will be constantly reminded of the perils outside his door, where wicked forces combine to thwart his victory, even though the Conservative Party has no other choice or purpose than to elect him and is, in fact, eager and anxious to do so. But like a man who rapes his mistress, the Diefenbaker forces bring to the convention a peculiar hostility, as though they must first prove their manhood to the Tory Party in order that the prize be worthy.

It is part of the lore of the Diefenbaker forces that their man has never lost, other than by conspiracy and trickery. Memories are rekindled and there are fierce vows that it shall not happen this time, or ever again.

Gordon Churchill has become remote and inaccessible. The Young Conservatives, who are for Diefenbaker nearly to a man, or boy, wear their belligerence like a winter's garment, keeping their ardour warm. They are contemptuous of the identifiable supporters of George Drew, and of his personal staff, and of the party headquarters' personnel. "Old guard" becomes a scornful epithet.

The Young Tories are packing the delegates' lists with adventuresome contemporaries, some of whom have not been to a Tory meeting in their lives. They are well financed and highly organized, and they give to the Diefenbaker campaign a spirited presence and muscle that is unique to the convention. More important, if less audible, the Ontario organization of Leslie Frost discreetly signals its preference for Diefenbaker; to Maritimers and Westerners, it is like a sign from Above.

Diefenbaker easily, Diefenbaker early—Diefenbaker on the first ballot.

The first afternoon is like the re-enactment of a long, tortured dream. The speeches fall like echoes upon the ear, a parade of familiar faces marches past the eye, transfigured in this ghostly ritual, relieving the party of its leader, and him of it.

Drew has come to say farewell. The platform is crowded with his own—his wife, Fiorenza, and the women's national president, Elizabeth Janzen, Earl Rowe and Bill, Grattan O'Leary and Dick Bell. All the things one has longed to hear said about him are now said by those who have been closest to him in the eight hard, barren years of his leadership.

Grattan O'Leary's voice is so beautifully tuned to the old cowbarn that its extravagant richness stirs the sluggish blood of the delegates, few of whom have come for this event and most of whom do not enjoy afternoon politics. O'Leary, one of the very few to know the man of whom he speaks, commands the crowd with the sheer lyrical force of language.

And it occurs to me, listening, that I am responsible for the decision that he be replaced as keynote speaker to the convention by Robert Stanfield. O'Leary had given the keynote speech at the Drew convention, and I had debated the wisdom of making it a custom by repeating it at this one. Besides, Stanfield was young and victorious—who better

233

to signal a party's renewal? Reluctantly, Dick Bell had agreed. Leon Balcer had telephoned O'Leary in Rome to ask him to withdraw for Stanfield.*

All for the best, I tell myself now, because O'Leary could not have done both the eulogy of Drew and the keynote address. And only O'Leary could have delivered this eulogy: Drew "probably saved the party from extinction." It is axiomatic in Canadian politics that unsuccessful leaders, having failed to win, have at least survived and have, therefore, "saved the party" and, as O'Leary adds, "preserved our two party system." It is a poor truth, at best, but it is safe for the delegates' applause.

How was the system preserved by Drew? It was because he spoke "the same language in Chicoutimi that he spoke in Saskatchewan and Ontario." But the true glory of George Drew lies in the fact that, in 1953, the Conservative Party ran its own candidates "in every Quebec riding from Gaspé to the Ottawa River and gained . . . one-third of the entire vote of that province."

Only O'Leary could have made such a summation sound triumphant.

George Drew, O'Leary continues, the voice growing stronger, more eloquent and earnest, instructed the Canadian people in the "dignity and sovereignty of Parliament." And here, O'Leary is in full flight:

George Drew lost that battle, but there are times when to fail is more
than to triumph, when victory is less than defeat, and it was
George Drew, not the hollow men on the treasury benches with their
serried ranks of robots, not that fortuitous collection of conflicting
ingredients held together only by common lust for power, who
emerged from that battle with the respect of Canadians.

Now George Drew–this strange, unknown, devalued man of paradoxical belligerence and shyness, of aloof and lonely image, who knew the "merciless and inscrutable fortunes" of public life (O'Leary's phrase) – rises to accept the last tribute of his party, and it occurs to me that the realities of party politics are personal, sometimes deeply private, and must first be felt to be truly understood.

One searches in vain, listening as Drew speaks, for clues to his emotions, his true feelings, as one hears the familiar sonorous, muscular voice delivering the phrasing wrought by O'Leary's ghosted prose.

*Extract from O'Leary letter to R. A. Bell, November 13, 1956:
". . . I had a call in Rome from Leon Balcer telling me the committee felt that Stanfield should make the 'Keynote' speech and with this I agree completely, in view of Nova Scotia. But, I think Stanfield should be briefed. This 'Keynote' speech will be different from any of its kind in the past . . . Stanfield will not merely be giving a 'Pep' talk to a few hundred of the faithful in a hall; with T.V. and Radio he will be talking to perhaps a million people . . . roughly to the entire nation."

(How must it feel to introduce the man who will make your own speech? Better, I suppose, than thanking the man who has done so.)

There are occasional words which betray the feelings buried underneath, the deliberate, quick reference to Kay Kearns, for example, who finds her place among a special few of those identified and thanked for their support–Balcer, Janzen, Tom Bell, Earl Rowe, and Fiorenza.

"There are no shortcuts to power," says Drew, who speaks with authority. *"In politics, nothing is sacred but the integrity of our own minds."*

What a pity that in all the words, all the marshalled, mustered sentiments, among all the invocations to history and the future, a pity that a sentence like that should be lost, never heard, much less remembered. But then:

"Now the time has come for me to say farewell." And, abruptly, the era of George Drew is over.

On behalf of the party, Earl Rowe presents the retiring leader with a painting, a Quebec winter scene by Clarence Gagnon; Mayor Whitton gives him the "Key to the Capital of Canada," Elizabeth Janzen adjourns the meeting until 8:30 p.m. George and Fiorenza Drew move down directly in front of the platform while a reception line forms on their left. The Drews, standing in front of the painting, shake hands and struggle for the last time to recollect the passing faces and names. It is their farewell to party politics, a way of life of which Fiorenza has said, "is given to so few people that we feel truly blessed."

On that evening another of the convention's ghost-writers takes his unseen turn upon the stage. When the message had come that O'Leary had stepped aside so that Stanfield could give the keynote address, the Premier did not seem overly keen.

"I'd be happy to do it, but I haven't got the time," he said, impressing his caller as to the pressing problems of his new administration.

Finally, "If you help write it, I'll give it."

What a business it all is; none can tell the illusion from the reality, or which is which. What would Stanfield have said if someone else had written it? What would Drew have said? What would King have said, if Pickersgill had not been there?

"In politics, nothing is sacred but the integrity of our own minds." Imagine Drew at Stornoway, in his easy chair in the library, writing that. Or saying to Marion Wagner, "Ah, now put this down–in politics, nothing is sacred but the integrity of our own minds."

Why would you tell that to a delegate from Arnprior? Only an Irish poet could write it; one could hardly imagine George Drew confessing it before two thousand Tories gathered in an oversized musty barn. And yet, possibly, it was Drew's, sprung from the recesses of his soul.

Stanfield, too busy to take mere words seriously, and wary, as usual, of abstractions, has never been seen nor heard before by the

235

Tory Party. Because he does not seem to be cast from the mould of their sort of politician, nor turned on the lathe of their kind of politics, nor burnished by their sort of rhetoric, the crowd is puzzled by him.

First, they must strain to listen; second, they must struggle to understand; finally, they must remind themselves that this spare, ascetic, dour, and barely audible man is a winner, the victorious leader of a party raised from ashes, from extinction, and the youngest Premier in the land.

Because at this time more than any other I am annoyed by the memory of the failure of Ontario's Tories to support Drew, I have put my annoyance into the speech:

There were those who stood with George Drew, both in victory and defeat; through circumstances, I stood with him during those days when this party knew mostly defeat. But speaking for a provincial party that rose from the ashes after the war, with not one sitting member in the legislature of our province, I am proud to admit that the growth of our party in Nova Scotia is due in great measure to George Drew's inspiration and his encouragement. George Drew knew, and I agree, that this party will wither and die, and the two party system with it, unless we are prepared to stand together in the support of those common principles we cherish. In defeat or victory, in office or out of office, the Conservative party of Nova Scotia, Mr. Chairman, has in the past, and will in the future, so long as I am its leader, and I believe long after, fulfill in good heart those obligations we believe every Conservative owes to his party.

And then a warning to the lusting Diefenbakerites:

The Conservative party of Canada and Conservatives in every province enjoy the prospect of victory tomorrow because of the honour and distinction George Drew brought to this party through the years of his leadership. We are united, strong and in good spirit. Whoever succeeds George Drew will do well to maintain and stimulate this unity, for without it we are unworthy and incapable of success.

Then, after the amenities and subtleties, at the heart of the speech the fusion of the writer's conscience, the speaker's mind and natural inclination, and the common purposes of each give resurgent strength to the words. Slumped in a chair in the back of the hall, I hear Stanfield's voice edged with a new earnestness, and I think it much the best part of the speech:

Now, my friends, there are in Canada today problems and issues of the most pressing kind.

The prosperity which propagandists tell us is everywhere in evidence is nonetheless not everywhere felt. And that, I may say, is an understatement.

There are many Canadians who, despite this rich abundance, live in mean and helpless circumstances. There are those who are in want, those handicapped by grinding poverty, those deprived of good fortune by the simple lack of opportunity. There are those made helpless by circumstances beyond them, the infirm and the sick. There are slums and depressed areas, and in them there is suffering and despair enough to be a blight upon any democracy.

And yet there are those in public life today who believe they have exhausted government's capacity to uplift and elevate the state of mankind in this society. There is no sadder spectacle than the politician holding office who truly believes his own propaganda. Now, Mr. Chairman, the people of Nova Scotia are among those who believe that some of the present policies of the federal authority are either inadequate or unacceptable. We live in that area commonly referred to as the Maritimes.

We are determined to impress upon the other governing body that shapes and conditions our daily lives the need for a program which will allow us to play a larger role in the development of this great nation. [Applause.] We are eager to co-operate with any authority which will implement such a policy, regardless of party politics. And we will resist and combat those policies which we believe are either harmful or useless to our people.

When it is over, Dick Bell and Balcer offer thanks, and the delegates ebb toward the doors while the business of the convention continues. Stanfield handshakes his way down the aisles and out into the night. Within minutes he is aboard an aircraft and returning homeward to Nova Scotia.

"What did you think of the speech?" someone asks Ted Rogers, Diefenbaker's deceptively gentle-looking youth organizer.

Unaware that he is speaking to the author, Rogers turns to me. "What did you think, Dalton?"

"I'm prejudiced," I reply truthfully.

"Well," Rogers says, caution showing, "I thought it was all right but, my God, it sure was quiet."

Some are more critical; they miss the hellfire and damnation of the customary keynote address.

O'Leary, when the convention is over, says on the CBC than Stanfield's speech was the best of them all. No higher accolade could come to the ghost-writer.

27

AT THE LIBERAL CONVENTION, ONE HAD FELT SMOTHERED BY A VELVE-
teen arrogance; this one was flawed by an undercurrent of malice, a
sense of an impending blood-letting, in which the victorious would all
avenge the past.

Diefenbaker long ago had chosen Hugh John Flemming to move
his nomination. I heard the news from J. M. Macdonnell, who had
called me to complain that a provincial Premier should have been
neutral in an affair like this.

Curious, I had telephoned Carson, who had also been discom-
fitted. "Hugh John didn't discuss it with me at all," he said. "Diefenbaker called him and asked him to do it, and Hugh John agreed right
on the spot. I must say I don't like it much."

It was a violation of the Leslie Frost example: If the Premier of
Ontario could remain above the politics of the federal party, why not
the Premier of New Brunswick?

Diefenbaker's seconder turned out to be General George Pearkes,
an amiable, vaguely blimpish man, a caucus colleague, and a man with
a First World War record of conspicuous gallantry. Pearkes had nominated Diefenbaker eight years ago at Drew's convention. Now the
seconder, he nonetheless becomes the *cause célèbre* of the convention.

Pearkes was not, obviously, French Canadian. The press, searching for an issue to enliven the reportage, found it in the choice of
Pearkes, who was very nearly the perfect non-French Canadian, with
his slightly British accent, his Victorian attitude, and his splendid
military reputation. Most Conservatives did not know that custom
dictated that a leadership candidate be either nominated or seconded
by a French Canadian, and few of them believed it when they read it
in the Ottawa paper.

The Quebec delegation, largely unnoticed in its forlorn support of
Donald Fleming, the certain loser, now focused its discontent on the
issue of the seconder, since it exemplified the cause of Quebec's chronic
complaint. When the provincial caucus was called, the delegates were
obliged to wade through waves of pressmen and, once inside and
gathered together, it occurred to them that they were *dramatis per-
sonae* to the convention.

In this crisis, which had erupted from ennui, the man who had
briefly been a candidate himself for the leadership, the party's national
president, co-chairman of the convention, and a brooding legate for
the rights of Quebec, now found himself as their champion and spokes-
man. With this new prominence thrust upon him, Leon Balcer was

cast for the first time in the role so many had expected he would some day assume, and which he himself had listlessly, aimlessly sought.

It was as their natural leader, then, that Madame Sévigny appealed to him in the caucus, saying imploringly, "Leon, you must speak for all of us." And hearing the cheers and applause through the closed doors led the press to describe the caucus as "stormy."

It was the first of a number of times the Quebec Conservatives would turn to Balcer, discovering and rediscovering what almost everyone already knew, that he was their only leader. But each time he would fail them, or they him, as the passions of the moment waned, as the crisis passed, and the need for him seemed less urgent. Always he found a way to blunt the challenge, to deflect his opportunity as though he, himself, had only half a mind to be a politician at all, that behind those limpid, dark eyes, the handsome, white-toothed smile, and the soft, gentle voice was some private restraining influence that would not let him act, much less succeed.

But if nothing else, the Quebec delegates discovered the real intensity of their enthusiasm for Fleming, which Diefenbaker's rejection of them had kindled anew.

Sensible men, searching for Diefenbaker's reasons, were puzzled. Perhaps he did not choose a French Canadian because he did not know one upon whom he could rely. His support from that part of the nation was thin, and he was always too proud to canvass for more. In the eyes of the candidate, Pearkes had been a perfect choice. The Diefenbaker backers would point out that he came from the Pacific, while the mover, Flemming, came from the Atlantic—one Canada from sea to sea, or at least from one sea to the Bay of Fundy, they would say.

Anyway, what the party should have read from this was the price Diefenbaker put upon personal loyalty. And it was revealing to him to see, in this brief tempest, who doubted him and who did not. Churchill and Grosart were firm in support of his decision; a fellow like Roblin was not.

In the corridors, off the convention floor, I met Roblin and we discussed the choice of Pearkes.

"Don't you think it's a mistake?" he asked.

I thought it was, but worse, it was unnecessary. Everything had been going Diefenbaker's way until now.

"Do you think I should talk to Churchill?"

I agreed and we went into my makeshift office.

"I don't suppose it will do any good," Roblin said, "but I'll talk to him anyway."

Which he did, saying that, of course, it was none of his business but, "I think John is making a mistake. It has nothing to do with Pearkes, Gordon. You know what I mean. I think it's unwise, and I think you should tell him."

Churchill's reply was not a long one, and the two rang off. "Just as

I thought," Duff said. "Gordon says Diefenbaker refuses to reconsider, and he agrees with him."

Better one trusted friend than one hyphenated Canadian. Anyway, it did not seem to make much difference, at least for a time. But sooner or later everything makes a difference in politics.

As an immediate result, the Quebec caucus became an enclave, finding solace and assurance in their solidarity. They were cheered when Fleming came to see them, and when that was followed by a visit from Earl Rowe, they were ecstatic.

Both they and Rowe had been celebrating the evening, and both they and he shared the same sense of misgiving about the convention. The only survivor from the regime of R. B. Bennett, the good earth of Ontario in the marrow of his bones and the simple principles of Toryism engraved upon his soul, found himself greeted with such fervour and effusive affection by the Quebec delegation that it moved him nearly to tears. He responded by endorsing their candidate, Donald Fleming, something he had wanted to do but had pledged his caucus colleagues, when they had made him acting leader, that he would not do.

After which, when the cheers had done, they all sang "Il a gagné ses épaulettes."

Bill Rowe and I, with our wives, were relaxing quietly in the national director's suite when the telephone rang and Bill learned of the elder Rowe's public endorsement of Fleming.

"Well," the son said, half proud and half dismayed, "I guess father has gone and done it."

Meanwhile, the Nova Scotia delegation was behaving badly. On the second day the delegates had paraded before the convention wearing badges which gratuitously proclaimed their attitude: "Who cares?" It was believed that Nowlan was to blame for this heresy, and the affront was not soon to be forgiven nor forgotten.

So even before the new leader could be chosen and pray for unity, Balcer, Rowe, and Nowlan had been marked for retribution. In the new order, all my friends and allies would appear to be hell-bent for exile.

It is cold, but after all it is December, and if you hate the taxi queues and hanging around the draught-ridden, dank exhibition building, you go out late to the convention and leave early, like a banker, and avoid the crowds.

Upstairs in the Chateau are men so sure of their power they can afford not to care about the proceedings, or about their vote; they sit in the warmth and comfort of the hotel's old suites and enjoy their cigars, late morning coffee, the first drink at the noon gun, and the conviviality of one another's company.

This is not their first convention and, so far as they know, not their last. Politics is a game, a spectator sport, and these men sit in the reds, as becomes shareholders with seniority and leverage. One notices they address as "mister" those who are beneath them, a formality which helps to maintain distance.

The senior bagmen are there, wise in their secret experience and with a view of politics uniquely their own. They prefer the company of winning politicians: thus, Leslie Frost is there, the winningest of them all, and Hugh John Flemming, something of a new boy, who has won but twice. The room smells of fresh cigars, mixed with something like Aqua-Velva, and the blunt, easy speech of men among their peers.

They are talking about Diefenbaker and about "poor Donald" Fleming—someone expressing a twinge of regret that Donald cannot win. It would be nice if it could be Donald, if only because they know him and he's such a decent fellow.

Diefenbaker?

"Listen," growls a senior bagman, shifting his weight forward in his chair, "if Diefenbaker wants it, let the crazy son of a bitch have it. There's lots of time for Donald."

It had become a philosophy for the reconciled—Diefenbaker could not be stopped. Though he would be difficult, if not impossible, as a leader, and a failure, after one election he would retire and the party could then find a younger, abler man. Diefenbaker had been around a long time, so let him have it. The Grits would win the next election anyway.

For those who spend their time at the convention in the warmth and privacy of their suites, such an argument seems credible, and it sustains a number who have come to the convention without a satisfactory candidate for the leadership who can win, and they are resigned to the fact that they will leave in the same condition.

28

*Each nomination shall be in writing, signed by the mover and seconder
who shall be delegates, and the candidate shall consent in writing.
Nominations and the written consents of the candidates shall be
delivered to the office of the National Director addressed to the
Chairman of the Nominations Committee by 6:00 p.m., Thursday,
December 13th, 1956.*

—from the Report of the Nominations Committee

IN THE LATE AFTERNOON, DICK BELL, AND BILL ROWE AND I ARE IN THE
convention office of the national director, receiving the nomination
papers of the candidates. Churchill arrives alone, his manner curt and
his brow stormy. It is as though the clouds have covered the sun and
the dingy room is darker for his presence.

After he has turned over Diefenbaker's nomination papers to Bell
and Rowe, Churchill demands a receipt. In the shocked silence, the
convention chairman and the national director improvise one. No one
has ever asked for a receipt before. (During the convention, and for
some time before it, Bell refused to take a drink. That night, he told
Rowe later, he fell off the wagon with a crash.)

Rowe and I sit together in the stands, among the spectators, to hear the
speeches. I lean forward, into the gusts of oratory coming from the
platform, trying to extract the strategic essence. Diefenbaker has the
luck of the draw, so that he and his mover and seconder speak last.
The nominations precede the addresses from the candidates.

Murdo MacPherson moves Fulton's nomination and one recalls
that all his life he has opposed Diefenbaker. MacPherson comes from
Saskatchewan, which must annoy Diefenbaker, and might be part
of the reason for his persisting with Pearkes, who is from Fulton's
province.

Both MacPherson and Fulton's seconder, Jean Methot (who
speaks entirely in French save for the last seventeen words), put
heavy stress upon Fulton's comparative youth.

"He is only forty years of age," MacPherson says, adding that
Stanfield is forty-two, Roblin is forty, John A. Macdonald became
leader at thirty-eight, and Tupper led his party in Nova Scotia at the
age of forty.

Methot echoes the theme:

"Macdonald, devenu chef à 38 ans . . ."

"Borden, devenu chef à 46 ans . . ."

"Laurier, devenu chef à 46 ans . . ."

"Mackenzie King, devenu chef à 44 ans . . ."

What they are saying is clearer to Diefenbaker than to anyone else. It is that Diefenbaker is now sixty-one years old, and since it is obvious to this convention that St. Laurent will win the next election, the Tory leader will be sixty-five before there will be any real prospect of a Tory victory, and his age will by then be a liability.

Always the questions of age and health would stalk Diefenbaker, and even now, if the balloting is close, it will be a crippling handicap. But it is not, and Diefenbaker's supporters listen in disciplined silence, refusing only to join in the applause for those who talk politics like actuaries.

James Maloney of Ontario moves Fleming's nomination, vigorously perspiring, loudly emphatic–giving a near-perfect parody of the ritual performance. But it develops into a cruel and cunning speech.

Even Rowe must smile at the attempt to cast Donald Fleming's lot with that of the common man and the farmer:

So, ladies and gentlemen, I say to you that he knows the problems, the troubles, the trials and the tribulations of the ordinary man who has to earn his living by the sweat of his brow. And even today his eldest son is a student at the Ontario Agricultural College at Guelph and upon graduation he will take his place in the agricultural development of this country.

Then, like a boxer in the ring who knows from long experience where to find his opponent's scar tissue, Maloney attacks the question of Diefenbaker's health and, in deeper innuendo, the question of his stability:

Those of us who were here in 1948 will remember George Drew when he stood before us in the full flower of his vigorous manhood, the picture of health, and we heard him make his eloquent plea to the delegates. We saw him yesterday when he said farewell to us and when he spoke those words of warning, namely, that the position of leader of a political party is an exacting one requiring a strong and healthy individual, one who can stand the rigours of leadership and all that it entails. So that I suggest to you with great respect that we should now choose a man who not only has great ability but one who is old enough and yet not too old, one who is strong and healthy and who is of a disposition and temperament that he can stand up to the grave responsibilities and discharge the tasks that lie ahead, and we have such a man in Don Fleming.

There are many levels and layers of understanding in politics; both those who are closest to Diefenbaker and those who are the most

243

fiercely opposed to him feel the thrust of Maloney's words. The air is electric, charged with the furtive, futile satisfaction of some and with the fierce resentment of others who only know their time is coming.

Henri Courtemanche seconds the nomination of Donald Fleming; the gods of irony smile at their private joke.

The audience brightens again, released from its anxieties and from the wounding attacks on the party's next leader as Hugh John Flemming moves to the rostrum to nominate Diefenbaker; the welcoming cheers are not unlike a deep, profound sigh of relief. The worst has passed and the best is now to come.

The Premier of New Brunswick is a big man, massive through the shoulders, draped in tweed, handsome, visibly victorious, with a winner's uncomplicated smile, and the poise and cool detachment of a one who wants nothing from his audience but its pleasure. Furthermore, he is a politician, unabashedly loving the lights, the roar of the crowd, and the task he is to perform.

Straight off, then, Flemming makes the big man's characteristic gesture:

I wish to make it very clear that nothing that I may say in supporting the man of my choice is intended to detract or subtract anything from the other men who have been or will be nominated. They are friends of mine and they have my respect and esteem—and they know it.

It is absolution and doxology, and the crowd responds to this powerful, prescient man who has so quickly released them from the burden of the anguished, bitter sentiments which had fallen on their ears like a rain of oaths.

I thought of Carson, pencil clutched between his fingers, writing those words a week ago, a day ago, or perhaps only hours ago. How could he know how apt, how excruciatingly right, they would be now?

After that, it becomes a "man who" nomination in the strict tradition, the crowd rising to its feet like a cresting wave at its breathless climax:

Proven winner in his own province, next winner in the nation, great citizen of the West, great citizen of all Canada, great parliamentarian, great humanitarian, I present to you as a candidate for the leadership of this great party and as the future Prime Minister of Canada, John Diefenbaker of Prince Albert, Saskatchewan!

Then the last of the legates' pleas, and this from Pearkes, who begins his seconding speech, considering his circumstances, in the worst of all possible ways; one flinched at the gaucherie of it:

244

Mr. Chairman, ladies and gentlemen, I hope you will forgive my inability to *parler français*.

But he is brief and the resolute frenzy of the Diefenbaker floor demonstration swiftly erases the anti-climactic bathos of the moment.

The demonstrations cast up the mirror image of American politics and reflect the pubescent demands of the new electronic media. Like an old person taking up with a nubile child, the delegates prance and parade in the aisles, grinning self-consciously, recognizing the superfluity of this unfamiliar exercise, blindly hopeful it will somehow advance their cause. Expectedly, Diefenbaker's demonstration is the best, bearing the impresario's touch of Grosart.

The speeches of the candidates confirm the wisdom of the convention's choice. Since Bennett, and despite the bright promise of George Drew, the party has been without conspicuous successors to the leadership but obliged to search for them among lesser men. And here, after conventions in 1938, 1942, and 1948, the party is confronted with a choice of three men, one of whom has been twice rejected and one of whom, Fulton, does not seem to many to be a serious consideration.

Certainly his speech does nothing for him and I conclude, in my disappointment, that he must have written it himself. It bears the self-conscious limitations of a mind corrupted by the certainty of defeat; the style is convoluted, too many words substituted for thought and feeling:

For what we see here is the acceptance by our party of the challenge that confronts us and of the opportunity that awaits us. That challenge and opportunity are so to build our party that we can discharge our duty of forming the alternative government, ending the period of Liberal drift and damage and setting our country's feet firmly on the path of the future on the basis of sound Conservative principles.

Even his supporters find it difficult to infiltrate his text in order to launch applause:

It is a manifest absurdity to see what we see today, the federal government embarrassed by surpluses running to hundreds of millions of dollars while provincial administrations in periods of prosperity lack the very means to meet their own just needs, let alone their developmental requirements. This is an intolerable situation and it must be rectified as speedily as possible in the interests of the nation as a whole. It is the Conservative party's pledge to rectify this situation by implementing the principle of partnership in confederation.

When he has finished ("I have the honour to submit my name to you for your decision tomorrow afternoon."), his opponents on the platform zealously lead the applause, their hands beating like vacuum cleaner brushes, sweeping up the votes Fulton has left behind him on the convention floor.

Donald Fleming is sustained by his own virtue, the faith of the true believer, which has tempered his ambition; furthermore, he is still young, the legitimacy of his aspirations not yet fully ripened, and while he would like to win, feels duty-bound to try to win, he is consoled by knowing this is not his last, final bid for power. He comes to the convention no worse than the second most powerful figure in it, gifted in speech, sturdy in health, dogged in purpose, and pure in spirit. If he must, he can wait for Diefenbaker.

"Let me at the outset make it clear," he tells the convention, "that I have made no deals or bargains with anyone . . . I am perfectly free, ladies and gentlemen of the Conservative Party, to do my duty in all respects as a Canadian."

From a man in whom there is so little mystery, these cryptic words flutter against the walls of consciousness. If Donald Fleming has made no deals, who has? Has Diefenbaker promised something to Hugh John Flemming?

But as the speech progresses, the real Donald Fleming emerges, the busiest man in the caucus, the most dutiful member on the front bench of the opposition, the man with the neatest office, the most efficient files, the cleanest air, the most precise mind, and the purest tongue. There is so much to admire, and envy, in Donald Fleming and yet, truth to tell, one feels a vague, unresolved sympathy for him.

"What, I ask, is our aim?" Fleming is saying.

The aim is, as with Winston Churchill, "victory," but on Donald Fleming's terms: "We shall seek that goal by every honourable means. In pursuing that goal, however, let us beware of shortcuts."

In the disavowal of shortcuts comes the obligation for honest toil:

"What we must do is work . . ."

"In my nineteen years of political experience I have never found any substitute for hard work."

". . . I will call this party to toil and sweat, believing that victory will be our reward."

"I enjoy working with other people in the same cause."

"In a word, we must ever seek to out-think, out-serve, and out-sacrifice all other political parties."

"I have been told that I am a fighter. I admit it."

Fleming's campaign reeks of hard work, of an excess of energy, of grimacing faces and bulging eyes, clenched fists, and sounds of fervent exhortation. So that when it is over, one feels the muscles relax and the shoulders fall while the storm of applause, like passing thunder, recedes into the distance.

Donald Fleming, I recall, reminds me of Thomas E. Dewey, who reminded Talullah Bankhead of the groom on the wedding cake, and both remind me of Duff Roblin, who reminds me, vaguely, of Henry Hicks. It has to do with politicians of smaller stature; they all appear to have the same speaking style, which is one of strenuous exertion, as though the world's lecterns and microphones have been built too high for them and they are forced to speak while straining on tip-toe, bringing their voices up from the floor. Nonetheless, many people are impressed by their style. But always, it seems, something less than a majority of them.

For Diefenbaker, who appears to be nervous, so taut and vibrant with anxiety that his voice twangs like a guitar string, it is the last hurdle in a torturing, lonely marathon. He knows, out of the depth of a long-gathered experience, and from the assurance the crowd has given him, that he needs only to finish the course to win his prize.

Yet to do so, he must run the gamut of the organized hostility of the Quebec delegation, he must speak in his miserable French, and he must explain the Pearkes decision, which he is loath to do. The speech is the last hurdle, and it matters not how cleanly nor how gracefully it is done, so long as he clears it and does not fall.

So, as the Quebec delegates ceremonially express their displeasure, Diefenbaker begins with his explanation:

Mr. Chairman and fellow Conservatives: In my first words of thanks to my mover and seconder let me say that they were chosen in recognition of the fact that this party extends from the Atlantic to the Pacific. I would remind you of the fact that the last time we won a federal election was in 1930. I was at the convention in 1927 when the party chose Mr. R. B. Bennett. The winning combination in 1930 was the nominator and seconder in 1927, the mover of Mr. Bennett's nomination being the Honourable Mr. Tilley from New Brunswick, afterwards Premier of that province, and the seconder being a westerner, a friend of Mr. Bennett's. That was the winning combination in 1930.

And soon after he appeals to them directly, even if some of them are not there to hear him:

May I therefore in all humility say a few words in the mother tongue of those of French descent who over the years in my own province have been my devoted friends.

A mes amis de langue française, j'ai tenu à m'addresser à vous dans votre belle langue maternelle, car il m'est difficile de penser en français. Je vous remercie de votre indulgence, et je vous dis merci . . . .

When the last of the 160 words has been laboriously pronounced, Diefenbaker describes the ordeal of both speaker and listener, saying:

... that is my tribute to the French-speaking people of Canada who,
with those of us who speak English, make up the fond embrace
of our country.

None of this has seemed real to most of his audience, who have endured numberless hours of obsequies, but the speech has been crafted to discharge the more painful and necessary duties first. So that now as the voice and inflection change, Diefenbaker moves to the central theme of his candidacy, the sure note which will summon his majority:

My purpose, if chosen your leader, will be to banish any spirit of
defeatism in this party so that we may cease living our yesterdays
and look forward to our tomorrows. That will be my purpose, not
to win the election after the next election or the next election after
the next but, with your co-operation, the next election.

The applause is genuine, from the hearts of those stirred by the prospect of an election campaign in which the prize may be victory and not survival. It is Diefenbaker's genius that he has told them not merely what they wanted to hear, but what they desperately want to hope, if not believe.

Sitting in the stands, above the enthusiasm on the floor, looking down at the milling delegates making their way to the exits, I wonder at their response to the speech, with its curious abjectness, and its appeal for a "winning spirit," which few will understand better than I. But it was a poor speech, poorly organized and poorly spoken. Based upon the oratory, the party does not appear to have much choice, even while it is clear that its mind is made up.

"Well," I say to Rowe, "I guess that's it."

"You're right," he says, "that's it."

29

WHILE THE BALLOTS WERE BEING COUNTED, DICK BELL INVITED LESLIE
Frost to the platform, and the Ontario Premier, smiling broadly, made
his leisurely way up the aisle from the back of the hall, bringing an ovation with him to the podium.

His distinctive, slightly nasal voice lulled the hall into silence, as
no one else had done excepting Diefenbaker. He spoke softly, con-
versationally, in measured, even tones, the platform manner exuding
a personal geniality, although underneath, I suspected, was an indomitable will.

He remarked that he had been sitting in the back of the hall, "with
my old friends who have fought with me in many battles," and he
paid tribute to "my old friend and supporter, Arthur Frost," who was
no kin and whose wife had been killed in the convention's only tragedy,
an automobile accident on the way to Ottawa. Then he spoke of "my
great old friend and mentor, George Henry," who had been Premier
of Ontario before Drew, and of "my great old friend, John Bracken,"
who had been leader of the national party before Drew. Then a
reference to "Macdonald and Cartier," and a tribute to Arthur Meighen
(prompted, he said, by something he'd seen in the Ottawa papers),
followed by a mild endorsement of the convention's choice, whom-
ever it might be, and Leslie Frost returned to his seat amid glowing
smiles and warmly enthusiastic applause.

Strange, I thought, that he did not mention Drew's name; he was
the only speaker of the convention to fail to do so. The oversight
seemed deliberate, had to be deliberate with a man so cool and poised
as Frost. The enmity between them, I concluded, must be intense and
enduring.

The results of John Diefenbaker's victory were first reported to
the convention in French by Ross Drouin, but they were plain in any
language: John Diefenbaker, 774; Donald Fleming, 393; Davie Fulton,
117. The losers were quick to make it unanimous. In doing so, said
Diefenbaker, in his acceptance address, they "showed and typified
that unity which, my friends, I want to see in every part of this country
from the Atlantic to the Pacific. . . ."

It was to be a recurrent note:

"I have enjoyed [friendship] from members of this party everywhere across this country. . . ."

". . . I now ask you to join with me in a dedication on behalf of

249

this party and on behalf of Canadians everywhere in our country."

". . . my friends, we can win and that is what we now set out to do from one end of this country to the other."

"You have given to those associated with me from one end of the country to the other the chart."

". . . one appeal I want to make to you today is that we unite from one end of Canada to the other."

". . . I need above all other things, the abiding presence and support of my colleagues and the representatives of this party everywhere across the country."

C'est mon intention d'unir tous les Canadiens de l'Atlantique au Pacifique . . . ."

"My hope is that he [Drew] will join me as my seatmate in the House of Commons to unite this party from one end of Canada to the other."

"Let us raise for this party from the Atlantic to the Pacific the flag of freedom. . . ."

". . . unite from one end of Canada to the other. . . ."

It was, for most of the delegates, a powerful and compelling speech, made more so by the evidence that it appeared to be impromptu–only the French had been scripted–and by the moving intonations of emotion. It was not a speech to be heard, but to be felt, and when it was over, one applauded its mood and spirit, which seemed to capture the moment and quicken already racing hearts.

But it was not so much a speech as a cry of relief, that at last the ordeal was over, and no longer was ambition the prisoner of opportunity. And while inwardly Diefenbaker would give thanks to others, including the Keeper of his destiny, outwardly he thanked his lieutenants in a measured, cautious way, belied by the hoarse sincerity of his voice:

. . . no one will mind my referring to my colleagues in the House of Commons and to two of them in particular, Gordon Churchill, who devoted himself incessantly to my support for weeks on end, and George Hees, and all the others. . . ."

His invitation to Drew to be his seatmate in the House of Commons was momentarily satisfying for its dramatic effect but, on reflection, one recognized it as theatrical. The idea was undoubtedly someone else's.

"I do not intend to say anything on this occasion regarding policy," the new leader said. "Our policy has been drafted as the result of . . . the application and thinking of every Conservative at this convention and many more who were not privileged to attend. It is representative

250

of the viewpoint of every walk of life and people from every part of this country. It deals with the needs and aspirations of every Canadian."

Hearing that, no delegate could have concluded that the convention policy was soon to be abandoned.

For the first time the delegates heard one of their leader's favourite aphorisms; it struck most as high-sounding, but would puzzle some the more frequently they were to hear it:

I will make mistakes, but I hope it will be said of me as was said of another in public service, when I give up the highest honour that you can confer on any man, he was not always right, sometimes he was on the wrong side but never on the side of wrong.

Like the speech itself, it did not bear profound analysis, yet the words carried conviction and the speech left its impression upon the delegates–the appeal for unity and, as deeply felt and earnestly expressed, the plea for a winning spirit.

It was not, of course, precisely true that the party had, as he described it, "a spirit of defeatism." The resurgence of its fortunes had been marked in the Maritimes, its strength had been reinforced in Ontario. It even seemed to have a more sympathetic press and public. The plainer truth was that the party did not think it could win with John Diefenbaker and, for that matter, neither did he.

But he sounded convincing, as the convention now recognized and the country would soon find out:

Ladies and gentlemen, from the bottom of my heart I thank you.
I know what the responsibility is. I know how formidable the task.
I know that some have a defeatist attitude. I leave you with the
message that raised the spirits of Canadians in the first great war.
The officers were asked to do a formidable task and each one in
turn, after having reviewed the actual situation, was fearful of the
result and said it could not be done. Finally, the officer commanding
said: "Now, gentlemen, you have given me every reason why it
cannot be done. Now go and do it." My friends, let us unite and
go and do it.

After that, the galleries and the delegates on the floor hushed and motionless, Olive Diefenbaker spoke of her husband. She too had been prepared with a few words of French which concluded:

*Je vous donne ma parole que, le prochaine fois que je vous verrai,
je parlerai mieux votre belle langue.*

But when the results had been announced, Leon Balcer and some of his fellow delegates from Quebec had risen from their chairs and walked off the floor. In the turbulence of the convention at that moment, only a few were aware of the gesture, and the time would come when most of the delegation, including Balcer, would deny that it had happened at all.

And then it was over. The first televised convention, the klieg-lit dawn of the Diefenbaker age, the new leader, dazed with the sense of triumph, moist-eyed and trembling at the podium, one hand held high overhead, at his side, Olive Diefenbaker, on her face a beaming smile, and in her arms the eternal bouquet. They stood in the winners' circle, basking in the cheers cascading down upon them from the galleries and welling up from the floor, engulfing them in a flood of affection, the new agents of all their hopes.

How many times how many men would remember the moment. At least one of the press gallery wept—for the last time, perhaps, any of that membership would do so for John Diefenbaker. For most, in the darkness beyond the platform, there was the rare, sweet, satisfying moment of euphoria, for each of those who held shares in Diefenbaker's victory believed that all would be different now, the party would be different, and their place in it, and politics for them would never again be the same. And they were right.

There were others who smiled—sporting smiles, anxious smiles, perfunctory smiles—while the eyes were dulled with a kind of private pain; they, too, knew that the party would be different, as would their place in it. And they, too, were right.

I had listened to the acceptance speech, hearing the first, quavering notes of evangelism, the muffled sounds of angels' wings, hints of martyrdom and invocations of righteousness.

But then there was diminutive Wilfred Dufresne bounding down the aisle, slipping between the cheering delegates, like light threading through a forest, to mount the platform and leap into Olive Diefenbaker's empty chair when she stood to take her place beside her husband. The diversion interrupted introspection. Within moments, I heard the press enthuse upon Diefenbaker's speech and I put aside doubt.

Dick Bell's voice was the last to speak. "We would ask you to close the Convention with the singing of God Save the Queen and O Canada. I will ask George Hees to strike the note."

30

"Your committee was unanimous in expressing its confidence in the imagination and effort which has been put into our organization by the National Director, Mr. William L. Rowe and in our public relations and publicity by Mr. Dalton Camp. A formal resolution to this effect was moved and appears later in this report, but the appreciation of the committee was greater than can actually be expressed in a mere formal resolution."

–Convention proceedings. Report of the Organization and Public Relations Committee

ROWE WROTE OUT HIS RESIGNATION AS NATIONAL DIRECTOR. IT SUR-prised me that no one seemed to care when I mentioned it. The balance of the night was spent in absent-minded socializing, leaving a trail of half-emptied glasses around the Chateau, until the celebrant's smile became a grimace as his mask began to sag.

"By God, a great speech, eh?"

"Yeah, great."

"Jesus, it's good to see those Drew bastards get theirs."

"I guess that goes for a lot of us."

"You know who I mean."

"I thought we were going to be a united party."

"Goddam right. As long as those bastards aren't running things, we'll be a united party."

The Rowe family came in for a lot of abuse–the former House Leader, the former national director, and Clair Casselman, Earl's son-in-law. But victory means little unless there are losers. The Rowes were the losers.

I met Hugh John Flemming and congratulated him on his speech and on the success of his candidate.

"Rowe is quitting," I told him, "and so am I."

"Now, I wouldn't do that," he said. "They'll need you."

"I think they've been damned unfair to Drew and to Rowe," I said. "I'm going out with the people I came in with."

"Now," said Hugh John, "don't talk nonsense."

Later he came to Rowe's suite, beaming goodwill and warmth, shaking hands around the room. "The Rowe family," he said, in a loud, clear, public voice, "is the salt of this earth."

I never liked Hugh John Flemming more than at that moment.

He told me he had gone to Diefenbaker to urge that he see me. As a result, I was to meet with the new leader in his hotel room at eight o'clock the next morning.

The hour appalled me. "What does he want?" I asked.

"He wants to talk to you," Hugh John said, speaking gently, like an uncle. "You see him now, and I think you'll change your mind about things."

Almost everyone in the party establishment had a suite at the Chateau Laurier; the Diefenbakers, however, had only a room, which was commendable in an egalitarian sense, but awkward for the practical purposes of conversation. I found the new party chieftain stretched out upon one of the twin beds, wrapped in his dressing gown; the sleeves were too long and flapped around his hands. The window blinds were drawn, the room illuminated by two feeble lights, one over the bed and the other from a floor lamp. The dresser was piled high with a collection of telegrams.

There was no place to sit, so I stood by Diefenbaker's bed, looking down at his reclining form surrounded by newspapers.

"I want to thank you," he said, as the conversation became business-like, "for a comment you made about me which has since been reported to me."

Oh? "What was that?"

There was a half-smile about the lips. "Never mind," he said. "That doesn't matter, you see. I just want you to know that I heard about it and I appreciate it."

What came to mind, first of all, is that I could not recall saying anything of such significance about Diefenbaker to anyone. From that, I concluded this was some sort of mysterious strategy–he was telling me that *if* I spoke of him, he would hear about it. Was that it? He is, I thought, a very complex–perhaps dangerous–man, and possibly the things they have been saying about him are true.

Then he began to talk about Drew; my senses were now alerted and I could hear Olive rustling in her chair. He was only interested in the unity of the party, he was saying, and bringing everyone together. It had not been that way with Drew, back in 1948, at the last convention.

Nor was he blaming Mr. Drew, he said, his voice tinged with the memory of his private sorrow; perhaps Drew was not to blame. But after the balloting, at the 1948 convention, he had come to Drew's suite–right here in this hotel–and knocked upon his door to congratulate him personally and offer him his loyalty and co-operation.

When he stepped into the room, the celebrations stopped and everyone fell silent. Then he spoke to Drew and left, because he was not invited to stay. And when the door had closed behind him, he heard the room erupt in laughter. Laughter, you see; they were laughing at him, mocking his gesture, his decent gesture to Drew.

It was, I suspected, possible. If it were true, it would explain a lot of things and perhaps I am being told this, by someone who is very nearly unknown to me, as an explanation. But supposing it is not true?

254

I could find nothing suitable to say.

Now about headquarters: Bill Rowe–whom he had always liked
–had resigned. He understood that and it was all right. He wanted me
to take charge of headquarters for him, for a time at least. He had a
lot of speeches to make in the next while and he wanted my ideas.

But there was one thing he particularly wanted me to do: he
wanted to see all the mail that came to headquarters. He wanted me,
personally, to show him all the incoming mail and–the faint smile
returning–I should also give him copies of all the letters I wrote in
reply, of course.

"I just want to know what's going on down there, you see."

I felt a nearly overpowering sense of claustrophobia and a desperate urge to escape this dim, stale-smelling room; perhaps it would
be different later in the day, in an office, in the sunlight.

"Will you do that?" John Diefenbaker asked.

Shortly, I left him, hastily, clumsily, and without saying yes or no.
Maybe, I told myself, he is exhausted, or maybe I am, or perhaps, as
some are saying, this party is now in deeper trouble. Olive saw me to
the door, smiling graciously, her lips moving, but I did not hear what
she was saying because I was listening to the alarms signalling in my
own mind.

I went to Stornoway to see Drew, to say good-bye to him and to
Fiorenza, but more urgently I wanted to talk to him about Diefenbaker. There were already rumours about Drew–that he would go to
the Senate (a seat was offered by St. Laurent but he refused lest it
embarrass Diefenbaker and the party) or that he would, like R. B.
Bennett, leave the country and never return to it.

When I repeated Diefenbaker's account of the night of the 1948
convention, Drew seemed genuinely shocked. To the contrary, he said,
he had made every effort to be conciliatory and had invited Diefenbaker's company in the evening celebrations, but Diefenbaker had
begged off. There certainly had been no scene in the suite as described
by Diefenbaker.

Eight years ago it had happened, or not happened. I persuaded
myself that perhaps both men were right. A deeply sensitive and defeated man, such as Diefenbaker, could be easily wounded by the
mere sight of Drew's forces in jubilant celebration, and he could as
easily have been slighted or ignored by them. Or perhaps Drew, who had
changed a good deal during the eight years of his luckless leadership,
from the crusading, conquering hero of the Ontario Tories to this
presently spent and uncertain man preparing to leave Stornoway–
perhaps, eight years ago, he might have affronted the man he had
defeated, even without being aware he was doing so.

If none of this had happened, why would Diefenbaker have told
me? If he did not believe it himself, why did he want me to believe it?
I decided I did not know, but that sometime, later, I might find out.

31

Dear Dalton:

It seems rather strange to write you a letter about your resignation after talking with you at length about it by telephone in the past few days. But I do wish you to know that up to this point everything we attempted was accomplished. I still recall the luncheon we had at Simpson's Arcadian Court when you persuaded me to accept my own position and I remember your own acceptance and the decision that it would be a team effort. It has been in every sense of the word and, may I say, a good team.

In a way I hope that our retirement from the organization field is a permanent one. On the other hand, I hope sincerely that as a team we may contribute in other ways to the success of this Party....

I believe we both made the only possible decision at this time and I am pleased that you have been rewarded by your Company with a vice-presidency. I congratulate you and know that you not only deserve it but will go on to even greater responsibilities within your Company....

William L. Rowe

THE AGENCY, WHICH ONLY A YEAR AGO HAD POLITELY SUGGESTED firing me, reconsidered and promoted me instead. Perhaps they were influenced by the successful campaigns in New Brunswick and Nova Scotia, both of which had been billed through the agency. Perhaps they had intuitive glimpses of things to come.

Advertising agencies proliferate executive titles; I looked upon my elevation to a vice-presidency much as I did on becoming a lance-corporal in the army–an assumption of greater responsibility without any apparent corresponding benefit. But it seemed to please my employers, who wished, perhaps, to make amends by their own lights for their earlier, darker impulses.

Through most of January I found myself conspiring with Churchill to have him placed in charge of party organization at national head-quarters. We appeared to be ranged against George Hees and Allister Grosart. Ostensibly, Diefenbaker had to decide between Churchill and Hees and, by doing so, choose as well between myself and Grosart.

Strange that men who were to work so closely, and effectively, in a great enterprise should be eternal strangers to one another.

If there was a man in the caucus of the Twenty-second Parliament whom I thought I knew, apart from Nowlan, it was Churchill. But the longer I knew him, the less I understood him. He had been staunchly allied with Rowe during the brief two years Bill had been national director, yet he saw him leave without so much as a personal word. Churchill had been one of the foremost Drew loyalists, outspokenly critical of Diefenbaker's selfishness and diffidence, but he had rushed to Diefenbaker's banner immediately Drew had resigned, and he now sounded like a western YPC with his prattle about "the Drew clique" and "the Bay Street boys." Although he had once been considered one of the authentic "conservatives" in the caucus, suddenly there were intonations of radicalism in his rhetoric. For one who seemed so stubbornly set in his ways, these abrupt changes in attitude and outlook which came with the change in leadership were puzzling.

However, one consistency remained; Churchill did not like Hees. Convinced that Hees, abetted by Grosart, was conspiring to seize control of the party's organization and ultimately the party leadership, Churchill pressed his own claims, in his own way, upon Diefenbaker. I had no such suspicions of Hees; I simply did not want him in charge of party organization any more than I wanted Grosart in charge of party publicity.

Throughout this period Grosart played a strange but obviously crucial role. At the outset, he had insisted he did not want to be national director of the party. Indeed, he claimed to want no part in the future of the organization. Instead, he adopted the role of conciliator between Hees and Churchill, professing to be acting under Diefenbaker's instructions. I could not tell whether this was true or not; Diefenbaker did not appear to be talking to any of them.

I was not wholly convinced that Grosart did not want the job of national director, and I remained unforgiving of him for his part in the federal campaign of 1953. By this time, with two successful provincial campaigns immediately behind me, I had a good deal more confidence in my abilities than was perhaps warranted and a good deal less appreciation of Grosart's value than was deserved.

Hees and Grosart sought to recruit Mel Jack as Bill Rowe's successor at headquarters. Jack was then a civil servant in the Department of Indian Affairs; after having been fired by Drew, he had been given a post in the department, allegedly by a compassionate Jack Pickersgill.

Now it appeared he was the unanimous choice of Hees, Grosart, and Diefenbaker for the position of national director. Churchill listened with furrowed brow to Grosart's recounting of the negotiations–the terms were high, apart from salary, and included a prepaid annuity. Diefenbaker was reportedly piqued at this latter demand, although it had not been made because the prospective party organizer doubted the future prospects of John Diefenbaker but, as his wife pointed out, because his previous experience with the party had been very nearly a personal disaster.

However, none of this was to be. The party's finances could not be committed to so ambitious an undertaking; there were a number, Diefenbaker included, who were relieved, as they did not relish the precedent. As for Mel Jack, he would later find his way back into Tory political circles by more graceful and less hazardous means; soon after the Diefenbaker victory he became the ubiquitous personal aide of the Hon. George Hees and the prime favourite in the new order of things among the members of the Ottawa press gallery.

Whatever the uncertainties—and they were numberless—during the early weeks of Diefenbaker's leadership, there were no doubts that there would be a spring election; it would probably come just after the budget which, we wrongly guessed, would be full of good news for taxpayers, pensioners, and farmers. Before the writs were issued in the spring, the new Tory leader was anxious to have his house in order, including Bracken House.

Diefenbaker's hostility towards the party's national office persisted, made up of old grievances, past convention defeats, memories of slights imagined but nonetheless real. So anxious was he to have headquarters under control that he ordered everyone around him to "take charge of the place." As a result, the office was being managed by a number of untitled and competing individuals, including Grosart, Churchill, and myself.

While I had very little authority from Diefenbaker, as compared to Churchill or Grosart, I was clearly the favourite of the headquarters' personnel, especially Miss Kearns, who actively feared Diefenbaker. The staff had known me through associations in happier days; as well, I had hired some of them, and all of them had worked for me at one time or another. Finally, I was the only holdover from the Drew era who had political leverage of a sort which allowed me to be independent of the Diefenbaker people and outwardly contemptuous of their prejudice against the party's continuing employees.

I had no hesitation in making clear my affection and loyalty toward these underpaid, apprehensive servants of the party. Allister seemed aloof and heedless of their concerns, and Churchill remained an outsider. I was determined to see that all were fairly treated. Hindsight reveals they were not much threatened anyway, although in transition mistrust was natural to both the staff of the former leader and the retinue of his successor.

For a time the uneasy triumvirate of Churchill, Grosart, and myself managed the party's organization, none of us thoroughly, each of us fitfully. All the while, I waited for Diefenbaker to choose between

258

Hees and Churchill, spending most of my time in Toronto, commuting only occasionally to Ottawa to renew my sporadic vigil over the organization. I never saw Diefenbaker.

My own motives were as obscure as they were complex. I wanted Churchill to become national director because I did not want the responsibility to go to Hees or his designate. My antipathy to Hees was persistent, if irrational; I could not think of him without recalling a remark attributed to C. D. Howe, but widely circulated by Tories, that he had "the build of an Adonis and the brains of a gnat."

My objections to Grosart were more tangible, though not much less superficial. I suspected that he was incompetent in matters of advertising. But then, he cheerfully admitted to it. My experience with him had been that he gave too quickly the impression of agreement and understanding when, in fact, none existed. Should someone express an opinion, he would be the last to say that, in truth, his was the opposite. Possibly he had been so long in public relations–for such clients as the tobacco growers, George Drew, Leslie Frost, and John Doyle–that all causes and all men had become the same to him; like a lawyer, he could take any case and champion either side. I could not.

So while I marvelled at his toughness, accommodated by a masculine, roguish charm, I considered him cynical and uncommitted. Politics on that basis was impossible to me. I wanted the Conservative Party to become an effective, efficient political instrument–such as could bring down a Liberal government. I was not certain that it could be built on the forensic skills of John Diefenbaker, the bonhomie of George Hees, and the huckstering pragmatism of Allister Grosart.

On the last day of January an agreement was recorded between Allister, myself, and Gordon which, apparently, suited us all. It was neatly typed on the back of personal stationery bearing the embossed name "John G. Diefenbaker."

January 31, 1957.

Plans re Publicity
I. (a) Budget–$800,000
   (b) Two agencies are necessary for the major tasks, namely
       McKim's and Locke-Johnson's. Other agencies may be
       required for regional assignments. The three (Churchill,
       Camp & Grossart) to decide what other agencies shall be used.
   (c) Gentleman's agreement that G. C. to be referee of any dispute.
       The responsibility will be shared equally between McKim
       & Locke Johnson.
II. Decisions re Publicity to be made by Churchill, Camp
    and Grossart.
III. With regard to Policy and Platform, the group of three to be
     given the opportunity to discuss any policy decision that is to be
     communicated to the public.

IV. (a) Caron to be called by Al and asked to report to Dalton.
   (b) French speaking Ad man must be at Headquarters.
V. Al Grossart to be available for duty in Ottawa 2 days per week
   until Writ is issued; after issue of Writ he will act in any capacity
   that is desired.

The document was composed and typed in Churchill's office; in those days, everyone misspelled Grosart's name.

The agreement suited everyone, including Diefenbaker, or so I was told. It gave Churchill at least *de facto* control of the organization, an objective he sought with an intensity as fierce as it was mysterious, and it allied with him two men who were vital to an election campaign.

It suited Allister because it left him free to pursue his private interests in Toronto while retaining equal shares in the campaign billings and the option to serve "in any capacity that is desired" when the campaign began.

It suited me because it appeared that the threat of Hees had been turned aside; furthermore, it seemed I would get my way in particular matters of personal interest affecting the party organization, because, I thought, I had Churchill's ear. And I, too, was free to come and go as I pleased between Toronto and Ottawa, at least until the election seemed imminent. I spent much the greater part of my time in Toronto.

I began to make plans for the campaign. By mid-February I had completed a media assessment, including costs, evaluation, and closing dates based on the three dates which seemed to me most likely for the election–May 27, June 10, and June 17.

I urged Churchill to get out of Ottawa, and see the party organization at first hand and begin to acquire some personal contact with the membership at the grass-roots level. I sent him memoranda which, I assumed, would also be shown to Diefenbaker.

Churchill dithered. He could not be prodded from his House of Commons office. To Gordon a discussion of a problem was indistinguishable from decision; memoranda became plans in progress; a private understanding was immediately assumed to be a wide consensus; he would not answer mail, all communication was verbal. Gordon spent his days confronting his problems and considering the possibilities; at the end of the day, nothing had been untouched and everything had come under the close scrutiny and the intense, frowning gaze. Yet nothing was decided, nothing achieved.

"You're darn right," Gordon would say, having received your advice. "We'll have to do that."

And he would smile, rubbing his bald head, his hand removing the wrinkles as it passed over his brow. And all passed with it, including the resolution.

I prepared a lengthy memorandum for him, both as a means of mobilizing my own thoughts and organizing his. Some of it makes interesting reading, in view of subsequent events:

Memorandum to Gordon Churchill, M.P.
From Dalton K. Camp

Herewith a resume of my thoughts on the subject of campaign
publicity, organization and related matters.

The ideal end product of political advertising and publicity is
that it be effective in persuading voters to support candidates of the
party. There are, of course, other benefits. Good publicity has a
direct influence on the morale of both candidates and organizations.
Good publicity maintains party support, even as it increases it,
and good publicity has a direct effect on the percentage of voters
who do indeed vote on election day.

There is obviously no simple, inexpensive and mechanical means
by which one political party may triumph over another. Otherwise
elections would be won by the best mechanics. Instead, elections are
won by qualities of leadership, public attitudes towards political
issues, and party organization, and all of these are equally important.
The lack of one of them cannot bring success.

The tendency in discussing publicity is to over-simplify. But
simplicity is helpful to basic understanding. So let us consider the
various instruments of publicity. And these are advertising in daily
newspapers, magazine advertising, television, radio, weekly
newspaper advertising, pamphlets and outdoor posters.

(1) *Daily Newspaper Advertising*
There are slightly less than 100 daily newspapers in Canada. These
newspapers have a total circulation of nearly 4,000,000, a readership
audience of more than 12,000,000.

The daily newspaper is basically the most accessible of the media
of publicity. Naturally it is also expensive. For example, to buy a
full-page newspaper advertisement in every Canadian daily
would cost about $40,000. . . .

(2) *Magazine Advertising*
As my earlier memorandum indicated, it would seem possible for us
to use magazines if we wished. But whereas a newspaper advertisement
may be prepared and run nationally within 10 days, magazine
advertising must be prepared from one month to six weeks prior to
the magazine's publication. This means that as a rule advertising
copy in magazines is usually general in its appeal, and runs the risk
of being somewhat dated by the time it reaches the reader. . . .

(3) *Television*
There are 31 privately owned television stations in Canada, reaching
nearly 2,000,000 homes. Five of these are French. If they are

to be used they must be used individually, as few of them are interconnected by network facilities.

Perhaps an idea of the cost would be useful here. For one five-minute broadcast on each television station, the cost is $2,477.50. For a ten-minute broadcast, $2,913.75, and similarly for fifteen minutes, $3,374.00.

With the exception that television time is purchasable from these stations, the regulations regarding political broadcasting set forth by the C.B.C. apply. These regulations prevent the use of film clips, cartoons or animation of any kind, unidentified or anonymous spokesmen, or the use of pictures or photographs not considered previously published material. All photographs must be identified.

The larger use of T.V., that is of the C.B.C.'s major market T.V. stations, is a matter which is not yet resolved. The C.B.C. may well provide only a minimum of free time on the Toronto-Montreal-Ottawa network, or it may make available purchasable network time in addition. This is a decision that the C.B.C. will make known only when the writ has been issued.

Television, as we all know, is an intimate, personal medium, and the nearest thing to direct contact aside from a personal canvass. Its impact in both the Nova Scotia and New Brunswick elections was substantial. It is a distinct advantage to the party that uses it resourcefully, and disastrous to the party that doesn't.

This medium represents a heavy surcharge on publicity expenditures, but more important, it adds a further burden to the Leader of the party. Since he must use television, and can reach directly a larger audience personally by its use than through any other medium, he must be given ample time to prepare for his television appearances. It means, as well, that he must have, if he is to use television as he should during the campaign, someone with him competent to act as his producer. It would be unwise and unfair to leave him to the mercy of individual television stations.

We are, as you know, considering a series of five-minute filmed television talks by the Leader. These can only be done, if they are to be done, at some time before the House dissolves and he becomes fully engaged in the campaign. . . .

Television is the most pervasive and influential medium of all. It is likely that the Liberals will use television in the "commercial sense," since it is apparent I believe even to them that the Prime Minister does not like the medium. This affords us the opportunity for a certain advantage. But the medium cannot be used to wage an argument and to win one. What it does do is to create an impression, and it is always possible to leave a good impression, whereas it is difficult to leave a message. It is very nearly as simple as this. The question that begs at every occasion of a political television broadcast in the viewer's mind is, "Do I like and do I trust him?"

262

Speech material and technique of delivery, which answer this question affirmatively, are what we must seek. . . .

(4) *Radio*

. . . still a useful medium, and it is obvious that it remains one of our basic publicity considerations. First of all, we will have the usual amount of c.b.c. network time at our disposal. Unlike television this will be national in scope rather than regional. It is possible because of this that the Leader may use as much of this time as he chooses, since his address may originate from any station in any province he happens to be in at the time.

The French language radio for the c.b.c. has always been something of a problem because of the dearth of speakers. . . .

(5) *Weekly Newspapers*

There are 555 weekly newspapers in Canada. As I have said to you before, there is no other form of advertising so extravagant. I am hopeful that we can remain entirely outside of this advertising medium. I say this because it is abundantly clear that weekly newspapers will be heavily used by our local candidates, and they are ideal for that purpose. I am hopeful that we can keep out of weeklies because they are an administrative problem, and oddly enough, far more expensive than daily newspapers if they are used on a national basis. But staying out of some and going into others is hardly a solution, because the discrimination arouses as much animosity and more than the goodwill created with those that are used.
In our publicity advice to our candidates, we shall, if possible, inform them of our policy and advise them to use weeklies on their own behalf.

(6) *Pamphlets*

The following general pamphlets are planned for:
1. Constituency organization.
2. Scrutineer's Manual.
3. Diefenbaker pamphlet.
4. Speaker's Handbook.
5. Platform pamphlet.
6. Pocket Politics.

As you know, I am inclined to be frugal about pamphlets. No Conservative has entirely recovered from the pamphlet blizzard of 1949. The pamphlets listed above fulfill basic needs and will be generally speaking in universal demand. Broadly speaking, to produce these involves the distribution of some 6,000,000 pieces of literature, even though three of the above pamphlets have restricted circulation. It is apparent, however, that one or two other pamphlets will likely be produced. This is a budget expense difficult to assess and impossible to avoid.

A Consideration of Campaign Issues

Having done with this general survey of publicity, we come now to a consideration of the use we can make of these media. In other words, we come to a discussion of the basic issues involved, so far as we know them now, in the forthcoming election. These are, I submit, some, if not most of them, and they are not rendered with any sense of priority.

1) To use the chief's expression, "the rights of the people in Parliament."
2) Restoration of the two-party system.
3) Canada's natural resources and human resources as well.
4) Economic problems of the have-not provinces.
5) The social services and social security benefits, assuming, of course, that all is not attended to in the next budget.
6) The impasse in dominion-provincial relations.
7) St. Laurent–a lame duck Prime Minister.
8) The personal appeal of Diefenbaker, both to latent Conservatives and independent voters.
9) The United Nations, the Commonwealth and the United States.
10) Credit restrictions, fiscal policy, and inflation.
11) Agriculture.

There are, of course, others.

The important consideration with regard to all these issues is, to me, the fact that only one of them can honestly be said to be truly national in its scope, and that is the personal appeal of the leader himself.

Consideration of any one of the others on the basis of regions or provinces in Canada will lead one inevitably to an area or province where it can barely be called a serious issue. It would seem to me, for example, that in certain parts of Canada a discussion of the issue of American investment would appeal to the voter as either rhetorical or inflammable. Further, there are areas within provinces where we are hopeful of good results, where this issue risks giving offence to large numbers of persons employed by or beneficiaries of American capital.

The only other issue with any direct appeal to the Atlantic provinces is the one which concerns federal assistance for economic development. Some of these issues, such as the first two, appeal to our partisans and have a certain appeal to what might be called the politically sophisticated. They are lost on the rank and file.

In all candor, it has not always been possible for a political party to consider its leader as its first asset and best issue. Flattery is useless here. But in actual fact there is every evidence that what we describe as the average voter appears to have an intuitive confidence and liking for this party's leader. Translated into publicity it means that

264

our newspaper and magazine advertising, if it is to have the greatest effect on the greatest number of people, will give the highest priority to Mr. Diefenbaker. Thus, of all these issues, the one with the widest common denominator is the leadership issue. It is perhaps especially timely since our intelligence is that the average voter believes or is willing to believe that Mr. St. Laurent is not long for his office even if elected, and, further, that television has shown him in a less benevolent light than did radio and newspaper publicity in the past.

Thus, the election is not even a contest between Diefenbaker and St. Laurent. It is perhaps a contest between Diefenbaker and Pickersgill.

It is because of these considerations that I would urge such strenuous use of television and that I would hope as much of our radio broadcasting as possible be done via regional networks and actual political gatherings.

This kind of campaign strikes a national note that is affirmative. We can be positive rather than negative, and we can advance our cause rather than defend it. No one has entirely recovered from the taxation plank in the 1953 platform. This was the result of trying to make a national issue out of an issue that at best applied to Toronto and vicinity. Tax cuts reminded voters in many areas of Canada of government retrenchment, of loss of government services, of military and civil service personnel without hope of increased wages. The issues we campaign on, like the platform we campaign on, must be complementary to the main theme of the campaign, i.e., Leadership. It seems almost incredible that in 1953 they were in fact contradictory.

Some Basic Considerations of the Campaign
It has been suggested that we "decentralize" our campaign activities as much as possible. This is desirable. But, of course, and some-times unfortunately, election campaigns are decentralized right down to the level of the poll. Some of the most effective issues will be peculiar to individual constituencies. Nevertheless, there has to be:
1) A national publicity campaign
2) A national tour by the leader, and
3) An organizational appreciation of the overall situation made with a national eye, so that both (1) and (2) can be used to the most judicious advantage.

1) National Publicity Campaign
Tactically, administratively, and financially, there must be fairly rigid control of national publicity. There must be both authority and direction, effective communication and liaison. The wastrel son usually lives farthest from home. We can only direct and control those

activities best that are under our immediate jurisdiction. Local candidates and associations are of course free to do what they can and will, but they cannot be held responsible for activity on a national basis.

2) *The National Tour*

This is a strategic campaign consideration. I am, of course, anxious to know the composition of the chief's staff and, as well, the itinerary itself. He will require the following personnel:

Personal secretary and administrator (Bedson)

Press relations and TV and radio producer (Grosart)

Research assistant (Eldon or Morrow)

Detail man for local arrangements (This can be done perhaps by regional appointment.)

Assistant for preparing speech material (Finlayson or other)

Regional advisers (Probably caucus members where advisable)

Liaison with National Headquarters will be less of a problem with Derek Bedson, and with regard to publicity we shall rely on Al Grosart. In research, there will be an opposite number remaining in Ottawa.

3) *Organization*

Basically, when the writ is issued and the campaign is then well under way, there is no longer, so far as the national organization is concerned, a federal election, but rather 265 by-elections. We are here to coordinate in whatever way we can the various conduct of these constituency elections. We come closest to direct involvement when the leader is in a candidate's area, when we assist them with regard to publicity, and when we deal with them on matters involving finance.

We should have here at Headquarters a staff member who will be delegated the task of agency liaison with regard to publicity and another who will do the same with regard to French language publicity. The staff is already available for handling the liaison with the campaign tour itinerary so far as its administration is concerned. We shall need of course additional staff for clerical duties and for the mailing room.

Our campaign intelligence will be based largely on our direct relations with responsible persons in the various provinces concerned. These vary both in degree of responsibility and in usefulness. To sustain the substantial contact we have and strengthen the weaker ones is an immediate organizational task.

Interim Resume Re Provincial Organization
Newfoundland–We should have no illusions about our organization

266

here. Our latest reports confirm that the usual situation obtains in Newfoundland, i.e., an obsession with Smallwood and provincial considerations. They do not think federally and could not reasonably be expected to. We have sent the Y.P.C. organizer to Newfoundland, and are sending the Women's President there. They are of course extremely anxious to have the chief or, failing that, a federal member of substance who will stress the federal aspects of politics.

The most promising area is St. John's with marginal opportunities in Cornerbrook. The old guard remains in the saddle and they are not so much Conservatives as Anti-Confederationists. There are, however, promising young people coming forward.

Nova Scotia–At the moment the organization is potentially of the highest order, but our fortunes are low because of the obvious aftermath of the change in government and the resultant dislocations throughout the rank and file of the party's membership.

We shall get help from the organization and even financially, and I am of the opinion the picture will be much brighter before long. The chief's visit in March will have a tonic effect.

Prince Edward Island–All our candidates are in the field, although one of them is in Toronto. The opportunity for gains is apparently good. There has been a chronic history of organizational strife, largely in the women's organization. Elizabeth Janzen is visiting there shortly.

New Brunswick–Infinitely better off than 1953, but they will need prodding. The organization, however, seems to be whole-heartedly committed, and they have come to like defeating Liberals. The possibility of some self-financing beyond their 1953 contribution needs to be explored.

Quebec–Now that Normand is busy again, we shall be getting accurate reports on individual ridings. The Quebec district picture will be much clearer after Perron returns. One need hardly comment on the activity in the Montreal district.

Ontario–We are informed daily as to progress in Ontario through both Harry Willis and Dorothy Downing. We have managed to generate Y.P.C. activity by helping them in an organizational task with financial assistance.

Manitoba–No comment.*

Saskatchewan–Personal "on the ground" intelligence has been lacking, but the chief's tour should produce a great deal of helpful information as well as the visits of John Hamilton and Walter Dinsdale.

If the Saskatchewan office is to be kept open and Alvin Hamilton is going to be involved in his own candidacy, we should find out as early as possible what plans he has for that office. As discussed previously, our liaison here is somewhat tenuous.

*In deference to Churchill, a Manitoban.

Alberta–Much the same as Saskatchewan.

British Columbia–When Davie Fulton returns, he will no doubt have a great deal of information for us. You and I have discussed this to-day and are, I believe in mutual agreement as to the need of more extensive conversation with the B.C. members.

Yukon and North West Territory–We are in remarkably good contact with Eric Nielsen who seems very keen and also reliable.

32

IN THE EYES OF SOME, I OUGHT TO HAVE BEEN A CANDIDATE. LUCY
Sansom, wife of the General whose election posters of the 1948 campaign still clung to the posts along the Saint John River, wrote to report
a conversation with Michael Wardell:

... Today I had a longish talk about political matters with Michael
Wardell. He feels as I do, that we can take York-Sunbury at the coming
federal election if we have a good candidate. The only one in sight
at present is Aulder [Gerow]. Michael asked me what I thought
about you as a candidate and of course I think it would be a
splendid idea.

Michael's support, in my opinion, helped greatly in the provincial,
as witness our greatly increased popular vote in York County
where the Gleaner is widely read.

I do hope you will consider this Dalton.

Michael used to like Milton Gregg but he is browned off with him now.

I had not seen Lucy Sansom since the party's last annual meeting, in
January, 1956, when Rowe had given me the painful task of telling her
that she should not seek re-election as national women's president because strong factions among the women had other plans, and because
another New Brunswicker, Tom Bell, had become YPC president. It was
a thoroughly unpleasant experience, relieved only by the fact that Lucy's
reluctant withdrawal prevented an unpleasant scene. No one could
remember an officer of the party association being defeated for re-
election.

I replied to Lucy's letter, thanking her but declining the suggestion.
I also thanked Wardell, with whom I was corresponding on other
matters. (I had wanted him to carry the view of the Liberal and Tory
leaders in his magazine regarding policy for the Maritimes; "We will
have much the stronger point of view," I wrote, "if you will pardon the
partisan observation.")

As for my entry into politics: "I had a note from Lucy Sansom
reporting a conversation with you which was most flattering to me. If
this was a true report, I thank you for the kind thought."

To which Wardell replied, not without perception:

You do not say what your reaction was to Lucy Sansom's suggestion; but from your letter I fear you may have found the idea impossible.

This was not quite so, as I informed him:

With regard to Lucy Sansom's suggestion, I do not quite find the idea impossible, but rather unlikely. . . . I am informed that there is a possibility that Dr. Bev. Jewett might consider being a candidate. It would appear he would do extremely well. In any event, I have replied to Lucy's letter, and if you are interested, I am sure she will tell you about it.
Gordon Churchill, M.P., who is Diefenbaker's appointed Director of Organization, expects to be in Fredericton February 21st or 22nd. . . . I am hopeful that you and Gordon can meet.

Drew's secretary, Derek Bedson, had remained on with Diefenbaker, and his ability to keep the channels of communication open between the headquarters and the leader's office was never more sorely tried. It was not always easy to know who, if anyone, was in charge. Derek lived on the upper floor of the three-story house on Cooper Street in which Rowe and I had also lived, sharing a flat on the floor below which now, alas, I occupied alone.
"Dear Bill" I wrote Rowe:

I am sending you two letters which came here. One . . . is a bill from the laundry. I have paid the Hydro as I should have, and the office has paid the telephone bill, but I am not going to pay your laundry bill. . . .
As ever,
Your best friend.

While most of the Tory caucus looked to the election, in the main, as another struggle for personal survival, there was a different feeling among some of Diefenbaker's admirers in the press gallery.
I had great respect for Jim Oastler of the Montreal *Star,* whose opinions on politics and politicians were rarely clouded by bias. Jim had worked for R. B. Bennett and had since seen a lot of Ottawa politics. He was optimistic about Diefenbaker's chances and, when I occasionally talked to him about my returning to full-time private business, he strongly urged me to stay on for the campaign.
Oastler had an interesting theory about Diefenbaker; he thought the Tory leader might win because he would get "the railroad vote," which Oastler described as the votes of employees of the railroads and their families. Jim thought there was an average of a dozen or more "railroad votes" in each poll in the country and he thought they would go to Diefenbaker's candidates in the election.
Ron Nickerson was the second of two reporters in the British United

Press Bureau on the Hill, the bureau chief being Norman MacLeod. Nickerson was an acquaintance of many years; we had been in the army together. While I addressed him as "Corporal," he was the only person in Ottawa to call me "Butch," a nickname acquired at university before the war. Nickerson had only praise for Diefenbaker and thought he had a chance to win.

The Chief was spending much of his time outside the House, exposing himself to the country and trying out his new mantle. The press liked him; the doubters in his party were still unconvinced and suspicious of him, but they were silent. He was also making progress in settling his followers in positions that were satisfactory to their pride, position, and ambitions. When he issued a communiqué which finally appeared to settle the contest between Hees and Churchill, the press gave it scant attention. Not many knew of the fierce struggle within the party for position in the new pecking order:

In order that the Progressive Conservative Party may prepare as rapidly as possible for the forthcoming federal election, it has been necessary for me to delegate certain important responsibilities with regard to the Party's National Headquarters and the Party's Organization across Canada.
Gordon Churchill, M.P., Winnipeg South Centre, has been placed in charge of all activities at National Headquarters and will be in direct charge of party organization.
To bring our organization up to fullest efficiency in view of the impending campaign, an extensive tour throughout Canada is immediately necessary. This task I have deputized to George Hees, M.P., Toronto-Broadview, who has already rendered valuable service to the Party in organizational work.
I appreciate the fact that these tasks represents [sic] considerable sacrifice of time and energy and that both Mr. Churchill and Mr. Hees will assume these duties in addition to their responsibilities as Members of the House and their obligations to their own ridings in the forthcoming campaign. I am sure all members of our Party will extend to them full cooperation.

The voice was that of the leader, but the composer, I suspected, was Grosart. At last Allister had succeeded in his mission and given both of the Chief's lieutenants what each most wanted–a command position for Churchill and a cross-country junket for Hees. I marvelled.

The sorting-out was endless. Perhaps the most difficult questions to adjudicate were those claims for preference which were accompanied by reminders of a lifetime of personal fealty. Diefenbaker, his destiny at last ripening, had as long a memory for his friends as he was suspected to have for his enemies.

Ideally, to qualify for the highest rank among the few who had been constantly faithful, one should have been among the seventy-nine who voted for Diefenbaker on both ballots at the 1942 Winnipeg convention, who stood with him before the Drew steam-roller at the Ottawa convention in 1948, who were among the few who attended his grief at the burial of his first wife, and who now, jostled by newcomers in the hundreds, would ask nothing of him but to continue to serve him as always.

The trouble was that the ardour of their faith was not matched by usable skills. Bill Brunt and David Walker, both of Toronto, could be helpful in Ontario, provided they did not interrupt the smooth functioning hum of the Frost machine; friends in Saskatchewan felt more passionately about their non-partisan support of him–and they coined a slogan to match: "Not a partisan cry," it went, "but a national need." It was perfect for Prince Albert.

M. J. "Mickey" O'Brien, president and founder of O'Brien Advertising, was another of the faithful few. He had always been helpful where he could, promoting Diefenbaker's interest, solacing him in defeat, hailing him in victory, consoling him in his private sorrows. When the leadership convention was over, O'Brien returned to British Columbia to outline the advertising campaign for the next election–"a few thoughts" and "rough ideas" which he thought would communicate to all Canadians in the few weeks of the campaign his own life-long feelings and admiration for the new leader.

Diefenbaker, aware that other commitments had been made, referred the matter of the O'Brien presentation to Grosart, who deftly passed it on to me. I did not want to see it, but asked Dick Coates at National Headquarters to review it and give me his opinion:

February 22, 1957

To: Dalton Camp
From: Richard Coates
Subject: National Advertising and the O'Brien Agency
As you know, Mr. Kelly gave a preview consisting of a tape recorded talk and slides in order to suggest the type of national campaign which the O'Brien Agency feels the Conservative Party might use on both radio and television to attract voters to our Party at the coming election. . . .

The general method suggested by the O'Brien Agency is that any advertising should first concentrate on the national leader, John Diefenbaker, then on the national leader and his team and finally on the candidate. This, I believe, is quite sound. . . .

However, where I do have considerable reservation is in the method of presentation by the Agency.

Their slogan seems to be "A Vote for John Diefenbaker is Best for Canada, Best for the West and Best for You."

I am not at all convinced that that is what we want.

The television portion of the presentation would be a series of five minute films on various subjects such as agriculture, industry, natural resources, etc.

The method used would be John Diefenbaker interviewing the average citizen with a screen background to give variety and the proper locale.

The example shown by the Agency was a farm interview between Diefenbaker and a farmer by the name of Dick Peters, with close-ups and a question and answer exchange between the farmer and Mr. Diefenbaker.

The idea is perfectly all right but I have reservations as to whether the O'Brien Agency has the necessary political understanding to be able to present this properly.

Throughout the whole television portion there is a horrifying smugness and a shocking naïveté in the final conclusion, that after a brief interview this farmer can appear completely happy, completely sold on the Conservative Party and with all his questions answered.

... I believe we should think about the adoption of a slogan or theme for this election. The O'Brien Agency used the maple leaf as a suggested slogan and while I believe they can come up with something better, none the less I feel we should have a definite slogan for this election which would identify our Party and John Diefenbaker.

One was never sure when Coates was being serious and when he was being droll; the memorandum could be read either way. But O'Brien was serious. He had a curiously imperious style, which led him to dispatch a man to Ottawa to pitch for the account while he himself remained in Vancouver, apparently standing by the telephone.

Meanwhile, his man in Ottawa would tell us, "Mickey says Mr. Diefenbaker has an excellent radio voice."

Or, as matters developed, "Mickey thinks Mr. Diefenbaker will be very disappointed."

Without warning, consultation, or explanation, Gordon Churchill suddenly withdrew from his headquarters role. Grosart was placed in full command. It came to me as a blow from the darkness. I felt that Churchill had betrayed our understanding, that Allister had been merely cynical in all our deliberations and, finally, I felt it was a mistake.

It had been my feeling that Grosart should have accompanied Diefenbaker throughout the campaign, acting as speech writer, television consultant, sounding board, and press relations manager. I thought he would be wasted in headquarters during a campaign where, in my experience, there was largely talk but little action.

273

I did not think I could work with him alone, or under him, in preparing the campaign advertising. I wanted Diefenbaker to know of my decision, since so much had been done allegedly in his name. I had not had any personal contact with him since the convention.

March 15, 1957

My dear Chief:
I am given to understand by Gordon Churchill that you have appointed someone of your own choice to take over all direction of publicity for the forthcoming campaign as well as to direct the activities at National Headquarters in Mr. Churchill's absence from Ottawa when the House is dissolved.
This being so, the person you have appointed, of course, replaces me and is therefore responsible for my present duties.
It is my pleasure to submit forthwith my resignation as Director of Publicity. This I do with best of goodwill.
I wish you godspeed and every success.

Cordially yours,
Dalton K. Camp

I returned to Toronto and informed the agency that my career in federal politics was now done. It was a complete withdrawal; I even convinced myself, along with others:

I was sorry to hear that you found it necessary to resign. Although I am not suggesting your indispensability, I feel the party will have considerable difficulty finding another who combines the art of the publicist with the values of an intellectual.
Enough of that–back to the gray flannel suit and your nightly pilgrimages to the Martini Belt.

Yours,
Finlay MacDonald

The Prince Edward Island Conservative Association have learned of your resignation from National Party Headquarters.
During our last Provincial Campaign we were indeed pleased to have had your assistance. True enough, our combined efforts proved unsuccessful in defeating the old regime. However, we have not in any way held you responsible and we sorry that you have at this time, found it necessary to terminate your association with us.

Yours sincerely,
H. B. Carr
Secretary

Churchill called. What was I doing in Toronto?

"For God's sake, Gordon," I said, "you should know."

"I hope you'll think it over. Darn it all, we need your help down here."

"Gordon, why did *you* quit?"

"Well–"

"You know Allister and I won't work well together. It just won't work, Gordon. I've tried it."

"Well, I just want to do what the Chief wants me to do."

"I think that's great, Gordon. But what does he want me to do?"

"Well, darn it, he wants you to give us a hand here."

"Why doesn't he ask me? He's told everyone else what to do–you, Hees, Grosart–why doesn't he tell me?"

"I'm telling you."

"Gordon, I don't think you know what he wants. I don't think he knows." I was being miserably difficult, but nothing could shake Gordon's calm.

"I'll speak to John. You know, golly, there's no doubt about it. He wants you and Grosart and me to work this out."

"I'll think about it, Gordon."

"I'll speak to the Chief. Goodness, that's easy enough."

Allister called, the conversation was more of the same.

"Diefenbaker is a funny guy," Allister told me, in a smiling voice. "He never asks anyone to do anything. You just hear about it."

"Did he ask you to take over headquarters?"

Cough. "Well, only for the campaign." Cough. "I hate the place, you know that."

"I think it's a mistake."

"You may be right, but he's the boss." Cough.

And there the matter stood.

On March 18, I went to the annual Press Gallery Dinner with Ron Nickerson, my first invitation to this traditional event. It was a pleasant, strangely mellow evening; the skits were good-natured, and the speeches were uniformly excellent.

It was Diefenbaker's first appearance as party leader, as it was to be St. Laurent's last.

In those days, before the reconstruction of the innards of the West Block, the guests to the dinner assembled for drinks before and after the dinner in the Railway Committee Room, which was eminently suitable for the purpose, both in its ample physical dimensions and its acoustics, which were as good as those in the Mormon Tabernacle.

And here in the midst of this cheerful din, as I entered the room with Nickerson, I met Diefenbaker, who was standing in a dissolving receiving line with the gallery president. I had not seen him since the morning after the convention.

Immediately he saw me he flung his arm around me, locked my

head in the crook of his arm and drew me against him. It was a sudden and surprising embrace. I was close enough to him to smell his shaving lotion, or was it mouthwash?

"What is this?" he demanded, staring down at me with those intense blue eyes. "What is that letter all about? (My letter of resignation.) I have not read it, you understand? I have not received it. It does not exist."

I said nothing.

"Now, I want you with me. Do you understand? I want you with me, and that's all there is to it!"

What could I say?

33

Statement by John Diefenbaker, National Leader
The National Campaign Committee of the Progressive Conservative
Party will meet in Ottawa on April 7th and 8th to outline campaign
strategy for the coming Federal Election. The National Committee comprises representatives of all ten provinces.

It is expected that the meetings will cover all phases of the general
campaign plan including policy, candidates, advertising and publicity.
Decisions reached will be placed before the entire party Caucus
for amendment or approval on the second day, April 8th.

Preliminary planning for the meetings will be undertaken by a
Planning Committee of Caucus consisting of the following Members of
Parliament: G. R. Pearkes, D. S. Harkness, Gordon Churchill
(Chairman), G. H. Hees, J. M. Macdonnell, D. M. Fleming,
Dr. W. G. Blair, Mrs. E. Fairclough, Leon Balcer, R. Perron, Wm.
McL. Hamilton, A. J. Brooks, G. C. Nowlan, and J. A. Maclean.
D. K. Camp and A. Grosart, National Campaign Manager, will also
serve on the Committee. Mr. Camp, formerly Director of Publicity,
has undertaken important special responsibilities for the Atlantic
provinces and for creative planning of national advertising.

Provincial committees have been actively engaged in all
provinces organizing nomination meetings and other activities. This is
in line with a general policy of decentralization of campaign duties
and responsibilities.

IT NEEDED A SLOGAN.

Hank Loriaux, Bill Kettlewell, and I shut ourselves up in the agency
boardroom, with its long, gleaming, bare table, and the incongruous
revolutionary print by Diego Rivera hanging on the wall. We racked
our minds for a suitable slogan, something to wrap around the campaign, like binder twine, holding together all the condensed, compressed stuff of the campaign, the advertisements, posters, and pamphlets.

We liked what we had—a spare, uncluttered full page bearing a
square-cut photograph of Diefenbaker with a solid paragraph of tributes to him distilled from the press, including citations from the Vancouver *Sun* and the Winnipeg *Free Press,* rare sources for homage to
a Tory politician. The bottom of the ad was blank, awaiting the magic
of inspiration—the slogan.

We had taken Reidford's *Globe and Mail* cartoon, portraying the

Peace Tower as a guillotine, as the motif for another full page, with the stark headline, "BLACK FRIDAY." The copy was a summation of the Tory position on the pipeline debate with supporting statements and cartoons from the newspapers. Kettlewell had also adapted this to a pamphlet, reversing the Reidford cartoon white-on-black. It was strong stuff.

But the slogan.

Brain-storming was the vogue in agency practice. Creative minds were encouraged to think spontaneously and aloud, to express whatever entered their minds, without inhibition, order, or relevance. The only rule was that no one else should criticize or question anything said by another.

The agency had assigned Loriaux as account executive to our two-man creative task force. Since Kettlewell and I were on the "creative" side, our activities seemed to require the presence of someone like Loriaux who would represent the agency in the correct, professional sense. We were likely to be flighty. The other trouble with Bill and me was that we were committed Tories.

We had all been together previously at J. Walter Thompson's, so that we were accustomed to one another's work habits and thought processes. I considered Loriaux to be thorough and diligent as a contact man, but uninspired creatively.

The brain-storming around the campaign slogan began.

"Too bad," Kettlewell said, "that it can't be, 'Let's clean house.' "

"It's something like that–an invocation," I said. "Like the Republican slogan, 'It's time for a change.' "

"Okay, a change to what?"

" 'King or Chaos'–that was a great slogan."

"Now is the time for all good men. . . ."

"What this country needs is a good five-cent cigar."

"What this country needs is a change of government."

". . . a Conservative Government."

". . . a Diefenbaker Government."

"It's time for a change."

"Canada needs a Diefenbaker Government."

". . . needs a Diefenbaker Government *now.*"

"Next!"

"Now is the time for a change to Diefenbaker."

"It's time for a change to Conservatism."

"Now is the time for Diefenbaker."

"Canada needs Diefenbaker."

". . . needs Diefenbaker now."

"Let's have a Diefenbaker Government for a change."

"It's time for Diefenbaker."

"That's close," I said.

278

"It's time for a Diefenbaker Government," Loriaux said.

"Of course!" I said. "It's time for a Diefenbaker Government."

The slogan was Loriaux's.

I knew it was right. It was positive. It echoed what we took to be the greatest common denominator of the campaign—the belief that the Liberals had been in office too long, that it was time for a change.

But "time for a change" begged a question—change to what? The answer ought not to be "change to the Conservatives," which invoked partisan loyalties and repelled Liberal sentiments. Better a soft answer: change to "a Diefenbaker Government."

Diefenbaker was obviously a better word than Conservative: it had no history; it was non-WASP, more acceptable to Liberals.

The name had the proper cadence—better than Drew, because Diefenbaker rhymed with nothing, did not make the same kind of sound, like disapproval, and Diefenbaker suggested ethnic origins, a social order other than Toronto, and politics other than Conservative. The words "Diefenbaker Government" had a strong, positive, credible ring. They were confident words, carrying the thought beyond winning elections to forming a government; not a Conservative Government, mind you, but a Diefenbaker Government.

Painless change, buoyant hopes, a new order, glints of strength and fresh promise!

"It's time for a Diefenbaker Government. . . ."

"Golly," said Kettlewell, pencilling it in the roughs, "it lays out beautifully."

34

DALTON CAMP
LOCKE JOHNSTON & COMPANY
TORONTO, ONT.

NATIONAL CAMPAIGN COMMITTEE MEETINGS QUEBEC
SUITE CHATEAU LAURIER SUNDAY APRIL 7 AT
10:30 A.M. STOP MONDAY APRIL 8 CAUCUS ROOM
HOUSE OF COMMONS 9:00 A.M.

A. BURNS
OTTAWA

THE NATIONAL CAMPAIGN COMMITTEE WAS COMPOSED OF THE SENIOR
officers of the national associations, designated members of caucus, and
a number personally chosen at large by Diefenbaker. It was his creation,
and the committee continues to function to this day—possibly Diefenbaker's only contribution to party organization.

It had one principal attraction; it allowed the leader to create his
own campaign committee, without seeming too rude about it, simply by
superimposing his friends upon the formal structure which he had inherited from his predecessor.

Leadership conventions make politics new again, and this old
committee sensed the newness of others around them. The Quebec
Suite was dark with inscrutability, the old pols wearing masks, like
visors, which cast their faces in expressionless immobility.

The new Diefenbaker men were there—Bill Brunt, Pierre Sévigny,
Paul Lafontaine, Norman Genser, Mickey O'Brien—the converted
Diefenbaker men—Grosart, Churchill, Harry Willis—and the rest, the
remnants of the Drew era, their offices and titles somewhat faded
now—Elizabeth Janzen, the women's president, Leon Balcer, the
national president—all gathered in the suite to hear plans for the campaign and to explore the footing in the new, unknown terrain of Diefenbaker's leadership.

Since I was to make the advertising presentation, I took Loriaux,
Kettlewell, and Jim Mumford, the agency's media director, with me.
I looked down the long table to see Grosart (McKim's) who was
chairing the gathering, and Art Burns (Burns Advertising), and
Mickey O'Brien (O'Brien Advertising). It occurred to me that Diefen-

280

baker had more advertising agencies than General Motors.

Politicians know nothing about political advertising, but they all know what they like, and they begin their appraisal of advertising campaigns with brooding suspicion. Elections, they feel, are too complex for the public, and they would rather contest them by the conventional means–the emotional rallies, noisy parades, and the partisan rhetoric which are, more than anything, comforting in their simplicity. Politicians fear the instruments of advertising, even while recognizing them as a necessary evil which must be borne, like journalism, during elections.

The trouble with advertising was that it threatened a political system that was fundamentally a private matter. It introduced strange new circumstances, most of them unpleasant; it had the capacity to publicize everyone and everything, including those who wished to be anonymous and preferred to conduct their politics in secret.

But not only that, advertising meant that there was less room in the club-house (or else it would be empty); the hierarchy was obliged to make way for young men with alien manners, full of self-assurance and incomprehensible jargon, and demanding large sums from party campaign funds for doubtful enterprise in publicity. They were dangerously close to running things.

And now one of them was appearing in the Quebec Suite, on that warm and quiet Sunday forenoon, delivering to sixty-two members of John Diefenbaker's campaign committee the outlines of the election advertising strategy, fully illustrated.

I explained to the committee the essential wisdom in a campaign in which nearly all the promotional copy was not of our own creation but written by unimpeachable authority, the press of Canada–editorial testimonials, strung together like pearls, giving rounded, lustrous tribute to the new leadership of the Tory party:

A Canadian with a spirit of true Canadianism . . . a reformer with
a keen sensing of changing needs for his country . . . a man of breadth
who has been tested in the trials of pioneering and progress.
He is an indefatigable worker. He is independent enough not to be
swayed by sectional appeals. And he is buttressed in his task by the
declared loyalty of exceedingly able lieutenants.
An incorrigible defender of human rights. His record pleads
eloquently for him. Since the day when he first hung out his shingle
as a young lawyer in Wakaw, Saskatchewan, in 1919, he has been
fighting with clear-sighted vision for those elements in Canadian life
which he believes are vital for the well-being of the individual.
He has first-hand knowledge of the trials and problems, the hopes
and dreams of ordinary people. He is profoundly dedicated to belief
in individual rights and human dignity.

John Diefenbaker would fill the post of Prime Minister with dignity, with courage, with fairness and with honor, those same inflexible qualities which already won for him the instinctive trust of ordinary people everywhere.

All this explained the slogan, which needed no explanation. Election campaigns which feature policy are for parties with unpopular leaders; parties with popular leaders do not have to campaign on reckless, irresponsible promises. Besides, as everyone knew, people do not understand politics, but they do know who they like.

I was brimming with confidence and something like indifference. Not only did I know the campaign was good, very good, but it was, at that precise moment, unimportant to me whether anyone else in the room thought so or not. As the visuals were presented, confidence, fueled by arrogance, brought to the presentation a commanding authority.

There was not too much copy in the ads ("Did the Vancouver Sun *really* say that?"), the photograph of Diefenbaker was handsome, the Kettlewell layouts were bold and clean, mounted and matted so that they commanded the eye.

When the presentation was done, applause broke out in the room, swelling to an ovation. I had to take a bow. Harry Willis liked it. More important, so did Brunt. Eddie Goodman gave his enthusiastic endorsement. Even Mickey O'Brien smiled–only a little ruefully. Grosart, his face flushed with relief and satisfaction, adjourned the meeting for lunch.

He came over to me and said, "You can have anything you want. Just name it."

As I said to Kettlewell, it sounded good but what did it mean? "It means," Bill replied, "that he liked it."

Diefenbaker had a rule. The party was not to publish anything in his name or about him unless he had first approved it. I could not blame him for that, but I warned Allister that magazine closing dates were already upon us and the material was due. If Diefenbaker had to approve of the laudatory newspaper citations of himself, he would have to do it soon.

Earlier in the day I had met him. He said he had heard enthusiastic reports about the advertising campaign, but he reminded me of his stricture and said he would like to see the material on the following day. I decided, rather than press for an earlier meeting, to gamble.

"To hell with it," I said to Kettlewell, "send out the material. If Diefenbaker finds anything wrong with it he will either have to live with it or live without his creative consultants."

Within hours, the material had gone out from the Toronto suppliers –to *Maclean's* and *Reader's Digest,* to a half-dozen publications–for the farmer, the veteran, and Daughters of the Empire, all proclaiming "It's Time for a Diefenbaker Government!"

Diefenbaker liked the campaign; when it was explained that none of the glowing copy in the first ad had been produced by mere copywriters but by the press, he liked it even better.

He began to read it, word for word, Allister looking over his shoulder and clucking approvingly, aware of the fact that it was a *fait accompli,* and eager to hurry Diefenbaker through the material, especially the first ad, already gone to press.

But the leader's eye rested on a single sentence, half-way through the copy. The great head shook negatively, the eyes, shrewd, cool, and lit by an inner glow of justification, raised from the proof.

"No," he said, casually but with firmness, "no, we can't have that."

"Can't have what, sir?" asked Allister, with a hint of indulgence.

Diefenbaker pointed to a sentence in the text. "I want that taken out."

Allister and I squinted fiercely at the offending passage. Had we missed something? some typesetter's error? some obscenity–*double entendre*? what?

The sentence read, "Since the day when he first hung out his shingle as a young lawyer in Wakaw, Saskatchewan, in 1919, he has been fighting with clear-sighted vision for those elements in Canadian life which he believes are vital for the well-being of the individual."

"That's good stuff," Allister was saying.

"I want that reference to Wakaw taken out," Diefenbaker said, not hearing him.

I decided to plunge into the fog of unseen danger. "Wakaw? Isn't it true?"

Diefenbaker's level gaze met mine, the smile slight, the voice a decibel stronger. "I want it out, that's all." Then, perhaps wistfully, "Someday I'll tell you why, but for now, just take it out. Just that one change. Now," turning to the next advertisement, "what about this?"

There was nothing left to say. "Just that one change." I thought of Kettlewell, possibly trotting on his horse over the countryside in King, blissfully unaware. The first advertisement had been dispatched, would, indeed, now be on the presses. Tens of thousands of impressions of John Diefenbaker, the man from Wakaw, rolling off the big drums, still wet, already racing through the printing plants of the nation.

I then explained that I must leave immediately to ensure the sentence was expunged from the campaign. I cursed the unknown editor who had written it, and myself for putting it into the copy. Who would give a damn anyway? Only Diefenbaker.

Somehow, Kettlewell had the changes made, so that no one would know, or be reminded, that John Diefenbaker began the practice of law in the Saskatchewan town of Wakaw.

What was so offensive about the reference to Wakaw? Someone once suggested that it had to do with the coming of the Ku Klux Klan to the Prairies, that possibly Diefenbaker was peripherally involved in its early activities. Peter Newman had another suggestion; it was that Diefenbaker had once been the secretary of the Liberal Party Association in Wakaw. The mystery remains.*

Politics is largely made up of irrelevancies. Politicians, when they have nothing else to do, immobilize themselves and everyone near them, obsessed, like Spanish border guards, with the continuous assertion of their authority. It is a mechanism for self-preservation.

Diefenbaker enjoyed the adaptation of the Reidford cartoon into the Black Friday folder and newspaper advertisement. But Olive thought the copy might be made stronger. In the Diefenbakers' bedroom in the Chateau, Olive and I grappled with the copy. She rearranged sentences, shortened them, suggested stronger words. She had an eye for words and an ear for nuance. Finally, she was satisfied with it. The national advertising campaign was at last complete. Not only had John approved, I told Kettlewell, but Olive, too.

The campaign was a model of simplicity, efficiency, economy, and reach. The editorial testimonial advertisement would appear in every Canadian magazine of record, and in every daily newspaper. *Reader's Digest,* where it would appear as a double-page spread (one page made up of Diefenbaker's picture), ran off extra copies in the hundreds of thousands to be shipped into the constituencies as pamphlets. When folded, the inside was blank for local use. The second advertisement, Black Friday, was another full page scheduled for later

*"He hung out his first shingle at Wakaw, Saskatchewan, north of Saskatoon and almost overnight became a successful lawyer."
It's right there, in the red-and-blue, one-fold campaign pamphlet. Long after the election, I read the copy, presumably written by Allister. ("JOHN is a natural winner . . . JOHN is nationally known . . . JOHN is a man of high principles . . . JOHN has the common touch.") I recalled the scene in the leader's office, and the argument about the mention of Wakaw in the advertisement. Three possibilities:
(1) The presentation having been unanimously acclaimed by the Campaign Committee, Diefenbaker felt he must assert his authority, and reinforce his commandment that all advertising must be cleared by him. Thus, desperate to find some caveat in the fulsome praise in the copy, he found only Wakaw, which reminded him of something.
(2) Allister had already written the pamphlet copy with the offending reference to Wakaw and it was already at the printers. Thus, Allister gently argued the point, but did not press too hard, convinced, as I have been for a lifetime, that no one reads political pamphlets anyway, except authors, original or post hoc.
(3) Allister did not write the pamphlet and did not read the proposed copy for it. Certainly I did not, nor, obviously, did Diefenbaker (unless we accept explanation No. 1). Anyway, some hundreds of thousands of pamphlets were circulated throughout the country; the reference to Wakaw appears to have passed unnoticed. Perhaps readers were beguiled by this: "As P-C foreign affairs expert he has travelled widely in Europe and elsewhere and lectured by special invitation on 'Freedom' at the University of Jerusalem in 1954."

in the campaign, for the newspapers only. It, too, was converted into a pamphlet.

All in all, there were less than a thousand words of copy in the entire campaign–and less than fifty of them had been written by me (and Olive). There was but one photograph–Diefenbaker's–and one other illustration–the cartoon by Reidford. Everything bore the slogan, which was the agency's chief contribution, the product of group brainstorming and Loriaux's inspiration.

The national campaign had been done even before the first speech of the campaign was to be made. Still, the Tory Party's new leader remained a stranger to me, the more so after the Wakaw incident, when the man's inscrutability and secretiveness gave hint to future troubles.

Notwithstanding, Diefenbaker was cheerful, friendly, and entertaining. Everything reminded him of a story. He conveyed to those who were to be close to him in the campaign the sense of their being needed, of his depending upon them, which Drew could never seem to do. So the Diefenbaker political family, of which Grosart was the ranking member, was surprisingly free of friction and small jealousies. Each felt secure in his role in the campaign and satisfied that he enjoyed the leader's trust.

Diefenbaker was a changed man. He had once held brooding, resentful doubts that he would ever lead the Tory party. Now the doubts were gone, and although he was profoundly uncertain as to whether he might ever lead the country, he was, in 1957, content with his immediate prize, enjoying his new role to the full, eager to campaign in the country; the exhilaration of it was enough so that he greeted each day with zest, and revelled in the quickening pace of precampaign activities.

Elections are neither fought nor won by personal arithmetic. Even so, everyone does their own sums, exploring the calculations for victory. It is a feckless exercise, like tic-tac-toe, but politicians practice it compulsively.

The most artful, optimistic calculations could not add up to a Diefenbaker victory.

"How many seats you figure in Ontario?"

"Ontario? Sixty."

"Sixty out of what?"

"Sixty out of eighty-five."

"Okay. How about Quebec?"

"Twenty-five."

"You're kidding."

"Fifteen for sure."

"How many for the Grits, then?"

"No more than fifty. Absolutely."

"So, after Quebec and Ontario, we have seventy-five seats and the Grits have eighty-five?"

"Well, the CCF will get some."

"So how do we win the election?"

"I didn't say we could win the election. I said it would be close."

Once, in a spasm of annoyance with Grosart, I said, "Come on, Allister, tell me where you think we can win the election. Give me the arithmetic."

Allister looked hurt. "You know I can't do that," he said.

But I was coming to like him, despite his vagueness, the circumlocutory responses, the studied cough that allowed him time to respond, time to think, time to duck. He was smooth, shrewd, patient, and resourceful.

"You divide up the billing," he said to me. "It's your campaign. Take what you want and allocate the rest."

I told him I did not want to do it. He persisted, assuring me that he had no commitments to his own agency, McKim's, nor to any other.

"Just as a suggestion," he said, helpfully, "you might give the pamphlets to McKim's. They've done it before. They're big enough to handle it."

All the pamphlets had been done. Allister had produced one himself–about Diefenbaker (one fold, for a No. 10 envelope, with space for the candidate's imprint, all in red, white, and blue). It was corn, which was Allister's forte, but the faithful loved it.

McKim's was obliged to fill the various pamphlet orders from the constituencies and ship them out. It did not impress me as being an especially complex operation, although there had never been an election in memory following which there had not been a chorus of complaint from Tory workers about the pamphlets–either because they did not get the pamphlets in time to use them in the campaign, or sometimes because they did.

I dutifully carried out Allister's request to divide the budget. McKim's was given the pamphlets and the placing of Ontario daily newspapers; I assigned all radio to Foster's together with western daily newspapers; I gave my own agency all magazine advertising, plus Quebec English daily newspapers and the daily newspapers in the Maritimes. Based on the estimates, the money worked out almost evenly among the agencies.

Allister thought it was a fair proposal; he was "personally" delighted with it–which meant there was something wrong. It was Diefenbaker, who had insisted that his friend, Mickey O'Brien, be "given something."

Agencies, not without reason, worry about their money when dealing with political parties, who, unlike their normal clients, are not legal entities and cannot be sued for debts.

286

It was difficult, if not impossible, to educate party authorities to the function of the agencies and to convince them of the legitimacy of campaign costs. They would not, or could not, understand who paid whom, and sometimes they did not understand why anyone was paid at all.

The advertising agency (I used to hear Allister explaining) *creates* the advertising for the client, and pays the media for the cost of publishing or broadcasting the advertisement, less fifteen per cent which the media allow the agency to keep because it is an agency. The client must then pay the agency the cost of the advertising, which is the total cost, including the fifteen per cent. In short, the client does not pay the agency anything, really. He pays for the cost of advertising, and the *media* pay the agency.

Simple, isn't it?

Grosart knew enough about advertising and about politics to appreciate the earnest requests of the agencies that, in a swift-moving campaign, they be paid promptly by their political clients.

In my own agency, I spent a good deal of my time reassuring the principals that the Tory Party could, and would, pay its bills. Often the amounts of money in receivables were staggering, because campaigns are brief, and funds are quickly committed and quickly spent. In these anxious periods I would receive frequent calls from the agency, all chuckles and encouragement but, before hanging up, a closing plea for reassurance that, win or lose, "we'll get our money *back.*"

Finally, the agency "responsibilities" were so finely drawn they could be reduced to a memorandum which Allister issued from headquarters:

MEMORANDUM TO: Progressive Conservative Members of Parliament
　　　　　　　　　Members of National Campaign Committee
　　　　　　　　　O'Brien Advertising Agency
　　　　　　　　　Locke Johnson Advertising Agency
　　　　　　　　　Burns Advertising Agency
　　　　　　　　　McKim Advertising Agency
　　　FROM: Allister Grosart, Campaign Manager
　　　RE: ALLOCATION OF ADVERTISING RESPONSIBILITY

(1) Some misunderstanding appears to have arisen about the respective responsibilities of Provincial federal Campaign Committees, National Headquarters and the various agencies re the above.

(2) The following general statement of policy is issued to clarify the situation.

(3) The creation and media selection of National Advertising is the responsibility of Dalton Camp of Locke Johnson. National

Advertising comprises national magazine, daily newspapers, Radio-TV, pamphlets and national farm papers. Mr. Camp will seek help at his discretion from other agencies in obtaining best space and time.

(4) Placing of national advertising will be shared by the following agencies: Locke Johnson; O'Brien; Burns; McKim and possibly others to be named (including a French-language agency).

(5) O'Brien will place all daily newspaper, TV and radio national advertising as defined and conditioned above in the four Western Provinces. Locke Johnson will have the same role in the four Atlantic Provinces. Similar agency service will be performed by the other agencies in Ontario and Quebec.

(6) All national newspaper advertising will be submitted in advance to the federal Provincial Committees in each province. The Provincial Committees in each case may reject the suggested advertisements and submit to National Headquarters new copy for use in their own province.

(7) If budget permits, appropriations will be made for provincial advertising under the control of Provincial Committees. This will be handled in all respects at the discretion of the Provincial Committee subject only to copy clearance from National Headquarters.

(8) All local advertising (paid for by local funds) will be under the control of the Provincial Committees and/or Candidates. They may request and arrange for assistance from the above named regional agencies as they see fit.

(9) All publicity and public relations activities on the provincial level will be controlled by the Provincial Committees, which may request and arrange for assistance from the regional national agency as they see fit.

(10) Arthur Burns at National Headquarters will act as National Co-Ordinator of agency activities.

April 13, 1957.

35

April 10, 1957.

Miss Kathleen Kearns,
National Headquarters.
Ottawa, Ontario.

Dear Kay:
I recall an advance of $175.00 for the purposes of my trip to Halifax
the week of March 25 from Toronto via Ottawa, returning
March 31. As itemized, my expenses were:

Hotel	$ 66.65
Other Meals	36.00
Taxis, T.C.A., etc.	11.85
Entertainment and Incidentals	13.00

I hope this comes to $128.30
On that understanding, I enclose a cheque to the amount of $46.70.

As you know, I am going there again next week, and since you
have sent me a cheque for $200.00, I shall consider that
as an advance on my travelling for that purpose.

Thank you for your kind words and interest on the last weekend.

Best regards,
Dalton K. Camp.

April 11, 1957.

J. H. Morrow, Esq.,
Brighton, Ontario.

Dear Mr. Morrow:

This will acknowledge our telephone conversation of Tuesday last.
I am told that your request is the responsibility of the Ontario
Organization Committee, Harry A. Willis, Q.C., Chairman.

I have passed on to Mr. Willis your request for an outside speaker
for a meeting at Campbellford or Cobourg during the latter part
of May on behalf of Ben Thompson. I recall that you expressed
a preference for Donald Fleming.

I am sure you will hear further from Mr. Willis.

Sincerely yours,
Dalton K. Camp.

April 10, 1957.

Dalton Camp, Esq.,
Locke Johnson Advertising Agency.

Dear Mr. Camp:

You have asked for authorization for the use of Mr. John Diefenbaker's
picture on book match covers. I have discussed this with him
today and he has given me the authority to authorize the E. B. Eddy
Company to use the official campaign picture taken by Gaby
of Montreal on book match covers produced by them for
the Progressive Conservative Party. Will you be good enough to pass
this on to the Company.

Yours sincerely,

Allister Grosart
Campaign Manager

April 11, 1957.

Wally West, Esq.,
Eddy Match Company Limited,
Toronto, Ontario.

Dear Mr. West:

I enclose a letter of authorization from Mr. Allister Grosart,
Campaign Manager, with regard to your use of Mr. Diefenbaker's
picture on matchbook covers. I trust this is sufficient for
your purposes.

Yours sincerely,
Dalton K. Camp.

April 11, 1957.

Henri Loriaux, Esq.,
Locke Johnson Advertising Agency.

Dear Hank:

Further to our orders for the Diefenbaker poster, would you
please send 10 large and 10 small to:

Roy Hall, Esq.,
Diefenbaker, Guelenaere and Hall,
Bank of Montreal Chambers,
Prince Albert, Saskatchewan.

Sincerely,

Richard Coates
Department of Publicity

April 12, 1957.

Dalton Bales, Esq.,
Toronto, Ontario.

Dear Dalton:

I hope that I can serve some useful purpose in the interests of
Frank McGee's candidacy, but I am sure you will realize
the difficulties involved. Nevertheless, I was very pleased to meet you
and Frank last evening, and I look forward to being of some
small assistance to you in your efforts in this campaign.

Yours sincerely,
Dalton K. Camp.

April 10, 1957.

Mr. Allister Grosart,
Campaign Manager,
National Headquarters.

Dear Allister:

I enclose for your signature and for your records media commitments
for magazines and weekend publications, English and French
languages.

The space has been booked, as you know, following verbal agreement by yourself and Gordon Churchill.

The advertisement is the copy on Mr. Diefenbaker. The total space commitment is for $44,196.50.

This must be a novel experience for an agency man.

Cordially yours,
Dalton K. Camp.

April 10, 1957.

Mr. Allister Grosart,
Campaign Manager,
National Headquarters.

Dear Allister:

I am enclosing photostats for the Black Friday pamphlet. Some changes have been made in the copy, and I will discuss them with you at our proposed weekend meeting. I also enclose the photostat of the basic magazine advertisement re Mr. Diefenbaker. I shall proceed to adapt the latter to a pamphlet for candidates and prepare printing estimates for your approval.

We have not determined the size of the Black Friday pamphlet. Some of the National Committee members suggested that it be done in an envelope size and in a larger size as well for distribution at meetings and for canvassers. They were presumably impressed by the dramatic size of the blow-up. What is your opinion?

Yours sincerely,
Dalton K. Camp.

April 20th, 1957.

Mr. Dalton Camp,
Ottawa, Ont.

Dear Mr. Camp:

We have received pictures of Mr. Diefenbaker, both with and without the name imprinted, and thought we would let you know we think they are grand.

The simplicity of the one with the name imprinted is terrific, and is far more impressive than a picture with slogans, etc. We can certainly use this type of publicity, keep it coming!

Sincerely,

Mrs. A. J. Bickerton,
South York Conservative Association,
Toronto, Ontario.

April 22, 1957.

Dalton Camp, Esq.,
Locke Johnson Advertising Agency.

Dear Dalton:

Donald Fleming has indicated that he would be willing to travel in the Maritimes and the Province of Quebec from May 14 to May 18. Would you please let me know your views on this as soon as possible.

Best wishes.

Sincerely,

Richard Coates
Chairman, Speakers' Bureau,
The Progressive Conservative Party of Canada,
National Headquarters.

April 23, 1957.

Oakley Dalgleish, Esq.,
Editor-in-Chief,
Toronto Globe & Mail.

Dear Mr. Dalgleish:

John Diefenbaker has asked me to write you and request your permission to reproduce certain cartoons by Mr. Reidford for use by the Progressive Conservative Party of Canada in the forthcoming election campaign. These cartoons we should like to reproduce in both pamphlets and newspaper advertisement. The usual credit will be given both the artist and the publication, unless you wish otherwise.

It would be genuinely appreciated if such permission could
be granted.

Yours sincerely,

Dalton K. Camp,
Director of Public Relations.
The Progressive Conservative Party of Canada.

April 23, 1957.

Dalton Camp, Esq.,
Locke Johnson Advertising Agency.

Dear Dalton:

Concerning the local C.B.C. television time which is being made
available in Halifax to candidates, I assume that Rod Black
will take responsibility for these broadcasts.

Would you arrange some system of control so that either you or
George Nowlan could see scripts in advance in case of any
controversial statements by a candidate.

Sincerely,

Richard Coates
Department of Publicity.

ST STEPHEN NB 24 203P═DALTON CAMP TORONTO═

HAVE ARRANGED FOR DIEFENBAKER TO ATTEND AFTERNOON MEETING
AT ST STEPHEN ON THIRD NOT A CONVENTION═
LORNE GROOM═
1957 APR 27 PM 1 33

DALTON CAMP═
BEAVERBROOK HOTEL

ANGUS MACLEAN PLANS RECEPTION AT MONTAGUE KINGS COUNTY
AT TEN O'CLOCK BEFORE AFTERNOON MEETING STOP CHIEF TO
LUNCH AT RCAF OFFICERS MESS SUMMERSIDE STOP PLANS TO
HAVE HIM APPEAR TEN MINUTE TV PROGRAM AT FIVE FORTY PM
WITH FOUR CANDIDATES ALL TIMES ATLANTIC STANDARD═
ALLISTER GROSART CAMPAIGN MANAGER═

April 30th, 1957.

The Progressive Conservative Party of Canada,
National Headquarters.

TO ALL CANDIDATES AND CAMPAIGN MANAGERS

The enclosed newspaper clippings are from the Toronto Telegram
and the Toronto Star after Mr. Diefenbaker's meetings there
last week-end.

The Toronto Star particularly, is most gratifying. We all know that
this paper is recognized to have strong Liberal tendencies and
yet with the right kind of publicity even they have gone overboard to
publicize the success of the meetings in that area.

Both John and Olive Diefenbaker are giving their all on a forty-three
day tour so that we will be victorious on June 10th. Won't you,
while they are in your area, give of yourself unstintingly to make the
reception of them as successful as those in the Toronto area.

A suggestion would be to have one man in your area whose specific
job would be to contact all local radio stations, daily and weekly
newspapers, television stations, if any, and have photographers at all
meetings, while another is ensuring that enough local newsworthy
dignitaries are in attendance so that your local press will carry
a maximum of publicity.

If there is anything that we can do from this end have no
hesitation in contacting us.

Arthur Burns,
Co-ordinator of
National Advertising.

April 30, 1957.

Mr. Arthur Burns,
National Headquarters,
Progressive Conservative Party of Canada.

Dear Art:

I am sending you a stat of a paste-up of the full-page farm
advertisement tentatively scheduled for Free Press Weekly Prairie
Farmer, May 15 issue. The closing date on this is May 9.

295

April 30th, 1957.

The copy in this ad has been derived from farm policy speeches made by John Diefenbaker. They are direct quotes and, as far as I know, nothing has been added.

We need a very rapid approval of the copy in particular and the layout in general if we are to make our closing date. If approval is given within a day or so, we may also be able to make Country Guide. We must have material in Winnipeg by Friday. Please call me on this.

Cordially yours,
H. Loriaux.

MEMORANDUM TO HENRI LORIEUX [sic]

Sometime past I asked when any order of pamphlets etc. was shipped that the agency involved immediately notify us of the quantity shipped, to whom, how shipped–C.N. or C.P. Express, and the date of shipment.

So as to expedite things from this end would you please in future do this for me.

Arthur Burns.

May 1, 1957.

Mr. Arthur Burns,
Campaign Headquarters,
The Progressive Conservative Party of Canada.

Dear Art:

I enclose herewith a budget which is pretty much the same budget which was the basis for our proposals presented by Dalton Camp at the meeting in Ottawa. Some of the figures are fairly accurate, such as newspapers, magazines, farm papers; others such as contingencies, production, printed matter are "guesstimates" and probably high. Call me if you have any questions on this.

In addition, I am sending you several copies of a memo from our

TV and Radio Director, which I am sure will be of some interest to the people at Headquarters.

Cordially yours,
H. Loriaux.

The Progressive Conservative Party of Canada,
National Headquarters.

MEMORANDUM TO ALL PROGRESSIVE
CONSERVATIVE CANDIDATES

For your information sample of "POLICY" pamphlet for general distribution will be mailed to you Tuesday, May 7th.

Arthur Burns,
Co-ordinator of
National Advertising.

Ottnwn,
May 2nd, 1957

1957 MAY 2 AM 10:22
HENRI LORIEUX LOCKE JOHNSON ADVERTISING═
255 DAVENPORT RD TORONTO═

SHIP TODAY SEVENTY FIVE LARGE DIEFENBAKER POSTERS TO
ADRIAN CLOUTIER KAZABAZUA P.Q. C.P.R. EXPRESS═
ARTHUR BURNS═

May 6, 1957.

Hon. Richard Donahoe, Q.C.,
Minister of Health and Welfare,
Halifax, N.S.

Dear Dick:

Thank you for sending on to me the material with regard to the hospital program in Nova Scotia, which I found on my return to the office today.

As you may know, I spent last week touring the Maritimes with Diefenbaker. I must say the response was exceptionally good.

I am leaving on Wednesday for Halifax and look forward to the possibility of seeing you there.

Kindest personal regards,

Yours cordially,
Dalton K. Camp.

May 7, 1957.

Mr. Richard Coates,
Progressive Conservative Party of Canada,
National Headquarters.

Dear Dick:

For your information, the posters cost 37¢ each for the large and 15¢ each for the small. I have ordered a re-run of 2,000 large.

Cordially yours,
H. Loriaux.

May 7, 1957.

Mr. Arthur Burns,
National Headquarters,
The Progressive Conservative Party of Canada.

Dear Art:

This morning I have ordered a re-run of 200,000 English "Reader's Digest" pamphlets. Would you please send me a confirmation order.

Cordially yours,
H. Loriaux.

TORONTO ONT
MAY 7 1957

MR FINLAY MACDONALD
RADIO STATION CJCH
HALIFAX NS

ARRIVING MAY EIGHTH TCA FLIGHT 426 THREE FIFTY FIVE PM
LOCAL TIME
DALTON K CAMP

May 8, 1957.

Mr. Arthur Burns,
National Headquarters,
The Progressive Conservative Party of Canada.

Dear Art:

Further to your instructions on insertion of the first newspaper ad,
would you please supply me with a complete list of candidates
in the Maritime Provinces with the following information:

(a) Name
(b) Riding
(c) Province

We need this for local listings.

Cordially yours,

H. Loriaux,
Locke, Johnson & Company Limited.

May 8, 1957.

Miss Kathleen Kearns,
National Headquarters,
The Progressive Conservative Party of Canada.

Dear Kay:
I enclose various vouchers collected during my travels. These are
paid out of the advance from you. I also enclose my home telephone
bill for the months of February and March, and I have indicated
on each bill the amount which should be charged to your office. Would
you be good enough to check my addition and have a cheque to
this amount deposited in my current account in Toronto, The Bank
of Nova Scotia, King & Victoria Branch.

With kindest personal regards.

Cordially,
Dalton K. Camp.

May 8, 1957.

MEMO TO: Mr. Art Burns
FROM: H. Loriaux

The remainder of the account was sent to Allister last week.
You can get the original account from him or you can give this
portion to him, but the two pieces have to be put together.

1957 MAY 8 PM 7 32

=DALTON CAMP ORGANIZER
PROGRESSIVE CONSERVATIVE HQTRS 215 ROY BLDG HFX=
WE DIDNT GO TO CAMPBELLTON TO MAKE A SPEECH BUT THATS
ALL WE GOT NO OYSTERS NO BEER NO NOTHING=
=THE DISAPPOINTED DIEFENBAKER PRESS=

MAY 9TH 1957

FRED DAVIS
SECRETARY=DIEFENBAKER PRESS
JOHN DIEFENBAKER SPECIAL TRAIN=CPR NO 3 OR 5
MACTIER ONT

REFERENCE YOUR WIRE=MY INFORMATION IS YOU ATTENDED THE
WRONG CAMPBELLTON MEETING NAMELY RALLY FOR INDEPENDENT
SOCRED J CLYDE VAN HORNECASTLE STOP AM RELIABLY INFORMED
REAL J C VAN HORNE IS ATTENDING EMERGENCY SESSION NATO
COMMITTEE AT UNITED NATIONS FLUSHING MEADOWS STOP HAVE
DONNELLY INVESTIGATE STOP TORY NOMINATION IN WINTERS RIDING
BIGGEST IN HISTORY STOP HOWE LAID EGG IN HALIFAX STOP PRIVATE
AND CONFIDENTIAL

BOB KID

1957 MAY 11 AM 7 41

OTTAWA ONT MAY 10 518P=
DALTON CAMP LOCKE JOHNSON AND CO LTD=
255 DAVENPORT RD TOR (MISROUTE)=

300

PLEASE BE ADVISED THAT NO COMMITMENTS OF ANY KIND
WHATSOEVER WILL BE HONOURED OR PAID FOR HERE UNLESS
APPROVED IN ADVANCE STOP THERE ARE NO EXCEPTIONS OR
QUALIFICATIONS WHATSOEVER TO THIS DIRECTIVE==
ARTHUR BURNS   COORDINATOR   NATL ADVERTISING==

May 13, 1957.

Mr. Arthur Burns,
National Headquarters,
The Progressive Conservative Party of Canada.

Dear Art:

Do not forget we still have 15,000 Pole Cards available for
distribution. Let us not throw them away–give them to someone.
As you know, we have already shipped the French.

Cordially yours,
H. Loriaux.

May 15, 1957.

Mr. Arthur Burns,
National Headquarters,
The Progressive Conservative Party of Canada.

Dear Art:

With the holiday being on Monday, May 20, you realize, of course,
that no one will be working on Saturday or Sunday previous.
So, in order to get out all the requests that you may receive in your
office on Friday morning, I am asking you to put someone on
the telephone with them and phone them all in so that we can get them
out on Friday afternoon, rather than on the next Tuesday when
we could expect to receive orders mailed by you on the
previous Friday.

Let me know if you go along with this so that we can have someone
ready to take orders on Friday morning, and if you agree to this
try to have all your orders assembled on Friday morning so that we
can take the whole batch at once and process them.

Cordially yours,
H. Loriaux.

May 15, 1957.

Mr. Richard Coates,
National Headqquarters,
The Progressive Conservative Party of Canada.

Dear Dick:

Here is a copy of an inter-office memo which I sent out after our
conversation this morning. If you detect any errors in my
reasoning here, please let me know.

Cordially yours,
H. Loriaux.

May 15, 1957.

Mr. Arthur Burns,
National Headquarters,
The Progressive Conservative Party of Canada.

Dear Art:

1. Please note that the responsibility for the shipment and
administration details of posters and pamphlets within Locke
Johnson has been assigned to Dave Patton. Please direct all requests
whether by mail, wire or telephone to him. I will continue to
supervise this operation, but Dave Patton will handle all detail work.
If any major problems arise, please contact me.

2. So far as media print advertising is concerned, please contact our
Media Director, Jim Mumford. He is fully conversant with the
media situation as it pertains to national advertising and will be able
to cope with all your requests or enquiries. If he is not immediately
available by telephone when required, please contact me.

3. On major policy matters, contact Mumford or me.

Cordially yours,
H. Loriaux.

The responsibility for outside speakers rests on each provincial
headquarters, with Dalton Camp the final authority. It is strongly
recommended that contact from a constituency level to outside speakers
be restricted except in case of local speakers. Dates of meetings wherein

special speakers are desired should be forwarded as soon as possible to said headquarters after noting the availability of speakers.

Committee members: Harnett, Hayden, MacDonald, MacRae & Bell.

Every effort should be made to obtain speakers who understand the problems of the Atlantic Provinces and whose approach will be appreciated in each area and not in conflict with united nature of that meeting. Particular attention should be given to the movement of members both federal and provincial as special speakers to other Atlantic Provinces, possibly by way of exchange.

ATLANTIC PROVINCES
CANDIDATES MEETING,
MONCTON

May 15, 1957.

Mr. Arthur Burns,
National Headquarters,
The Progressive Conservative Party of Canada,

Dear Art:

I enclose herewith a memo on printed matter. Please note that the 100,000 Portrait Only Reader's Digest pamphlets were shipped en masse to Montreal. Would you be good enough to initial one of the copies of this memo, and we will take this as your authorization for the printing of all quantities and materials as stated. We will continue to inform you of quantities on hand periodically.

Cordially yours,
H. Loriaux.

May 15, 1957.
PRINTED MATTER
These figures do not take into account under or over runs.

Diefenbaker Posters Ordered–	5,000 small
	4,000 large
Shipped as of May 14–	4,167 small
	2,682 large
Pole Cards Ordered–	15,000 English
	5,000 French
All Shipped	
Reader's Digest Pamphlets Ordered–	1,000,000 English
	100,000 French
	100,000 Portrait Only

Shipped as of May 14–	670,000 English
	48,000 French
Black Friday Pamphlets Ordered–	250,000 English
	100,000 French
Shipped as of May 14–	196,000 English
	15,000 French

May 17, 1957.

Mr. Dalton Camp,
Lord Nelson Hotel,
Halifax, Nova Scotia.

Dear Sir:
If you are interested in accuracy of name for ballot reproduction,
I should point out that your listing is incorrect in so far as it
refers to the Junior Candidate in Queens.
Without division or exception, I spell my name with a Mac.

Yours in the service,

Heath Macquarrie.

1957 MAY 16 PM 3:38
OTTAWA ONT
HENRI LORIAUX=LOCKE JOHNSON ADVERTISING CO LTD
HOLD INSERTION FOR DIEFENBAKER AD SCHEDULED MAY 21ST
INSERTION DATE NOW TO BE 27TH MAY INFORM PAPERS THAT
WE ARE HOLDING FOR NOMINATION DATES ALSO IF YOU MORTISE
FOR LOCAL CANDIDATES ENSURE PROGRESSIVE CONSERVATIVE
PARTY IS STILL IN AD=
ARTHUR BURNS COORDINATOR NATIONAL ADVERTISING=

1957 MAY 21 PM 2 30
SUMMERSIDE PEI 21 213 P=
DALTON CAMP=
LORD NELSON HOTEL HFX=
PLEASE CONFIRM DON FLEMMING [sic] FOR THURSDAY MAY 23RD=
W CHESTER MACDONALD=

1957 MAY 27 AM 9 14
LUNENBURG NS
DALTON CAMP=
PROGRESSIVE CONSERVATIVE HEAD QTRS 215 ROY BLDG HFX=
SUGGEST VERY IMPORTANT TO MARITIMES THAT DIEFENBAKER
PLEDGE IF ELECTED TO ESTABLISH PROPER COASTGUARD

SERVICE COST NEGLIGABLE [sic] IF PRESENT INEFFECTIVE
DUPLICATION OF SERVICES ELIMINATED FURTHER SUBMISSION NOT
SO VITAL THAT SHELBURNE NOVA SCOTIAS MOST SOUTHERNMOST
PORT BE BASE══
JIM HARDING══

1957 MAY 28 PM 7 42
OTTAWA ONT
MR DALTON CAMP══
LORD BEAVERBROOK HOTEL══DIEFENBAKER
ARRIVAL TIME SAINT JOHN JUNE FIRST TWELVE NOON STOP
PLEASE CONFIRM WHEN RESERVATIONS ARE MADE AT LORD
BEAVERBROOK LORD NELSON══
ARTHUR BURNS══

1957 MAY 29 AM 9 28
SYDNEY NS
DALTON CAMP══
══RALLY PLANS AWAITING YOUR DECISION PLEASE WIRE OR PHONE
IMMEDIATELY══
══R B MACQUARRIE══

SYDNEY NS MAY 29
DALTON CAMP FREDERICTON NB.
THANKS FOR YOUR WIRE TONIGHT STOP HAVE BEEN HARD
PRESSED BY CONSTITUENCIES BUT REALIZED WHAT WAS PROBABLY
HAPPENING WIRED NATIONAL HQ TODAY IN DESPERATION FOR
ASSISTANCE BUT HAVE ADVISED THEM OF CHANGED SITUATION
TONIGHT STOP NEW TARGET DATE WEDNESDAY JUNE FIFTH AND
SOLICIT EXERCISE YOUR TALENTS TO PRODUCE BEST RALLY
EASTERN CANADA.
R B MACQUARRIE CAMPAIGN MANAGER.

1957 MAY 30 PM 2 56
HALIFAX NS
══DALTON CAMP══
BEAVERBROOK HOTEL
REGRET TO ADVISE MONCTON TIMES REFUSES TO DELIVER MAT
TO ANYONE WITHOUT AUTHORIZATION FROM SENDER. KINDLY
WIRE MONCTON TIMES TO RELEASE SAME TO AMHERST DAILY NEWS
══W T HAYDEN══

MAY 30 1 07 PM '57
RS TROIS RIVERES QUE
DALTON CAMP

WE ARE NOT COMING TO MAKE A SPEECH STOP REQUIRE
POSITIVE DIRECTIONS CORRECT MEETING THIS TIME STOP HOPE YOU
PLANNING HAVE US MEET LOBSTER AND OYSTER CANDIDATES STOP
DIEF SAYS ACTION NOW STOP WE SAY AMEN
THE HUNGRY DIEFENBAKER PRESS

1957 MAY 31 AM 8 32
SYDNEY NS MAY 30
DALTON CAMP==
TELEPHONE CONVERSATION NATIONAL HEADQUARTERS THIS
THURSDAY MORNING STATE THEY WERE CALLING YOU AND
NOTIFYING ME OF RESULTS THEREAFTER STOP UNDERSTAND
PREMIER NOT AVAILABLE TUESDAY CAN YOU OFFER ADDITIONAL
ATTRACTION WITH VAN HORNE TUESDAY JUNE FOURTH STOP
RALLY ARRANGEMENTS AWAITING YOUR DECISION==
R B MACQUAIRRIE CAMPAIGN MANAGER==

MAY 31 2 00 PM '57
OTTAWA ONT
DALTON CAMP. CARE LORD BEAVERBROOK HOTEL FREDERICTON NB
C.D. HOWE MAKING ELECTION PREDICTIONS IN PORT ARTHUR
ONTARIO SAID THE LIBERAL PARTY SHOULD BREAK EVEN IN THE
MARITIMES STOP RE ST LAURENT SPEECH YESTERDAY IN
ST JOHN'S HE REFERRED TO A DIEFENBAKER STATEMENT THAT A
ROYAL COMMISSION WAS NOT NECESSARY AND SHOULD NOT HAVE
BEEN APPOINTED STOP I RECOLLECT DIEFENBAKER SAYING TO A TV
QUESTION ABOUT THE IMPENDING REVISION OF FINANCIAL TERMS
OF UNION THAT A ROYAL COMMISSION WAS NOT NECESSARY TO
SEE HOW FAR NEWFOUNDLAND LAGGED BEHIND OTHER PROVINCES
IN THE LEVEL OF SERVICES IT COULD PROVIDE ITS CITIZENS STOP
THEN HE PROMISED A BETTER DEAL FOR NEWFOUNDLAND THAN WAS
PRESENTLY PROVIDED BY THE LIBERAL GOVERNMENT STOP.
G G SEDGWICK.

1957 MAY 31 PM 2 44
SAINT JOHN NB
DALTON CAMP==
LORD BEAVERBROOK HOTEL==
I UNDERSTAND LOUIS LEBLANC CONSERVATIVE REPRESENTATIVE
IN KENT COUNTY NEEDS ASSISTANCE TO PLACE FACTS BEFORE
THE ELECTORS IN A FORCEFUL MANNER STOP A MR ROBERTSON
FROM KENT COUNTY SAYS HE WROTE MR CARSON SECRETARY TO THE
PREMIER FOR INFORMATION BUT HAS NOT RECEIVED ANY REPLY.
PLEASE HELP MR LEBLANC. MR BELL HAS SUGGESTED I WIRE YOU==
B BLOOMFILLS JORDAN==

306

JUN 1 7:54 AM '57
MONTREAL QUE
DALTON CAMP. PROGRESSIVE CONSERVATIVE PARTY
LORD BEAVERBROOK HOTEL FREDERICTON NB.
MRS DIEFENBAKER NOT ACCOMPANYING CHIEF ON MARITIME TRIP
(STOP) PLEASE ALTER ANY ARRANGEMENTS ACCORDINGLY.
GEORGE HOGAN.

1957 JUN 3 PM 2:37
SYDNEY NS
LOCKE JOHNSON AND CO LTD
255 DAVENPORT RD══
TV STATION CJCB HAS NO ORDER OR TIME SCHEDULED
JUNE 7 RE P C DIEFENBAKER BROADCAST OKAY JUNE 5 KINDLY
ADVISE RADIO STATION OR HERE REGARDING JUNE 7══
R C DUCHEMIN CAPE BRETON POST══

JUN 3 4:14 PM '57
R C DUCHEMIN
SYDNEY CAPE BRETON POST
SYDNEY NS
TV STATION CJCB HAVE EIGHT OCLOCK BOOKED FOR PROGRESSIVE
CONSERVATIVE ONE MINUTE SPOT JUNE SEVENTH
LOCKE JOHNSON AND CO LTD

1957 JUN 11 AM 10 41
TRURO NS
MR DALTON CAMP LOCKE JOHNSON══
TORONTO══
YOU MAY KEEP YOUR HEAD AND ON IT I PLACE A TEN DIAMOND
CROWN══
DICK HATFIELD══

July 12, 1957.
Mr. Allister Grosart,
National Headquarters,
The Progressive Conservative Party of Canada,
Ottawa, Ontario.
Dear Al:
Enclosed herewith is a completely itemized account of Locke
Johnson's part of the National Campaign. All insertion orders
are attached.
Two items not previously billed to Headquarters are included in
this account:

1. The Black Friday newspaper ad in Maritime papers–$4,316.42
2. The series of 10 TV flashes on each of 5 Maritime
     stations–$2,630.00.

The amount outstanding is less than the total for these two items, due
to credits and adjustments to previously billed and paid-for accounts.
Still to be billed is the time, space, etc. bought on the spot in the
Maritimes by Dalton Camp and for which I understand a separate
reserve fund had been set up. The invoices for Dalton's operations are
still trickling in from the Maritimes. As soon as these are all in, we will
submit a complete accounting.

We would appreciate it if you can arrange final payment of the
National account.

Best regards,
H. Loriaux.

July 17th, 1957
Mr. H. Loriaux,
Locke, Johnson & Company Limited,
Toronto, Ontario.
Dear Hank:

Attached is cheque as per your June 28th account for $6,614.12.
I note that you refer to this as "final payment of National account".
For the sake of the record, the arrangement as I understand it was
that Dalton was given a total fund of $10,000 for advertising in the
four Atlantic Provinces over and above the national advertising
campaign. I take it, therefore, that the total of the two items mentioned
in your letter of July 12th (6,946.42) is an expenditure against this
special allowance.

Please let me know if this agrees with your record.

Sincerely,
Allister Grosart.

36

BY GORDON CHURCHILL'S ARITHMETIC THE PARTY HAD TO WIN WITHOUT Quebec, which meant that it had to win nearly all Ontario, and sweep the Maritimes and the West. No one could argue the logic, although it was subsequently deemed to be bigoted.

In 1957, Quebec could not produce any significant result to the benefit of the Conservative Party. To argue otherwise was ludicrous. I agreed with Churchill's essential point; if we were campaigning to win, we ought to campaign where we were most, not least, likely to win. Quebec would be the last province to turn against Louis St. Laurent. Diefenbaker was little known in Quebec and the least desirable of the candidates among Quebec delegates to the convention. The party had no French-speaking lieutenant, present or prospective, and the more one saw of Balcer the more one marvelled that he had come this far.

Furthermore, the major issues of the campaign appeared lost on the voters of Quebec. The Quebec Tories, nearly all of them members of the Union Nationale, were unmoved by the pipeline issue and the rights of Parliament. English-speaking Tories talking about "government arrogance" only made them uneasy. Authoritarianism was neither alien nor hostile to them. After the advertising presentation, a few of them had sidled up to Allister to murmur that, while the Black Friday advertisement was "very nice," it just wouldn't do for Quebec. Allister assured them that their sensibilities would be respected in this, as in all such matters.

Similarly, suggestions of government mortality and themes such as "time for a change" or "too long in office" or simple arrogance found them unresponsive. While they were prepared to be fiercely anti-Liberal, Diefenbaker was not. And while Diefenbaker was prepared to challenge the leadership of St. Laurent, they were not.

So that all that was in common was the bond of anti-Liberalism, unredeemed by any realistic prospect for success at the polls. It was not the sort of thing I cared to admit, even to myself, but there it was. In politics, one can seldom invent the issues out of whole cloth and only rarely can one choose one's allies. The frail Quebec wing of the Tory party was of little concrete help, and its attitude was a not insubstantial hindrance.

Poor Gordon Churchill! Loyal to Drew, now devoted to Diefenbaker, a decent, pleasant man with modest qualifications as a strategist, he was to endure many years of obloquy for providing his highly obvious, simplistic analysis for the campaign of 1957. And I have no doubt his detractors drove him to occupy the position they accused him of having, as though, out of hurt or perversity or both, Churchill preferred notoriety to anonymity. And so he became, in so much that followed, hostile to Quebec's interests, within and without the party.

But Churchill was right—there was nothing so costly, enervating, and frustrating as this compulsive habit of re-enforcing failure in Quebec. The Quebec organization, newborn with each election, comprised minor functionaries from the Union Nationale. While the Conservative Party easily gave them a certain status, a higher rank and station, there were vast disparities in the perquisites, as there always must be between losers and winners. But U.N.-trained organizers brought to the Tory cadres expensive habits, a total disregard for the need to budget for campaign expenses, and a touching faith in the accident of success; their demands were insatiable, their optimism unquenchable, and the political results negligible both during and after every campaign in living memory.

No one knew how to arrest it, much less turn it around or improve it. The terrible cost of campaigning in Quebec came to be accepted as a necessary hazard of politics, some sort of actuarial loss to be endured, a cost of doing business, like pilferage on the docks. It was not that the cost was so substantial in itself, but it seemed inordinate when measured against the results; as a dreary footnote, it was a cost always greater than estimated or imagined, since it inevitably left a legacy of unexplained, non-attributable debts.

"I'll check out Yarmouth and let you know, Arthur."

"Don't call me until tomorrow night. I have to go to Montreal."

"Oh?"

"It's the usual blackmail dodge. We've got a lot of token candidates there, and every election the bastards go right up to nomination day and then threaten to pull out unless we come through."

"More money for their campaign?"

"More money for *themselves,* for crissakes."

"Where do we get people like that?"

"Sometimes that's all you can get, baby."

"I'd tell them all to go to hell."

"Sure, and read in the papers the next day that a half-dozen of Diefenbaker's candidates have quit on him?"

"What reason could they give?"

"Any goddam reason. He's anti-French, anti-Catholic, anti-Christ. Anything."

"Good luck, Arthur."

"Thanks, pal."

Or the campaign auction of the leader's time:

"Listen, you got to bring the Chief in here. If he doesn't come, they will say he doesn't care, or worse than that, he's afraid to campaign in Quebec."

310

"You know he's not afraid."

"I guarantee it. You bring him in here for a rally and we'll fill the place, pack them in–ten thousand people! And we'll win the seat."

"You mean we can't win the seat unless he comes in?"

"Oh, no. We're going to win, although it will be very close. But if the leader comes, we will win very big and everyone will know he cares about Quebec and it will help the other candidates. You can be sure of that."

"Well, say we did it–you can get ten thousand?"

"No trouble."

"Okay, we'll try and do it your way."

"Can you get us George Hees too?"

"I'll see."

"George is popular here."

"Well, I think it will be okay."

"The only thing is, we need about five thousand dollars."

"Five thousand dollars?"

"If the leader comes here, it has to be a big success. So we need money for advertising, and for bands and things like that."

"Listen, for God's sake, I thought you wanted Diefenbaker to. . . ."

"Don't *worry*! Leave it with us. When he comes here, it will be the greatest rally in history–and we will win the seat easy."

In the politics of Quebec, money was a constant imperative. It was, one realized, always Toronto and Montreal money–another currency– so that whether it was a federal or provincial election, the source of campaign funds was the same. All that changed were the spenders, and often they were also the same.

It was English money, of course. In Canada, there is no other kind for politics. The financial institutions, the big resource industries, the national manufacturers and distributors, the distillers and brewers (and the "international" trade unions) finance Canada's elections, bear the campaign expenses of the party leaders, pay the costs of advertising, pay the rents of the constituency headquarters, the salaries of paid workers, and also for the votes that are hustled to the polls by car, coercion, or persuasion on election day.

The trouble is, goes the frequent lament, the French Canadian doesn't give a damn about election expenses. After all, it's not *his* money, but the coin of another realm, that of the WASP, Jew, American, or corporate Canadian. There has never been enough money in Quebec, it could be said, to fight a by-election in the College of Cardinals, other than the currency of English capitalism.

And of course, English Canadians knew that Quebec politics was different. (English Canadians could not forget Hector Langevin as they had never remembered Thomas McGreevy.) The mention of Duplessis made them shudder. If the politics of Quebec seemed lacking in broader issues–seemed, instead, to devolve fiercely upon the small matters of jobs, patronage, and public works–the reason was thought to be in the make-up of the French Canadian rather than in the nature of Canada itself, and in the structure of its commerce and society. No one realized that politics in Quebec was all that was left to them by the English, who paid for that as well.

Anyway, while I could occasionally brood on it, nothing could be done about the condition of the party in Quebec, or about the state of politics there. If the party was to do well in the election of 1957, it would have to concede the logic of Churchill's strategy.

From the Itinerary of John Diefenbaker, 1957.

Sunday	
April 28th	
12:10 a.m.	*Leave Levis*–c.n.r. *Ocean Limited.*
1:15 p.m.	*Arrive Moncton. Dalton Camp meets train and stays with Party through Maritimes trip.*
7:15 p.m.	*Leave Moncton, Maritime Central Airways. Reservations for press on plane from Moncton to Charlottetown. Arrange enough cars to move party of 15 from railway to Moncton Airport.* p.e.i. *Headquarters to arrange for enough cars to hotel from Charlottetown Airport. Reservations for Party and press at Hotel Charlottetown.*
Monday	*Leave Charlottetown by car for Summerside*
April 29th	*noon-time meeting. Night meeting in Charlottetown. Other arrangements in* p.e.i. *to be made by Dalton Camp. Cars to be supplied by* p.e.i. *Headquarters.*

Diefenbaker was an indiscriminate collector of paper–so far as could be seen, he never threw any away. Every evening, when he walked onto the platform of a filled auditorium, he had with him, jammed between the covers of a single file, all the speech material he had gathered along the way, including the latest day's contribution, newspaper clippings, letters with paragraphs underlined, and scraps of hotel stationery and foolscap with handwritten impulses of the mind or memory logged upon them. As he spoke, his hands ceaselessly rummaged through the file, picking over the papers looking for something suitable to the

312

moment, for inspiration in a heading. (All his prepared speeches were organized under topic headings: "unemployment," "welfare payments," "wheat," or, if they were not provided, he wrote them in himself.)

When the speech was over, he would have used some of it, sometimes a lot of it, but all of it was then in a litter about him, tucked under the lectern, fallen on the floor, stuffed into his pockets, or scrambled in the file. It was one of George Hogan's first responsibilities to retrieve the file and put it in order again. Diefenbaker would call for it the next day, asking, "Where's my stuff?"

Procedures and standing orders for Diefenbaker meetings were simple: There must be a lectern (to hold "the stuff"); the auditorium lights are to be left *on* when he is speaking ("I want to see their faces."). After the Chief has spoken, no one else is to be called upon to speak. ("I put forward what I want to say, then someone else gets up, you see, and says something else which I do not agree with. Well, it's the last thing the audience hears and it's the first thing the newspapers report! You see?")

Nevertheless, occasionally there was no lectern–there are towns in Canada that have never possessed one–and sometimes an aesthetic janitor turned out the auditorium lights when the Chief began to speak. And frequently some damfool would ramble on after Diefenbaker had spoken, ostensibly in the act of thanking him, and say something to make your blood run cold. But these incidents were unimportant, except to those who seek perfection–no one listened to anyone else but Diefenbaker; his audiences were left limp and sated, so that no local Demosthenes could move them after the leader's sixty to ninety-minute oration.

I wrote speech material for Diefenbaker somewhat in the way that Bob Newhart's apocryphal ghost-writer did for Abraham Lincoln–"on the backs of envelopes." My material went directly to him, by hand, as taken out of my portable. Raggedly typed, on yellow copy paper, the text was full of strike-overs and the marks of instant editing to which, of course, Diefenbaker would add his own.

He seemed to prefer getting "stuff" this way; in the morning while travelling, I would sit beside him and hand over the speech notes and, as well, a briefing on the day's activity–who he would meet and their place in the hierarchy–and anything else I thought might be useful to him, including items of political interest from the local press. Sometimes these capsule reviews served as stimulants, other times as tranquillizers.

I would wait while he read it all, at his accustomed breakneck speed, circling words and underlining phrases as he raced through it, pausing for questions: "Where did you get that figure?" Or, about a candidate: "Is that fellow working?"

In those times, when he was either myth or stranger to most of his party, Diefenbaker appeared eager for advice, whether as a man who needed it or who merely wanted to establish himself as a man who sought it. Conservatives, schooled in pessimism and caution, seldom gave him the advice he wanted to hear.

After he had won, of course, the doctrine of infallibility was swiftly proclaimed and contrary advice was volunteered under pain of instant dismissal, while those who brought bad news would, like the king's messengers of old, have the wrath of God upon them. But in 1957, arriving in Moncton for a week's campaigning in the Maritime Provinces (having survived two harrowing days in Quebec), he looked to me uncertain and vulnerable, and needing help.

With him on his special train were Mrs. Diefenbaker, George Hogan, the train manager, Fred Davis, a professional photographer who was listed in the headquarters' manifest as "Public Relations" (which meant the care and feeding of the press), and two secretaries, Marion Wagner and Connie Irving.

About eight journalists were covering the Maritime swing, including Murray Gart of *Time* magazine, who was to be the first, so far as I knew, to sense the possibility of a Diefenbaker victory. But if there was a common sentiment among the press, it was one of friendliness for Diefenbaker and the natural sympathy of the journalist for the underdog. The Tory leader, in response, was accessible and cordial in his relations with them. He was his own public relations man and he was, in the campaign of '57, very good at it.

The campaign was only five days old; it had begun in Massey Hall, Toronto, with Leslie Frost sharing the platform. The national headquarters rushed out tear sheets of the ecstatic Tory press in Toronto, celebrating the renewal of the *bonne entente* between Ontario provincial Tories and the new federal leader.

Allister dispatched a memorandum the next day to all candidates: dates:

April 26th, 1957.

MEMORANDUM TO: *Candidates and National Committee.*
Attached is a paste-up of the news coverage by one Toronto newspaper, the Globe and Mail, of John Diefenbaker's opening campaign meeting in Massey Hall, Toronto.

We think you will be interested in knowing that the campaign got off to such a fine start and that Premier Leslie Frost left no doubt in anybody's mind as to his all-out support of our federal campaign . . .

This well-planned occasion is sure proof that we have a Leader who can arouse tremendous enthusiasm in his public appearances and win plenty of front page publicity when local organizations really put on a show.

One of the most effective parts of the opening meeting was the

use of banners, placards and demonstrations by Y.P.C. and
student groups on behalf of area Candidates. Also, good advance
planning with press, radio and T.V. yielded great results.

Allister Grosart

Campaign Manager.

But still there was a long way to go.

I had my first briefing session with Diefenbaker on the way to
Prince Edward Island, sitting beside him in the chilly DC-3 as we
lumbered out of the Moncton Airport. The small plastic windows
vibrated noisily as the plane struggled for altitude. There was a little
chop, as usual, as we headed over Shediac Bay and into Northumberland Strait, but I forgot to be nervous, watching instead the leader's
face as he studied my speech notes. Then he turned to the briefing
report:

In Nova Scotia, Pictou and Colchester-Hants are the likeliest
prospects. Cumberland, with a young candidate named Coates
(29-year old Dalhousie law graduate) is a possibility.

The best that can be said for Halifax is that the two candidates
mooted two weeks ago–inferior to the standard required–have
been discouraged and an earnest search is being made for better
material.

The South Shore is Stanfield's bastion but solid Liberal federally.

Antigonish-Guysborough, Tory only once since Confederation
and again last year, provincially, shows surprising promise, especially
in Antigonish.

PRINCE EDWARD ISLAND

Angus [MacLean], who is not noted for optimism, is very sanguine
about the dual riding of Queens. Kings is good fighting ground
but I doubt that Prince is.

John A. MacDonald, the candidate for Kings, is a former member
of the Legislature with a good war record (Army) and the public
reputation for hard work, integrity and stability. He was a victim in
the provincial debacle, running with a man whom the Liberals
were determined to defeat at any cost (Walter Shaw, retired deputy
minister of agriculture), and he went down with him.

The situation on the Island now is that both Liberal Governments
are shaky. The last provincial budget raised the gasoline tax and
was eloquently pessimistic about the Island's fiscal problems. As you
know, the federal-provincial agreements resulted in the discovery
that P.E.I. had been "overpaid" some $1,400,000. They were asked to
pay it back–an impossibility. The net result has been that P.E.I.'s
position has been to return to the status of the previous agreements and

it has been given five years to "repay" Ottawa although it has been assured that it will never, in the life of the new agreement, get any less than it did under the old agreement. All this has not only hurt Island pride but it has hurt them financially. It would be no rhetorical statement to describe their fiscal situation as critical.

This fiscal situation is one of two dominant issues. The other, and it is only secondary, is agriculture. Here, it is the same story. Lost markets, rising costs, dwindling profits. Also, certainly, the present credit restrictions are working some real hardships on this predominantly "seasonal borrowing" economy.

My hope is that Premier Matheson will show little enthusiasm for the Liberal cause in this election. I would extend sympathy, if anything, even though he has been a gullible soul to say the least.

The Provincial Tory Leader is R. R. (Reg) Bell–Q.C., M.L.A., who is ineffective and unpopular.
There are three Tory M.L.A.'s–the pick is a Dr. Dewar (Prince).

The Provincial President is Mel McQuade, a defeated provincial candidate from Souris but one of the most effective men in the organization. A lawyer, McQuade will chair the Charlottetown meeting.

Col. David Stewart, DSO, is Mayor of Charlottetown, (second term by acclamation), past president of the Canadian Association of Mayors, etc. He is a Lincoln-Mercury dealer and will provide the transportation for you. His father was the last Tory to be elected Premier of P.E.I. He needs to be encouraged in order to make him as effective as he should be in the campaign. Refused nomination.

Others I suggest you give special encouragement to:

Reagh Bagnall–former provincial president, an excellent grass-roots organizer and the backbone of Angus' rural organization. A plain good Tory.

Bennett Carr–one of the few promising young Conservatives, from Charlottetown, an insurance agent. Needs encouragement and needs pushing.

The YPC organization is largely a paper one. The women's organization a perpetual feud. No real leadership in either and trouble from both.

Re Prince County: Summerside is always sensitive to the fact that Charlottetown gets the best of the political visits. It also offers the least promise. In the last election we were badly hurt by the tax cut promise, especially on the RCAF base–a vital factor in the economy.

Re Press: There are three papers: The Guardian of the Gulf ("Covers the Island like the Dew") is easily the leading daily. Now a Thomson paper, and always good to Angus. Politically neutral and inclined to be pollyanna. Has an old, seasoned editor named Walker, an R. B. Bennett Tory. The other Charlottetown daily is

The Patriot, pathologically Grit. The editor's name is Gaudet (pronounced Goodie). Summerside has a tri-weekly, the Journal, which finds your itinerary incompatible with its publishing dates. They want to phone you Monday morning and get a brief interview of some kind. The man who will call will probably be Elmer Murphy. Politically the Journal is neutral-Liberal.

The Charlottetown radio and television station is owned and operated by the Island Broadcasting Company which is Mrs. Large and her son, Bob. She has had some mild infatuation with Social Credit. Bob is a do-nothing Conservative.

There have been some minor changes and elaborations to your itinerary:

Monday: Leave Charlottetown (9:00 a.m.) by car. Stop at Montague (Kings) for informal (10:00 a.m.) reception to be held in a restaurant. One-half hour stop. Proceed to Summerside for lunch at the RCAF Officers Mess (12:30). Public meeting at 2:30 in theatre. Chairman not yet known. Return to Charlottetown for ten-minute TV appearance with four candidates at 5:40. Public meeting at Charlottetown at Rollaway (dance hall). Speech will be taped. Mel McQuade—chairman; Angus says he (Angus) will introduce you. Propose to have meeting over by 10:00 p.m.

The television facilities are primitive.

He worked through it, flourishing his pen, busily making marginal symbols, underlining key words. He wrote "Selkirk" at the first of the P.E.I. section, underlined the names of his candidates and, coming upon the reference to Reg Bell as being "ineffective and unpopular," he scratched out the words with great deliberation. Then, putting the speech notes in his pocket, he handed back the other material:

"That's wonderful," he said. "Thank you."

"Fine, sir," I said.

"I'd better not carry that kind of thing with me," he said. "You see, there might be an accident and someone would find that I was carrying it."

"That's right," I said, looking out to check the wings.

Yet he loved gossip, enjoyed hearing the small talk about the petty conflicts of party politics. He knew little about the Maritimes, a fact made evident by his conversation, which employed only the safest and most sweeping generalizations for local consumption. Maritimers, listening to the campaigning politicians from central Canada, found the essence of their speeches devoid of meaning, though occasionally stuffed with patronizing deception.

When the Prime Minister went to Halifax and spoke of the "big things going on in Canada today," he was able to list them for his audience—the St. Lawrence Seaway, the Trans Canada Pipeline, the

317

Northern Quebec-Labrador Railway, for example–but even his partisans would wince when Mr. St. Laurent went on to say, in his best grandfatherly fashion:

Now, you may think that none of these projects I have mentioned
is of particular value to Nova Scotians. Not at all. Whatever
helps stimulate activity in any province and region is good for all
provinces and regions in Canada. So in the Atlantic Provinces there
are sound grounds for welcoming these great developments.

In a nation in which the rich got steadily richer and the poor got poorer, it was the sort of rhetoric for patriots, especially for the self-satisfied and well fed.

To add insult to such injury, the Prime Minister went on to charge that Diefenbaker and Frost had made "a deal" which would, if consummated, discriminate against the Maritimes. *Time* magazine later quoted Mr. St. Laurent's speech-writer, Maritime-born Rhodes Scholar Dan Wallace, as saying, "That's the kind of stuff they go for down there."

He did not have to say it to have it believed. Such appeals to Maritime paranoia are common enough. Nor was there much new in the Conservative approach, which was to exploit the sense of discontent and grievance. What *was* new, perhaps, was the fact that the Tory ghostwriter not only knew the grievances intimately, but felt them keenly– and there was no public man in Canada so capable of airing another's grievance and injustice as John Diefenbaker. It had been his stock in trade, so to speak. There had to be more than that, of course, if the Liberal dominance of this part of Canada was to be overturned. But in the short list of absolute essentials, this was one of them–that of a convincingly sympathetic leader who appeared to understand the problems.

As the DC-3 bearing its political cargo lowered its flaps to land at Summerside, the Maritime campaign began.

Looking out the window at the ground below, fallow and wet in the early spring, the Tory leader reflected further on my memorandum. "I agree with you about the Premier–what's his name. . . . That's right –Matheson. I'll have nothing to say about him other than the most genuine expressions of concern."

He smiled at that.

"When will our people ever learn," he said.

I shook my head in reply.

"You cannot beat Grits by attacking them. I never use the word 'Liberal' when I speak," he said.

It would be a new sort of political campaign for the Maritimes.

318

37

I HAD NOT SEEN HIM CAMPAIGN, AND NOW I WATCHED HIM AS HE PICKED his way between the factions of the Island Conservatives with the big man's determined cordiality. He was their Chief, and he made it plain that he needed all of them. He reminded me a little of Harry Truman–embattled by the odds, but seemingly inexhaustibly confident and cheerful.

He shook hands firmly, not aggressively; there was always something kept in reserve. He did not invite constituents to touch or embrace him, but kept his distance by playing his role–the leader, a little taller than the rest, the one dressed in black, with the hard black hat, black coat, subdued tie. He smiled and frequently said things that made people laugh, even though they were not that funny.

At Summerside, Angus MacLean welcomed him to the Island. About fifty of the faithful stood on the tarmac and smiled and waved when he stepped from the plane during the station stop. He had a quick eye for the elderly, particularly those who looked hard-used by life, and then the smile was more sympathetic, the gaze more penetrating and voice more deliberate in saying, "Hello, how are *you*? Glad to see *you*."

When you fly into Charlottetown, if the sky is clear and you are sitting on the right side of the plane, you see it all below–its four hospitals, five funeral homes, three cemeteries, twenty-four law firms, six banks, five trust companies, six loan companies and–as a centrepiece–the Province Building where, in 1864, the Fathers of Confederation met and, making history, agreed to meet again at Quebec.

Today on the second-floor where the talks took place, where the Cradle is, where Macdonald sat with Tupper and with the eight gents from Upper and Lower Canada, visitors may see on one venerated wall in the hall (which once knew the tread of Confederation's Fathers) an oil painting of the Provincial Building.

The painting is accompanied by a plaque, and visitors will read that this is "an original oil from the Seagram Collection of Paintings . . . a Centennial Gift from the House of Seagram." Drinkers of Crown Royal, Golden Gin, or Seagram's 83 will recognize the coat of arms ("Integrity-Craftsmanship-Tradition," it says.)

The painting, says the plaque, is a gift "to the people of P.E.I. *and accepted on their behalf by The Honourable Alexander Campbell,* B.A., LL.B., *Premier."*

(Have you not seen the Guinness Stout plaque at Runnymede? The Beefeater's plaque at Westminster?)

But on this earlier day, Monday, April 29, 1957, Diefenbaker is opening his campaign in the Maritimes, and Seagram's is still only a distillery and not yet known for cultural benefactions.

The Rollaway Club is a dance hall, bowling alley, and bingo parlour. Diefenbaker is to speak upstairs in the dance hall, from the platform upon which the orchestra plays on Saturday nights. The place is dark and smells of creosote and age. But it's the biggest hall in town, except the rink, which is too cold this time of year, and too big anyway.

I have been at the Rollaway before; the Tories held their little wake at the Rollaway on election night, 1955. It's really more suitable for a wake than for a rally.

But for Diefenbaker the chairs are filled, and people are lined against the walls and standing at the back. There are as many people on the platform as there used to be in the whole hall at Tory meetings. It is raining outside, but the place is packed; there is the smell of damp clothing, heavy breath, and a vague odour of urine and chemicals from the two toilets at the back.

I have heard him speak before, know his style, but I listen with fresh interest as he deliberately arranges his papers in the bulging file, putting his speech in order, while the tongue runs on with the ceremonial observances. He pays tribute to Chester McLure, the former member, who ran and lost in 1953, while Angus won, leaving the bitterness which is characteristic of dual ridings.

He trades on the Selkirk Settlers, establishing blood relationships.

He has been told to remember that Angus is not the only candidate in Queens, but is running with Heath Macquarrie who is a newcomer. (Macquarrie impresses me; one of the party's rare academics, he is writing a book about Robert Borden.)

Diefenbaker gives them each equal time, spreading it thick, voice drenched with sincerity. "Angus MacLean is one of those who over the years has given that measure of service to this nation which will live in the hearts of all those who. . . ."

Everyone, it will be discovered, is "one of those who over the years has," including Diefenbaker.

I am one of those who over the years, having regard for those things
without which this nation could never have come to the greatness
of its destiny, I have loved Parliament.

The sentences are like eggs rolling on a table, unpredictable, circumlocutious, errant, creating their own suspense, sometimes falling off, breaking on the floor. The audience sits fascinated and motionless, heads uplifted. The janitor, an old hand at Saturday night dances, has killed the house lights. It is like theatre, or a minstrel show. Macquarrie and MacLean (MacLean and Macquarrie) are the end men; Angus, sitting on the platform with his short legs crossed at the ankles, a fixed, dour smile on his square, dark face, motionless, his white socks gleaming. Heath looks inscrutable, his mouth turned down at the corners but smiling. White hair grows around the sides of a pink bald head, seeming like a halo under the spotlight, and grows long at the back. Macquarrie looks more like a Father of Confederation than Cartier.

Diefenbaker is the magician; he suspends sentences in the air, makes people laugh and applaud by the sudden inflection of his voice, like a wand, as he casts a spell in the old Rollaway dance hall and bingo parlour, over the crowd, over the press, and over me.

Of course, I wait for him to use my stuff. Even political ghost-writers have their egocentricities. Besides, the Maritime issue is really all I care about here, in the context of issues. The pipeline thing has come to bore me; it is not the pipeline controversy that proves the arrogance and indifference of the Government of Canada, but the conditions in this part of Canada, the state of people like those sitting in this dark, dismal, stinking hall which is now suddenly brightened by this man's rasping, thrusting voice, the fierceness of his eye and the glow of his indignation and passion.

An old man, seated on the aisle half-way down the rows of chairs, is carried away by Diefenbaker's oratory and he punctuates the speech with shouted agreement, "Tha's right, John, tha's right!"

Diefenbaker cannot see him in the darkness and does not hear the words and thinks he is being heckled. The audience, which is wiser about the old man—and knows he is drunk—laughs and applauds. Before it is over the old man rolls off his chair and into the aisle. He is chastened by this and becomes silent.

My yellow pages emerge from the file and Diefenbaker begins to read. The author's phrasing and the speaker's style mesh; sometimes you write for people who can't read more than one word at a time, but Diefenbaker faithfully follows the thread of the text even while weaving another one around it. When he falters, or loses his place, he converts it into a dramatic pause, shaking his head in mock sorrow, changing the pitch of his voice, changing the torque, before resuming the full flight of his oratory.

When it is over, the crowd seems reluctant to leave; the streets outside are black with rain and people hover around the door before plunging into the confusion of the traffic.

"Boys, he tells 'em!" a man says.

Watching them come out, I see two Grits shuffling toward the exit, smiling wanly, being nudged by friendly Tories.

"Glad to see ya here. Do ya a world a good!"

321

Back to the hotel; Diefenbaker likes to eat before retiring. He drinks milk and munches a cold beef sandwich.

This is the winding-down process, cooling out after the evening's exertion. The staff hovers about the suite, venturing praiseworthy opinion on the meeting, personalizing it with anecdote. Hogan has been talking to Allister and he forwards optimistic reports from Ontario. A cabinet minister is campaigning in Saskatchewan; Diefenbaker wants to hear about it, in detail. He makes a western phone call, dictates a note, gathers up his mail and a clutch of newspapers and starts for the bedroom.

"Good night," I say to him.

"How was that for a meeting?"

"It was great," I tell him, once more.

"Wasn't it a wonderful meeting?"

"No one ever saw anything like it here."

"What's that?"

"That's the best meeting anyone has ever seen here."

"Who said that?"

"Bennett Carr said that," I tell him, lying harmlessly.

He pauses at his bedroom door, savouring the last morsel of the day's success.

"Well, you see me tomorrow."

The door closes and I hear him sigh. "Oh my," he says, getting into bed.

The press are unwinding too. After the meeting they write their stories and file them at the telegraph office, or they phone them in. They disappear for an hour, then come together again in a room booked by Fred Davis, "Public Relations," and stocked with ice and glasses, mix, and liquor. It is much the best part of the day, when the cause of all our concerns has gone to bed and the staff is released from duty and the press knows that at last the man they are covering is silent with his own thoughts or dreams.

So most of them gather, as one day runs into another, for drink and badinage and gossip. Hogan drops in to test the room temperature, to listen for complaints about travel arrangements, beefs about staff services, criticisms of Diefenbaker. He is young, zealous about his job, and uneasy with the press who, in turn, find him aloof.

"Jesus Christ," the Toronto *Star* man says, "no wonder the Tories aren't getting anywhere—here's this guy Diefenbaker and he's put his whole life in the hands of two admen and a used car salesman." Meaning Grosart, Camp, and Hogan.

"Hogan," someone says, while George listens, "is a bloody fascist."

"What the hell," someone else says, "he makes the trains run on time, doesn't he?"

"Hey, Camp—how could a guy like you *ever* live in this part of the world?"

Gart is filing his story for the week and I sit in his room, sipping Scotch, while he rereads his copy. Gart is *Time*'s man from Toronto, an outsider among the press, but he sees things clearly, I suspect, because he is seeing it for the first time.

"That was quite a meeting," Gart says. "What do you think it meant?"

Well, you cannot always level with the press, but this is not one of those times. (They would come later.)

"Honest to God, Murray," I tell him, "this guy is quite a surprise. Things are happening. We can win here with Diefenbaker."

Gart thinks about that, about his source, I suppose, and the time of night. "You may be right," he says.

Of course, we are only talking about Prince Edward Island. One tenth of one per cent of all the land of Canada. And four seats, three of them Grit.

38

THE MORE OFTEN I THOUGHT ABOUT IT, THE MORE CONVINCED I BE-
came that the key to Diefenbaker's electoral possibilities–and my role
in the campaign–would be found in the Maritimes. There were twenty-
six seats in the three provinces and twenty of them were held by Grits.
In this part of Canada, the political ground was occupied almost
exclusively by the two major parties; Liberal losses therefore meant
Tory gains. In the simple arithmetic of politics, this made each seat
doubly significant. If Diefenbaker was to win–or come close to winning–
the seats in the Maritimes would be decisive.

In Ottawa, early in April, some of the Maritime members had
gathered in the office of Col. Alf Brooks to discuss prospects and
strategy. I had not been impressed by the discussion, a conclusion confirmed by a memorandum circulated afterwards to the participants:

Statement of Policy
A meeting of representatives of the Maritime provinces was held on
April 8, 1957, in the office of A. J. Brooks, M.P.
The main objective of this meeting was to carry out the Leader's
wishes for a statement of policy, with particular reference to
each province.
(A) The following problems are of great importance to the Maritime
     economy, and should be considered for our statement of policy.
1.   Subvention of coal for transportation *within* the Maritime
     provinces.
2.   Cheaper freight rates.
3.   Cheaper electrical power.
4.   Assistance to municipalities through grants in aid to the provinces.
5.   Decentralization of industry.
6.   Construction of the Chignecto Canal.
7.   In Prince Edward Island the important issues are Agriculture
     and Fiscal Need.
(B) The main areas of *criticism* of the Liberal Party are:
1.   Its attitude toward the Commonwealth.
2.   Contempt of Parliament.
3.   Neglect of the Maritimes.
4.   We are opposed to the Government's inflexible bank credit
     control.
cc: T. M. Bell
     A. J. Brooks

D. K. Camp
J. A. MacLean
G. W. Montgomery
George Nowlan

A more significant result of the meeting had been omitted from the memorandum. I had achieved agreement that there be "a central meeting of the candidates in the Maritime provinces." The week of May 6 had been proposed as a suitable time, and the site preferred was Moncton. I now longed to take matters in my own hands and to invite the assistance of the fresh and vital forces that were to be found in the victorious provincial organizations of New Brunswick and Nova Scotia.

I proposed to Grosart that we mount a special campaign in the Maritimes. I had already persuaded both the Nova Scotia and New Brunswick organizations to contribute $10,000 each from their own provincial funds on the understanding that the federal party would contribute a like amount. With this agreement, we had a $30,000 budget for a regional publicity campaign. It would go a long way, provided we had something to say.

Bill Rowe would have been impressed by the ease with which this was achieved, how effortlessly the gears had meshed. Stanfield's organization, fresh from its provincial triumph, was eager for more action; and the new Premier, well aware of the willing help he had received from the national headquarters, matched the eagerness of his own followers to enter the federal campaign.

Nowlan, the acknowledged leader of the federal party in Nova Scotia, also saw the need to create an effective, cohesive campaign in the Maritimes. There had never been such a campaign before. Nowlan now found himself an outsider in the new party of John Diefenbaker, but the remedy for that, knowing his man, was to identify himself with a successful fight against the Grits. I urged Nowlan to lend his prestige (and approval) to the concept of an overall Maritime campaign, and George, now detecting in me magical properties, quickly gave the project his blessing.

In New Brunswick, Flemming and Carson were also agreeable. Flemming had his own reasons: the New Brunswick Power Commission was building a $30-million dam on the Saint John River at Beechwood. It was Flemming's personal political project, and had become something of an obsession for him. In Ottawa, where he had appealed for assistance in financing the project, the response had been negative. Meanwhile, Carson told me, Flemming was building Beechwood "on an overdraft."

Others, especially Flemming's provincial treasurer, Donald Patterson, were concerned about New Brunswick's financial condition. Unless something changed for the better, provincial taxes would soon have to

325

be substantially increased, or else services and capital projects would be severely limited. The best, indeed the only, prospect for improvement was for a change of government in Ottawa.

The federal election provided such a possibility, and Patterson, a diligent and ingenious man, wrote a lengthy memorandum to Diefenbaker proposing the federal formula that was later to become the special Atlantic Provinces Grants:

Honourable Sir:

I want to express to you my appreciation for your courtesy in granting an interview to me during your busy visit to Fredericton. As agreed upon, the purpose of this letter is to put down on paper a summary of the points mentioned in our conversation that day. . . . We feel there should be what might be called a sliding scale system of grants supplementary to the tax rental agreements and designed to assist the poorer provinces to improve their relative position. We refer to such grants as national adjustment grants. Our particular formula submitted to the federal-provincial conference in the fall of 1955 was one based on supplementary payments going to those provinces whose per capita income was below 85% of the national average. Incidentally, New Brunswick's per capita income is approximately 2/3 of the national average, and only slightly over 50% of that of Ontario. Under this formula, at that time, four provinces would have benefitted—the four Atlantic provinces—and the cost to the federal treasury, $33,162,000 (see statement I of the Case for National Adjustment Grants). In the Budget Speech of this year we said—"I have spent considerable time again on this subject for this very important reason—that we see no way our budget problems of the future can be met, except through acceptance of the principle of a national adjustment grant." In other words, this subject is really a life and death matter to the less wealthy provinces. We do not see how it is possible for such a province and its municipalities to meet their peacetime obligations, having in mind the narrow tax base and low taxable income— without the adjustment grant. I respectfully suggest to you that this whole field of the tax sharing relationship is one that could very well be a top issue in the election if the Conservatives wished to take up the side of the provinces. As you know, Ontario does not feel that they are getting back from Ottawa the money they need for essential peacetime growth services. Obviously, this would apply to all provinces (although I suppose Alberta is in some sort of special category by itself). Thus I would suggest there are two problems—(a) that even the wealthier provinces are not receiving back a proper share, and (b) that the poorer provinces need special help in addition to the regular per capita distribution being made to all provinces.

The reply from Diefenbaker was cordially encouraging:

Dear Donald:
Thank you very much for your letter of April 3rd with your full and
helpful views on the National Adjustment Grant which we discussed
briefly when I was in Fredericton last month.
I believe you know that my own thinking on the necessity for this
grant follows your own very closely. I shall draw upon your letter and
the material forwarded under separate cover when I speak on this
subject during the coming election campaign.
With kind regards and again my thanks.

Students of the techniques of political leaders dealing with matters of
this kind will be quick to note that Diefenbaker had promised every
satisfaction to Patterson except a commitment to his proposal. But it
was not to be the end of it. Patterson also sent a copy to me, and while
I did not concern myself with the detail of his proposal, the letter helped
fix my resolve on the need for a Maritime policy manifesto.

Prince Edward Island had also been included in the Maritime campaign, although they made no contribution to it. Their provincial party
was still in leaderless disarray, but Angus MacLean was now leading a
strong Island federal ticket. To help matters, Ottawa had found that a
statistical calculation regarding population growth had proved to be
in error and, as a result, the federal payments to the provincial administration had been excessive. Thus, the government of Prince Edward
Island now owed the government of Canada one and a half million
dollars, which the Island treasury did not have. The federal government,
as though determined to strengthen its growing reputation for arrogance, pressed for repayment, much to the embarrassment of the
provincial Liberals. What was needed, it seemed to me, was a policy
statement that would exploit the mounting difficulties heralded by
examples of this kind in a part of Canada where grievances had become
the inevitable harvest of each Liberal electoral landslide.

Rod Black, by this time the acknowledged leader of the party organization in Nova Scotia, was anxious to bring all the Atlantic provinces'
candidates together for a briefing. They were, in a word, green. Most of
them had never run for office, and some of them had barely enough
political experience to know which party they had joined. "You can
say one thing," Black remarked mournfully. "If we can elect any of
them it will only be because we out-organized the Grits."

In addition, Nowlan thought it would be a good idea to bring all
the Maritime candidates together so as to integrate Diefenbaker's two
visits to the east coast, and to talk about policy.

Talk policy, hell; I intended to write it.

There was little use trying to get through to Allister about policy

327

while Diefenbaker was concentrating on attacking the government. The convention policy of last December, as we all knew, had been ordered by the leader to be withdrawn and burned–a psychological bonfire that was to light a new era of spontaneous conservatism. Nevertheless I explained to Allister the purpose for this gathering of Maritime Conservative candidates.

"It's your show down there," he said affably. "You run it." It was the slogan for the new "decentralized" party.

The candidates' meeting was scheduled for Moncton on May 11. Moncton was not only suitably central, a fact confirmed long ago by the CNR, it was also easier for Hugh John Flemming to attend, and bring Carson with him.

Black and I drove to Moncton from Halifax. Black, at the wheel, piloted the car as he did a poll workers' meeting, with consummate caution, deliberation, and at minimum speed. He did not talk much about the election, which did not interest him. Organization, however, did: man-management and practical means of getting things done in a thorough, systematic way. He liked to beat Grits, and he relished the rough conflict in politics, but, like a lineman in football, Black considered the contest to be a personal one, head to head, poll for poll. The stars in the backfield did not matter to him; he would often forget the names of politicians.

Many of the candidates brought their campaign managers to Moncton with them. The four Island candidates were all present; Nowlan, the only elected member from the last Parliament, headed ten Nova Scotian candidates.* All of the New Brunswick candidates were present, with the conspicuous exception of Charlie Van Horne.

Moncton is a railroad town, built beside the mud tidal flats of the Petitcodiac River. It boasts a "magnetic hill" in its western precincts, and a "tidal bore," which twice a day runs up the Petitcodiac River, past the main street and a mid-town park. Someone called the bore "the most aptly named natural phenomenon in the world." No matter, Moncton is a busy town, bustling with transients en route to Nova Scotia, the Island, southern New Brunswick, or the North Shore. And you could always get fresh lobster in Moncton, and a glass of cold beer with it, even when the law prescribed otherwise.

Politics had long since moved from the private clubs and the halls of the loyal orders to occupy more functional and more neutral grounds. Better suited to the purposes of contemporary politics were hotels like the Brunswick, which offered meeting rooms, hot and ready meals, and open lobbies with their conversational groupings of comfortable chairs, where senior statesmen could hold court, oversee and be seen, and withdraw gracefully to their private rooms for more intimate discussions whenever they chose. Hotel lobbies also offered access to travelling salesmen who volunteered interesting intelligence, such as the

*Two were not yet nominated.

328

information in 1952, in New Brunswick, and later in Nova Scotia, that the government was going to change. The salesmen said the merchants were saying so, and they in turn were hearing it from their customers.

The Tory candidates were greeted by opening statements briefly and cheerfully rendered by Nowlan, Brooks, MacLean, and Bill Browne, each speaking for his own province. Nowlan obviously enjoyed the uniqueness of his having been the only Tory member from Nova Scotia—a recent Chambers cartoon in the Halifax *Herald* had portrayed him as the "Lone Ranger." MacLean was the only Tory from the Island to have sat in the last Parliament. Brooks, not to be outdone, could say that after the election of 1935 he had been the sole Tory elected east of Montreal. Bill Browne, one of two who had come from Newfoundland, could only add that no federal Conservative had ever been elected in his province. The fledgling candidates measured their prospects against this meager legacy, but did not seem depressed by it.

This encounter was my first view of many of the party's standard-bearers. They were young, personable, and surprisingly articulate. They knew very little about politics, but seemed to know about their constituencies. All had in common an earnest, innocent optimism. When Black rose to speak on poll organization, he held their rapt attention. None are so fascinated by technique as the novitiate.

Carson and I hastily withdrew from the meeting to an upstairs room where he propped himself up on the bed, pen and notebook in hand, and I sat before my portable typewriter. We began to compose the "Atlantic Resolutions." Carson knew what he wanted, which was what Flemming wanted—a federal commitment to assist in financing the Beechwood power project. In addition, there was mention of a special subsidy on the movement of Maritime coal for the use of thermal power, a more equitable share of defence production contracts, a federal capital projects commission (which later was realized as the Atlantic Development Board), a Canadian Coast Guard (ardently advocated by the candidate for Lunenberg-Queens, Lloyd Crouse, who was Bob Winters' opponent), and the Patterson proposal which was to lead to the special Atlantic Provinces Grants.

While we wrote, read, and corrected each other's drafts, Nowlan commuted from the downstairs meeting to our upstairs room, offering encouragement, topping off our glasses, and refilling his own. When we had drafted a resolution to our common satisfaction, Nowlan would bear it downstairs, place it before the candidates who cheerfully and promptly gave their consent. After the resolutions had been completed and approved, we drafted the preamble:

We the Progressive Conservative Candidates from the 31 federal constituencies in the Atlantic Provinces, believe the just demands of

329

the Atlantic Community for recognition of their economic problems and special needs urgently require more united and forceful representation in the Parliament of Canada.

In keeping with the growing co-operative spirit of the people of the Atlantic community, which has already led to the creation of APEC and to the Conference of Atlantic Premiers, we are resolved to stand together in support of these measures which will help to overcome the historic disabilities which have limited and even denied opportunity to this area. We believe our young people have the right to opportunity at home and we are convinced that only by united action by all individuals and at all levels of government and through the constructive efforts of private organizations, can this right be made real.

We believe that all those who live in this Atlantic community are entitled to the benefits of opportunity and security which shall be no more, but certainly no less, than all Canadians have the right to enjoy.

Amendments and changes were few. Bill Browne, representing the unknown and isolated Tory Party in Newfoundland, asked only that his province be specifically mentioned in the manifesto and this was cheerfully agreed. But, apart from that, the words remained largely as they were when George Nowlan brought them from our hotel room to the meeting below. The Brunswick Hotel meeting of the Atlantic Provinces candidates was a feast of harmony and cordial agreement.

Hugh John Flemming, never more urbane, self-possessed, and handsome, appeared at the meeting's end to endorse the new policy, as well he might. The candidates were warmed as much by his presence as by his words.

We departed the meeting in high spirits. The manifesto had been carefully drafted, specific enough to be meaningful, general enough to be broadly appealing. And all were agreed on it.

"What," I asked, "do you think Diefenbaker will say about all this?"

"Well," George Nowlan said, snapping his fingers in a characteristic sign of impatience, "we'll see about that."

I returned to Fredericton by air, my plane bouncing upon the updrafts rising from the rolling countryside below. I had, it seemed to me, completed a full circle, from the Liberal convention of 1948 to this gathering in Moncton, some nine years later. At last, the circle being drawn, a major commitment to policy had been made, if not as yet by the party's leader, by a solid phalanx of his candidates. And whether Diefenbaker wanted it or not, or whether he won or lost, Tories in the Maritimes might have a cause worth their patient efforts and loyalties.

Memorandum to Mr. Diefenbaker from: Dalton Camp
Re: Tuesday, April 30th, 1957

Arrive New Glasgow–9:05 a.m.

Will be met by:–

Russell MacEwan and Mrs. MacEwan (Pictou candidate)

and

Angus R. Macdonald (Antigonish-Guysborough candidate)
and Mrs. Macdonald

MacEwan is 32 years old–a lawyer

Macdonald is about 55–St. FX graduate

Transportation will be supplied by the Antigonish-Guysborough
people for a 40-mile drive to Antigonish.

Enroute from the Airport to Antigonish Mrs. Diefenbaker is to stop
at the Baptist Church to see a plaque in memory of her grandfather.
She will be accompanied by the Mayor, Mr. Bennett (a relative
of R. B. Bennett and a member of the church). The Pastor is likely
to be there. He is the Rev. Mr. Harvey–an "old country" Scotsman.

The party will arrive at the Royal George Hotel in Antigonish for a
"semi-private" luncheon. About 15 persons have been invited.

The public meeting is at 2:30 p.m. at the Capital Theatre. The
Chairman of the meeting is–Clem O'Leary–who is also the Riding
Campaign Manager.

Mr. Diefenbaker will be introduced by William (Bill) McKinnon,
M.L.A. for Antigonish–a radio station announcer and one of
the youngest of Stanfield's caucus.

The entire meeting will be broadcast live.

The meeting is scheduled to be over at 4:30 p.m.

The party will then be met by cars from Pictou and Mr. and Mrs.
Diefenbaker are to drive to New Glasgow to the Hotel Norfolk.

The Pictou meeting is scheduled for 8:00 p.m. at the Junior High
School. The party is scheduled to leave the Hotel Norfolk by car at
about 7:50 p.m.

The Chairman of the meeting will be–John A. MacGregor, the
Association President and Campaign Chairman.

Mr. Diefenbaker is to be introduced by the candidate, Mr. MacEwan.

Other Platform Guests will be:

Mrs. Tom Hayden, President of the Women's Provincial Association

Harvey Veniot, M.L.A.

Don R. MacLeod, M.L.A.

(Pictou Provincial Members).

This meeting will also be broadcast.

The meeting is supposed to be over by 10:00 p.m. The party will
stay the night at the Hotel Norfolk.

Transportation from New Glasgow to Truro will be handled by the
Colchester-Hants Organization.

The party is scheduled to leave the Norfolk Hotel at 10:00 a.m.
Wednesday, May 1st.

We depart Charlottetown early and fly under a warm morning sun to the Nova Scotia mainland. Diefenbaker is cheerful and his mood infects his staff and the press. Long after, he will confess to a friend that the meeting in Charlottetown was the critical moment when he suddenly realized he might win–if he won Prince Edward Island, as now seemed possible, he could win anywhere.

At New Glasgow, we are parcelled out among a number of cars for the drive to Antigonish. After lunch, we find the Capitol Theatre filled for the afternoon meeting, an audience of old people, a number of men dressed in frayed wool shirts, open at the throat, a few days' growth of beard on their faces. The theatre is dark, a heavy dankness in the air, and it smells of dried sweat, the barn, and stale popcorn.

It is a poor place for a meeting but the local organization had no other choice for the afternoon, they said. They refer to the candidate, Angus R. Macdonald, as "Angus D.D." When someone asks what that means, he is told it stands for "Angus Dead Doctor"–in an area with so many Macdonald's, and so many of them with the Christian name Angus, the Tory candidate needs be further identified as the late Doctor's son. Diefenbaker is intrigued by this; so far as anyone knows, there are only four people in all Canada named Diefenbaker.

On the way back to New Glasgow from Antigonish, I think of my wife and young children at home, and the possibility of their being left widowed and orphaned on this day. Our driver is determined to demonstrate to the newspapermen who are my fellow passengers that he is the legitimate successor to Barney Oldfield. We hurtle over the roads at seventy and eighty miles an hour, taking curves on the wrong side of the road and overtaking cars on blind hills. The driver has been drinking; along the way he asks if we mind if he stops for a booster shot.

When I arrive in New Glasgow, alive, I retreat to my room and offer a silent prayer of thanksgiving. And I resolve never again to be driven by unknown chauffeurs.

Stanfield joins us in Truro to spend two days campaigning with Diefenbaker. All along the way, the halls are filled, and the people in them friendly and responsive. Stanfield stands at Diefenbaker's side in the crowds, smiling shyly, looking like a favourite cousin who is along for the ride. But on the platform he is unequivocal in his support of the federal party.

Driving from Truro to Amherst, we stop to mainstreet in the town of Parrsboro. By chance, Diefenbaker meets Bob Winters and the press is exultant; the two men shake hands for the photographers, exchanging pleasantries. Canadian Press and BUP race for the telegraph office; with the Liberal Party visibly crumbling in the Maritimes, the biggest news they have yet to stumble upon is that Winters and Diefenbaker have crossed paths in Parrsboro.

Studying Winters' blandly handsome, smiling face, I cannot recall seeing anyone so supremely self-confident. He must not have the least idea of what is happening around him. His continual attacks on Stanfield have made it easier for the new Premier to enter the federal campaign and have intensified the feelings of the provincial organization. As a result, Stanfield's people are beginning to work, encouraged by Diefenbaker's surprising acceptability and provoked by Winters' speeches.

Perhaps I am imagining it, but as the week progresses the crowds seem to be growing. Even in the rain, in Amherst ("Busy Amherst, watch it grow!" proclaims a faded sign), the hall is filled. I stand in the back, near the door, listening with a clinical ear to the speeches. The local candidate, Robert Coates, speaks in a hesitant, high-pitched voice, almost a falsetto. I wait to hear the crowd's reaction to Stanfield's reply to Winters, who has accused the provincial government of being unresponsive to a federal proposal to assist in building thermal plants. Stanfield personally considers the proposal as purely political and next to worthless, but he conceals his contempt to say:

We will agree to the federal proposals immediately they produce a contract which guarantees the use of Nova Scotia coal and guarantees a reduced price for power to Nova Scotia.

The audience applauds his firmness, impressed by the strength in his lean, rugged face, the cool, laconic speaking style, and the deliberately understated platform manner—there is a quality about Stanfield that people find reassuring, even though they are always surprised at his modesty and his strange diffidence.

Amherst is a town in which industrial activity and prosperity are of recent memory. It is now a little down at the heel, and the townspeople listen, fascinated, to Diefenbaker's comprehensive cataloguing of the area's problems—the chronic plight of the coal industry at Springhill, doomed to be shut down; the abandoned ferry service from Parrsboro to Wolfville; the loss of local industry; the decline of agriculture; the out-migration of the young; the plight of the old, and the problems that are being created as the life is slowly squeezed from the Cumberland towns and the once-prospering villages along the Fundy shore.

In the close, damp stillness of the packed hall, the only sound is Diefenbaker's vibrant, emotive voice, his the only face in the crowd—his eyes lit by the ceiling lights and by the inspiration of his calling. He invokes Suez and St. Laurent's scornful "superman" epithet, directed at the British; he excoriates "the six-buck boys" who cheated the pensioners of their just deserts. "I love Parliament," he says, abruptly, turning to the mysteries of the pipeline controversy and the secrets of parliamentary procedure.

All these concerns, vaguely felt by wounded spirits, become

focused on this single man, whose face quivers from the suppressed torments of having known and suffered the rape of Parliament, the despoiling of the British connection, the humiliation of the old, and the long, steady, inexorable decline in the prospects of Cumberland County and the town of Amherst.

In Diefenbaker's passion is incorporated all the grievances of his audience; he absorbs their indignation and, at the end, after they have laughed with him, cheered him, felt their nerve-ends respond to his voice, they find that he has repossessed their hopes, and they believe in him as they have not believed in anyone in a long, long time, if even then.

I leave the hall, as the crowd's ovation begins, to find a taxi to drive me to Moncton. I sit in the back, remote and silent, discouraging conversation with my driver. It is a little like watching a nightly miracle, this recurrent chemistry between Diefenbaker and his audiences. I had not expected it, but, of course, there are explanations, and not all of them have to do with Diefenbaker. Tory meetings in Nova Scotia and New Brunswick have recently become respectable, now that provincial Premiers are in attendance. More than just the hard core of party supporters come; some are coming out of curiosity, to see this new voice and prophet of the Tory party, while others are coming to be seen, to offer by their presence testimony to the new order of things. One overhears various versions of:

"Guess who was at the meeting tonight?"

"Who?"

"Jack Shute."

"I haven't seen Jack at a Conservative meeting in years."

"I thought he was a Grit."

"His family were always Tory."

"Anyway, there he was. With his wife."

Long-absent friends, political strays, and those heretofore timid are suddenly comfortable at Tory meetings chaired by the local member, with the Tory Premier sitting on the platform. They are in the company of others in like circumstances, whom they previously had only seen at the curling rink, or the downtown businessmen's luncheon club, or in church.

The new Tory machines in Nova Scotia and New Brunswick have the sleek, shining allure of bandwagons; after the victorious elections, the word is out that Tories, too, are treating folks, and the fellows around Liberal headquarters aren't quite as friendly as they used to be. Times change, and power shifts, and the first to sense these currents are the luckless and the poor who must always know where their best chances may be found, where the distant job prospects are, and where the possibilities of favours are likeliest. And then there is the competitive lust of men in a newly triumphant party organization. Pride will not let them lose, not while the taste of winning is still fresh, as is the memory of defeat, each made keener by recent, exhilarating experience. All this is Diefenbaker's unexpected inheritance in the Maritimes, something which came to him quite by accident, which he had not earned, expected, or even understood.

But, in fact, men who hardly knew him, including some who vaguely mistrusted him, now commit themselves entirely to his success. They come to his meetings not only to hear him, but to swell the crowd, and they cheer him not just because they share his opinion but because the fierceness of their partisanship has to be communicated to others, including the opposition, who must be watching.

And there are those like myself, caught in the fastness of another man's driving ambition, swept along in the tidal flood of all the hopes and urgent desires which powered his campaign. Even though still half-doubting and yet uncertain, I have come to serve this strangely compelling, puzzling man with a fierce and unrelenting concentration I find difficult to explain, even to myself.

Rain streaks across the beam of headlights as we race over the Tantramar marshes, through the quiet college town of Sackville, through Dorchester, with the formidable walls of the ugly prison silhouetted against the sky, past darkened farm homes and cross-road stores, until the lights of Moncton appear ahead. We slow our speed to drive along the empty streets to the station, and to the waiting railroad cars, standing at a siding. I order the steward to bring lobster to the train for the press when they return.

Four days, two provinces, a dozen meetings, thousands of smiling faces–and New Brunswick tomorrow–we are like a conquering army, returning home.

John Diefenbaker's campaign cars, joined to Train 14, moved out of Saint John City on its return to Moncton, destined for Montreal and Ottawa, with a stop in Campbellton in the interests of Charlie Van Horne. I would leave the train at Moncton and return to Halifax, but I seized upon this brief journey by rail to find the solitude of my bedroom to recover an hour or so of sleep.

Life aboard a campaign train is very special, offering a privacy and remoteness which, together with other comforts and consolations, both the politicians and their company find deeply satisfying. On the Diefenbaker train, the kitchen never closed; it provided, on request, cold chicken, ham and roast beef, fresh milk, hot coffee, fresh fruit, and rich cheddar cheese. Elsewhere, Fred Davis operated a bar which never closed. As the train moved through the countryside, one could relax, tieless and shoeless–and mindless–feeling the slow ebbing of tension and fatigue.

We made our leisurely way out of Saint John and into Alf Brooks' loyal constituency of Royal, under a high blue sky in which white clouds hung suspended and becalmed, the late morning sun drying out the soft green fields drenched by night rains. On the horizon, clusters of chestnut and cherry blossoms gladdened the eye, and wild violets bloomed along the tracks. Passing through this slowly unfolding, superb New Brunswick spring, secure in the comfort of the train, gently rocked by its leisurely passage, I seemed to have come upon a moment in time that was, like a pearl, the perfect product of a long, grinding travail.

All had suddenly come miraculously into place, a hundred separate energies were now harnessed as one, working with the sun, the tides, and the sweep of the rivers to change the shape and course of history. No one would have believed it possible, nor believed it yet, but, like the promise of summer on the land outside the window, one felt the faint, uncertain pulse of change.

In Moncton, the cars were switched to the Ocean Limited, and Diefenbaker withdrew to rest and to read his daily papers and the mail. Later, when the crowd which came to see him had dispersed and the departure was announced, the passengers, standing in the sun, moved reluctantly back into the coaches and the train began to move.

I stood on the platform, quite alone, watching it go. I saw Diefenbaker standing on the end of the last car, with Olive.

"There's Dalton," he said to her. "Wave goodbye to Dalton."

They both waved and so did I, as the train disappeared in the distance and I discovered, unaccountably, my eyes stinging with tears.

Dear Dalton:
When I left you yesterday at Moncton I thanked you personally.
This letter is merely to underline and re-emphasize my appreciation
for the good work that you did in arranging for the tour of the
Maritimes, and for the valuable and helpful suggestions given by you
so generously.
I hope the campaign continues upward and upward in the days ahead.
I know I was very much inspired by the reception at all the meetings.
Again thanking you and with best regards,
I am,
Yours sincerely,
John Diefenbaker

The John Diefenbaker who returned to the Maritimes twenty-seven days after his first visit was a man subtly changed by the changing composition of his self-evaluation of his prospects. At the beginning, he had desperately needed help, now he commanded it. He had already become just a little imperious, his temper and patience shortened by his long ordeal.

Arriving in Saint John, on the first day of June, he was full of doubts and torment about western Canada. Alvin Hamilton, he said, was certain to lose; Saskatchewan was not at all promising. It took some time, while he paced the floor of his bedroom in the Admiral Beatty Hotel, for him to refocus on the Maritimes where, I told him, his prospects could hardly be improved.

Hugh John Flemming, Ted Emmerson, the party's provincial bag man, and Ken Carson came to visit him in his suite. Hugh John's intention was to inform him of the Atlantic Resolutions and to ask him to endorse them publicly. The request was made with unaccustomed bluntness.

Diefenbaker seemed to bite his tongue. No, he said, he could not. He did not mind if his candidates made their own policy, but he could not be responsible for it. And anyway, he had had no opportunity to discuss it with his colleagues–what would Howard Green think?

Flemming could be tough too, when he needed to be. "Come on now, John," he said, languidly, "you wouldn't talk that way to Leslie Frost."

"Wouldn't I?" he said. "You just ask him."

But the tension soon dissolved in laughter, and Diefenbaker agreed to consider the matter. A few hours later, in a television appearance with Tom Bell, the former member and candidate, Diefenbaker volunteered the information that he thought the Atlantic Resolutions were wonderful and that he was cheerfully in support of them all.

He was plainly tired, drawing upon all his reserves to finish the last week of the campaign. In New Brunswick, speaking to the embattled miners at Minto, he depended almost entirely upon my text, which dealt with one of St. Laurent's characteristically off-hand remarks about the Maritime coal industry, and which both Michael Wardell and I had been making into a major issue.

After the meeting, Ralph Hay drove us back to Fredericton, with Diefenbaker stretched out in the back seat. We heard the late newscast from CFNB which began: "Progressive Conservative leader John Diefenbaker said tonight in Minto. . . ."

"I didn't say that," remarked the voice in the back seat, chuckling. "Dalton Camp said that."

Then to Halifax, the next day, to meet the two Tory candidates, Edmund Morris and Robert McCleave, both from the newsroom of Finlay MacDonald's radio station. Neither had been nominated until mid-May. (McCleave, in fact, had earlier written an article for the press predicting "slight" gains for the Tories in the Maritimes.)

All that day, an exhausted Diefenbaker was driven along the south shore of Nova Scotia, through Bridgewater and Liverpool, in the heart of Bob Winters' constituency. It looked promising; people gathered along the highway to wave to the Tory chieftain as his motorcade passed, and when young girls saw Lloyd Crouse, seated beside him, they jumped up and down and screamed with delight. Someone re-marked that the contest between the handsome Winters and Crouse, who bore some resemblance to Robert Taylor, was more like a beauty contest than an election. But Winters was plainly in trouble.

Along the way, Diefenbaker tried to doze between towns. But our driver, who was also the campaign manager for Crouse, kept the national leader awake by signalling the appearance of any and every constituent seen ahead on the road.

"Wave y'arm, John," Rhodenizer would call out, and Diefenbaker, half asleep, would feebly raise an arm to the window as yet another citizen of Lunenberg-Queens was rewarded for his vigil.

Then, at Liverpool, on a breathless, sunlit afternoon, while I strolled in the park with a friend from my prep-school days, Diefenbaker un-expectedly launched into an attack on the government for allowing the Liberal Party access to the voters lists of military personnel which had been denied the opposition.

The press, at last given something new, rushed to communicate this sensation across the country. Diefenbaker, asked to prove his allega-tion, found he could not. But he could point an accusative finger at me, since I had put the thought in his mind, showing him a "personal letter" from the Prime Minister to members of the armed forces and telling him that when I had sought to get the names and addresses of armed forces voters some months ago, I had been told, at NDHQ, that such lists were not available.

But he could hardly say to the press, "Dalton Camp said that." In-stead, he kept his distance from the press, and from me, and declined further comment. His last day in the Maritimes, in the 1957 campaign, was given over to bitterness and recrimination. In Kentville, he and Nowlan argued and the exchange was so heated that, overhearing it, I could not even discover the subject of their obvious disagreement.

As for me, Diefenbaker could hardly bring himself to speak. (Afterwards, Hogan recalled that my name was banned from the campaign train; hereafter, Diefenbaker pretended he had forgotten my name, referring to me, when necessary, as "that Toronto advertising fellow.")

In the jammed high school auditorium, outside of Kentville, I sat high in the galleries and heard Stanfield pay his tribute to Diefen-baker (which I had written) and heard Diefenbaker pay his tribute to Nowlan and Stanfield (which I had written) and when it was all over and the crowd was leaving the hall, I climbed into the back seat of a car, and Norm Atkins, my brother-in-law, drove me back to Halifax, in silence and darkness.

The second coming of John Diefenbaker to the Maritimes had been a complete political success, but he took his leave of this mother lode for his pending triumph full of complaint and abuse for most of those

338

who had helped him. He left Halifax by air at 6:45 Tuesday morning; I had left a call at the hotel so I could be aroused in time to see him off. But when the message came, I turned over and went back to sleep.

None of us had ever thought of the possibility of minority government– a Diefenbaker minority government. But, in the unpredictable whims of the democratic process, such it proved to be: 112 Conservatives elected, 105 Liberals, and 48 from among the third parties.

Tory representation from the Atlantic provinces leapt from five members in Parliament to twenty-one; Ontario's rose from thirty-three to sixty-one. On the prairies, the numbers increased from six to fourteen, while in British Columbia, seven members were elected as compared to three in the election of 1953.

For years afterwards, the illusion would persist that the West had yielded up Diefenbaker's triumph in 1957. In fact, his party was third in the popular vote in both Saskatchewan and Alberta, and only fourteen out of forty-eight prairie constituencies elected Diefenbaker candidates. Where he won in the nation was where the party was already strong.

On election day, I was awakened early by the explosion of a gas furnace up the street; the shattered house was the polling booth and a neighbour's living room had to be hastily commandeered for the purpose. I was one of the first to vote, marking my ballot for Frank McGee.

Then, as the polls closed in the Maritimes–an hour before Toronto's time–I made the first of several calls to Halifax. Finlay, who was reading the reports coming to his radio station, answered.

"Who's ahead?" I asked.

"You know about Newfoundland, of course?"

"No, I don't. The polls are still open here."

"Browne and McGrath elected in St. John's."

"How about Nova Scotia?"

"We're ahead," Finlay said, simply.

"Where?"

"Everywhere."

"I don't believe it."

"Neither do I."

"Anything from the Island?"

"What would you like?"

"I'd like them all."

"You've got 'em," Finlay said, dissolving in laughter.

Ralph Hay called from Fredericton. "We've licked Gregg," he said enthusiastically. I had to be glad of it–defeated cabinet ministers count for more–yet I had an odd feeling about Gregg, a twinge of regret, deeply buried in a dimly remembered past. But it was there, summoned quickly to the surface and as quickly returned.

Arthur Burns called from Prince Albert:

"What do you hear from the Maritimes?"

I told him, seat by seat.

"My God," he said, disbelieving.

"Give my congratulations to Grosart," I said.

"To hell with that," Burns said, breathing hard. "What have you got now for a total?"

The night became a ceremony of surprise, of shouts of disbelief, of glasses raised–the victors toasted and the vanquished celebrated–until, at last, it was over. Gregg, Winters, C. D. Howe, Stuart Garson defeated; the resignation of St. Laurent imminent. Diefenbaker triumphant. Conservatism restored.

All after this would be for me somehow anticlimactic, even though the political struggles to come would be more fierce and would involve an intensive, highly personalized contest within the Conservative Party, which some considered epochal; but as of the moment of this narrow victory of the Progressive Conservative Party, it was to me the triumphant conclusion of a long crusade. There was now nothing left of the power of Liberalism which I had found entrenched in the country only five years before.

And it seemed the triumph was sweeter for the fact that my own part of Canada–the Maritimes–had contributed so substantially to the result; and because we had wrung from the new rulers of the country substantial commitments to policy, it seemed certain that Maritime members, such as Nowlan, would have positions of considerable influence in the new government; Balcer would have yet another opportunity to prove that he was a leader of substance as well as promise, and this would have bright and hopeful implications for the party in Quebec; and, in Diefenbaker, the party obviously had a leader, and the country a Prime Minister, with humility and compassion bred in his bones, and one whose victory had been a product of a small miracle of co-operation involving all the elements of his party.

TORONTO ONTARIO
JUNE 12, 1957
MR. JOHN DIEFENBAKER
PRINCE ALBERT SASK
I COULD HARDLY ADD ANYTHING TO THE PERSONAL TRIBUTE OF A
HOST OF YOUR FELLOW CANADIANS. NONETHELESS PLEASE ACCEPT MY
PERSONAL CONGRATULATIONS AND BEST WISHES. IT HAS BEEN A GREAT
PRIVILEGE TO HAVE BEEN ASSOCIATED WITH YOU IN SUCH A GREAT
CAMPAIGN AND SUCH A GREAT CAUSE. KINDEST PERSONAL REGARDS TO
MRS DIEFENBAKER. . . .
DALTON K CAMP

340

There would be neither acknowledgment nor reply—ever.

But the triumph was complete. The tragedy was only beginning, as with the first flicker of sensation too fleeting to be recognized as pain, but which heralds the certain death of a dream.

Index

343

345